The
Lyotard Reader

Janet Bayne
bought Edinburgh
"Waterstones"
25TH November 1990

The
LYOTARD
READER

Jean-François Lyotard

Edited by
Andrew Benjamin

Basil Blackwell

Copyright © introduction, editorial matter and organization Andrew Benjamin 1989
First published 1989

Basil Blackwell Ltd.
108 Cowley Road
Oxford, OX4 IJF, UK

Basil Blackwell, Inc.
3 Cambridge Center
Cambridge, Massachusetts 02142, USA

British Library Cataloguing in Publication Data

A CIP catalogue record for this book is available from the British Library.

Library of Congress Cataloging in Publication Data

Lyotard, Jean François.
 [Selections. English, 1989]
 The Lyotard reader / edited by Andrew Benjamin.
  p. cm.
 "Select bibliography of Lyotard's writings"; p.
 Bibliography; p.
 Includes Index.
 ISBN 0-631-16338-7 ISBN 0-631-16339-5 (pbk.)

 1. Philosophy. 2. Philosophy, Modern—20th century
3. Aesthetics, Modern—20th century. I. Benjamin, Andrew E.
II. Title.
B2430, L962E5 1989   89-110
194—dc19   CIP

Typeset in 11 on 13 pt Plantin
by Times Graphics
Printed in Great Britain by T J Press Ltd., Padstow

Contents

Foreword

Andrew Benjamin asks me for a short – very short – foreword for his *Lyotard Reader*, nothing much, only four or five pages. Just like that, quite casually. As though it was the most natural thing in the world. But there's nothing natural at all about this *Lyotard Reader*, or about the idea that Lyotard himself should write a foreword for the *Reader*. You say *foreword*. Let him say a word before you read his words. A key word that gives the reader a key to the words in the *Reader*.[1]

They say that anyone who writes – an *écrivant* or, more rarely, an *écrivain*[2] – is *his/her own first reader*. I've been known to say so myself. It can be argued that reading has priority or primacy over writing. It seems to be a coherent argument. You cannot write without reading what you have written. Of course you cannot write without rereading, but first you have to read what you are writing. Of course you hear yourself writing. Even if you try not to listen to yourself.

Sometimes you do listen to yourself writing. That is not the same thing as hearing yourself writing. When you hear, you merely hear something that has to be written. You can't do it. You go on. You don't pay much attention to style. You let the style take care of itself. You're ahead of the writing. You merely point it in some direction. Set a course. The style will follow. It can look after itself.

You end up listening to yourself writing when you have no faith in your style. You tighten it up, make it severe, classical, academic. You argue. You address someone. Or, contrariwise, you take less care over it in the sense that you try to make it look careless and casual. That form of listening has a bad press amongst the censors, but I'd like to defend it. It indicates that you are not sure of your direction, unsure of where you are, or completely lost, that you're afraid, that you don't seem to have the strength to think. And that is only right and proper. It is not just that you feel unworthy and anxious, but that you show it by overwriting, by being either too severe or too careless. It annoys the reader. But his/her anger is a good thing. So are the worries of the one who is writing. He's not too sure where he is either. Overwritten, unreadable.

And sometimes, it seems, you do not listen to yourself when you are writing. Sometimes you seem to have no ear for what comes into your head. That's a blessing for all concerned, reader and writer alike. A state of grace. The joy of writing. But it is also a big mistake; it is presumptious to place blind faith in writing. You act as though your sole concern were with the loftiest works of the mind. You leave to the servants the task of putting some order into what has to be thought before you reach the writing line. What has to be thought lies on the edge of the words that are beginning to take shape, where they come into contact with the empty horizon where thoughts appear. The lowly task of administering what the pen is setting down is left to craft and talent, to the knowing reader you have already become.

There's something presumptuous about this talent, about this preliminary running in. About thinking that words fall into line all by themselves behind your back as you walk along. And then there is the further presumption of believing that you can allow yourself to be cut to the quick by what you are trying to think while you are writing, that it can touch a raw nerve. It's never like that, thank God. You are rereading what you have written.

You reread it in advance. You will have reread it. The thing that has to be written does not come along like some artless *ingenue*. It is already dressed. Sometimes scantily dressed in only an epithet or an adverb. Alternatively, a whole sentence may suddenly come to you out of the blue. And sentences or words that come out of the blue may hide the thought that was about to speak its name. You think you recognize them, and fail to see it. And so, instead of hearing it, or reading it properly, as properly as possible, you reread it. Already expressed in readable words and sentences. That kind of rereading is a prereading, a *foreword*. It drives to distraction anyone who tries to hear as they write. A form of interference on the edge of thought, pleasant or unpleasant, easy or difficult, but recognizable, that prevents you from hearing its silence properly, or for long enough at a stretch. The servants have done the housework too quickly to give thought a proper welcome, rushing to do the cleaning before the thought comes to you. On the contrary, they have gagged it, disfigured it. Too much order, too much language, too much talent, too accustomed to writing.

But there again, how do you know that a thought that comes along ready house-trained isn't the right one? How can you compare it with what it should be, except by accommodating what it should be. And in any event that will put an end to the moment of grace and the 'joy' of writing. The only alternative is to move house. To hire new servants. To refuse to put your trust in home comforts. And to listen to yourself writing once more. Make different domestic arrangements. Find less or more disciplined servants.

The constant changing of the verbal guard is thought's modest, honest tribute to writing. It is a never-ending process, like translation. You have no idea of how to go about the task of so-called 'correction', a task which implies adopting an incorrect attitude towards any recognized or recognizable language. Anyone who writes and then rereads what he has written in a constant attempt to write 'better' has no idea of what he is doing when he does his duty, adds corrections, throws pages into the wastepaper basket, replaces a word he has written and which seemed fine with another word, disowns a word he liked and in doing so deauthorizes himself so as to be authorized by a different word, which may be more ordinary, more learned, more banal or more unexpected. He can't know what he is doing when he does his duty. What he does know is that you cannot hear thought if you don't listen to the words.

Now imagine a friend, someone like Andrew Benjamin, who decides to go through all the scribbles you have produced over the last forty years and picks out a few texts that suit his purpose. And puts them together for publication in English.

He comes along and says: write me a short *foreword* to the collection. In other words, and as I have just explained, he asks me to do the one thing that has to be avoided, the one thing that prevents the advent of thought. Pre-vention. (Everyone knows that *forewords* are *afterwords*. But there are ways of ensuring the presentation is not too much of a representation, neither too early nor too late.) I therefore have to give the reader a preventive warning about (or against?) how the spirit moved me. Or the letter. A word of warning to my English-speaking readers.

An English-speaker who tries to think faces the same struggle as the *écrivant* or *écrivain* I have just described because he/she too is surrounded by servants who are either over-zealous or too disorderly. But they are not my servants; they work in a different language. And when I say language, I do not just mean grammar, vocabulary, or phonology; I also mean the immense network of words and sentences in the midst of which, in the face of which, he/she struggles to make room for the thoughts that come to him/her. Every individual in a given language has his/her own specific network, but there are also collective differences between languages. Cultures, as the saying goes. Worlds. I know perfectly well that English-speakers think, but they have different domestic arrangements, different accommodation and different ways of changing accommodation.

Their thoughts are as translatable as mine, because languages are, hypothetically, translatable. And their style is therefore translatable too. But when you look at the style of a foreign text, it is hard to tell the difference between accommodating language and a change of accommodation. To do that, you have to be familiar with its *home*, but also with the way it lives in it. And everyone lives differently; hence their singularity. It is also possible that two different languages may not offer the same range of styles of accommodation, or at least that the range of styles they offer may not overlap. Hard to tell.

What we do know is that you are not at home when you are in someone else's house. That you can't think at your ease, create order and disorder at ease. That you have little control over what you have reread and what you have not yet read, over representation, presentation and appresentation. That you don't quite catch what the servants are saying. I speak from experience, having once been bold enough to write in English.[3] Not that there is anything exemplary about that. Even so, I did have the reassurance of knowing that an English speaker would reread my text before it was published, and that he was a friend. I could rest assured that David Carroll, the friend in question, would laugh at my English, albeit in kindly fashion, and that he would devote all his competence, skill and time to making sure that an English reader would not laugh too loudly. That he would only laugh at the content.

Does that mean that Carroll was a translator? No; he corrected my English. A co-author? He didn't write the book. A rewrite man? He didn't alter the tone, and didn't adapt the text to the norms laid down by an editor-in-chief or a series editor. A corrector? As it happens, he corrected my language, not the proofs. He might be called a *co-writer*. Given the cosmopolitan and Babel-like situation in which we find ourselves, there's a great future for co-writers. We live in a situation in which the *writer* or *writing agent* addresses allophones directly. And in which he necessarily addresses them clumsily. The situation calls for allography; the circumstances call for clumsiness.

When it comes to housework, the allograph will have a lot to do. You can say that again. He has to deal with a foreign language which does not automatically tidy itself up behind his back. On the contrary, it constantly begins to say something other than what was meant to be said, to connote at random – not to mention the solecisms and barbarisms. It rebels and goes astray without him knowing how or when. A rereading of Swift's *Directions to Servants* suggests that the household he describes is a good metaphor for my allography. Swift directs servants to be arrogant, to do as they please, to be felons and vandals.[4]

An allograph cannot reread his work in the above sense. The staff who are supposed to clean up after him when he tries to think do so in a different language. And they are in an awkward mood. What gets thought above stairs by the master, and I assume that Swift's master is English, bears little relationship to what gets done (written) below stairs by the servants, who are presumably Irish. Or if it does, it is pure chance. It is the same with a French speaker who writes English without being fluent in the language. He has a peculiar feeling of irresponsibility. He does not reread what he has written. He knows it's a waste of time. That he cannot do any better. Only that he will do something other, yet again. God alone knows which other! A master who despairs of mastering and therefore feels free of all responsibilities. I remember my unhappy experiences as being a bout of infantilism or linguistic drunkenness.

To go back to translation. Another case of Swiftian housekeeping, but for different reasons. Not that a translator is a bad servant. Quite the contrary. A translator is as zealous as an old manservant, as faithful as an incorruptible chambermaid. Like them, he/she has known and loved his/her master or mistress for a long time, and his/her probity and self-effacing manner mean that he/she can do the housework as it should be done according to the orders that have been given. It is as though the master were carrying out his own orders.

Few things are more admirable than a good translation. Because of the air of self-abnegation it gives off. That is much more important than any consideration as to technical competence (the one inevitably follows from the other). It inspires moral respect. For someone who could and did prefer what came into the mind of the other to what might have come into his/her own mind. Not preferring what the other writes as it stands, once the housework has been done, to what the translator can write on the same subject. Preferring rather, the thoughts that come into the other's mind before the housework is done, if that is possible. A translator prefers, then, the other's disorder not only to his/her own order, but also to his/her own disorder (you do not think or write any the less for being a translator). The wonderful effects of love. Of loving not only that which is born of the other, but that which demanded to be born. And of doing it again. Not only does a translator help to give birth; he/she helps something demand to be born in the so-called target language. A good translator loves and respects not only what has been thought [*le pensé*] but also a 'way of thinking', as the saying goes.

Is the author any judge of the quality of a translation? Certainly not, unless, they say, he writes both languages equally well. Only someone who is perfectly bilingual or, to be more accurate, perfectly digraphical, is in a position to judge. And that person does not have to be the author. Perfect bilingualism, like perfect hearing, is a dream of a pre-Babel state, of an ideal form of interlinguistic communication in which there is no need for translation. That is every translation's ideal. To render itself useless, impossible even, and to erase the interlinguistic gap which motivates it.

It is in fact a never-ending task, as any given state of the target language text has to be reread and corrected, and as a result the translator stops, not because he/she is satisfied but because he/she is tired. All translations, even famous translations which are recognized to be unsurpassed, have to be begun again years later.

The real problem is that, as in writing, the grace of the word which seems to suggest itself is suspect and has to be suspected in the name of the very thing that comes with it: its finery. As in writing, one would like to reconstitute whatever comes in all candour (but in the case of translation, it came into the mind of the other, into the mind of the person you are translating). Its nudity. You struggle to respect the freedom of the nascent thought, to free it from being travestied by its inscription in language. But the child never comes naked into the world. Neither in translation nor in writing, and language never dresses up anything that has not already been formulated. But the very fact of having been formulated means that it has already been badly formulated.

That is why translation and allography are fairly good illustrations of the relationship between writing and rereading. By providing examples of, respectively, extreme fidelity and extreme infidelity, they show that advancing towards inscription means having prescribed, that advancing towards writing means having reread in advance. The conclusion to be drawn from this is not that the *écrivain* or *écrivant* who turns towards the empty horizon when he is writing finds a ready-made text which he simply reconstitutes or, at best, translates. Nor that he reads it as it stands. If that were the case, prereading would simply be a matter of prejudice.

The *écrivain* or *écrivant* no more encounters a text than a translator deals with a text. We might say that both *écrivain/écrivant* and translator find themselves faced with a thousand texts. A texture of texts. Not even a texture, not even texts, as that would imply a high degree of order, the seemliness created by a weft passing over the warp at regular intervals. One structures, the other intrigues. One displays competence, the other performance. Etc. They do not encounter this neat arrangement. They do not even encounter a mere multiplication of that arrangement. They find texts in rags and tatters. In other words, their culture, be it English, French or Irish. Their store of literary knowledge, as they say, as though it could all be packed into a suitcase. Their past readings, to the extent that the passwords are not present, but are prepared to come to the mind of the *écrivain/écrivant* or translator. Their own texts, their own translations are obviously part of the same heap; they too are in rags and tatters, neither more nor less recognizable than the rest.

Not their entire pasts, of course. Scraps of the past. The scraps that came to mind, or are about to come to mind, when a word has been set, or sets itself, as a 'thought', as something to be thought. I mean a topic that you have been asked to deal with (for a colloquium, a lecture, a journal, a book). A commission. Andrew Benjamin, for example, commissions me to write a *foreword* for the *Lyotard Reader*.

I immediately ask: what precisely is the theme I am being asked to write about? *Foreword*, *Lyotard* or *Reader*? Or any possible combination of the three? Each word and each combination will give rise to writing, reading, rereading, translation, allography and betrayal.

It may be the case that there is no set theme, that nothing seems to have been set. That you write and translate of your own accord. You do sometimes seem to write or translate without being told to do so. But it is an illusion. There is always a word, or words, usually something you have picked up elsewhere, usually something taken out of context, which does not help you to isolate a semantic field, and which tells you to sort through your tattered old rereadings (the empty horizon) in one way or another. Either it goes well, or it won't come. It is a question of direction. If nothing comes, you listen to yourself writing (and a translator is the classic example of someone who cannot write without listening to himself). If it is going well, you have no time; you are chasing after scraps of text which fly from your pen on to the page; you quickly note them down, and you say to yourself: we'll see about that, we'll see later. Clean it up later.

Even when the scraps do come together, some housework has already been done, and there will be more to do later. Because the work that has been done will already have been undone, because you only come up with scraps. The work you have done in accordance with your sense of order will have been done as you write according to your sense of order. But creating tidiness is another way of tidying up. The order sabotaged by your unruly servants is sabotaged in accordance with a different order. They disobey because they are obeying something else. You are not their master, but that is not because they have another master who is similar to you, the only difference being that you have different names. It is not because they simply commit the felony of working for someone else that they are unruly. They do not betray you out of respect for another, but out of another respect. They are not wearing a different livery beneath the livery which you claim is yours. They are obeying their own memory, out of respect for the below-stairs element in thought. Words remember words.

This is a different kind of memory, and it is more faithful than the good memory a writer or translator needs. The treachery of your servants, who reduce the order of your thoughts to tatters, who countermand your commands and your command, is a faithful memory. This is how words stick together in their civil and disordered disobedience. They support each other, but at the same time they retreat. There is no longer any prince or general to draw them up in ranks and to make them fight a frontal battle with their eyes fixed on the horizon. They helped one another as they fell back, already wounded in a war that has already been fought, already wounded in many a war. In as many wars as there are texts. But only wounded, as they seldom die. They are in tatters, but that is good for them. It is as though they had been allowed to become children again, after having pretended to obey, to be grown-ups and to go to war. That is how you find them; already read and organized by warlords (*écrivains, écrivants*, translators), unreadable in defeat (for any text is a defeat), left to their devices, hobbling along together, clinging together to form groups of idle survivors, saving their skin. That is your famous store of knowledge. That is your past, a past which does not belong to you and which, as is only right, is older than you and other than you. Neither your son nor your father. And it has nothing in particular to do with you.

And what about you? What are you going to be? Their general? In command and giving commands? A weaver who will combine weft and warp anew as you weave your text? A master who sends orders to the kitchen? But no matter what you do, even if you have no alternative (given that you do presume to think, write or translate), let me tell you that they will do as they please, or almost (they are obviously under a certain obligation to negotiate the terms of their rebellion), and that you cannot count on their goodwill. That you will constantly have to reread them, perhaps in the hope of correcting them, of adapting to your order what happens when they carry out your orders. And there will never be an end to it.

So, you reread while you are writing, and you reread what has been written. Whatever you do, you rewrite. Whatever you do, there is an element of allography. Not yet written, already written; not a great deal of difference. I was saying that you cannot not listen to yourself writing.

Listening to yourself means listening to the din made by a horde of words running wild. You cannot hear yourself think unless you listen to that din, the din from whence comes thought, which makes thought come, the din from whence emerges thought, into which thought strives to enter.

That is what every translator who worked on the *Reader* did with his/her French text. That's what the editor, Andrew Benjamin, did when he was putting together these scraps of texts. And (I hope) that's what the author, Lyotard, did with his thoughts. Did he have to return, not to give the disorganized troops lined up here for embarkation to Anglophonia their reading orders, but rather (if he is faithful and sincere) to impose a new disorder? To add to it the perpetual debacle which serves (in his case) as a substitute for thought. He certainly didn't have to, but he did.

NOTES

1 Italic script in this paragraph indicates English in the original.
2 For the distinction, see Roland Barthes, 'Écrivains et écrivants', in *Essais critiques* (Paris: Seuil, 1964). The *écrivain* performs a function, the *écrivant* an activity. The terms are rather unhelpfully translated as 'author' and 'writer' by Richard Howard in Barthes, *Critical Essays* (Evanston: North Western University Press, 1972).
3 See Jean-François Lyotard, *Peregrinations. Law, Form, Event* (New York: Columbia University Press, 1988).
4 Jonathan Swift, *Directions to Servants* in *The Prose Works of Jonathan Swift*, ed. Herbert Davis, *Volume the Thirteenth: Directions to Servants and Miscellaneous Pieces* (Oxford: Basil Blackwell, 1959).

Translated by David Macey

Und So Weiter:
In Lieu of an Introduction

... the rule of the philosopher's discourse has always been to find the rule of his/her own discourse. The philosopher is thus someone who speaks in order to find the rule of what s/he wishes to say, and who by virtue of that fact speaks before knowing the rule, and without knowing it.

Jean-François Lyotard

The temptation that resides within – as well as presides over – the strategy of an introduction envisages the type of coverage that provides a history. The temptation therefore harbours and seeks to enact the restrictive and restricting borders of an historical continuity. (Though it is one where both history and the nature of continuity remain, of necessity, unexamined.) Each text is thought to need a location; a positing prior to interpretation. The tireless and indeed tiresome effort of giving the text a position would involve sketching its contours and providing it with a predetermined interpretive flotilla of dates and proper names; mapping and therefore stilling its movement, surrounding it and thereby hindering its drift. Assistance can always be given but the cold, bleak and humourless gesture of specifying in advance the project of reading – and hence of interpretation – will, in this instance, be resisted. There is, in addition, no need to reduce these texts to that which has already taken place. Here, there is a real sense in which they are taking place *again* for the first time.

The problem of introductions and forewords, of requests and compliance, will have already been noted. It is therefore possible to move forward rather than repeat the chatter of the desire for cultural and historical specificity. It has been replaced by the demand stemming from Lyotard's work. A demand that is, perhaps, also an imperative. Think.

> ... our role as thinkers is to deepen our understanding of what goes on in language, to critique the vapid idea of information, to reveal an irremedial opacity at the very core of language.[1]

The work, shreds of which are presented here, can be described as centring around the possibility of a philosophy that takes place in and after – though not simply in and after – the refusal of both the complacency of tradition and the determination in advance of meta-narratives (or grand-narratives). They are coupled to the more positive need to think in response – as well as the response – to the experimentations within the arts and especially the visual arts. Part of the difficulty here is thinking the 'in' and the 'after' as not designating simple temporal locations within an unfolding sequential continuity. Rather they need to be understood, at least initially, as moods or to use Lyotard's own expression as states of mind. These simple observations are an adequate preparation for reading. They are because they are not. The deferral before – in front of – is pointless. There is no way in but the way in itself. The only introduction that can be written is the one that will be written – though not by me – after having read these texts. This is a point made elsewhere.

What is intended by this *Reader* – intended for any reader – is the simple presentation of texts.[2] The order, while not random, reflects no more than what I take to be central in his work. My taking it thus does not make it central. I gathered, collected from a position. My position is both obvious and obscure. A growing recognition – perhaps personal perhaps not – of the importance of dwelling philosophically on Judaism coupled to an acceptance of Lyotard's own arguments concerning the necessity, for philosophy, of the visual arts, inter-spersed with the consequences of recognizing the need of being able to make claims about justice, still, and therefore of the indispensability of the political. That said, all that remains is propriety.

NOTES

1 Jean-François Lyotard, 'Rules and Paradoxes and Svelte Appendix', *Cultural Critique*, no. 5, winter 1986/7; p. 218.
2 For an introduction to Lyotard's work see G. Bennington, *Lyotard. Writing the Event* (Manchester University Press, 1988) and D. Carroll, *Paraesthetics* (London: Methuen, 1987). Bennington's book is, at this stage, the most important philosophical confrontation with Lyotard's work. It repays careful attention both in its mode and its presentation of argument.

Acknowledgements

There are a number of people who must be thanked for their help in compiling this book. In no particular order I would like to acknowledge the assistance I received from: Rachel Bowlby, Geoff Bennington, Paul Buck, Homi Bhabha, Tim Murray, Daniel Brewer, Ruth Francken, Andrée Lyotard, Tony O'Leary, David Macey, Luigi Bowen, Jean-François Lyotard, and Stephan Chambers. Whether they answered letters, answered phone calls, translated, provided wine, cigarettes and roses, just seemed to possess obscure journals or simply listened with remarkable tolerance to an editor (a collector of scribbles?) whose manuscript was always just about to be ready, may I extend my sincere thanks to them all. All errors, mistakes, sins, misjudgements, omissions, etc., I wish, naturally, to embrace and call my own.

The editor and publishers would like to thank the following for permission to include the material collected in this edition: for 'The Tensor', translated by Sean Hand, *The Oxford Literary Review*, 7: 1–2 (1985), 25–40; for 'The Dream-Work Does Not Think', translated by Mary Lydon, *The Oxford Literary Review*, 6:1 (1983), 3–34; for 'Passages from *Le Mur du Pacifique*' and for 'One of the Things at Stake in Women's Struggles' the editors, *Substance*, 20 (1978), 9–19, and the University of Wisconsin Press; for 'Beyond Representation', Paladin Books (a Division of Collins PLC), for 'Acinema' and for 'Judiciousness in Dispute, or Kant after Marx', Columbia University Press; for 'Philosophy and Painting', the editors, *Camera Obscura*; for 'The Sublime and the Avant-Garde', the editors, *Paragraph* vol. 6, reprinted by permission of Oxford University Press; for 'Analysing Speculative Discourse as Language-Game', translated by Geoff Bennington, *The Oxford Literary Review*, 6: 1 (1983), 3–34; for 'Levinas' Logic', the State University of New York; for 'Discussions, or Phrasing "after Auschwitz" ', which first appeared as a Working Paper (1986), the Centre for Twentieth Century Studies, University of Wisconsin–Milwaukee; for 'The Sign of History', from Attridge and Bennington: *Poststructuralism and the Question of History*, Cambridge University Press.

Acknowledgements

1

The Tensor[*]

Semiotic sign

Let's take up yet again this business of signs, for you haven't understood, you've remained rationalists, semioticians, Westerners.[1] So let's have it out again, it's the road leading to a libidinal currency which must be opened up by force. What the semioticians retain by way of hypothesis beneath their discourse is that the *thing* they speak of can always be treated as a sign; and this sign in turn is indeed thought of in the network of concepts of the theory of communication, it is 'what replaces something for someone' as Peirce and later Lévi-Strauss both said, which means that the *thing* is posited as a message, that is a physical medium equipped with a sequence of coded elements which its addressee, himself in possession of this code, is capable of decoding, in order to retrieve *the information* which the sender aims at him.

Therefore, immediately, *ex hypothesi*, we have a hollowing-out of the thing, which becomes a *substitute*; it replaces the 'information' for the someone who is the addressee. This replacement, of course, can be conceived of in two ways, along two very different lines of thought. We can say that the sign replaces what it signifies (the message replaces the information): that is the most brutal way of putting it, the Platonism of the theory of Ideas, for example: the sign at once screens and calls up what it both announces and conceals. Port-Royal has said it all on that score. Or we can think of the substitution not metaphorically, but in terms of the interminable metonymy which Saussure or any political economist understands by the name of exchange; then it is no longer signification (what is encoded) which the sign substitutes, for the following trick is conjured up: signification itself is also only made of

* This essay was first published in Jean-François Lyotard, *Economie Libidinale*, Editions de Minuit (1974), pp. 57–115.

signs, and goes on forever, so we never get anything but cross-references, signification is always deferred, and meaning is never present in flesh and blood. We are filled, then, with compassion for good old Husserl, and we say: no, there are only divergences [*écarts*], and if there is any meaning, it's because there is a divergence, not any old divergence of course, we don't move from one element to the other any old way, on the contrary it is a journey organized from one term to another, and involves the extreme precision of a system or structure, and eventually, in this process, if we have religious souls like Freud or Lacan, we produce the image of a grand signifier forever completely absent, whose sole presence is formed by the absentification, reserve and relief [*relève*] of those terms that make it into signs – all substitutes for one another – the image of a grand zero which holds these terms apart, and whose obviously unpronounceable name will be translated in a libidinal economy by that of Kastrator.

Look what you've done: straight off the material is annihilated. There is no material, where there is a message. Adorno said this admirably when speaking of Schoenberg: the material, he explained, in serialism no longer has a value as such, but only as a relation or link between one term and another. And in Boulez we no longer have anything but relation, not only in pitch, but also in stress, timbre and duration. Dematerialization. Here a long examination is necessary: is this dematerialization the equivalent of the work of capital in the affairs of sensibility and affect? Is this thus simply the abstract version of the pieces of the band of drives, and the cutting-up of the latter into comparable and countable parts? Or is it rather the case that, under *cover* of this squaring off and through it, it gives rise to an indiscernible refinement and intensification of the affective passages? And if this is the case, isn't this 'determination', at the same time and within the same space, the cartography of a *material* voyage, of new regions in the space of sound, but equally of chromaticism, sculpture, politics, eroticism and language, which thanks to the *sign-representation* are conquered and crossed by the paths of impulses, offering the libido new opportunities to intensify itself, while the fabrication of signs by 'dematerialization' causes an extension of the tensors?

We tend to think that this last hypothesis is the right one, but let's first of all pursue the description of the few notable effects of the process of sign-representation in its own field.

It's not only the material which is commuted to a sign-term, for the 'thing' that the sign replaces for someone is itself another sign, and so we no longer have anything but signs. The first consequence is that the relationship is therefore based on an infinite postponement, and so recurrence is installed as a fundamental trait of the system, the reiteration of the *signifying postponement* guaranteeing that we never get presence itself and also that we always have a job on our hands to determine the terms to which, in a given *corpus*, the term under study can and must lead. The other consequence is that with the sign begins the *search*. In the past it might have been the search for God, or meaning, when it was the *metaphorical* organization of signifyingness that predominated. For us moderns, when this metaphor is absent from our thought and when the object of our admiration is to be found in the structured metonymic substitution, the search is no longer for God or truth, it is the search plain and simple, scientific research, in fact not a search for causes, since we know very well that that is not a good concept, but a search for 'effects' in the scientific sense, a search for a discourse that can produce locatable, predictable and controllable metamorphoses, a search, then, for discrimination. There is no sign or thought of a sign that is not about power and of power. The journey of this search is not that of the wandering ship of fools and lepers, nor is it the transpatial exodus of the uncanny, but it is the well-equipped venture of the explorer, who clears the way for the curate, the soldier and the shopkeeper, it is the avant-garde of capital, which is itself already capital only to the degree that it is always pushing back its frontiers, always incorporating new bits of its circumference into the system, but so as to yield a return and a revenue. The sign goes along with this business trip, and the business trip creates the sign: what is an African for a British explorer, what is a Japanese to an eighteenth-century Jesuit? Organs and partial drives to be reabsorbed into the one normal organic body called Humanity or Creation. Materials to be dematerialized and made to signify. Do you really believe, say the white thinkers, that when the Noh actor sidles forward on the stage as though he were not moving at all, that it means nothing? It's a sign, it is there in place of something else, there is a code, and the addressees are familiar with it, or at all events, even if it is unconscious, it exists, and we, the semiologues, Jesuits, Stanleys and conquerors shall have triumphed only when we have this code and can *reproduce* it, *simulate* it – the model for all semiology is not *The Purloined Letter* but *The Gold-Bug*. These dead Africans and Orientals leave behind them precious messages, and we simulate their codes. Lévi-Strauss: I want to be the language spoken by the myths.

And so with this voyage of conquest which the process of sign-representation cannot fail to inspire (unless it is the opposite, a certain sort of voyage inspiring the process of sign-representation, but we are not very partial to these futile priorities, for all of this is a great package of little arrangements focusing on this or that thing, or material, or person, a set-up in which everything moves together), so along with this quest and conquest, where the latter is constantly postponed, there is also an indissociable intention, the intention to forge a link, the intention to yield a high return. To work out the code of signs *for power*, power as a cause, power as aim. All those risks, living with cannibals, being stationed in a frontier post, the heat, the flies, all the deaths incurred, all the sins involved, like the Jesuit in the *Supplément au voyage de Bougainville*, are taken with intent, and so there is a split. Not the zone and the taut moment, but the zone traversed, the moment of a movement, the tensions, with the risk and pain that go with them, *paid for* in the hope of an ulterior gain, perceived and experienced as a *loss*, as the concession that must be made for the sake of health, progress, knowledge, enlightenment, socialism. The wasted flesh hanging in shreds on thorns is not the essential point, the important thing is rather the *final return*, what we can get out of it, which as we know is the attitude adopted nowadays on their holidays by wage-earners, as well as by the rich, their bosses and masters: the desire to *bring back* images, photos, film, prestige, the tourism of the return, retourism, a succession of explorations that always follow the same outline. Here we come up against the question of interest. For tourism or conquest is interesting–interested inasmuch as *the expenditure*, which covers not only the cost of equipment and its maintenance, but also *affective expenditure*, which can be very heavy, Caesar at the Rubicon, is no longer any more than an *advance*, inasmuch then as desire is lost only to be at that point the better recovered.

But it must be stressed that it will not simply be recovered, but recovered *at that point*, where? no other than in the account book, in the space-time *open* (like a book) as a result of the intention of the sign-representation. I will not be recovered, since there is only deferment and different, and since there is never any question of desire and its own modality in the constitution of signs: semiology as a preamble to all the sciences ignores, as they do, the desire realized within itself. Another consequence, then, is that with the sign, if we have intention and postponement, we also have the opening up of diachrony, which is merely a result of drawing out the compact immobile tensor time into the *no longer* and the *not yet*, the *even yet* and the *not already*, in the game of de-presence which is the very game of semiotic nihilism. Where does signification lie in relation to its signs? Before them, since they are only its offspring; and yet always behind them since their decoding is endless. But in this apparently insane pursuit, which is the constitution of meaning, while some hermeneut or pessimist will come along and tell you: look, we never *have* meaning, it escapes us, transcends us, teaches us we are finite and are going to die – well, while the edifying pastor is telling you all that, his soldiers and tradesmen are gathering in organs, drives, bits of membrane, and are stockpiling and capitalizing them. And the time we 'know so well', Freud's 'secondary time', Kant's a priori form, the conscious Bergsonian-Husserlian-Augustinian unfolding, is woven in the double game of this despair and this building up of capital, the despair of the lost-postponed meaning and the treasure-trove of signs that are but lived 'experience', the Odyssey.

With Ulysses the *thing* which the sign replaces has already become a sign; look at Ulysses's episode with Nausicaa and you will see the *love* of which the Westerner is capable with his wretched *conqueror's* virility, for women are to him, like the Negroes and the Chinese, a contest, with success guaranteed, a brief moment in the continuous hoarding-up, an essential exteriority in an endless process of *sign-representation* and the accumulation of things which have become signs in systems. We, however, didn't want Ulysses to go back; we wept with Nausicaa, and told him he was being too Greek. There was no need for submission or domination, just being-alongside, and only then could he have *gone astray,* and been rendered incapable of getting his return and making his report [*de faire du rapport et de faire son rapport*]. But, she replied, is it even possible not to enter into the virile Greek capitalist game of domination? Just being there, said the beautiful princess, isn't just being alongside, it's being inside and yet indissociably marginal. Anyway, was it up to me to save this stupid bugger? By wanting me to save him, you are treating me as he has done, you are subordinating me to your designs. Sure, you don't want his return and revenue, you want his 'perdition' – but in your eyes that would be his salvation, and so I remain his slave, his moment, his spring-board. So you're still maintaining me in a dialectic. She's right, to want Nausicaa to 'ruin' Ulysses is still to be a Westerner, it's still the sign, scarcely displaced. After all there are explorers who became negroes, priests who became heathens, Jesuits who became Polynesians, the Bounty mutineers – do you really think that the intention to redeem is any the less pressing in those people than in their masters in the City, in Rome and in the Royal Navy? Any the less urgent in our friend Jaulin than in his master-enemy Lévi-Strauss? There is still something *saved* in these paths to perdition, still an intention in these quests for intensity. You don't get rid of *return* and profit through departure and export. Here, my friends, let us take note of duplicity and cultivate it.

Another consequence of the informational constitution of the sign is that there is someone for whom the message *replaces* the thing specified, there is a subject (two subjects), that is an agency to which all predicates, all postponements of meaning, all events experienced and touristed, are related. This someone is something which will expand as *experience* accumulates (an experience in which, if you recall what Hegel says, the subject will not fail to say how it is constantly perishing, oh hero!, oh Self!), as the events, tensors, passages of intensity find themselves split into signs – and then these signs will be taken care of by their 'receptor' or addressee, who will supervise their storage and ownership, and who will say: there you are, I've been in Egypt, there you are, I've sailed between Charybdis and Scylla, there you are, I've heard the sirens, there you are, I've gone out of my abode and into the wilderness, or: all that stuff, all these emotions, are messages which I have heard and received, I must understand them, somebody has spoken to me, it has spoken, who is the sender? The I is constituted in this sign relation both as an addressee (what Kant calls *Sinnlichkeit, Rezeptivität*) and as a cracker and investor of codes (intellect, *Selbsttätigkeit,* autonymy). Receptivity is here no more than the indispensable constructive *moment* of autoactivity. The I is first and foremost a self, but it makes *itself* by *constructing* what it or the other says (since it is not there). The same 'dialectic' of the intense and the intentional which splits those things encountered, also splits the self constitutively, and this split, receptive/active, sensible/intelligent, donee/donor, is its constitution. All that, let us repeat, is of value only in the configuration of the sign, the split of the Self is the constitutive split of the sign, part passivity part activity, part message received part decoding intelligence, part meaning part understanding, part emotional opacity part intentional capacity, and even Husserl with all his intentionality has to inject a passivity or a passive synthesis into his meditation. And, of course, it will be no more than a moment in the construction of intentionality, the jolly little movement of the jaw by which the head grasps meaning, catches up on it, oh formation of capital, gracious game of sublation [*relève*].

Two more things about semiotics. It thinks in concepts. The fact is that the sign is itself exactly the concept. Not only in its stable static constitution of terms whose connotation and denotation are ascribable only through a series of orderly relationships with other terms, and through a set of propositions which are themselves reputed to be well-formed with an explicit formal system; but also in its conceptual dynamism, the concept is the sign to the extent that there is a conquest, for like the sign, it *works*. It is uneasy, it searches out its own limits and frontiers and moves outwards towards its edges, touching them without ever attaining them (since as soon as it reaches them they cease to be exterior), while at the same time this allows it to be amazed at the power of the negative, oh stupid imperialism disguised as tragic laborism, oh comic 'work of the concept'! OK, you will say, we get the same so-called work with the sign: it's not as simple as you've made out, the relationship between one term and another in metonymy is not only endless, it is constantly confused, traversed by other chains, Freud taught us that, and in fact each term is a crossroads, a vertigo, and the network is a text or texture where not one, but many meanings are woven, each one pulling the term to itself, and that's your sign-work. Oh exquisite polysemy, tiny rift among the *bien-pensants*, little rebellious disorder, sugared deconstruction. Don't expect to catch the libidinal in those nets.

One last thing, which has already been made clear a thousand times: semiotics is nihilism. It is the religious science *par excellence*. Open your Victorins at the twelfth century and there you will see a beautiful example of semiotics, the attempt to read creation in all its details, to interpret statements as messages and to build up a code from them; and already we have a refinement, for Hugo and Richard de Saint-Victor know that they do not and never will *have* the code. With this refinement, then, they already love in things that element in things which denies them the code, they love the negative of the code in the message, they valorize the work of this negative, the text, the *dissimilitude* of things, and they find beauty in this. A religious science since it is haunted by the hypothesis that someone is speaking to us in these statements and, at the same time, that its language, its competence, or at all events its performance capacity, transcends us: the very definition of the unconscious that we find in the boldest semioticians, Lacan, or Eco. Thus the sign is wrapped up in nihilism, and nihilism proceeds by signs; to continue to stay in semiotic thought is to remain in religious melancholy and to subordinate all intense emotion to a lack and all force to a finitude.

Dissimulation

We know what your objection is, semioticians: whatever you do or think, you tell us, you make a sign of your action or reflection, you can't avoid it, simply by the way in which it is regarded on the referential axis of your action-discourse, hollowed out into a two-sided thing that is meaningful/meaningless, intelligible/sensible, manifest/

hidden, and has a front and a back; as soon as you speak, you will say, you excavate a theatre in things.

Fair enough, we don't deny it, we've been over that and we keep going over it, we have no wish to establish a new domain, another field *beyond representation* which would be immune to the effects of theatricality, not at all, we know very well that you're waiting for this piece of 'stupidity' (but such an error wouldn't merit this name; stupidity is instead something we wish to claim for ourselves) which would consist of saying: let's get out of signs and enter the order of the tensors beyond the reach of semiotics. We know very well that in saying that we should fully accomplish your desire, for it would be easy for the first semiotician to come along and start again on our apparent exteriority with the little African imperialist's work of exploration and ethnology, of the mission and the trading post, of pacification and the colony. We know that such is the fate you prepare with a smile for our libidinal economy, just as it is the fate that capital prepares for workers' demands, the Whites for *coloured people,* adults for children, normal folk for the mad, 'men' for 'women'. Very intimidating. It is here that *everything* is played out at present, here that we must fight and work out where we are going, a course that would trace not the frontiers of our empire, but our escape routes, as Deleuze says.

We must grasp this first: signs are not only terms, or stages, related and clarified in a voyage of conquest, but they *can* indissociably be the singular and vain intensities in an exodus.

Are we talking about another sort of sign? Not in the slightest, *they are the same* as those with which the semiotician carries out his theory and textual practice. The first thing to avoid, comrades, is to claim that we have taken up a position somewhere else. We're not moving out of anywhere, we're staying right here, we occupy the terrain of signs, we are just simply saying: that ritual death among the Guayaki, which you interpret as the counterpart of an exchange between the living and the dead designed to keep the world in balance and which you then make into a sign related to other terms in the general structure of Guayaki culture – well, we receive it *differently.* You say it speaks to you? It sets us in motion. Marcel's father climbs the stairs with his lamp: you hear in the agitation of his son the effect of the Oedipal structure, but we seek to continue this agitation in the fabrication of other things, texts, images, sounds, politics, caresses, which are, if possible, *as productive of movement* as Proust's text. And when I say '*as* productive' it is ill said, since it's not a question of quantity, we must see it as the singular quality of this text giving rise to repercussions, ramifications, and the invention of new libidinal pieces, which no other object would have been able to engender. First of all, then, a different reaction, a different reception. We do not suppose, to begin with, that the signs, in this case Proust's text, or Clastres's, are the vehicle for messages that are in principle communicable. We don't start off by saying to ourselves: someone or something is *speaking* to us here, so I must try to understand. To understand, to be intelligent, is not our overriding passion. We strive instead to be set in motion. This is why our passion would be more like the dance that Nietzsche wanted, and that Cage and Cunningham continue to look for. (And you understand at once that on this point of method we shall encounter the greatest difficulty and the greatest misunderstanding, since, first of all, we shall have a load of false dancers who will call themselves our friends, and then we shall have the censors who will explain to us, as if we didn't know, that to dance we must hear; but to that we say that it's not the same thing to dance by transit and to hear in order to comprehend; and lastly at this point we shall come up against the exiguous analysts, who will say: ah yes, you extol the *transition to the act*, that's what they call dancing, you are *acting out* in order not to be *working in:* I'm afraid this last lot will be the most difficult to subvert.)

A dance, then, not composed and written down, but on the contrary, one in which the body's gesture would be, with the music, its timbre, pitch, intensity and duration, and with the words (we dancers also sing), in a relation that is always singular, and which creates on each occasion an emotional event, as in Cage's *Theater Piece* or in the execution of a Noh play by an actor inspired by Zeami's *Flower of Interpretation*. We can sit a long time completely inert waiting for the moment of this flower, or encounter, the *tuchè* where something flares up on what is called the body, and we must also love this wait, which is just as beautiful, and this immobility which is barely less prompted and motivated than the display provided by the graceful gestures of delicate pale hands or their violent movement as they beat on the drum in the Korean courtly dance named *Yu Ch'o Shin.*

For it is also the case that we look for something in a face seen at night in Montparnasse, or in a voice on the telephone, something that will appear, a contour or a tone in the voice, a silence, a fixity, a sudden flash, and we never get it. And that, far from feeling resentful or disgusted, we love this reserve, with the greatest feeling of impatience.

A dance that includes suspense, as music includes silence. The important thing not being the fact that it is 'well composed' (although it needs to be) but that precisely at the moment of this semiotic perfection, there be tension. That the structure is only what 'covers' the effect, in the sense that it acts as a cover; that it is its *secret* and nearly its dissimulation. That is why we must love our enemies the semioticians and structuralists, for they are our accomplices, since in their light lies our darkness. Here, if I were composing, a eulogy of dis-simulation would be grafted on.

Let us content ourselves with recognizing in dissimulation exactly what we're looking for, difference within identity, the chance encounter within the composition's foresight, passion within reason – and between the two, so absolutely foreign to one another, the closest unity: dissimilation. Just as the Antichrist preaching in the square that Signorelli painted in a fresco at Orvieto completely resembles Christ, so is it true that Christ *dissimulates* the Antichrist in the sense that he conceals his formidable mission even in his choice of words, so that when he says: love one another, it would take no more than a word for the most disastrous misunderstanding to ensue (which in fact it does); and the Antichrist also dissimulates Christ in that he more or less simulates him, this being the *dis-* of dissimulation, or dissimilation. Our reception of the sign dissimulates the semiotic reception which in turn dissimulates our own, although not in the same way, without our having to decide if there is an Antichrist, and which one it is.

But let it be understood, to change our reference, that the two principles of Freud's late theory of drives (*Jenseits . . .*, 1920), namely Eros and death, are not simply two ways of proceeding, each of which is equipped with a different working principle that would allow us to identify them from their respective symptoms or effects in the 'psychism' or in the body. It is not true that Eros is a forger of groups and systems, a composer and master-binder, and that the death drives *on the other hand* are the destroyers of systems, the deconstructors and unbinders. When on the body of the hysteric pieces of the great band are circumscribed and excluded from the normed circulation of affects, and placed outside regular intensity, 'insensibilized', when muscles contract and remain tense, when respiratory channels become choked and provoke asthma, it creates small drive networks (a fragment of the organic system of breathing, a bit of the organic system of a striated or smooth set of muscles) which form interdependent groups: shall we say that it is Eros that is responsible for these collections? or death, because these sets have seized up? But seized up in relation to what, what normality? The respiratory system of Dora the organic is seized up, the respiratory system of Dora the hysteric works wonderfully, and there is no need to seek a *secondary benefit* in her distress. The benefit is immediate, there is no benefit, there is a drive-machine set in place, which functions *for its own sake*. This machinery does not obey either death or Eros, but both, and is erotic in so far as it is an orderly machine (whose discourse will try to produce a rational simulacrum in the texts of Freud or Lacan), and lethal in so far as it is a machine with a fault (which the analyst wishes to repair) – but also deadly in so far as it is orderly (because it condemns Dora to a sterile repetition), and lively since it is lacking in order (because it attests that the libido can circulate and invest itself on the organic body with complete unpredictability). There are, then, two principles, and these principles are not identifiable moments because of their respective functions, since Eros can untie and set free, while death is capable of tightening the knot to the point of strangulation. Freud himself, who didn't see this clearly, nonetheless recognized it at the end of *Jenseits* when he says in the space of a few lines first of all that the pleasure principle is subordinate to the death drive: here he understands the latter to be a system of repetitive compulsions which make *everything* return, even the most painful experiences, as in the dreams of a traumatic neurotic, and that we must assume a *liaison* through repetition before every discharge if it is true that the latter de-mands specific and orderly means by which to produce satisfaction; and then, a little later, that the Nirvana principle is subordinate to the pleasure principle, meaning now by 'Nirvana' that excess of force which pushes the discharge beyond the metabolic rule to which the 'psychic apparatus' (or the body) is submitted, and which threatens to rupture the latter. The functions are indefinable on each particular occasion; it is a question of always reserving the possibility of being incapable of assigning an effect, *that is, precisely, a sign,* to one drive principle and one alone. And it is clear that it is no longer a question of *polysemy,* or overdetermination, we won't get out of it by saying: death will add its effects to those of Eros, or vice versa; it has got nothing to do with the fact that the sign, Dora's cough, is caught up in *several networks* or structures creating meaning.

It clearly has to do with the totally different fact that the sign is in one respect indeed caught up in these networks, and so localizable in metonymic systems (or, in Freud himself, still often metaphorical systems) which are different from one another, and that it is heterosemic or heterological and consequently subject to semiotics – but *beyond* this fact, *jenseits* . . . . , that it is *not* assignable to such and such a function nor therefore to the play of its effects of meaning, that it is indiscernibly a sign of referral and by referral, but without an assignable referral. It is at once a sign that creates meaning through divergence and opposition, and a sign that creates intensity through strength and singularity. One might almost be tempted to give priority to libidinal intensity (but we shall not, for we are too much the old fox that has been trapped once too often to do that) and to say: but after all, if you, the semiologues, have any cause for weaving your networks of meaning, it is *first of all because* there is this positive incandescence, because Dora's throat first of all seizes up, because there is, in short, a datum, which is indeed the intensification of a certain region of the beautiful Dora's body, and the fact that this region has become an intelligent-intelligible sign! But we're not even saying that, indifferent as we are to questions of priority or causality, those forms of guilt, as Freud and Nietzsche called them. The other doesn't matter, but what is very important, however, is the fact that from this same symptom two receptions are simultaneously possible, inevitably.

Is there any need to point out the amusing perspectives opened up by this idea of dissimulation, notably in the matter of theoretical discourse, but also in the case (blandly accepted these days under the label Marxo-Freudian) of the dialectic of theory and practice?

Intensity, the name

If an example must be given of the way in which the tensor can dissimulate itself in the semantic which it in turn dissimilates, we could take that of the proper name. It is first of all that name of which Frege and Russell speak, which creates a problem for the logician because it refers in principle to a single reference and does not appear exchangeable against other terms in the logico-linguistic structure: there is no intra-systemic equivalent of the proper name, it points outwards like a deictic, and either has no connotations at all, or else an interminable number of them. A slight hitch which the logicians resolve with the concept (not having any choice of means) of the predicate of existence. Hegel already knew this: the *meinen,* and the obstacle that the gift of existence, flesh and bones, as Husserl will say in turn, can set up in opposition to any systematization of signs. So to those who will ask: what about Flechsig? we can reply: there is at least one existent individual such that he can be called Flechsig, and he was Schreber's doctor, anchoring ourselves firmly to the reference. But the name of this same individual gives rise to *dividuation* when Schreber's delirium takes hold of it. It will render compatible a multitude of incompossible propositions regarding a single 'subject' of the utterance [*énoncé*]. Of the predicate Flechsig it will be said simultaneously that he is a cop, God, and a lover seduced by the feminine charges of Schreber, that he does everything to prevent the President from shitting, and that he is a member of a noble family that has had long dealings with the Schrebers. What makes this a delirium? Only the fact that it is uttered.

That the same delirium displayed by a writer, barely more prudent for having placed a subject of the enunciation between himself and his text, called Marcel, that same delirium revolving around the proper name of Albertine.

The same delirium expressed by Octave regarding the proper name of Roberte,[2] the MP whore, the virtuous libertine, the indefinable body offered and refused, a body of dissimulation *par excellence* because it is a dissimulation in two senses: on the one hand the Huguenot and pleasure-seeker capable of standing as a sign in the equally thinkable networks of respectability and sensuality; but on the other hand each of these assignations dissimulating something; not the other as such, to the extent that it belongs for its part to a network that is itself ordered, similarly ordered, and merely displaced, the MP being as thinkable as the whore, each according to its own nature – no, each assignation dissimulating the sign as a tensor, and not the other sensate sign, and the tensor-sign, consisting of the fact that the proper name of Roberte covers an area where the two 'orders' (at least two, there are probably more) are not two, but indiscernible, where the name *Roberte* is like a disjunctive bar spinning at top speed around some point, the look, the vulva, the gloved thumb, an intonation, while itself travelling erratically along the segment formed by this line. If Roberte is a tensor, it's not because she is at once a broad and a bluestocking, but because she exceeds *jenseits both* of these assignations in the vertigo of an intensity where, if the inner thigh is revealed at the edge of the skirt, if the flesh of the thumb strains towards the seducer's mouth, if the nape of the neck leans away from his teeth, it is certainly for reasons of genuine prudishness and sincere sensuality, but also for a reason that is not qualifiable, a figure propelled by drives where impulses that do not belong to Roberte, nor to anyone else, are disposed and dispersed. If Roberte is not the name of someone (a predicate of existence), even if it is double, it is the name of this unnameable, the name of the Yes and No, of the neither Yes nor No, and of the both the first and the second, and if the proper name is a good example of a tensorial sign, it is not because its singular designation creates difficulties when one thinks in concepts, but because it covers a region of libidinal space given over to the undecidability of energy impulses, a region of fire.

The same goes for Schreber. If we concentrate on his *Memoirs of my Nervous Illness*,[3] we see the vertigo that is localized, as it were, around the name of Flechsig. I must be a woman, thinks Schreber, so that God can impregnate me, and so that, by giving birth to new men, the salvation of humanity can be accomplished through me. This change of sex is a miracle; but any modification of the body is in the eyes of Schreber a miracle and must be imputed to a singular power, at all events to the singular decision of a power (in this Schreber's religion is totally Roman, closely related to the intercession by divine authority in the most simple, daily acts, to that secularization of the sacred or sacralization of the secular). The same applies to defecation: it gives cause for dissimulation, which will be extended to Flechsig (through God); and even if this continual ambivalence of the density of these drives can be described, the important point nonetheless remains the indiscernible nature of the incompossible elements at any given moment, giving and hold back shit, Flechsig the protector and Flechsig the executioner, God the lover and God the persecutor, my man body and my woman body, my divine self and my human self; and something else *besides.*

Defecation is not natural, but miraculous. And it is here, à propos this *miracle of shitting,* which Freud quotes in its entirety, that we see what *delirium* can accumulate around a single name. If defecation demands the miraculous intervention of a 'One' that is both Flechsig and God, of what is this the *sign?* Of the love that *one* bears Schreber or the assistance that *one* lends him? No; or rather yes, but very indirectly. This compassionate love appears only allusively in the President's discourse, and it appears back to front. If Flechsig-God makes defecation miraculous, and removes from Schreber's body the natural use of this function, it is in truth in order to be able to *demiraculize in extremis* the act of shitting, and thus to persecute the President: they send people into the toilets in front of him to occupy all the seats. In this way they cut short 'the extremely strong feeling of *spiritual voluptuousness'* that accompanies a successful defecation. And if they use it in this way, it is because such a jouissance *menaces* Flechsig-God, in that it subjugates them to the body of the President, as is the case with every intense feeling of bliss. For example: 'God would never undertake to withdraw from me (. . .), but on the other hand he would continually yield without any resistance to the attraction that pushes him towards me, if it were possible for me always to assume the role of a woman clasped in my own sexual embraces, if I could always *allow* my gaze to fall on feminine forms, always look at images of women, and so on.' It is not, then, through love that *one* makes Schreberian defecation miraculous, but in order to defend oneself against the seduction it exerts. Flechsig the lover, but on the defensive. But also Flechsig the perfidious persecutor, who asks Schreber: 'Why do you not shit?' in order to make him reply: 'Because I am stupid or something like that.' Flechsig who humiliates his victim. But as well as that the stupid Flechsig-God, incapable of understanding that a human creature has no need of a miraculous intervention of an omnipotence in order to defecate: 'The pen refuses to record this enormous absurdity, namely that God, blinded by his ignorance of human nature, could actually go so far as to acknowledge the existence of a man incapable of the one thing any animal can do: a man stupid enough to be incapable of shitting.'

Do all these contrasting properties still merely form a polysemy around the name of Flechsig? We shall see. But before that two remarks that herald what is to follow. The first: let us observe the immensity of this stupidity, which goes well beyond the bestiality of Bataille, since the latter continues to know what it is doing, even if consciousness no longer knows, wherein lies the whole *Acéphale*[4] secret of a tiny eroticism, while with Schreber we must flounder about in a swamp of uncertainty that shapes the instincts themselves, montages of the beast, where we are beyond the knowledge of the headless animal, where the 'body' no longer knows how to shit even though it 'needs' to, and where the shit doesn't know where to come out. The fantastic stupidity of the mad body, into which Flechsig plunges Schreber. The opposite of the organic body, montage of montages, functional assemblage, erotic edification, this libidinal body appears not to have any channel set up for the circulation and discharge of impulses. Not the profundity of stupidity, but the immensity, the absence of measure. *Libidinal stupidity* is something altogether different from that of Bouvard and Pécuchet which consists of recitation, of quoting anew by dipping into the *common fund* of platitudes, and something quite close to it, since, like it, it rests on the destruction of the subject capable of answering for its statements and acts, on the loss of identity (illustrated in Flaubert by the *duo* that makes up the stupid hero).[5] A stupidity inseparable from the dissimulation we are speaking about here.

The second remark: this stupidity can be found in the strange acceptance of femininity implied by the text quoted above from President Schreber; it is 'having' a woman rather than being one, this 'having' translating indifferently as: to act like a woman during coitus and *also to be this woman's man* ('to assume the role of woman clasped in my own sexual embraces'), to see woman, to see the image of woman – and no doubt even: to be seen as woman, and so on. Here again the stupid immensity of the libidinal band. There is a correspondence between the proper name of Flechsig, tensor *par excellence*, and the anonymization of Schreber's body: a body without any regular organic function, a body without a sex or with many sexes. Shall we now say that the name of Flechsig is but the predicate of several utterances which imply that, beneath it, incompossible drives are writhing about? Flechsig loves me, since he makes me shit-come; Flechsig hates me since he forbids me to shit-come; I love the fact that Flechsig hates me, since my own persecution is necessary so that I can bring about the salvation of future humanity; I hate the fact that Flechsig loves me, because I want defecation to be as natural for me as for anyone else . . .

Let us interrupt this list of statements which are already in themselves simplified. Ignore the reading that Freud makes of the relationship between Schreber and Flechsig: as a semiotic or conceptual reading it is exemplary, since it creates from all these statements and many more besides the terminal phrases resulting from the transformations of a single core which would be: *I (a man) love him (a man)*. Transformations due, as in the exfoliation of the fantasy *A child is being beaten* to the drives displaced by repression or regression, and consequently implying a use that is certainly not very generative, but is nonetheless perfectly regulated and regulating, of negation. Let us discuss instead the following point: do our statements (whether four or *n* in number, what does it matter, since who would claim to exhaust their potential series?) really give rise to what we are looking for under the name of dissimulation? Don't they rather provide a polysemy, on the one hand a homonymy, Flechsig the lover being the homonym for Flechsig the executioner, on the other hand a synonymy, Flechsig the lover and executioner being the synonym for God (a synonymic group to which Freud does not fail to add the Father) – so many relations which the semiologue knows well and will accept, not at all as an objection to his method, but as an encouragement to it. All this certainly leads us into those transformations by which we scarcely come close to a libidinal economy. If Flechsig, as our previous example, Roberte, illustrated a minute ago, is a tensor-sign, and not simply 'sensate', it is not because of the polysemy of utterances attached to his name, but because of the vertigo of anal eroticism which seizes the Schreberian libidinal body, of which the name Flechsig is an extension. A vertigo because it is once more around the anus that the revolution of the disjunctive bar will grow furious to the point where the President's arse will glow like the sun, above all to the point where it will henceforth become impossible to distinguish between facilitating or forbidding the passage of matter (the faeces or the divine member), since the two movements will be invested and activated together: 'It takes place in the following way: the matter is pushed forward and sometimes also backward in my intestines, and if there is not enough left . . .', to the point where in this agonizing strug-gle taking place between constipation and diarrhoea, hetero- and homosexuality, virility and femininity, it is the position of the sun, of the gods, of doctors, of men, which begins to turn on itself by denying any stable distribution and any 'thought'. This incandescent vertigo bears the name of Flechsig, and it is this way that he is of value as a tensor-sign.

It spins out the game of the top, beyond the organic body of Schreber, into unexpected regions of the libidinal band; this name grasps them or rather suddenly lets them exist as pieces of the vast *anonymous* fanatical erectile labyrinth. Ah, so you thought you were a doctor engaged in restoring my solar anus to the miserable dimensions of pre-genital Oedipal regression; by saying Flechsig, by building on Flechsig my metaphysical and historical novel, by placing Flechsig at the beginning and end of my loves and hates, I make you, doctor, not a piece in *my* paranoic game, as you think, but an unpredictable scrap of the immense band where anonymous impulses circulate. Your name is the guarantee of anonymity, the guarantee that these drives *belong to no one,* that no one, not even the 'doctor', is safe from their course and their investment. That's why you get scared and lock me up. What is woven by the name of Flechsig is therefore not only the wise polysemy that we find in the most banal statement but also the incandescence of a piece of body which cannot hold any more assignation, because the pros and cons invest it together, and even more than that, it is the transmission of this unthinkable burning to other libidinal regions, here namely the languages of history and religion, their invention and capture in the anal vertigo, their sexualization, as we used to say, the link forged between them and the mad anus, the extension made from the latter to the former. And so it is the supposed frontier of the body of Schreber which finds itself violated by the name of Flechsig (as much as the supposed frontier of the body of Flechsig). This limit itself is pulverized by the vertiginous turning, the President's body disinte-grates and its pieces are projected across libidinal space, mingling with other pieces in an inextricable patchwork. The head in all this is not more than any old bit of skin. Flechsig my arse. Beyond synonymy and homonymy, anonymity.

NOTES

1 Translator's note: in English in the original.
2 Translator's note: a reference to *Les lois de l'hospitalité*, by Pierre Klossowski.

3 Translator's note: *Denkwurdigkeiten eines Nervenkranken* (Leipzig: Oswald Mutze, 1903); first translated into English by Dr Ida Macalpine and Dr Richard A. Hunter as *Memorabilia of a Nerve Patient* (London: William Dawson, 1953).
4 Translator's note: the word can be translated as 'headless'. It refers to a review of that name, first published by Guy Levis Mano in June 1936, under the directorship of Bataille and Masson. Its cover bore a drawing by Masson of a headless man.
5 This is shown in an unpublished work on *Bouvard et Pécuchet* by Suzanne Lafont.

Translated by Sean Hand

2

The Dream-Work Does Not Think

It should come as no surprise that the problematics of work versus discourse is the nub of chapter 6 of *The Interpretation of Dreams*. In the course of this chapter Freud examines the dream-work and enumerates the essential operations by which it proceeds. It is easy to show that each of these operations is conducted according to rules which are in direct opposition to those governing discourse. The dream is not the language of desire, but its work. Freud, however, makes the opposition even more dramatic (and in doing so lets us in on a figural presence in discourse), by claiming that the work of desire is the result of manhandling a text. Desire does not speak; it does violence to the order of utterance. This violence is primordial: the imaginary fulfilment of desire consists in this transgression, which repeats, in the dream workshop, what occurred and continues to occur in the manufacture of the so-called primal phantasm.

The figure is hand in glove with desire on at least two counts. At the margin of discourse it is the density within which what I am talking about retires from view; at the heart of discourse it is its 'form'. Freud himself says as much when he introduces the term *Phantasie*, which is at once the 'facade' of the dream and a form forged in its depths.[1] It is a matter of a 'seeing' which has taken refuge among words, cast out on their boundaries, irreducible to 'saying'. We will dwell a little on secondary revision because the *Fliegende Blätter* inscriptions, in spite of their dismaying aesthetic impoverishment, provide an excellent opportunity for formulating the relationship between image and text. Considerations of beauty aside, art begins here.

I

At the end of chapter 6 of *The Interpretation of Dreams*, which deals with the dream-work, Freud recalls the question with which he began: 'whether the mind employs the whole of its faculties without reserve in constructing dreams, or only a functionally restricted fragment of them'.[2] His response is that the question must be rejected: it is badly put, 'inadequate to the circumstances'. On the basis of the terms in which it is stated, the answer would have to be in the affirmative in both cases: the mind contributes *both* totally and partially to the production of the dream. What Freud calls the *Traumgedanke*, the dream-thoughts, what the dream thinks, *what it says clearly,* its latent pronouncement (*énoncé*), must be attributed *in toto* to waking thought. It is 'perfectly proper thought' (*vollig korrekt*) which belongs to the same genus as conscious thought. Even if it retains some puzzling aspects, these have no 'special relation to dreams and do not call for treatment among the problems of dreams'.[3]

What the dream says *at bottom* is fully intelligible. Its motivating discourse is an intelligent one, subject to the same rules as waking discourse. No doubt that is why Freud believes that an interpretation (something quite different from pure invention on the interpreter's part) is possible, because such an interpretation does not have to recover a meaning (*sens*), but a *signification* just as explicit as that which pertains to 'normal' discourse. It is for this very reason, however, that the essence of the dream is not to be found in the dream-thoughts. Freud makes this clear in a note added in 1925:

Many analysts have become guilty of falling into another confusion which they cling to with equal obstinacy. They seek to find the essence of dreams in their latent content and in so doing they overlook the distinction between the latent dream-thoughts and the dream-work. At bottom, dreams are nothing more than a particular *form* of thinking, made possible by the conditions of the state of sleep. It is the *dream-work* which creates that form, and it alone is the essence of dreaming (*das Wesentliche am Traum*) – the explanation of this peculiar nature.[4]

This work, however, does not belong to the category of waking thought: 'it diverges further from our picture of waking thought than has been supposed even by the most determined depreciator of psychical functioning during the formation of dreams'.[5] It is a transformation. The dream-work is 'completely different . . . qualitatively' from waking thought, so that it is 'not immediately comparable with it'. The dream-work 'does not think, calculate or judge in any way at all; it restricts itself to giving things a new form'.[6]

It is advisable, if one wants truly to grasp Freud's intention, to take seriously the opposition he establishes between dream-thoughts and dream-work (*Gedanke* and *Arbeit*), and the transforming action (*umformen*) of the dream. The discourse which resides at the heart of the dream is the object of this work, its raw material. The dream-work does not relate to this primary discourse as another discourse, such as that of interpretation, might do; the gap between latent content (*Traumgedanke*) and manifest content is not the empty distance, the transcendence separating a 'normal' discourse from its object (even if that object is itself a discourse), nor yet that which separates a text from its translation into another language. That difference is 'intrinsic' according to Freud. The problem of the dream-work is therefore to discover how, from the raw material of a statement, a qualitatively different though still meaningful object can be produced. The work is not an interpretation of the dream-thought, a discourse on a discourse. Neither is it a transcription, a discourse based on a discourse. It is its transformation.

This statement of the problem sets the tone for all the descriptions of oneiric elaboration in chapter 6. From beginning to end of the study, Freud assimilates the dream-thoughts to a text and the dream-work to a sum of operations carried out on the ('correct') meaning of the text, but by means of procedures which are non-linguistic, and which hence must operate on the text as if it were material. How must a *text* be *worked over* in order for its stated meaning to be modified?

To begin with, a word about chapter 4, which deals with the notion of *Entstellung* (distortion). The help it offers might appear to be slight, given that we might justifiably expect it to contain the heart of the matter, if it is indeed the case that in the notion of *Entstellung* an entire way of working on the initial text is summed up. In everyday speech, the word indicates the use of force: *sich entstellen,* to disfigure oneself; *die Sprache entstellen,* to do violence to language. According to Sachs and Villate, the semantic field of the particle *ent-* is constructed along three axes: that of privation, of deduction (de-position); of distancing (ex-position); of progress from a given point of departure (trans-position). But Freud's thought in this chapter is focused elsewhere. He wonders why, if the dream is the fulfilment of a wish, it frequently contains failures, disappointed wishes and frustrated desires. It is at this point that he shows that the motive of distortion is censorship: a power exerted by an authority forcing desire to disguise itself. At the end of chapter 4, the canonical formula for the dream posited in its third section has to be modified as follows: '*a dream is a (disguised) fulfilment of a (suppressed or repressed) wish*'.[7] This is a statement whose parentheses at once record the chapter's acquisition and echo its tone: that of repression. It is therefore the first trace of the theory of repression, rather than an analysis of the concept of *Entstellung*, which is to be found in chapter 4. This is not to diminish the importance of the theory of repression. It teaches us the fundamental truth that repression and desire are born simultaneously.

There is, however, a short meditation on *Entstellung* in *Moses and Monotheism*,[8] Freud's last piece of writing. In it Freud advanced the hypothesis that the Jews, who had rebelled several times against the over-austere, over-paternal religion which Moses, allegedly an Egyptian, had imposed on them, killed him; and that after the subsequent reconciliation of the people with itself and with religion, under another Moses, oral and then written tradition indefatigably worked and reworked the story of Moses, the Pentateuch, in order to conceal the murder. The dream-thought in this instance is therefore parricide, and the work of disguise is called *Entstellung*. I am deliberately ignoring the other secondary operation, whose objective is the pious conservation of the text, thus interfering, so Freud presumes, with *Entstellung*. He writes as follows:

> In its implications the distortion (*Entstellung*) of text resembles a murder [in this instance a murder, that of Moses; but the latter was already an *Entstellung*: a distortion of the father's Word]: the difficulty is not in perpetrating the deed, but in getting rid of its traces. We might well lend the word *Entstellung* the double meaning to which it has a claim but of which today it makes no use. It should mean not only 'to change the appearance of something' but also 'to put something in another place, to displace'. Accordingly, in many instances of textual distortion, we may nevertheless count upon finding what has been suppressed and disavowed hidden away somewhere else, though changed and torn away from its context. Only it will not always be easy to recognize it.[9]

At first glance, Freud's remark appears to take *Entstellung* in the weak sense. The displacement of its fragments does not demand that the body of the text undergo the pressures, slippages and thrust faultings which arise in *The Interpretation of Dreams*. A bit of text may be displaced without interfering with the space of writing, of language. Consequently *transposition* would be an adequate translation of *Entstellung*: a piece is taken out here and replaced somewhere else. But that is to forget the act itself. On reflection, it seems that such an operation cannot fail to have recourse to a spatial dimension which is precisely excluded from the linguistic system. To erase a fragment from one place on the page (remove it from a particular point in the chain) and put it elsewhere (where space will have to be made for it) demands that the extract move *above* the text. This movement takes place, therefore, in depth, the same depth required by Kant for the superimposition, by rotation, of two triangles symmetrical with respect to a perpendicular, and which cannot be made to coincide by a simple planar movement. In what does the murder which is the *Entstellung* of the Pentateuch consist? In precisely this: a text is inscribed on a plane surface, the two-dimensional spatial limitations of which reproduce the linguistic restraints governing the units which constitute the text, while it symbolizes, for Freud, the strictures of the Law itself; and this text is still subjected to processes inscribed in a three-dimensional space. Writing belongs to a space of reading (letters without depth), the process of displacement has a gesticulatory, visual scope, and the result of displacement, which encompasses both the readable and the visible, is illegible.[10] It is this that constitutes a kind of murder: desire, with its dimension of depth, disfigures the *table* of the Law. And simultaneously, by the same token, it is illegible, hence hidden. Its concealment demands the depth which discourse excludes. Here, in the violence of the Law *vis-à-vis* desire, and the violence of desire's disrupting the space of the Law, we have the two demands of the dream-work: the wish and censorship, both violent, the former undecidable.

With this understanding of *Entstellung*, let us return to an inventory of the processes instituted by the dream-work. We know that Freud enumerates four of these: condensation (*Verdichtung*), displacement (*Verschiebung*), considerations of figurability (*Rücksicht auf Darstellbarkeit*) and secondary revision (*sekundäre Bearbeitung*).[11] It would be an easy matter to show precisely how each of these operations is based on a spatiality which, far from being the locus of the discourse's meaning (*Traumgedanke*), can only be the sensitive, plastic surface where the text is supposed to be inscribed. I will limit myself to the following remarks:

1 *Condensation* must be understood as a physical process by means of which one or more objects occupying a given space are reduced to a smaller volume, as is the case when a gas becomes a liquid. Consequently, when condensation is applied to a text, it has the effect of telescoping either the signifiers (the *Norekdal* dream, etc.),[12] or the signifieds (dream of the botanical monograph),[13] or both, into 'objects' which, in any case, are no longer specifically linguistic, and are even specifically non-linguistic. As far as the signifiers at least are concerned, Freud is categorical: condensation is a *Spielerei* (the dream of

the *Autodidasker*)[14] which treats words as if they were things, like the *Sprachkünste* of childhood and of neurosis.[15] Condensation comes under an energetics which plays 'freely' with the units of the initial text, freely, that is, relative to the constraints peculiar to the message, to any linguistic message. Hence condensation is a transgression of the rules of discourse. In what does this transgression consist? In condensation itself! To squeeze signifiers and signifieds together, mixing them up, is to neglect the stable distance separating the letters and words of a text, to scorn the distinctive, invariable graphemes of which they are composed, not to recognize, in a word, the space of discourse. This space, neutral and empty, plane of pure oppositions, does not appear by itself. It is invisible, but all the elements of language (or of writing) attain specificity in it, and it is thanks to it that we are able to 'hear' (or 'read').

Condensation is a change of 'state' (a difference in 'nature'). The geometric space of language, where the differential lines which lend order to the line of discourse (of the written text) meet, is invaded, as a result of this process, by a movement which violates its taboos, and constructs word-things, words that are 'comical and strange',[16] from the units it finds there. Their 'thingness' lies in their depth. Normally, in the linguistic order, a word is transparent: its meaning is immediate, and it is that meaning which is received, the phonic or graphic vehicle passing, so to speak, unperceived; the product of condensation, as its name implies, is, on the contrary, opaque, dense, hiding its other side/s.

Now this mobility which manufactures things out of words, is it not desire itself, pursuing its usual course, producing the imaginary? If this is the case, then we should not say that condensation is an exercise by means of which desire disguises itself, but rather that it *is desire working over* the text of the dream-thoughts. In the first of these interpretations, the force is located *behind* the manifest content, itself assumed to be a disguised text; in the second, and apparently correct one, the force, on the contrary, compresses the primary text, crumpling it up, folding it, scrambling the signs it bears on its surface, fabricating new units which are not linguistic signs or graphic entities. The manifest content is the old text 'forced' in this manner; it is not a text. Force occupies the very scenario of the dream as Van Gogh's brush-stroke remains recorded in his suns.

This hypothesis would appear to run counter to Freud's own explanation: that the force which crushes the text, pulverizing and combining its elements, is censorship. It would follow from that explanation that desire would be the initial discourse of the *Traum-*

gedanke, and the work of condensation (and all the revision) would be the product of censorship. But this imputation raises great difficulties: the censor understands what he reads before he cuts, and *in order* to cut. As far as pre-conscious censorship is concerned, 'meaning' belongs to articulated language; it is in the realm of the 'readable'. Cutting a text after having understood it is a parapraxis if it was a matter of not knowing it. This would be a regression to the Sartrian hypothesis of bad faith. The dream, however, is truly initially opaque: between the text from which it comes and the 'reader' (the interpreters), there is no third knowing authority which embellishes the first for the benefit of the second. It must not therefore be the agency to deceive which assumes the responsibility to disguise (transitive verb), but desire itself which disguises itself (reflexive verb). Only that reflexiveness is unreflecting, pre-reflexive, and one can understand how. Desire is a scrambled text from the outset. The disguise does not result from the alleged deceiving intent of desire; the work itself *is* disguise because it is violence perpetrated on linguistic space. There is no need to imagine that the id has an idea at the back of its head. 'The dream-work does not think.' The mobility of the primary process is deceptive in itself; it *is* what deceives, what sends the 'faculties' using articulated language into a spin: the figural versus the mind.

So much for the principle. It raises several difficulties, however, and Freud's thought on the subject is by no means unequivocal.[17] How do desire, dream-thoughts, and censorship interact? The hypothesis could be advanced that there is a de-centring of their relationship in the course of Freud's work, a de-centring which does not in any way prevent the terms from occupying different positions at a given period.

In the first kind of relationship, the dream-thoughts are the intelligible text which an exogenous censorship renders indecipherable, thus inviting the analogy with political censorship.[18] In this case it is censorship which represents force, which is exerted on an unconscious desire that speaks. In the second kind of relationship, the dream-thoughts (*Traumgedanken*) are always opposed to the dream-content (*Trauminhalt*), just as the latent is to the manifest content. But this latent content no longer possesses the limpidity of a text, the *Traumgedanken* are composites of text and figure. There are ready-made symbols in the depths of the dream,[19] material designed to lead censorship astray, because it already contains elements of the unreadable and the figural. There is, therefore, a precensorship, which is in fact the originary repression. Freud subsequently emphasizes the ambivalence of censorship,[20] which thus also serves the interests of desire. If we apply the capitalist/entrepreneur metaphor to this relationship, desire is the capitalist, furnishing the energy; the entrepreneur provides the ideas (the thoughts).[21] But, says Freud, it is only a question of two *functions*. They may both be embodied in the same man: there are capitalists with ideas (= the textual may be present in desire), and entrepreneurs with capital (= desire profits by the perceptions and traces that make up the *Traumgedanke*).

In other words, desire is forbidden long 'before' the censorship of the dream comes into play; it is intrinsically forbidden. And it is necessary to dissociate, not a pure force from a discourse, but the 'discourse' of desire (which, figural and figurative, constitutes the matrix of the primal phantasm) from the pre-conscious material, diurnal perceptions and traces, which this matrix attracts and works over to the point of making it unrecognizable, the objective being both to fulfil desire – repeating the matrix form by imprinting it on a material – and to disguise and to clothe that form with elements deriving from reality. The censorship that Freud speaks of in *The Interpretation of Dreams* is therefore the operation by which the silt of daily experience (the day's residues) comes to cover over archaic desire. But this desire already carries within itself its primary repression.[22] This means that it is a travesty from the 'outset', that it *has never spoken*, in any real sense of the word, that is, of emitting communicable utterances. This would even mean that 'to disguise' is a bad metaphor, since the word implies the identity of the thing under different clothing. This means that the correct metaphor would be 'to transgress', in the sense I have indicated.

On the other hand, the finality of the dream, wish-fulfilment (*Wunscherfüllung*) would be more satisfactorily explained. The principle of *Is fecit qui profuit,* formulated à propos of censorship in the case of displacement, ought to read: 'it is desire (and not censorship) that did it', since it is desire which the dream fulfils. It would be understood that the fulfilment of desire, an important function of the dream, consists not in the representation of a satisfaction (which, on the contrary, when it occurs, wakes one up), but entirely in the imaginary activity itself. It is not the dream-content that fulfils desire, but the act of dreaming, of fantasizing, because the Phantasy is a transgression.

2 *Displacement*   Freud calls it 'the essential portion (*das wesentliche Stück*) of the dream-work', 'one of the principal methods by which that distortion (*Entstellung*) is achieved'. There is no need to dwell on it any more than Freud does,[23] for displacement is treated in these pages as a preparatory step to condensation. The latter has been shown to be closely connected to overdetermination, but to overdetermine sup-

poses certain changes of emphasis in the initial text of the dream-thoughts. In condensing themselves, the dream-thoughts crush certain parts of the discourse, leaving others visible. Take a text written on a sheet of paper and crumple it. The elements of the discourse take on *relief*, in the strict sense. Imagine that before the grip of condensation compresses the dream-thoughts, displacement has reinforced certain zones of the text, so that they resist contraction and remain legible. The result is the 'textual difference' between dream-content (*Trauminhalt*) and dream-thoughts (*Traumgedanke*).[24]

We have a simple example of this in the poster for Frédéric Rossif's film *Révolution d'Octobre* (figure 1). The letters of the title are deformed in such a way as to give the impression that a wind is blowing the flat surface on which they are written. This is enough to make this plane movable, to turn it into a piece of cloth, the cloth of a flag carried by someone who is walking fast towards the left (which, as well as being politically symbolic, also carries a plastic value: the eye moves from the left when reading; hence the letters move ahead of the glance, complementing its movement). But this is only the beginning of condensation. If the wind were to blow harder, if the horse of the standard-bearer were to gallop flat out, if one were able to 'freeze' the inscription, certain letters would disappear altogether into the folds and others would undergo radical changes. B, whose base was masked by a fold, might be read as an R, D as an O, etc. Certain differential or graphically relevant features would be transgressed. It could happen that *Révolution d'Octobre* might read *Révon d'Ore* and be heard as *Rêvons d'or* (let's dream of gold). So much for condensation, which clearly requires the third dimension, that in which the flag forms its folds. But such a distortion would have required a preliminary choice; in our example, it is the beginning (*REV, D'O*) and the end (*ON, RE*) that must remain visible, must stand fast to windward. It is the work of

Figure 1

displacement that effects this choice by reinforcing certain parts of the cloth, stiffening them, enabling them to preserve certain sites of the – primary – text in position. 'Textual difference' might be imagined in these terms. It remains, however, to conceive of it. If desire is the mobile element (here the wind, elsewhere water) that crumples the text, can it also be the fixative which keeps certain parts of it readable? I know of only one notion which can satisfy these conflicting demands: the notion of Form, of Phantasy.

3 Look out for the figure: *Rücksicht auf Darstellbarkeit* (considerations of figurability). We must proceed cautiously here, because here desire seizes the text in a quite different manner. By condensation and displacement it acts on the *supposed site* of its inscription. One might say that by figuration, desire, in addition, takes words literally (*au pied de la lettre:* at the foot of the letter), the foot of the letter being the figure. Surrealist art might shed some light on this. I am thinking particularly of the paintings of Magritte, many of which are not plays on words but games played by the figure on the words which form its legend. For example, the painting called *Reconnaissance Infinie*[25] shows an enormous bare planet floating above desert mountains, bathed in a dull cosmic light, and on it a man in a double-breasted suit scanning the void, doing a reconnaissance of it. The examples which Freud borrowed from Silberer and which support his entire theory of figuration, show that exactly the same procedure takes place in the dream. '"Example 1. I thought of having to revise an uneven passage in an essay. Symbol: I saw myself planing a piece of wood"'.[26] The literal is the figure, at least if one accepts the hypothesis that all discourse aims at an object exterior to language, which may be presented (*darstellen*) as its referent. We rely, therefore, on the function of designation, rather than signification, in which the relation between the sign and the thing gels, where, as a result, magic (*magie*) can take place, the possibility of conjuring up the thing by the word, of making an image. *Image-magie,* the luck of the anagram, but objective luck, and Freud in any case was a firm believer in the relationship between the two. To become convinced of this one has only to read *Moses and Monotheism,* a meditation built exclusively on the opposition between the Jewish religion, sober and image-less, and the Egyptian one, full of magic and images. Beware of the figure because it is the thing supplanting the word, because it is desire fulfilled, not only childhood, but paranoia, hysteria, obsession.[27] Do not crumple the pages of the book! Do not illustrate it!

The *Rücksicht auf Darstellbarkeit* is that arrangement of an initial text which, according to Freud, has two objectives: to illustrate it, but also to replace certain portions of it by figures. In the illustration the figure is outside the text, and text and image are, as a rule, presented together (which gives rise to other problems). In the rebus, corresponding figures will be substituted for at least some fragments of the primary text. The *Rücksicht* is that operation on the text which consists in replacing 'colourless, abstract' expressions 'such as might be used in a political leading article in a newspaper' by expressions for which it would be permissible to use a figurative equivalent *or* substitute.[28] The text must become an 'imaged' text, by virtue of the fact that the 'imaged' (the imageable, *das Bildliche*) is, for the dream, 'particularly capable of being figured (*darstellungsfähig*).'

An imaged text is a discourse which is very close to the figure. It will be necessary, then, to analyse the different ways in which such a proximity may be established: the figurative power of a word, of course, but also the rhythmic power of syntax, and at an even deeper level, the matrix of narrative rhythm, what Propp called form. We will see revealed what I consider to be an essential paradox. At the lexical level, the figure is given as *outside the word* (Silberer's 'roughness', Magritte's 'reconnaissance'); at the (still rhetorical) level of syntax, the figure is the rhythmical schema (the rhythm of a given writer's sentence, Flaubert's as Proust studies it, for example). We are no longer in the domain of the visual. Here language communicates with dance by diffusing its range and frequency throughout the body of the reader: recitation, declamation, song are intermediaries between reading and dance. At the stylistic level, the figure is submerged in the words but only in order to support and control the articulation of the large units of the narrative. There is no longer anything visible, only the visual haunting narration. We are approaching the matrix. It is clear that the notion of the figure leads to image, configuration, form, and therefore a lexical and/or syntactical, but also stylistic, proximity, because there are figures which correspond to words, figures of style, of discourse, in each case, the figural surrounding the substance of language and permeating it. Pursuing this tack, we inevitably stumble, once again, on the question of the phantasm, which is pivotal. The great linguistic figures, of discourse, of style, are the expression, right in the heart of language, of a general disposition of experience, and the phantasm is the matrix of that ordering, that rhythm, which will henceforth be imposed on everything that happens on the levels of 'reality' and expression. Thus these figures figure a primary figure. It is through their agency that a discourse may enter into communication with the images that are reputed to be external to it, but which in fact depend for their organization on the same signifying matrix.

It is not fortuitous that Freud, in the passage under discussion, ends up spontaneously citing poetry as an example of the work of figuration, not on account of its powerful external images, but as an immanent rhythmic force (both rhythmed and rhythming): 'If a poem is to be written in rhymes, the second line of a couplet is limited by two conditions: it must express an appropriate meaning, and the expression of that meaning must rhyme with the first line'.[29] We will see that it is precisely this rhythm that Jakobson calls metaphor. The constraints of rhyme impose a scansion (*découpage*) on the signifier, and if the poem is a good one, on the signified, simultaneously. Similarly, there is a 'distribution and selection' of signs (signifier and signified) in the dream, which allows one particular sign to exercise an influence over the others by remote control, as it were, comparable to that which forces the poet to choose *retour* over *rentrée* because it must rhyme with *alentour* three lines earlier. This remote action, which takes place in the body of the work, is the very principle of form: all along the linear body of a text, an utterance or a piece of music, flat on the plane surface of a picture, in the volume of a sculpted object or a building, it is form which establishes communication between the parts, in keeping with certain constraints, and in order for it to be form, these constraints must not be inscribed in any *language*. Why? Because whatever is language is dedicated to communication between interlocutors, while the figure, as described above, has to jam that communication. By virtue of the fact that it sets up a closed circuit intercom system of the work with itself, the figure surprises the eye and the ear and the mind by a perfectly improbable arrangement of the parts. Thus there is no more restraint in the figure of discourse than in any other image. And it is futile to attempt to bring everything back to articulated language as the model for all semiology, when it is patently clear that language, at least in its poetic usage, is possessed, haunted by the figure.

II

Before dealing with the fourth operation of the dream-work (secondary revision), which I should particularly like to illustrate more fully, the most important implication of what I have just said must be examined, i.e., that the dream is not a discourse, because the dream-work is intrinsically different from the operations of speech. I have already indicated as much in the preceding remarks, but since this statement runs directly counter to what I believe to be Jacques Lacan's interpretation, as well as counter to the current tendency to stuff all of semiology into linguistics,[30] it is worthwhile confronting these positions.

The operations which have guided Lacan's interpretation of the dream-work are those elucidated by Roman Jakobson with regard to the speech act, in his article 'Two Functions of Language and Two Forms of Aphasia'.[31] The origin of the separation he makes in that article between metaphor and metonymy is to be found in the Saussurian thesis according to which meaning is ultimately reducible to a value, that is that the signified of the linguistic sign 'is only the resumé of the linguistic value, given the interplay of the terms'.[32] Saussure says, even more explicitly, that 'what the word contains is never determined by anything but the convergence of what exists around it, associatively and syntagmatically'.[33] In the table of language, what surrounds a given term organizes itself according to two kinds of relationships. The first, which are syntagmatic, determine the position and function of the term in every possible statement; the second, which Saussure called 'associative' or paradigmatic, link the term with others which may be substituted for it. I consider it very important to establish a link between the syntagm–paradigm opposition and the theory of meaning as a value because this theory, in turn, has meaning only insofar as a language refers back to a closed system (*la langue*) which is independent of its object, and precisely because of this exteriority can speak of that object. The closure of the system is pivotal to both these properties of language at once, the double internal function (paradigmatic and syntagmatic) and the external (referential) function.

Corresponding to the double setting of the term in language is the double operation in the speech act which Jakobson visualizes summarily as follows: the speaker chooses each term he utters from among all those which are linked to it by paradigmatic, substitutive relationships; and he combines the chosen terms according to the constraints of concatenation (syntagmatic relationships) which regulate the linking of each term used to its context in the line of speech. Thus for the speaker an act of selection corresponds to the paradigm, and an act of combination to the syntagm. Jakobson shows that given this disentanglement (*désintrication*), two forms of aphasia may be distinguished, according to whether the illness attacks the selective activity (disruption of similarity), leading to the loss of the capacity to define and of metalanguage in general, or whether, on the other hand, it affects the combinatory activity, leading to the disappearance of double articulation (agrammatism) by scrambling the relations of contiguity.

Jakobson's analyses are perhaps arguable for the linguist; they are extremely fertile for the philosopher. But in any case they make a strong assertion: that speech supposes twin, indissociable activities;[34] that it is illness which separates them in fact and the linguist who separates them in theory; and that it is the equilibrium of both functions in the speech act which guarantees, as a rule, the 'normality of the discourse',[35] that is to say, its communicability. Doubtless one function could gain precedence over the other without causing the discourse to become immediately aphasic. Jakobson attempts to apply his criterion of similarity/contiguity to literary discourse, an essential characteristic of which, in the eyes of linguists, is to 'unbalance' 'normal' discourse. He comes up with a classification on three different levels of discourse – rhetoric, genres, schools – which the following list summarizes:

Levels	Paradigmatic relationships	Syntagmatic relationships
Language	similarity	contiguity
Speech act	selection	combination
Trope	metaphor	metonymy
Genre	poetry	prose
School	Romanticism Symbolism	Realism

It has been noted that the extension of the criterion does not so far exceed the field of articulated language, properly so-called. But at the end of the article, Jakobson permits himself to take the plunge: 'The respective prevalence of one or the other of the two procedures is not in any way exclusive to literature. The same oscillation appears in sign systems other than language ... The competition between the two procedures, metonymic and metaphoric, is evident in every symbolic process, whether intra-subjective or social.'[36] It is at this point that he considers dreams: 'Thus in a study on the structure of dreams, the decisive question is to know if the symbols and temporal sequences used are based on contiguity (the Freudian metonymic "displacement" and synecdochic "condensation") or on similarity (Freudian "identification" and "symbolism".).'[37] The result of this formula is that displacement and condensation belong in the same column of our table, that of the syntagm, while identification and symbolism are consigned to the paradigmatic column.

Nicholas Ruwet, the translator of Jakobson's article, notes that this classification does not coincide with Lacan's: 'The latter identifies, respectively, condensation with metaphor, displacement with metonymy.'[38] In the table, therefore, condensation would go under paradigm, and displacement under syntagm. Jakobson and Lacan agree, therefore, in situating displacement in the syntagmatic order. The disagreement arises over condensation: syntagmatic for Jakobson, paradigmatic for Lacan. Ruwet adds: 'Roman Jakobson, to whom we have pointed this out, believes that the divergence is explained by the imprecision of the concept of condensation, which, in Freud, seems to encompass cases of both metaphor and synecdoche.'

This is to put the blame on Freud a little precipitously. Another hypothesis must be advanced, i.e., that the imprecision results from applying to one field of expression categories borrowed from another, an undertaking which is motivated by the desire to find in the dream-work the operations of speech. It is, I believe, that desire which is really 'imprecise', if it is to 'spell out' Freud's text that is involved without 'deducting anything from it'.[39] Failing recognition in the dream of a true discourse, true precisely because it conforms to the only two operations defined by the linguist – which the analysis of the dream as well as that of *The Interpretation of Dreams* preclude – the desire of which I spoke runs the risk of backfiring on the two operations of selection and combination in order to bend them to the project. The dream cannot be made to speak? Then we will try to make discourse dream. That is more accurate, closer to what really happens, and I am convinced that the figure dwells in discourse like a phantasm while discourse dwells in the figure like a dream. The only thing is that it must be agreed that the 'language' of the unconscious is not modelled on articulated discourse, which, as we know, finds utterance according to a language. Rather, the dream is the acme of the inarticulate, deconstructed discourse from which no language, even normal, is entirely free. Metaphor and metonymy must, therefore, be understood, not in the strict sense attributed to them by the structural linguist in his theory of the speech act, but in a sense which is itself metaphoric. From this it would follow that it is not Freud who is imprecise but Jakobson himself in his use of concepts which he had begun to construct, in all rigour, on the basis of a structural analysis of the language activity.

Let us limit ourselves to an examination of condensation, which seems to be the nub of the disagreement between Jakobson and Lacan. Here is what the latter has written about it:

Verdichtung, or 'condensation', is the structure of the super-imposition of the signifiers, which metaphor takes as its field, and whose name, condensing in itself the word *Dichtung,* shows how the mechanism is connatural with poetry to the point that it envelops the traditional function proper to poetry.[40]

First of all, what is metaphor? Its formula, as Lacan has already explained, is 'one word for another'. Its 'creative spark ... ignites between two signifiers, one of which is substituted for the other while taking its place in the signifying chain, the eclipsed signifier remaining present in its (metonymic) connection with the rest of the chain'. The example given is the line from *Booz endormi:* 'Sa gerbe n'était point avare ni haineuse.' ('His sheaf was neither miserly nor spiteful.')[41] A perfectly appropriate definition. And it includes the notion of substitution, the very one which according to Jakobson characterizes the paradigmatic, hence metaphoric, relationship between two terms. Nonetheless two observations must be made.

The first is that the essential feature of metaphor, for the poet at least, is not covered by this definition. In the poetic metaphor, substitution *is precisely not authorized by usage,* is not inscribed in the paradigmatic network surrounding the supplanted term (it is not, for example, common usage to substitute 'his sheaf' for Booz, if this line is accepted as metaphorical). When the substitution is authorized, we no longer have anything like metaphor in Lacan's sense of a *figure* of style. We have simply an instance of a choice between terms which stand in a paradigmatic relation to each other, any one of which would serve equally well at that particular point in the chain. Hence the choice of one of them at the expense of the others results in no overloading, no 'overdetermination' of the statement. The substitution will, however, determine the amount of information which the message conveys to its recipient. Thus: 'I dread – , or – hope for – , or – await – his arrival'. Here we are 'ante' style, in the realm of language (*langue*). The true metaphor, the trope, begins with the too-wide gap, the transgression of the range of acceptable substitutes sanctioned by usage. Jakobson starts off from a notion of substitution based on a strictly structuralist concept of language, and proceeds (unjustifiably, as we will see) to a rhetorical meaning of metaphor which is applied to discourse. Substitution is indeed based on usage, but the true metaphor defies usage. André Breton is right in this instance: 'For me the strongest (surrealist image) is the most highly arbitrary one. I don't deny it.'[42]

And he is doubly right. Lacan accuses the surrealist notion of the image, as it is implied in automatic writing, of confusion, because, he says, 'the doctrine behind it is false. The creative spark of the metaphor does not spring from the presentation of two images, that is of two signifiers equally actualized',[43] but rather, as we have seen, from the eclipse of one term for which another is substituted. Hence the sheaf of Booz. This is to appeal to the current meaning of the word, which must be called into question here, and in the name of the very Jakobson who is invoked on the same page in a footnote. In his essay on aphasia Jakobson distinguishes the metaphoric from the metonymic process, in keeping with psychological notions of substitutive and predicative reactions.[44] For example, in a word-association test, 'hut' is proposed as a leading word to the child. If the response is on the order of 'has burned down' or 'is a wretched little house', the reaction is said to be predicative. If it is on the order of 'hut, cabin, palace' the reaction is said to be substitutive. Let us examine the predicative response more closely. Its nature is to constitute a sentence, hence to open the possibility of a narrative. But two kinds of opening must be distinguished. 'Hut – has burned down' is a purely narrative statement. 'Hut – is a wretched little house' is doubtless a syntagmatic organization (Jakobson calls it syntactic) by virtue of the positioning of the terms within it. But semantically, the statement is paradigmatic: as far as meaning goes, 'wretched little house' could be substituted for hut; 'has burned down' could not. Jakobson, therefore, distinguishes a positional aspect (within the statement – *l'énoncé* – from a semantic aspect (within the table of meanings accepted by language). A metaphor may be a predicative reaction positionally, but it must in any case be semantically substitutive.

A statement such as 'his sheaf was neither miserly nor spiteful' would be entirely unacceptable as a metaphor for Jakobson. Not only do the terms constitute a clearly predicative statement, but on the semantic level they are not amenable to substitution, unless it were claimed that the signifieds 'generosity' and 'benevolence' are implicit in the signifier 'sheaf' – which is not, in any case, the thrust of Lacan's argument. The fact remains that for Jakobson metaphor is characterized precisely by what Lacan judges to be a surrealist error: the co-existence in the discourse, hence in a syntagmatic position, of two or more terms whose semantic relation is one of substitutability. The spark of meaning ignites, not perpendicularly to the axis of the discourse, in its encircling depth, but all along that axis, like a short-circuit between two poles of the same sign. It seems to me that 'his sheaf' is a good instance of metonymy, the sheaf being understood as an emblem of Booz, while the use of the imperfect confers, in addition, a typically narrative connotation on the statement.

Now, given Lacan's interpretation of metaphor, how can one say that condensation is one? Lacan formulates the metaphoric structure as follows:[45]

$$ f\left(\frac{S'}{S}\right) S \cong S\,(+)\,s $$

which reads: the metaphoric function of the signifier is congruent with the emergence of signification. The metaphoric function is transcribed $f\left(\dfrac{S'}{S}\right)$, the emergence of signification $S\,(+)\,s$. The plus sign placed in parentheses indicates the crossing of the bar – and the role that crossing consistently plays in the emergence of signification. The bar (——) is, in Lacan's algorithm, what separates the signifier and the signified, it is the mark of 'non-sense'. Crossed $(+)$ by the metaphor it re-establishes contact between signifier and signified and thus establishes meaning. As for the notation of the metaphor itself (S'), it conforms to Lacan's own definition: S' is the stated term which eclipses the signifier S, just as his sheaf is supposed to eclipse Booz. If I am not mistaken, finally, about the 'crossing of the bar', metaphor for Lacan is the trope by means of which the signified is adduced. It 'takes up its position at the precise point at which sense is produced in non-sense'.[46]

Can the same be said for condensation in the dream-work? Here we will be obliged to return to Freud himself, since his interpreter is not very forthcoming. At this point Lacan's real preoccupation and the root of the displacement of the term 'metaphor' in his account becomes clear. Obliged to explain how condensation is metaphoric, he explains how the subject is never present in discourse except metaphorically, and that it is in losing himself in it that he can be present. The signifier is *never given*, so he believes, and the 'unique key' to metaphor and metonymy is that 'the S and the *s* of the Saussurian algorithm are not on the same level, and man only deludes himself when he believes his true place is on their axis, which is nowhere'.[47] When he says 'signified', Lacan thinks 'subject'. The entire theory of the metaphor is a theory of the metaphor of the *subject*, which only apprehends itself through the ruse of the metaphor, that is, in missing itself, because it is signified by a signifier. And the signifier is the Other. It is this expressive repression which the bar between S and *s* conveys.

We have seen how the use of the word metaphor diverges from Jakobson's definition. We are now obliged to register the strongest reservations about such a reading of the Saussurian algorithm. To begin with, Saussure placed the signified *above* the signifier, and the line which separates them in the schemas, far from representing repression or censorship, has so little consistency that it will tend to disappear as the notion of value will supersede that of signification in the later lectures, the signified of a term being nothing more than a summary of its *value*, that is, of its syntagmatic and paradigmatic entourage. And that entourage is not hidden, but transparent. Lacan, preoccupied for his part with that deafness – the Greeks called it *Atè* – which constitutes the unconscious, omits to say that Saussure's reflection on the linguistic sign takes its departure from the transparency necessary to interlocutory experience. To such an extent that in the end one might wonder if the sign is indeed a sign, since it has no depth. In other words, it seems to me that here in Lacan's thought there is a confusion between *signification* in the strict sense Saussure accorded the term by shifting it back to linguistic value, a sense which, precisely because it reduces signification entirely to the ensemble of syntagmatic and paradigmatic relations surrounding a term, controlling its functioning in the statement and its place in the semantic field, robs that signification of all the depth of hiding/revealing and explains the enigmatic limpidity of words in use, a confusion, then, between signification thus isolated, and *meaning* (*sens*). When a French speaker says *La nuit tombe* (night is falling), the statement does not preclude signification, which is completely transparent to the French ear. The indissociability of the signifier and the signified which Saussure never ceases to underline, and Lacan to suppress, is complementary to that transparence. On the other hand, the statement may yield depth by virtue of its *meaning* (*sens*), but it will be necessary, most of the time, to refer to the context (whether, for example, the sentence has to do with the advent of Hitler to power) in order to interpret this meaning.

The manner in which Lacan understands metaphor has to do with meaning, not signification. That is why, incidentally, his metaphor is that of Hegel or Alain and could not be Jakobson's strictly speaking. The depth produced by the movement of a term shouldering aside another and eliding it, a depth in which I understand that the subject must lose himself at the brink of constituting himself (as a speaking subject), is absent from 'metaphor' if it is accepted that, for the linguist, metaphor is equivalent in the order of tropes to the paradigm in the order of the structures of language, and to selection in the order of the operations of speech. Or, if Jakobson's metaphor is already itself 'profound', the responsibility for the confusion ought to lie with the imprudent transition the linguist permits himself to make from language (*langue*) to rhetoric. According to his strict structuralism, there is no figure of language, only rules, no figure of speech, only controlled operations, and the figure enters language only at the stylistic level, when the units are sufficiently large so that the order to be followed is no longer constrained and the phantasm can 'freely' (that is to say, under constraints which are not linguistic) situate itself, not *behind* words, but *among* them, invisibly. And such is indeed the doctrine professed elsewhere by Jakobson with regard to the hierarchy of units: the freedom of the speaker growing in proportion to the size of the units.[48]

It seems to me that it is his overweening preoccupation with the theory of the subject, under the guise of the theory of signification, that causes Lacan to take metonymy for metaphor, as in 'Sa gerbe n'était point avare . . .', and metaphor itself as constituting a depth, a beyond, resulting from eclipse [of one term by another]. A structural theory of language could not agree with him on this point. Can the Freudian theory of dreams do so? The *Verdichtung* (condensation) for Freud is a genuine compression. It must be conceived of spatially. The given account of a dream takes up a few lines; its interpretation, that is, the exposition of the dream-thought, 'may occupy six, eight or a dozen times as much space'.[49] One must abstain, it is true, from measuring the coefficient of compression (*Verdichtungsquote*) failing direct knowledge of the 'real' scope of the thoughts. Nonetheless, we are dealing with a topography, having two superimposed levels, thought underneath 'content', the dream-work operating between the two, in depth, producing the latent/manifest opposition. Thus the need to reduce the second space relative to the first allows us to understand the two properties which Freud singles out in the *Verdichtung*: it is an 'omission' (*Auslassung*) and 'a multiple determination' (*mehrfache Determinierung*).[50] An omission of thoughts which cannot pass to a higher level, an over-determination of dream-elements which subsume several strands of thought. The topographical inspiration is so powerful here that it would seem that condensation is no longer motivated by censorship, but by limitations of space, in the strict sense, the locus of our dreams being narrower than the locus of our thoughts.

And by dwelling at length on the fate of words in the course of this compression, Freud assures us that it is a fundamentally non-linguistic operation. Where can we best grasp ('*am griefbarsten*') the work of condensation? When it seizes on words and names. The dream frequently treats words as if they were things (*Dinge*), subjecting them to the same combinations as representations of things (*Dingvorstellungen*).[51] And this is not a rare occurrence, it is 'extremely frequent', which is why the analysis of 'nonsensical verbal forms' (*unsinnige Wortbildungen*) is 'particularly well-calculated' to provide a grasp of the operation of condensation.[52] Here is formal proof that for Freud this work affects articulated speech (which gives at first silent, and ultimately, at the end of the interpretation, explicit expression to the dream-thoughts) in a deconstructive fashion. Substitution, for Jakobson, was *constitutive* of discourse; condensation, for Freud, is a transformation *dismissive* of discourse. Here we are at the opposite pole from Lacan, who writes: 'What distinguishes these two mechanisms [metaphor and metonymy] which play such a privileged role in the dream-work (*Traumarbeit*), from their homologous function in discourse? Nothing, except a condition imposed upon the signifying material, called *Rücksicht auf Darstellbarkeit* which must be translated by: "consideration of the means of representation". (The translation by "role of the possibility of figurative expression" being too approximative here.) But this condition constitutes a limitation operating *within* the system of writing; this is a long way from dissolving the system into a figurative semiology on a level with phenomena of natural expression.'[53]

It seems unnecessary to pursue the discussion with regard to metonymy; it leads to the same conclusion. It doesn't matter that Jakobson and Lacan agree, this time, to ascribe displacement (*Verschiebung*) to metonymy; it takes a real play on words to do it. Metonymy is already hard-pressed to play in rhetoric the role that Jakobson attributes to combination in the speech act and to the syntagmatic relation in the table of language. The difficulty is aggravated, if, leaving discourse behind, metonymy is required to function as a main-spring for oneiric displacement.

Neither is it possible to agree with Lacan about the dream-work's considerations of figurability. Not only does he relegate these considerations to the background, unjustifiably, in the light of Freud's text, but above all he refuses to concede to figurability its two functions: the one operative *inside* the writing system, creating figures with letters, heading not only in the direction of the hieroglyph, but in the direction of the rebus; the other, however, about which Lacan says not a word, trading on the designatory power of language, and simply replacing (as in the Silberer and Magritte examples) the signified by one of its designates, the concept by one of its objects. It is the prejudice in favour of the closure of the system that prevents justice being done to Freud's text.

It can be perhaps be said that the dream is articulated like a language. It must then be accepted that the word 'language' loses the precision conferred on it by post-Saussurian linguistics. It refers to a study not of language, but of enunciation. It is particularly the theory of signification as a value, and of value as a syntagmatic and paradigmatic framework that must be, if not abandoned, at least completed by a theory of meaning (*sens*). It is, at the same time, the doctrine of the indissociability of signified and signifier, that is of the transparence of the sign, which must be balanced by justifying the depth of discourse. The language to which one appeals must be 'weighty', labouring, concealing, revealing, in a metaphorical sense, no doubt, but metaphor must be understood here as in the case of an artistic work. So that, at first glance, the 'language' of the dream seems to be nothing more nor less than the language of art.[54] It is its primary cause, perhaps its model. The same distance separates Jakobson's substitution and Lacan's metaphor as exists between discourse and figure. On the one hand, the space of invariances, on the other the terrain where the plasticity of things 'seen' is deployed. Legible or audible space, open space of the visible (and invisible).

III

The fourth operation, *secondary revision*, remains to be explored. It seems to bear a paradoxical relationship to our thesis. Freud says of it that its function is to make a day-dream (*Tagtraum*) of the dream, to make it conform to the laws of intelligibility. He even goes so far as to maintain that it derives from normal thought,[55] the result being that this revision might indeed appear to be secondary, relative to the primary process, imposing articulated language on material to which, as Freud insisted in the section on figurability, nearly all the categories of rational thought were foreign. We have here, in a word, 'this work which does not think' resorting to the discourse of conscious or pre-conscious thought. How, then, can one continue to maintain that the operations which transform the dream-thoughts into the dream-content are real work? Must we not make an exception, at least, of the fourth operation, which seems to derive exclusively from language? But how can we understand this exception? The order of discourse which it is the function of the dream-work to render unintelligible, according to Freud, which in any case it violates, does this order participate in its own eclipse?

Freud is not as formal on the subject of this revision as the foregoing remarks may have indicated. It is true that he ascribes it to normal thought, that he entrusts to it the task of building the dream's facade.[56] But first of all he resists making it *posterior* to the three other operations,

> We must assume . . . that from the very first (*von allem Anfang*) the demands of this second factor constitute one of the conditions which the dream must satisfy and that this condition, like (*ebenso wie*) those laid down by condensation, and representability, operates simultaneously (*gleichzeitig*) in a conducive and selective sense upon the mass of material present in the dream-thoughts.[57]

And this is not all. The 'facade' which this revision must construct, the order it must impose on the chaos resulting from the upheaval of the three prior operations, may present itself quite unexpectedly. It happens, says Freud, that secondary revision may find that 'a formation of that kind (*ein solches Gebilde*) already exists, available for use in the material of the dream-thoughts'.[58] Thus the dream may wear its heart on its sleeve. 'I am in the habit', Freud continues, 'of describing the element in the dream-thoughts [he does indeed say 'thoughts'] which I have in mind as a "phantasy". I shall perhaps avoid misunderstanding if I mention the "day-dream" as something ana-logous to it in waking life.' A footnote to this sentence reads '"Rêve", "*petit roman*", – "day-dream", [continuous] "story." '[59] Some of these novels are conscious, others unconscious. It is around such phantasms constructed from memories, and not on the memories themselves, that hysterical symptoms are constructed. The essential characteristics of these novels are precisely those of the night-dreams. Freud writes: 'their investigation might, in fact, have served as the shortest and best approach to an understanding of night-dreams.' I indicated above that phantasms, rather than a discourse, should perhaps be classified as dream-thoughts. This passage invites such a conclusion. The dream's wrapping is also sometimes its core. The 'novel' is never an ulterior arrangement, and it is sometimes an archaic one, in which the memories themselves (or primal scenes) are involved, articulated. The phantasm is not only both diurnal *and* nocturnal, but belongs to the facade *and* to the foundations.

Clearly the recurrent 'sometimes' and 'it happens that', juxtaposed with the attribution of secondary revision to normal thought, scarcely constitute a coherent doctrine. But the hesitancy itself merits attention. We must be guided by Freud. Immediately after these reflections on phantasy, he states that secondary revision stands in the same relation to the dream-content as waking (pre-conscious) thought does to the material of perception: a quasi-pulsional ordering which obliterates the difference between the given and the anticipated and jams proper *reception*. Secondary revision is commensurate to that *pseudein* (to deceive, to cheat) which calls to mind what Plato said about painters and sophists, but which appears to be attributed by Freud in this instance to discourse itself.

And it is in order to illustrate this deceptive function that he cites the 'enigmatic inscriptions' which he takes as an example from the newspaper that had regaled Bavarian and Austrian households for a century, and of which, according to Lacan, he was 'an avid reader'.

> If I look around for something with which to compare the final form assumed by a dream as it appears after normal thought has made its contribution, I can think of nothing better than the enigmatic inscriptions with which the *Fliegende Blätter* has for so long entertained its readers. They are intended to make the reader believe that a certain sentence – for the sake of contrast, a sentence in dialect and as scurrilous as possible – is a Latin inscription. For this purpose the letters contained in the words are torn out of their combination into syllables and arranged in a new order. Here and there a genuine Latin word appears; at other points we seem to see abbreviations of Latin words before us; and at still other points in the inscription we may allow ourselves to be deceived into overlooking the senselessness of isolated letters by parts of the inscription seeming to be defaced or showing lacunae. If we are to avoid being taken in by the joke, we must disregard everything that makes it seem like an inscription, look firmly at the letters, pay no attention to their ostensible arrangement, and so combine them into words belonging to our own mother tongue.[60]

It is worthwhile to analyse the kind of hoax employed in these inscriptions: it presumes an interesting interplay of reading and seeing. Leafing through the issues from 1884 to 1898, years during which Freud was collecting material for *The Interpretation of Dreams*, I found thirteen of these inscriptions. They are all entitled *Ratselhäfte Inschrift* (enigmatic inscription). Some have no figure; the reader passes from the manifest text (which usually looks like Latin), to the latent text (in the dialect of the South), by a simple displacement of the divisions in the phonic continuum. For example: Integram addi coenam gymnasium ista nix vomia galata in trina (= In de Grammatiken am Gymnasium ist a' (auch) nix vom Jaga-Latein drinna!).[61] Freud is primarily concerned with figure-bearing inscriptions. Nonetheless, this first category teaches us something: that the passage from manifest to latent text takes place through displacement of the *phonic* reality of the original statement. We will see the importance of this remark. In order to classify the illustrated inscriptions, three elements, not two, must be taken into consideration: the latent 'text' (*Traumgedanke*), which is the solution of the enigma; the manifest text (*Trauminhalt* after secondary revision), which is the text of the inscription; and the scene illustrated (*Darstellung*).

Let us proceed from the manifest text to the scene. They can be joined in three ways: unity of place, when the linguistic signifier and the figure are inscribed in the same representational space; unity of culture, when both refer to the same civilization; unity of meaning, when the *signified* of the manifest text can be related to the *scene*. Hence, in theory, there are eight possible categories:

Categories	Unity of place	Unity of culture	Unity of meaning
1	+	+	+
2	+	+	−
3	+	−	−
4	+	−	+
5	−	+	+
etc.			

The categories preceded by the minus sign are excluded here. They would not be inscriptions, but legends, texts belonging to a space other than that of the figure. The categories 1–4 remain. The collected inscriptions fall into groups 2, 3 and 4. Group 1 would be typified by an inscription lodged in the same space as the scene, referring to the same culture, endowed with a signification which is related to the scene. The inscription of figure 2[62] comes close to being this type. Nonetheless, because the character is Austro-German rather than Latin, it would be better placed in group 4. The inscription of figure 3[63] belongs to group 2; it lacks unity of meaning, since the pseudo-Latin text is absurd. Finally, we will put the inscription of figure 4[64] in group 3.

If we now proceed from the scene to the latent text, two possibilities present themselves. Either the text is pronounced by one of the characters in the scene, or not, in which case the text becomes a commentary attributable to a third party (the author, the reader) who is outside the situation. Figures 3 and 4 are in the first category; figure 2 is in the second. This second criterion is independent of the first one. Figure 5 corroborates this.[65] Like figure 4 it belongs to group 3 by virtue of the relationship between the manifest text and the scene represented; but as regards the relationship of the scene to the latent text, it belongs in the same group as the enigma of figure 2: the hidden text is a commentary on the scene, not a statement issuing from it.

Clearly the link between latent and manifest texts and the figure is established in a great variety of ways. But we cannot really understand the function of the image until we have seized the nature of the relationship between the latent and manifest texts, a relationship which I touched on with regard to the unillustrated inscriptions. This passage consists in a double transformation: from one tongue to another, from phonics to graphics. First of all, the latent tongue is the mother tongue, a living tongue taken in its most common (phonic) manifestation. The manifest figure of the inscription is foreign, dead. Above all, it is a pseudo-language: the inscription does not conform to the syntactical and/or lexical restrictions of Latin. This first transformation should suffice to show the illusory finality of secondary revision. It puts forward a triply incomprehensible text: the majority of the *Fliegende Blätter* readers do not read Latin; it is a dead language whose statements remain unheard; it only *looks* like the language. We are thus discouraged from too hastily attributing secondary revision to a rational agency inasmuch as what results from its intervention is

Figure 2

Räthselhafte Inschrift.

SOCRATES ENSI AC ANSER LINAE
MANLI GERE SIS MIRA NE DEXTRA

(Auflösung in nächster Nummer.)

Figure 3

Räthselhafte Inschrift. (Schwäbisch.)

NOVAS PLASMA NUM EROS EX
HEBE DA.

(Auflösung in nächster Nummer.)

Figure 4

Räthselhafte Inschrift.

DIANA ISTA UNDA
SAEPE
ISTE DAT
ROMA:

VERE R
SIT SINE
T

(Auflösung in nächster Nummer.)

Figure 5

precisely not rational! Finally, this first transformation is in no way a translation. Every translation passes through the signified; here it is simply an equivalence in the order of the signifiers that is given.

This leads us to examine the second transformation, that from phonics to graphics, which is even more interesting. It is impossible to pass from the latent text to that of the inscription, or vice versa, without recourse to homophony. If you, an Austrian peasant, do not *pronounce* the text, *novas plasma*, you will never hear *No, was blas'ma?* This is half the secret (the other half is that the intervals must be displaced). The manifest text is the graphic notation, imitating another language, of a statement pronounced in dialect. The (oneiric) revision thus carries out a phonic analysis of the words and the redistribution of the letters (which are taken to be the written equivalent of the phonemes of the initial language) in words of another tongue. This operation is similar to that of the spoonerism (*contrepèterie*), with these two differences: one switches languages, and the resulting arrangement does not necessarily make sense (in fact it rarely does: see figure 2 for one example).

A comparison with the operation leading to what Saussure called a *hypogram*[66] might be more fruitful. For example in this line from the *Iliad:*

Λασεν ἀργαλέων ἀνέμων ἀμέγαρτος ἀϋτμή,

(Lasen argaleon anemon amegartos aütme) 'The dreadful breath of winds infatuated (him) ... '

the syllables of the name *Agamemnon* are disseminated throughout other words, so that the name is, so to speak, a sub-script, hypographed, in that line. Nonetheless what distinguishes our inscriptions from hypograms is yet again the switching of languages (although this is not essential); it is above all the fact that in the hypogram the manifest text contains repetitions, inversions, conversions of the syllables of the hidden name, whereas in secondary revision the space occupied by the manifest and latent texts coincides. As in a true anagram, the completed operation, in both directions, leaves no remainder. The repetitions, chiasmus, etc. of the anagram make it similar to a musical (the Ricercare of *The Musical Offering*) or literary (Raymond Roussel's *Impressions d'Afrique*) combinatory system, as Bally in a letter to Saussure, and Starobinski in his commentary (see note 66), suggest. The thing is that in these cases the manifest 'text' (in the broad sense of the word) must be 'readable', that is intelligible, audible by itself. It harbours the name, the canonical formula, but by allowing its scattered elements to reverberate within its own form, which must therefore be *similar in nature* to theirs. Hypogrammatic depth is of the order of resonance (assonance, consonance), and of harmonics: the line of the *Iliad* underlines the name of Agamemnon, and Saussure accepts for his hypogram this meaning of ὑπογράφειν (hypographein) which is 'to emphasize the features of the face with make-up'.[67] But the depth of our inscription is opaque. It is not a graph, but a pseudo-graph, homophonic with the originating text, like Saussure's hypogram, but at the expense of a double heterosemia. Transcribed from the phoneme to the letter so as to produce a presumptive other meaning, it supposes the transformation of the nature of the sign and of the alleged signification.

Provided with this scholarly definition – a homophonic, hetero-semic pseudo-graph – we can return to the function of the scene. The single constant which appears in the classification of these pseudo-graphs is, as we have seen, the unity of place joining scene and inscription. This unity constitutes the very stuff of the inscription. It is written in the same space as something else, in this case an image. Now the topical unity of writing and scene indicate that the text, having taken up a position on the same plane as the image, will submit to the strictures of that plane and betray the strictures of writing. By this simple placing of the inscription, we pass from linguistic space, that of *reading*, where one *hears*, to visual space, that of painting, where one *looks*. The eye no longer listens, it desires. Now the manifest text does not deceive, does not allow itself to be taken for another, except in the exact measure that one looks at it without hearing it. What is inscribed is a kind of non-writing; the space in which it moves is that of an object, not a text. An object's space is to be seen, not read. And this seeing is desiring.

The function of the image is to consolidate the pseudo-graph. Written, but written above all as an inscription, inscribed, a text lends itself to pseudology because by its letters it belongs to the object in which it is traced. It presents itself to view at the same time as that object, and it will remain graphic as long as the celebrant does not intervene to make it *heard,* as André Leroi-Gourhan suggests in the case of rock-paintings.[68] The support of the image casts a spell on the text; the image fulfils its antique function of deception (*pseudein*). But there must be an element of *pseudein* in writing. The text deceives not by the ear, but by the eye. An essential deception: the dream, says

Freud, makes use particularly of visual images. Seeing interferes with hearing and speaking, as desire interferes with understanding. Such, at least, is the Freudian algebra.

These observations ought to be expanded. The ambiguity of writing, object of reading and of sight, is present in the initial ambiguity of drawing. An open line, a line closed on itself. The letter is an unvarying closed line; the line is the open moment of a letter which perhaps closes again elsewhere, on the other side. Open the letter, you have the image, the scene, and magic. Close the image, you have the emblem, the symbol and the letter. These remarks find their commentary in the admirable treatment of capital letters in Romanic manuscripts, of which the R taken from the *Moralia in Job* done at Citeaux in the twelfth century (figure 6) gives us a glimpse. The letter is threatened, invaded by the line, the spirit by the eye, the Church by

Figure 6

the Barbarians, the very Book by the plastic ornament which comes from the Irish, while the repressive vertical of the Saint sets its face against the good-natured baroque of the dragon: the letter is opening itself up, we are heading towards the miniature and painting in depth. The birth and re-birth of painting from writing. That supposes the ambiguity of the line that André Lhôte talks about: it can delineate a contour, enclose a space, confer formal identity. That is called writing; it may be the trace of a gesture that creates a space, the wake of a movement that situates, organizes, and painting returns endlessly to that enigmatic gestation, endlessly offering it to the eye which desires it, so that it may err, and erring, may recover its spatializing truth. In Breton's words, 'We who have always preferred the shadow to the prey . . .'

The read-heard text is without depth, even without perceptible space; the seen text dwells over there, beside the image. That 'over there' is its mystery, renders it enigmatic. By virtue of its opposition within the range of vision it appeals to a distanciation of the eye from itself, which is the distance of representation, whereas read, it matters little from what angle, it is read from nowhere. From the read to the seen, we pass from a 'horizontal', flat, atopic negativity, to a 'vertical', deep, place-making negativity; the read belongs to the system of gaps which constitutes the language code; the seen requires openness, transcendence, showing and hiding. The enigma gives a sign to the eye, hence the dream's preference for visual images.

Let us return, finally, to secondary revision and try to understand it on the basis of this status of inscription. Where does its specific work come in? We have said above that Freud hesitated to place secondary revision within the topology of the dream-work: it acts from *as great a distance,* from as great a depth, as the three other operations; nonetheless it derives from normal thought. Is not this ambiguity the same as the ambiguity of the read, half-seen, half-heard inscription?

Freud says that the function of secondary revision is to expunge from the dream the absurd incoherent fashion in which it was produced by the three prior operations left to themselves. Desire, acting 'freely' within the constraints of the initial text, would leave in its wake the tortured, illegible relief of the 'content'. Secondary revision interferes with this operation by fabricating a manifest text like the 'Latin' inscription. This work consists in ostensibly *flattening out* the relief by using the humps and hollows, the peaks and valleys, to produce writing. Suppose that an upheaval of the earth's crust had distributed the figures of the relief so that, viewed from an aeroplane, they could be taken for letters, for words. Secondary revision would be the selective power directing these upheavals to deposit their products in a readable manner. At this point we pass from the energistic to the linguistic, which is readable. And this is how secondary revision belongs to normal thought, supposes intelligibility and intelligence.

But this readability is a pseudo-readability. The readable signification of the dream, its immediate content, cannot be read; and even when it is, it *ought* not to be: Freud reiterates that we must not treat the content as text, but as an object. The reason is that even when the inscription means something (in Latin, but this is an exception, as we have seen: figure 2), its meaning is suspect, and can only delude the interpreter. It is necessary to disbelieve 'rêvons d'or' in order to grasp 'Révolution d'octobre'. We must reconstruct a primitive text, hidden under the gilded text, which the work has deconstructed, or if you prefer, we must deconstruct the edifice, the figure which the operations have constructed. Thus what is intelligible in the text is pseudo-intelligible: that part of the text which is preserved in every case is precisely the distinctive unit (phoneme, grapheme) which is non-signifying, and it is the signifying unity (the moneme) which in many cases is destroyed. What is most often lacking is the unity of discourse, because the Latin syntax is not respected; and, finally, in those very rare cases (*Naevia*) where the entire architecture of the linguistic units is respected, the very meaning which emanates from the ostensible discourse leads the mind astray. The closer we get to true language, the more vulnerable we become to the true lie. The figure cannot lie, since it has no pretensions to univocality. Intelligibility is therefore rather simulated, aped, than truly satisfied. That is why Freud speaks of 'misunderstanding'.[69]

If he also says that secondary revision is like a pre-interpretation,[70] it is only because the content borrows its tool, articulated language, from interpretation, but only to divert it from its linguistic position and put it to criminal use, the text being taken as a thing, a phonic, visible thing, and not a conglomerate of empty signs, of cenemes. Secondary revision interferes with two functions: it introduces the textual into the plane of the figure (*Inschrift*), and it protects the figural implanted in the text. The text of the inscription is therefore false and deceptive, but it also bears witness: the oddness of its divisions, not counting the image itself, whose commentary it is supposed to be (we re-discover here the *two* modes of figuration: in the letter and in the designation), testify that something must inform this double figure: it is *a figure to be read*.

Now this double function, this double position, constitutes the very foundation of the dream. At bottom there is the *Gedanke* (thought), and for Freud it is a text which is lodged in the *Inhalt* (content) as in a figure. Only, and it is time to say so, no one has ever heard or read this text. The *Gedanke* is never rendered other than figuratively, in an *Inhalt*. The figure inhabits the allegedly initial text.

This remark allows us to understand Freud's hesitation about secondary revision: facade or 'foundation', *Inhalt* or *Gedanke*? The revision duplicates a deep-seated constitution. That is why it operates at once on the surface and at the heart of the dream, by a kind of analogy. If this is the case, it is because at bottom this movement of exchange, this whirlwind, has already occurred, continues to occur: the figural is immediately present in the context; the figural is always already there. The textual is already there in the core-figure. We are deaf at first. We do not begin by hearing in order subsequently to repel the awful utterance. Desire does not manipulate an intelligible text in order to disguise it; it does not let the text get in, forestalls it, inhabits it, and we never have anything but a worked-over text, a mixture of the readable and the visible, a no man's land in which nature is exchanged for words and culture for things. We must presume a primordial situation where repression and the return of the repressed are born together. Here, precisely, for Laplanche and Pontalis, is the phantasm.

Reverie, dream, phantasm are mixtures containing both viewing and reading matter. The dream-work is not a language; it is the effect on language of the force exerted by the figural (as image or as form). This force breaks the law. It hinders hearing but makes us see: that is the ambivalence of censorship. But this composite is primordial. It is found not only in the order of the dream, but in the order of the 'primal' phantasm itself: at once discourse and figure, a tongue lost in a hallucinatory scenography, the first violence.

NOTES

1 S. Freud, *The Interpretation of Dreams*, vols IV and V of *The Standard Edition of the Complete Psychological Works of Sigmund Freud*, ed. James Strachey et al. (London: Hogarth Press, 1953–74), V, p. 491 (henceforth: *SE*). S. Freud, *Gesammelte Werke* (Frankfurt am Main: S. Fischer Verlag, 1962), II/III, p. 495 (henceforth: *GW*).
2 *SE* V, p. 506; *GW* II/III, p. 510.
3 Ibid.
4 Ibid., underlined in text.
5 Ibid., p. 507; p. 511.
6 Ibid.

7 Ibid., p. 160; p. 166.
8 *SE* XXIII, p. 43; *GW* XVI, p. 144.
9 Ibid.

Es ist bei der Entstellung eines Textes ähnlich wie bei einem Mord. Die Schwierigkeit liegt nicht in der Ausführung der Tat, sondern in der Beseitigung ihrer Spuren. Man möchte dem Worte 'Entstellung' den Doppelsinn verleihen, auf den es Anspruch hat, obwohl es heute keinen Gebrauch davon macht. Es sollte nicht nur bedeuten: in seinen Erscheinung verändern, sondern auch: an eine andere Stelle bringen, anderswohin verschieben. Somit dürfen wir in vielen Fällen von Textentstellung darauf rechen, das Unterdrückte und Verleugnete doch irgendwo versteckt zu finden, wenn auch abgeändert und aus dem Zusammenhang gerissen. Es wird nur nicht immer leicht sein, es zu erkennen.

10 Ibid., p. 47; p. 148.
11 *SE* V, pp. 506–8; *GW* II/III, pp. 510–12.
12 *SE* IV, p. 296; *GW* II/III, p. 302.
13 Ibid., p. 281; p. 287.
14 Ibid., p. 300; p. 306.
15 *SE* V, pp. 294–5, 303; *GW* II/III, pp. 301, 309.
16 *SE* IV, p. 296; *GW* II/III, p. 302.
17 The discussion which follows is indebted to the contribution of Claudine Eizykman and Guy Fihman to the seminar on 'Work and Language in Freud', The University of Paris, Nanterre, 1968–9.
18 *SE* IV, pp. 142–4; *GW* II/III, p. 147–9; letter 79 to Wilhelm Fliess, S. Freud, *The Origins of Psycho-Analysis: Letters to Wilhelm Fliess, Drafts and Notes: 1887–1902* (New York: Basic Books; rpt 1977), pp. 238–40.
19 *SE* V, p. 491; *GW* II/III, p. 495.
20 See *New Introductory Lectures on Psycho-Analysis*, *SE* XXII, p. 28; *GW* XV, p. 29.
21 *SE* XV, p. 226; *GW* XI, p. 232. This volume contains *Introductory Lectures on Psycho-Analysis (Parts I and II)*.
22 Freud's clearest treatment of this notion occurs in *On Dreams* (1901), *SE* V, p. 667; *GW* II/III, p. 680. The relevant paragraph was added, according to Strachey, in 1911: 'In the erection of a dream-facade use is not infrequently made of *wishful phantasies which are present in the dream-thoughts in a pre-constructed form,* and are of the same character as the appropriately named "day-dreams" familiar to us in waking life.' Emphasis added. In the same vein, this passage from *The Interpretation of Dreams* may be cited: 'a succession of meanings of wish-fulfillments may be superimposed on one another, the bottom one being the fulfillment of a wish dating from earliest childhood' (*SE* IV, p. 219; *GW* p. 224). In a report presented to the seminar on 'Work and Language in Freud' mentioned above, Françoise Coblence and Sylvie Dreyfus emphasized the

impossibility of putting the different superimposed meanings in the same category. Censorship, which produces interference at the secondary level, must be distinguished from that interference by which desire is primarily led astray.

23 Freud devotes five pages to displacement as against twenty-six to condensation, ninety-five to considerations of representability, and twenty to secondary revision. *SE* IV, p. 308; *GW* II/III, pp. 313, 314.

24 *SE* IV, p. 307.

25 André Breton, *Le Surréalisme et la peinture* (Paris: Gallimard, 1965), p. 270.

26 *SE* V, p. 344; *GW* II/III, p. 350.

27 *SE* IV, p. 303; *GW* II/III, p. 309.

28 *SE* V, p. 339; *GW* II/III, p. 345.

29 Ibid., p. 340; pp. 345–6.

30 This tendency is clearly expressed by Roland Barthes in *Eléments de Sémiologie* (Paris: Seuil, 1964); *Elements of Semiology*, tr. A. Lavers and C. Smith (New York: Hill & Wang, 1968). See also A.-J. Greimas, *Sémantique structurale* (Paris: Larousse, 1966), p. 12.

31 R. Jakobson, *Essais de linguistique générale* (Paris: Minuit, 1963), pp. 43–67, in English in R. Jakobson and M. Halle, *Fundamentals of Language* (The Hague: Mouton, 1956), part II, chs 1–4.

32 Quoted in R. Godel, *Les sources manuscrites du cours de linguistique générale de Ferdinand de Saussure* (Geneva: Droz et Minard, 1957), p. 237.

33 Quoted in Godel, p. 240.

34 Jakobson, p. 45.

35 Jakobson, p. 61.

36 Jakobson, pp. 63, 65.

37 Jakobson, pp. 65–6.

38 Jakobson, p. 66, note 1.

39 Jacques Lacan, *Ecrits* (Paris: Seuil, 1966), p. 512; *Ecrits: A Selection*, tr. A. Sheridan (New York: Norton, 1977), p. 161.

40 Lacan, p. 511. At the risk of being pedantic, it should be pointed out that *Verdichtung* is related through *dicht* to the old German *dihan* (like *gedeihen,* to prosper); *Dichtung* comes from the Latin *dictare*. Of course it was simply a pun. But in that case it does not make a philological argument in favour of the classification which Lacan proposes. And in the same vein, *Verdichtung* could hardly be said to 'condens[e] in itself the word *Dichtung* . . .' On the contrary, it combines it with a particle (Sheridan, p. 160).

41 Lacan, p. 507; Sheridan, p. 156. (The reference is to a poem by Victor Hugo, '*Booz endormi*', which deals with the encounter between Booz and Ruth, an episode in the Book of Ruth in the Old Testament.)

42 'Pour moi la plus forte [image surréaliste] est celle qui présente le degré d'arbitraire le plus élevé, je ne le cache pas.' André Breton, *Les Manifestes du surréalisme* (Paris: Edition du Sagittaire, 1946), p. 63.

43 Lacan, p. 507; Sheridan, p. 157.
44 Jakobson, pp. 61–2.
45 Lacan, p. 515; Sheridan, p. 164.
46 Lacan, p. 508; Sheridan, p. 158 (tr. modified).
47 Lacan, p. 518; Sheridan, p. 166.
48 Jakobson, p. 47.
49 *SE* IV, p. 279; *GW* II/III, p. 284.
50 Ibid., pp. 281, 295; pp. 287, 301.
51 Ibid., pp. 295–6; pp. 301–2.
52 Ibid., p. 303; p. 309.
53 Lacan, p. 511; Sheridan, pp. 160–1.
54 The language of art, speaking as it does with things, making a figure with words, embodies an indissoluble link between discourse and the tangible. Consequently, if the dream is to be placed on the linguistic scale, its position ought not to be at the level of speech operations governing small units, but at the level of stylistics, as E. Benveniste has pointed out: 'It is in style, rather than in language, that we will find a term of comparison with those properties which Freud revealed as descriptive of oneiric "language"' (*Problèmes de linguistique générale* (Paris: Gallimard, 1966), p. 86). After some hesitation, Laplanche and Leclaire reached a similar conclusion: 'as for the *ontological status* of the unconscious thus constituted, is it necessary to recall that if indeed this status is that of a language, then such a language can in no way be assimilated to our "verbal" language?' 'L'Inconscient. Une Étude psychanalytique', *Les Temps modernes,* July 1961, pp. 81–129, p. 118. This last remark still lacks rigour. It is 'language of communication' which would be the correct phrase. In verbal language itself there are figures which defy communication and which are the offspring of the unconscious. Freud identified them from the joke (*der witz*).
55 *SE* V, p. 491; *GW* II/III, p. 495.
56 Ibid., pp. 491, 493; pp. 495, 497.
57 Ibid., p. 499; p. 503.
58 Ibid., p. 491; p. 495.
59 Ibid., p. 492; p. 496.
60 Ibid., pp. 500–1; p. 505.
61 *Fliegende Blätter,* no.2093 (1885), p. 78.
62 Ibid., no.2034 (1884), p. 20. The solution to the puzzle is: 'Nae (Nein), wie dies Ding da schön ist!' ('Isn't that thing cute, huh?') The Latin inscription means: 'Naevia adorned with reeds'.
63 Ibid., no.2277 (1889), p. 100. Solution: 'So, g'rad' essen Sie a'Ganserl?! – I' nehm'an Liqueur – es is mir a'net extra.' ('So, you're eating a little goose just like that?! – Me, I'll have a liqueur, for me it's no extra.')
64 Ibid., no.2241 (1888), p. 15. Solution: 'No, was blas'ma? – Numero Sechs – Hebet a'! ('What shall we play next? – Number six – One, two . . . .')

65 Ibid., no.2078 (1885), p. 168. Solution: 'Die Anna ist da und da Seppei steht a' (auch) d'rob'n, aber er sieht sie net.' ('Anna is there and Seppei is also standing above, but he doesn't see her.')

66 'Les Anagrammes de Ferdinand de Saussure: textes inédits', ed. J. Starobinski, *Le Mercure de France,* February 1964, pp. 243–62.

67 Starobinski, p. 246.

68 A. Leroi-Gourhan, *Le Geste et la parole,* 2 vols (Paris: Albin Michel, 1965), especially vol. I, ch. VI and vol. II, ch. XIV.

69 *SE* V, p. 500; *GW* II/III, p. 504.

70 Ibid., p. 490; p. 494.

Translated by Mary Lydon

3

Passages from *Le Mur du Pacifique*

The Kienholz story

There was the Kienholz story.[1] It was told to me by a young woman studying at the University of California, San Diego, when I was Associate Professor there. She had heard it from her mother, Mrs Greenstone, a widow from New York who had just visited the Documenta 5 exhibition in Kassel, West Germany, during the summer of 1972 with one of her friends, the son of a German Jew who had emigrated to New York in the thirties. The mother and the daughter had discussed at great length the implications of the piece that Edward Kienholz presented at this exhibition. It is this discussion which continued via other mouths and ears in California, in front of the wall of the Pacific. It led to the disclosure of a peculiar machinery, of a kind of conspiracy, a plot, one of its most striking effects being curious crossings or displacements – here a multi-looped coming-and-going between Europe and the US. Miss Greenstone recounted how much her mother had been struck by the fact that Kienholz, refusing to exhibit his composition in a room, had persuaded the organizers to put up an enormous tent in an area outside the Fredericanum,[2] a palace erected to the glory of Frederic II when Prussia had annexed the Electorate of Hesse-Kassel and one of the rare old buildings still standing after the bombing of 1944. This thick tent of dark green canvas, where the lighting was entirely independent of the time of day, was for the visitor if not a trap, at least an impasse: you had to leave by the same way you had come in. But this impasse, as large as a circus big top, was also movable; the crime it concealed could install itself everywhere, and in a very short time its itinerant character turned it into the revenge of wandering nations [*des nations errantes*] on the Imperial American-Roman-Germanic name, in complete contradiction to its content, the 'Tableau', which depicted the 'final solution' to the negro (nomad) question. But why did this space have to take the form of an impasse?

We found by talking that it was necessary *not* to be able to get through. To get through, to go around the exhibition rooms, means one should cast a prudent glance at the works on display. Here such a glance was impossible. After turning the corner of an ordinary door along a corridor where a thousand kitsch objects were on display, you went into a place, dark as night in daytime, whose gravel floor indicated, however, that you had left the museum. A luminous zone at the back of the tent caught your eye: some visitors were crowding together there, others were coming and going in the half-light, whispering. You went up close in order to try to make out the scene; when you succeeded, it was too late: you were part of it. The light from the back came from the converging headlights of a number of cars, parked in a circle. In the badly lit fringe some visitors were moving around slowly, trying not to make any noise; others seemed completely paralysed. Among the latter, you were astonished to see a man in shirt-sleeves, with a motionless face which you immediately realized was a mask, who was leaning on the open door of a truck and had a rifle under his arm; a woman, sitting in the cabin of the truck who was pre-venting herself from vomiting by endlessly pressing a silk scarf against her mouth; a ten-year-old boy, eyes gaping at this perversity through the glasses of an intelligent schoolboy, who was intently watching the scene from behind the dirty windshield of a car.

As for the dressed-up polyester sculptures that Kienholz had placed at the focal points of the headlights and gazes, they left no room for doubt: the three men holding down the nigger spread out on the ground, and the fourth, who was busy severing his penis, could not for a second have been taken for real. Their motionlessness was not even that of *tableaux vivants* because Kienholz, refusing to push the illusion any further, had put in place of the victim's belly, a rectangular basin of black water in which floated detached letters *which should occasionally drift into position to spell out* N·I·G·G·E·R,[3] and which took its liquid-supply from nothing less than the black penis twisted up into the form of a ghastly tap by the castrator's left hand, while his right hand plunged in the knife. *The shank of the penis was made of a piece of three-quarter-inch steel shaft which was then welded on the leg frame* and which had to be solid enough to resist attacks by vandals or souvenir hunters. The letters stirred up in the basin by the fall of the waterspout seemed to Mrs Greenstone and her friend to evoke what is ungraspable about the black continent and what white imperialism was trying in vain to root out. *I should explain that actually there is no black man. If you study the piece you will see that what appears to be the victim is, in reality, three separate white figures (each with part of the black body) shown up against the central 'pan body' which was welded from steel in the form of a human torso.* And even under torture, the parts of the black continent – the penis, the stomach – do not cease replenishing one another, which indicated clearly its independence. The paradox of the composition is that it is the victim, though tied and held to the ground like a pig prepared for slaughter, who is mobile whereas everything which was paralysed around him was part of the business of terror. And such was the trap that the visitor, whose fear stopped him in his tracks in front of this hallucination, tended by the very fact of his immobilization to become assimilated to the KKK figures that Kienholz had sculpted – stupidly persisting in trying to impose an identity on the liquid belly.

This is where the machinery begins its trick effects. Mrs Greenstone told her daughter how she and her friend found themselves observing the visitors, most of them German, who were getting themselves stuck in the network woven by Kienholz: they imagined that in place of the six letters in the basin's water, four other letters could form the word J · U · D · E and that SS uniforms had replaced the disguises worn by the Klan. Mrs Greenstone and her friend, watching the reactions of the visitors, spying on their emotions, saw them all as executioners – this young, distinguished-looking mother quickly rounding up her children to lead them to the exit before they could understand the horror, that young couple standing amazed for a long time; they suspected that if an old man put on a show of sympathetic attention it was only to hide his nazi past. No approach could be innocent in their eyes, all had to bear the mark of the exhibited crime, the latter spreading out continuously from the scene to the visitors by the mediation of a history [*histoire*] which was not only that of the destruction of the American blacks, or even only of the European Jews, but the history of an Empire which could only conquer itself at the price of destroying all those called minorities [*toutes les pulsions partielles*]. Mostly, I think of 'Five Car Stud', the title of the composition which is *symbolic of minority strivings in the world today* – provinces, subjugated nations, *métèques*,[4] slaves, the history of the Caesarist West.

But what were our two friends doing while they were regarding the other visitors with suspicion? Were they not in their turn perpetuating imperialistic obsessions? It was now they who, finding themselves positioned at the heart of a new Empire always the same, were throwing out the Germans, thus reduced to the position of a minority. They embodied the Caesarism of the West at the very moment that they thought themselves indignant at its racism and suspected it everywhere. They were reinstating the repellent whiteness. I never met Mrs Greenstone, but her daughter's skin, on which the Southern

Californian sun always left a silver-gold downy film regardless of the angle of its approach, and her bearing, devoid of all disgrace but obliging nonetheless, marked her for a white woman's destiny. Here it is necessary to know that the figure which seemed to be vomiting in the truck parked by the cars of the whites was a white woman with whom the black victim was supposed to have been seen drinking a beer. This detail, provided by Edward Kienholz, appeared to us to be important: it is a property of the Centre to arouse the envy of the periphery, and this is what the squint-eyed dubious managers called politicians busy themselves with. Under their guidance, the pale white skin, the indifferent skin, compromises itself by association with *métèques*. And since the desire such whiteness arouses in the latter can only be expressed in a compulsion to rape, the Centre also turns them into inhabitants of a no man's land, a frontier.

Of white skin

'Puisqu'il n'y a rien, Jarry, d'aussi blanc que le pelage le plus hivernal des animaux indéshabillables, si ce n'est la peau humaine,' the whiteness of skin carries no shadows, no values. Made of a tissue consistent with itself at every point, more than any other kind of skin – with the exception of a few dark black skins – it makes you aware that bodies are not volumes, but only surfaces. White skin is therefore impenetrable. Now, the idea of rape is that one must penetrate the impenetrable: that is, create a volume where no fold offers itself, make what is nothing but unproductive evenness resound like a soundboard. That the screen of skin should enfold itself (*s'invagine*), dark and rollicking, around the cock – that is what envy wants. Invasions from the outskirts create a metropolis, according to the permeability of its frontiers, the suppleness of its skin. And inversely, the naivete of whiteness, so central, blackens everything that desires its whiteness.

Kienholz's white men, by castrating the black man, intend to restore that surface to its monstrous, immaculate innocence. Mrs Greenstone and her friend, by suspecting the German visitors at the Fredericanum, do the same. If your cock is black, then you don't exist, only what is white exists. And what is white is woman. At that thin point where a woman's thighs come together, there is nothing but skin, skin like the skin at the bend of the arm or ankle, or the nape of the neck.

All this nourishes the consoling idea that woman has no sex (*pas de sexe*). But the point is that she is herself the whole of sex; unaware of it, she has the potential, the potency (*puissance*) to excite.[5] A little white girl would be astonished that eyes and swarthy fingers dare to open her panties, feel their way along the moist furrows to which she accords no capacities for pleasure. As surface, her body doesn't even have to offer itself, a gesture whose movement would require in turn withdrawal, hence a depth.

One will question this assimilation of sight to touch only if one's idea of touch is that of a precise collision between two bodies. But touch is a scanning which both effaces and gives rise to those who touch and those who are touched, transforming both just as the gaze changes those who are seen and those who see, and puts them into circulation. Those who have seen the vast white stretches of Californian beaches and deserts have been touched by them, have had one part of themselves blackened by them, the other whitened. That is their tactile force. These contacts blind you. The important thing about touch is not that it puts you in contact, but that it can or cannot stir up excitement, intensity.

How shall we understand the desire to rape which rises in the cock *métèque*? As that of a paradoxical touch, an inside touch (*un toucher de l'intérieur*) similar to that of the vaginal touch, except that the latter helps maintain the health of an organism, helps restore it to quiescence – that's what legitimates the vaginal touch – whereas the raping touch tries to bring it to life, to stimulate it, only in order to destroy its security. Put two or three fingers into your partner's mouth. It is no longer a casual allusion to fellatio – rather, it suggests dentistry, or laryngology. You touch his/her inside. Imagine that this touch has no purpose, no pretext to knowing, that it only seeks to crack open the fearlessness of surfaces, to open up a depth in them, to destroy their self-sufficiency, to call forth echoes: such would be the desire of the *métèque*.

With it comes the spirit of revenge, that is its weakness, the point at which it is attached to power (*pouvoir*). We imagined, Miss Greenstone and I, that the Greek tutors called to Roman Italy were obsessed with vengeance, determined to rape the inviolate skin of the younger members of the patrician class, to drill vertigo into it. The nomad, the immigrant, is in turn endowed with a fallacious prestige: he is made profound. Obscurity, subtlety, mobility, naturalization, penetration, the mask – that is his lot as *métèque*. A two-faced, divided body confronted with endless, even surfaces.

The *métèque* does not even recognize in the metamorphosis he undergoes his own spirit of revenge and desire for rape. It is Rome that makes him like this. *Césare*, the white female Caesar, engenders the existence of masks around her, at her peripheries, she raises depths, surrounds herself with signs (*signes*), with monkeys (*singes*), madmen, niggers, Greeks, Jews, Arabs, Chicanos, Wops, all of them swarthy. By making them desire her, she defines depth as their nature; by having them castrated, she affirms the sleekness of her vast surfaces, smoothed out to a tenth of a millimetre. White women have no sex (*pas de sexe*). They receive; they give nothing, they do not move. They live in a voluptuousness independent of touch. They are inviolable. In the arms of their slaves, their spasms do not resound. Do white women take pleasure in anything besides the very skin which they are? Rape would bring to this question, beyond the masculine imagination, the satisfaction of the last word thanks to the first penetration (*forage*).

Associate professors

On the function of culture: Why do the Romans want the Greeks as educators? They appropriate them for themselves, but they *métèquise* them. What do they want – the tutors, rhetoricians, philosophers, and sophists – who come to Rome?

To experience themselves as niggers, those who believed they were white. To travel and to make white space travel. To displace the Empire. To Rape.

At the same time, to make themselves commodities. As such, make no mistake: they are *métèques,* they speak Latin with a Greek accent, they sell their verbal merchandise.

And why do they sell like this? Peddle, export, import, transport? It is in their interest, they get rich; but it is also their passion.

Dependence on the vast skin, that is, potency (*puissance*), announces itself in the form of their servitude. They come to Rome because Rome is white power (*pouvoir*), capital (*le capital*), and they find in Rome white im-potence, potency (*puissance*). The emperors are oriental, barbaric, they speak Greek, Illyrian. Rome is no longer to be found in Rome. The United States is not a single country. The name of Rome is Caesar (*César*). Not one state, but states. Not one time, but times – Atlantic Time, Central Time, Mountain Time, Pacific Time. Not one law, but laws.

Im-potence is therefore found *in* capital. But you have to be – so they say – Greek to do that, *to have been* the white centre; every *métèque* is a citizen put to another purpose by potency, they say.

However, this nostalgic interpretation is itself profitable. It is precisely the interpretation of culture that Rome wants: teach us our origins, you are our past, etc. This point of view is the one that capital requires: origin is also a commodity.

In fact, this white skin has no past. The white woman has no past. Nefertiti = Marilyn.

The demand for an origin is a form of seduction practised today by the little white girl who opens her thighs with a whimper that tightens the Greek's underpants. But all this is controlled by the FBI and makes business tick. The *mètèquisation* of culture: it has to be critical, that is, the Greek tutor has to make himself appear older, more knowledge-able, more of a native and thus instruct (*paideutise*) the US.

The *mètèque* is obviously critical, by his very nature, since he is not an American-Roman citizen. So, Associate Professor, don't think you come to facilitate criticism. *Mètèque* criticism is the weapon of big companies; it determines boundaries, the outside and the inside, Romans and non-Romans, citizens and foreigners.

All your authors, all your assemblages of words, only reinforce this boundary, this frontier zone. The best you'll manage is the *mètèquisation* of a few citizens – pimps will become clients. Big deal. Potency is elsewhere.

Come, rather, to *lose* your culture, to de-culture yourselves. You are not the original nigger, the nomad of ancient times. The nomadism that is imposed on you is a role, it is the nomadism of those who live on the outskirts, who are marginal, who are sedentary, the kind of settlement that the Empire needs. But potency is white, 'central', not marginal.

Precisely off limits. But now consider this: the centre itself is the true nomad, it is where all cultures come to exchange their momenta and to lose themselves. Come, then, in order to raid that nomadism, in order to carry off potency. Make yourself a white woman. Whiten your skin.

Labyrinth at the centre

Unspoiled spaces regress constantly towards the West. The imperial borders of the Caesarist West, of Rome, spread out towards the Orient, the metropolis never stops moving westward. We were talking about Kassel on the shores of Southern California. This was the absolute West: the source of American capitalism, that is, Roman power; the beauty of bodies running on the beaches, in the hills, morning and evening, a soft tie holding back the infinite languor of green-blond hair, and moreover our trust in our discussion honoured by the sun, that is, the Greece of stadiums and schools; the urban garden between water and deserts, that is Phoenicia; the desire to try out new sentences, new terms, new forms of syntax, that is, Anglo-Saxon liberty – free enterprise, voyages of discovery into unknown territory. The absolute West is an island whose settlers have come from regions further east and where everything is imported from the mother-cultures, collected in order to get free of them. An island of forgetfulness. There was a time when Jefferson and Franklin prayed in Philadelphia's Independence Hall that God rid them of English rule. Today it is the men on the West Coast who are shaking off the old culture of New England. The population of this island does not constitute *a people* and must not do so. Whenever a culture starts to harden, to solidify, when anything like an organic attachment between people and institutions develops, this island then stops being the West; its population becomes wild, backward, rooted, European. One waits for a fragment to detach itself once more and head further West in order to reconstitute the white of surfaces devoid of all sentiment, of all fixed commitments. Even paganism would be foreign to it, like everything that stays put (*réside*), if it were only the religion of the peasants.

Exile, however, is not utopia. This serenity, always displaced, is always central not because it is the boundary which describes a point, but because, not having a reference point, it serves, for a while, as an origin for getting one's bearings. It is when it can itself be located, when its name begins to designate a character, that this area (*aire*) ceases to be seductive and a new one has to be opened up. From the new one, it will be possible to generate the previous one. It is the most western capital (*la capitale*), daughter of all those who preceded it, which engenders them all retroactively, which places them in a narrative (*un récit*), that of Western history; and this narrative recounts the expansion of the white Empire towards the East; but this East is never anything but an abandoned West and ancient centre for taking one's bearings, a darkened whiteness. So this imperial expansion, which is power, only creates itself by a lowly return to origins. Potency moves westward and nobody can make any mistake about it.

For at the impossible centre of the Empire (a centre which is not at the centre, but at one of the foci of an ellipse continuously stretching itself towards the West), there is no supreme authority, there is a jointing of surfaces, white, ephemeral, labyrinthine, purposeless. The word 'Rome' cannot be assigned to a single space. Los Angeles is the capital (*la capitale*) of the world because it is not a metropolis by

European or East Coast standards, not, in other words, a semblance of unity grouped around its ecclesiastic, administrative, economic navel; but a game of chess, whose squares are drawn by its highways and forty-mile-long boulevards, squares which are occupied only temporarily, as in the game. This chessboard is not the coat-of-arms (*le blazon*) of the feminine body (whose openings, whose eyes and ears, are emblems of depth), but rather of skin as white woman – a jointing harsh and by chance.

The white of the skin-woman is light, all colours (cultures) mixed. The blindness of the car in the labyrinth of LA is none other than the blindness of the palm as it traverses the length of thighs, the span of shoulders, of groins. The white body is not an organism. Without head, and without sex, it could pretend to be itself both sex and head, the capital (*la capitale*) and cold love, capital (*le capital*); but it is that only in one aspect, as the body is a unity, an entity, belongs to a sex only in certain respects: if one locates it. LA shows us rather what the ancient capitals lost, one after the other, in their wish, or their destiny, to be fixed permanently in one place: that a capital is not locatable, that it has no centre, that in the heart of the Empire lies the belly of a white nomad, that the survey of LA, an unsettled basin, always has to be done again and again.

The Greeks tell of the ruse of the fox-fish: 'It unfolds its internal organs, turns them inside out, skinning its body as if taking off a shirt.' Remarks the erudite white woman: this ruse is also that of Hermes who, stealing Apollo's herd of cows, puts on his magical winged sandals, makes the beasts and himself walk backwards, and moves from soft earth to rocks to efface all their tracks. Thus do the gods and the satyrs, who have thrown themselves into pursuit, turn in circles in this ruse, this aporia. The labyrinth is not an intricate building where one gets lost; it is a power (*puissance*) of the body to undo its apparent voluminousness and expel itself (*s'évaginer*): what is there exactly where once was the heart of the fox-fish when, its trick done, all its innards are on the outside? Under the fisherman's hands, as with the cock *métèque*, the prey vanishes, leaving them empty-handed, unable to do anything.

When you've reached or think you've reached LA by car, coming from the north-east or from the south, on Interstate 5 or on Highway 395, from arid lands or the desert, you come across exit signs such as Kennedy Boulevard, 48th Street, or Laurel Ave. These are organs expelled from a city in the process of turning its insides out. The deserts of the West are strewn with these unassignable parts. The names of the particular places to which these highways belong are never written on the road signs. No precise information is provided to indicate towards which city the highways lead, cities which might serve as stopping points along one's way. The exit indicating 48th Street leads you straight into the desert. At the end of the street perhaps you'll find a deserted canyon ready to be developed – four-lane highways, sidewalks, drains, water pipes, gas and electricity, streetlights, not a living soul – this is 48th Street. These empty lots are like the ghost towns preserved intact by dry air and sun after the departure of the last miner, towns that you meet in the desert at twilight and which frustrate your hope of ever finding a place to stop. Ghost towns by abandonment or anticipation: both belong to the vast white stretch of space that no one ever manages to occupy. Both attest to the excess of desire at the heart of whiteness, an excess of desire over time and space, an excess of potency (*puissance*) which renders every point in this continuum undecidable, which outrages every possible construction of coordinates.

As prove the white bodies which run in vain on the coastal skin of California, journeys here lead to nothing, everything leads to journeys. Cities have no boundaries, no frontiers, to separate them from the desert and dry lands. Today, in Europe, a road tells you where you are arriving, what place you are leaving, the smallest village introduces itself and leads you in. The designation of places is so meticulous that in certain suburbs the road signs indicating the names of the towns you're passing through come every few yards, stand back to back to each other, or are even juxtaposed side by side when two counties meet on the road. These designations signal a space dominated like a body of an animal intended for the butcher, like the body of a girl for the erotic war of the Chinese, every part destined to play its own role. This effort to contain the wanderings of the centre is the effort of local administrations and the State, tracing ins and outs on the white body of land, to pinpoint places which ought to be lived in, to attribute names to what ought to be countries. But (perhaps) this domestication leaves the mad belly unbroken. The Roman road system, the displacement of land, the eviscerated mountains, the entire traffic network, whose purpose was to centralize, to refer the vast stretches of land to a single head of state: all this happens (perhaps) completely in vain.

Genealogy of politics and sex

The octopus, the white octopus, begets fear which in turn gives rise to domination. Those silky thighs, moving endlessly, incite both rape and the urge to power: they produce the two poles of virility, that is, politics.

When the *métèques* appear, so do the pimps – the politicians, generals, emperors. They check the ruse of the white belly, they map the thrown-out surfaces of skin, they label them, they establish limits. They thus are the complement of *métèque* desire, they make themselves partners. Thus do we understand the nomadism of nations of marginals to be itself the other side of a desperate centralism. The Greeks of Philip and Alexander, Caesar's Gauls, Cortez's Indians, were *métèquisés*, 'pacified', decimated, humiliated, not because they were weak, but because the white men, in becoming their masters and relegating them to the edges of the Empire, were able to think they were expelling an uncertainty, a mobility they could not bear.

What is at stake in this relationship of complementarity between the citizen and the *métèque* is white skin. The citizens, the white authorities, become the pimps, the support, of this skin with regard to the foreigners: alright, we'll open to your tongues, to your eyes, to your commerce, the white thighs of our women, under certain conditions. What are these conditions? Nothing other than the differentiation of the sexes and the tripartition of roles. After Caesar femininity is confined to a single sex; it is offered the trap of being designated secondary or weak so that it will wear itself out wanting equality of power – absurd. After Caesar, virility is distributed between the police and robbers, between owners and workers, masters and slaves, and this doubling is offered the trap of understanding itself as the dialectic of inequality with itself – a stupidity by which is concealed the major oculation – that of the unassignable, inassimilable white skin.

The three players – the pimp, the whore, the client – pitch their tent together, erect their stage, their bulk, on the white surfaces of this uninhabitable space.

The proletariat, the *métèque* client to whom the status of pimp-citizen has been promised, has joined the game. Assimilate! You are neurasthenic marginals, we will look after you.

The white authorities pass themselves off as those who give. This trade, at the base of which is the enjoyment of women (may women enjoy and may we enjoy them! [*que jouissent les femmes et que nous en jouissions*]), allows the white authorities to take the place of the white female centre; but only the latter has potency – meaning, the potential to receive. Usurpation of potencies, imposture of functions. Every Caesar is this same impostor, this male more male than the others, more male than the *métèques*, who negotiates for what he believes are women, but actually he just negotiates for one of the results (himself being another one) of the auctioning of this white, empty expanse of space. Then he is faced with the endless ridiculous task of integrating all that into a social body.

The skin, thus distributed, fills these roles. Caesar usurping the potency or receiving and redirecting it into the power of giving. Immigrants, proletarians, *métèques*, marginals, standing by, outside of *jouissance*, left to the nightmares of rape and destined to the sinister distribution of virility. Finally, the invention of women, objects of exchange, at the base of all politics, women to whom at best (today) promises of power will be granted. And no sooner are the promises granted than women are neatly wedged into the doublebind of recognizing themselves as the objects they have been turned into and recognizing themselves in the would-be subjects they have been promised they will be – in prostitutes or proprietresses of brothels, in slavery or mastery – these white women who know the profound interlocking of dependence and potency. When this interlocking (which is indeed the skin, so fascinating, that I'm talking about) is concealed, then everything is in its proper place for the political game to begin.

Do we have to stress that this is precisely what's taking place in Kienholz's tent? That the white woman is suspected of having agreed to have a drink with the black man, the woman-object thus seeking to short-circuit her pimps but still showing that she and her supposed accomplice know – in spite of the positions (*postes*) granted them in political affairs – that they flaunt a potency which is indifferent to the power of the petty white Caesars? That these Caesars, the men of the *K*aiser *K*apital Amerika, only succeed in inventing the cock and that, believing that by severing the penis from the negro's pelvis, they make themselves the exclusive trustees of virility? But that nevertheless the black reservoir, which never stops nourishing itself, is also, as Kienholz says, the very source of their so-called separate beings as executioners? First, because they would not be anything if it were not for their victim. But most importantly, because the victim and the executioners are together creatures of true potency, here called white woman. *Actually there is no black man* = *actually there are no white men.* She vomits.

The black continent: when Freud compares feminine sexuality to it, he betrays that he belongs to the realm of the Caesars. The continent of intensities is white, it is not the Africa of conquests, the place of disturbances put on the outside, relegated and envious, the *métèque* or feminine thing – but it is the centralizing dizziness of Caesarism, as it is of *métèquisme* and of feminism, the undecidability of the pale deserts and of the limitlessness of skins. By considering the continent black, one has already cut it down to size, one is speaking as a white (*en blanc*), as an impostor.

We must move on; let's not start again, on women, the operation of *métèquisation* that the Austrian emperor forced the Jewish doctor to undergo. Let's not take the place of any emperor, even the *métèque* Hannibal. As soon as one becomes an emperor, this *métèque* becomes a white Caesar, invents his own *métèques*, and invents the blackness of his woman at the same time; immediately his empire distributes all the roles, so that when you say: the black continent of feminine sexuality, you too, like Mrs Greenstone and her friend, are only perpetuating imperialism. The black basin, the reservoir of Kienholz's nigger is white and turbulent, and it is woman, precisely because it is *jouissance* and self-potency, which are anterior to all virile sexuality.

NOTES

1 This 'story', which forms the second chapter of Jean-François Lyotard's *Le Mur du Pacifique* (Paris: Editions Galilée, 1979), is purported to be part of a manuscript written by one Michel Vachez and discovered in the foreign manuscript collection at the library of the University of California, San Diego.

2 After verification, only the desire of the Greenstones or that of the narrator, or both, can explain this error: Kienholz's Tableau was set up in the Neue Galerie, built after the Second World War and looking out (its name is *Schöne Aussicht*) on the park of the Fredericanum.

3 Translator's note: These italicized words in English are those of Kienholz, as are the other italicized words in English which follow in the text. In the original French text, they appear mysteriously, and without attribution, in English.

4 Translator's note: Lyotard frequently uses the noun '*métèque*' and the verb '*métèquiser*' in his text. *Métèque* is colloquial French for 'alien', connoting Greece and Athens, and originally denoting foreign residents living in Athens. To preserve the sense of foreignness, we have retained the French word wherever it occurs.

5 Translator's note: Lyotard uses the words '*puissance*' and '*pouvoir*' throughout *Le Mur*. We have translated them as 'potency' and 'power' respectively. *Puissance* is feminine and refers especially to sexual potency; *pouvoir* is masculine and refers especially to political power.

Translated by Pierre Brochet, Nick Royle, and Kathleen Woodward

4

Figure Foreclosed*

I cannot suggest at what point in this process of development a place is to be found for the great mother-goddesses, who may perhaps in general have preceded the father-gods.

Freud, *Totem und Tabu*

At a point in this evolution which is not easily determined great mother-goddesses appeared, probably even before the male gods, and afterwards persisted for a long time beside them.

Freud, *Der Mann Moses und die monotheistische Religion*

There have been two major attempts to disintricate power and knowledge and each in its own way lies at the 'origin' of the history, and of the historicity, of the West: one Jewish and the other Greek, Moses and Socrates. The former asserted itself to be religious; the latter appears to be the starting point for secular 'rationality'; both mark an irreversible break with the ambient religiosity of the Middle East, a religiosity which we can, by way of the cult of the chthonian divinities, relate either to 'savage' culture (Lévi-Strauss) or 'totemic' culture (Freud). On the one hand, the work of the so-called historical school of psychology (Détienne, Lévêque, Vernant, Vidal-Nacquet, and their masters) has shown how much the Socratic dialogue, that privileged locus for the critique of knowledge and power, owes to the organization of the *Polis*: a circle in whose centre precisely no one is placed by statutory right, and which breaks with all hierarchies; on the other, Freud, but also and with very different intentions, Bultmann and the demythologizing school, understand Judaism to be an effort to escape from myth, to emancipate an interpretative discourse from the *prestidigium* exercised by phantasmatic narratives and ceremonial. There were, and are, two ways to attempt to effect the disintrication we have mentioned: the *isonomia* of the round table in whose centre lack

* This essay was first published in Jean-François Lyotard, *Ecrit du Temps, 5*, Editions de Minuit (1984), pp. 65–105.

of knowledge is placed, and interpretation, which aims to dissociate that element in any word [*parole*] that comes from the drives of him who speaks or listens, and that element which is absolutely other, or truth.

But it is far from certain that we are dealing with well placed words in either case. Let us leave Hellenism. So far as Judaism is concerned, Freud may well see in it an advance in intellectuality, but he also stresses that it is still a religion and that, as a religion cannot be true or just (even though it may command us to live in truth and justice), it must in some sense be a deception despite its demythologizing force; in the case of Judaism, it is a deception precisely because it does emancipate itself from 'savage' phantasies. And there is more to it than this; to the extent that it is indeed Freudian psychoanalysis which Freud is psychoanalysing in *Moses*, we have to conclude that the science he founded has not fully recovered from the religious malady, and that it inherits from it that overestimation of the father which Freud sees as its major symptom.

The Jewish religion is not of the totemic, the Egyptian or the Christian type; in a sense it is closer to science than any other type; but insofar as it is a religion, and a religion exclusively centred on the father, it is an obstacle to the full development of rationality. Judaism is contrasted with totemism on the one hand and the Hellenism of science on the other. The former contrast is central to Freud's reflection; the latter appears to be marginal.[1]

There are at least two reasons for dwelling on relations between Judaism and totemism. In the first place, even an outline analysis allows us to reveal in it the operation of the fundamental categories which, in my view, govern Freud's thought and which relate to the opposition between discourse and figure; this same opposition constitutes the latent theoretical field of the *Traumdeutung*; Freud does not arrive at it for the first time in *Moses*,[2] but this is, perhaps, the first time he uses it in such a radically critical fashion. The final lesson of *Moses* is that even a discourse which tries to be as sober as possible, which does all it can to emancipate itself from the theatricality (*mise en scène*) of desire may still be haunted, albeit in a different way, by the 'figure'. Moreover, this critical approach to discourse in its opposition to the figure is couched in the form of a critique of a religion which Freud regards as one of the sources of rationalist Western civilization: Freud therefore appears to adopt (without, I think, realizing it) the critique Marx made of Feuerbach and, by implication, of all 'classical (Hegelian) German philosophy', on the grounds that it was a discourse which was falsely rational and effectively religious. And he even seems to adopt it at *precisely* the same point as Marx by applying it not at the

weakest point, or at the point where philosophy is merely a thinly disguised theology, at the point where the pastor peeps out from behind
the thinker, but at the point where thought seems to emancipate itself
from the religious sphere, and where it appears to accomplish the task
of demythologization. The Marxist critique of religious alienation was
not directed against Hegel, but against Feuerbach; similarly, Freud
does not merely attack Christianity which, in both *Moses* and *Totem
and Taboo* is simply reclassified as one more form of totemism, but also
primitive Judaism, which takes at least as radical a view of idolatry
(meditations) as Feuerbach does of the Hegelian dialectic. Nowadays,
no atheist critic of the religious critique of religion finds it surprising
that the current of thought in which the names of K. Barth and K.
Löwith figure so prominently can both draw sustenance from primitive
Judaism and take on board the work of Feuerbach. It is certainly
legitimate to establish a parallel between these two critiques – the
Marxist and the Freudian; the following reflections will establish the
point at which it has to stop.

In the second place, the opposition between Judaism and totemism
is also central because it should have allowed Freud to characterize the
former as a 'malady' which is not similar to but fundamentally
different from the latter. Now it is interesting to note that that
diagnosis is not made, even though the clinical picture is quite
complete. In Freud's work, religions are classified as obsessional
neuroses, primarily because of the importance they accord to ritual, in
which Freud sees an analogue to the compulsive ceremonials of the
obsessional. Now in theory Judaism proscribes such attitudes, which it
deems idolatrous, and Freud recognizes that perfectly well. As we shall
see, he devotes his energies to establishing that difference with
remarkable care. And yet the diagnosis he proposes of Judaism is still
one of obsessional neurosis. I would like to show that the clinical
evidence forces us to adopt the hypothesis of psychosis.

Analysis of the totemic religion/Jewish religion pair gives rise to a
sequence of remarkable oppositions.

Savage; Jewish: image; word

Among the precepts of the Moses religion, there is, Freud tells us, one
of great importance: 'the prohibition against making an image of God
– the compulsion to worship a God whom one cannot see.'[3] It is this
which introduced the 'characteristic development of the Jewish nature
(*des jüdischen Wesens*)' (223; 115). In effect, 'it meant that a sensory
perception was given second place to what may be called an abstract

idea – a triumph of intellectuality over sensuality' (220; 113); there was
an 'instinctual renunciation'. How is the exclusion of the visible bound
up with such a renunciation? Freud makes the connection seem self-
evident. The point is that the figure itself is bound up with wish-fulfilment. When the apparatus is under the dominance of the pleasure
principle it disregards reality-testing and wishes are equated with their
fulfilment.[4] The image is a hallucination; it bears the mark of shame[5]
because, being the terminal point of a regressive short-cut towards
wish-fulfilment, it is associated with the autoeroticism which accompanies hallucination. 'The motive forces of phantasies are unsatisfied
wishes, and every single phantasy is the fulfilment of a wish, a
correction (*Korrektur*) of unsatisfying reality.'[6]

Because it gives figuration a free reign, totemic religion (noble
savagery) is an expression of the pleasure principle or, like art, at least
of its reconciliation with the reality principle. It must be classed as one
of the products of phantasy, of the avoidance of reality, or at least of its
Korrektur.

The pertinent opposition here may seem to be, not as I am
suggesting image/word, but image/reality, that is, pleasure/reality.
But in Freud reality is never a matter for the perception-consciousness
system alone; its constitution also requires the intervention of
memory, which preserves traces with which sense-data will be
compared in order to determine whether it is real or not, and memory
in its turn can fulfil its function of reality-testing and can allow the psychic apparatus to free itself from the pleasure principle and to record
data other than data which is a source of a pleasure only when it is
bound to 'verbal residues'.[7] From at least the *Papers on Metapsychology*
onwards it is central to Freud's conception that consciousness is not
simply a perception of the object, but a perception or thing-
presentation of the object plus a corresponding word-presentation;
repression on the other hand consists solely of a thing-presentation of
the object, of its figuration-presentation, or in other words of the
withdrawal of the cathexis bound up with the word-presentation.[8] The
image–reality opposition thus masks the *image–word* opposition, and
that for Freud is the basic opposition. In his view, this opposition
provides the basis for the specificity of Judaism, as opposed to
totemism, and for the advance in *Geistigkeit.*

The savage represses and sublimates, thus producing a culture in
which almost the whole of the real symbolizes. Wishes are still
organized into phantasies; myth is the initial form of phantasy; the real
is precipitated into it, and is caught up in the matrix of meaning
precisely because that matrix is not a discourse but a form, an initial

compromise between a syntax and a scene. In addition to the method Lévi-Strauss recommends, we should perhaps apply to savage cultures a method of approach borrowed from the theory of the facade in the *Traumdeutung*, the theory that the 'content' of the dream or its latent 'thoughts' are hidden in its form.[9] This hypothesis implies that the content of the dream is not a discourse, but a form, a phantasy. And Freud will constantly move in the same direction from 1900 onwards. If we adopt this approach we may perhaps be able to justify the major opposition between savage and Westerner, and explain the great fascination the former exerts over the latter. Amongst savages, all, or almost all, 'real' material is so worked upon as to be fitted into the matrix form, into, that is, the cultural facade. And so, wishes do not come into their own as a lack; they are fulfilled through the reconciliation of the reality-principle and the pleasure-principle; this is the position of the *Dichter*. It follows that there is no philosophy or 'deliberative' politics amongst savages. The question of power is not *posed*, phantasy is bound up with the question of origins, with the question of fathers and mothers, and is simply repressed, exhibited in the facade of the myth which resolves the question, which, that is, ful- fils the wish couched in the phantasy. Nor is the question of knowledge posed; it is resolved by the social organization itself, by its hierarchy and by the ritual which satisfies the wish to know, and whenever, despite everything, the void of the *quid* threatens to appear, wish-fulfilment can be obtained through the symbolic efficacy of magic, or, in the most serious cases, through the invocation of *mana*, a free signifier. It does not seem impossible to integrate the Freudian doctrine of totemism with Lévi-Strauss's theory of the savage mind.

In theory, the effacement of the signifier (the killing of the father, to use Freudian terminology) does not give 'free' rein to wishes; the loss of meaning which is the original crime is, on the contrary, given thematic expression in the mythical formula which, directly or indirectly, orders all institutions and all relations men have with one another and with the world. The wish that is born along with the withdrawal of the signifier is immediately captured in a form – the myth – which allows the libido to be reconciled with reality in some way.

The West is the place where this form finally expires. Thanks to Judaism, but thanks also to Greece. It would be interesting to compare the two in this respect. What follows is not even an outline of such a comparison. If we accept the conclusions of the recent work men- tioned earlier, the decline or covering up of the mythic form in archaic Greece is accompanied by an upheaval in relations with space, time, the other, power and knowledge: religion is subordinated to politics, the earth to the sea, and the 'centre' of the city becomes an empty place in which the position of the speaker has to be won, and can be challenged. Truth undergoes a displacement: it is no longer something divine which is veiled and held back in the sacred word; now there are only interlocutors who believe they are challenging 'interests', combinations of passions and reasons, of drives and discourses – and who have to find an order in which they can coexist. Those who speak, the rhetors, the politicians, believe themselves to be or want to be subjects of the utterance; they claim that they are no longer spoken. *Aletheia* gives way to *doxa,* and perhaps to the new position of truth; and philosophy takes shape in the search for that truth.

With the Greek West, savage art, which reconciled pleasure with reality, disappears; what was once a naive reconciliation becomes knowing. The 'youth' of Greek art is the youth of the West because it is the last time that this reconciliation is seen. With the political, rhetoric, philosophy and the scientific, reconciliation is and will be impossible; art itself will have to be displaced; it will no longer be wish-fulfilment; it will become an openly unfulfilled wish, a wish for a wish, a wish to know, Picasso.

Was Freud right to compare Hamlet to Oedipus and to say that one was a normal dreamer and the other a hysteric?[10] Tragedy cannot exhibit the simple repression of savage art and dreams; it takes place in that instant of equilibrium in which the repressed returns, not as symbolized in the plastic element of reconciliation, but as articulated in the discourse of separation which announces science. In *Oedipus at Colonus,* however, that instant does end in reconciliation: symbolism comes into its own once more; all is reconciled in the religious. The tragic was a moment. Hamlet, for his part, cannot be reconciled; here, what is rejected is not reintegrated into a learned discourse or into a symptomatic practice; it remains outside, and it remains there in two forms; as an unreal reality, the ghost, and as inaudible speech, the paternal command which Hamlet does not succeed in obeying; it is therefore rejected both as an object of perception and as a signifier. Both the solutions offered by the tragic – knowledge, or the word heeded, and religiosity, or the symbolic realized – are disregarded: this is the sign of foreclosure, the sign of psychosis. Let us leave Hamlet. What Freud excludes from his characterization of Oedipus is the fact of theatricality. The religious ritual is a dream or a symptom; the theatre is the staging of a dream or a symptom, the staging of a staging. And this is why Freud can see in it, in addition to a dream, 'a process that can be likened to the work of a psycho-analysis'.[11] If Oedipus is a dreamer, *Oedipus Rex* is not only a tragedy but also the word's attempt to find its rightful place.

The historians mentioned earlier, and first and foremost their master H. Jeanmaire, have opened up another convergent way to interpret the youth of Greece. In his *Couroi et courètes*[12] Jeanmaire compares the 'circular' configuration of the warrior collectivity which gave rise to the archaic city (of which Sparta is a vestige) and where the norm is the instituting function of the word and *isonomia*, with the configuration adopted in many African societies by collectivities of young men who undergo initiation rites and who, during their period of retreat, are forbidden to enter the real and symbolic space of their village. This proscription merits attention; it might be seen as a dialectical moment of externalization within the self-development of savage society; but the archaic collectivity of the Greek horsemen distorted its function for integration (recuperation), and suppressed and dominated the village, practically by making the villagers its helots, and symbolically by subordinating ancestral law to the law of the word of the moment, to politics. The immobile old dialectic which once supported transition as rite is overthrown. Transition becomes the absolute position of the new collectivity; the city is transition, or in other words historicity. And there is no longer any mediation. That is the difference between repression, or rejection followed by incorporation into the symbolic, which corresponds to initiation, and foreclosure, an 'absolute' exclusion which offers no symbolic compensation and in which the foreclosed returns from the outside.

The Greeks Nietzsche retrojected existed only for an instant, for the instant in which Dionysiac savagery was in equilibrium with the Apollonianism of the warriors from the North, in which mystery had yet to give way to discourse. In the nocturnal, figurative and plastic current, we can recognize the old religiosity of reconciliation, which will transmit to Christianity its remnants of mediation and which will give Catholicism its pagan allure. The solar current which inspired the first founders of the city is the current which will, within their circle, permit the secular use of discourse, of a word which is 'reasonable' and discussed, and which will become the word of science. This instant of equilibrium, if it ever existed, is the youth of a youth. The equilibrium is broken, and savagery is abandoned; the symbolization of the repressed disappears along with it. For a long time Catholicism did no doubt restore this recognition and this profoundly Dionysiac paganism in the West. But paganism was not destined to remain there; whenever noble savagery is offered to us as a remedy, the offer is one of deception and alienation. When desire has once been manifested, revealed/ masked, as an infinity, any reconstituted totality that may be offered it in an attempt to make it come to rest and become reconciled to the world appears to be a lie. Even the early Greeks could not maintain this equilibrium, and the new barbarians Nietzsche was waiting for will not come, because historicity, being a disavowal of reality, does not arise from the ethics of slaves; it is a symptom of a madness which is very different from the phantasies of savages; it is the symptom of the western psychosis, and only art or play can provide a cure.

The horsemen who founded the city brought with them a myth which Lévi-Strauss incorporates into the Oedipus story, because this fragment is essential to any understanding of it, and which J.-P. Vernant finds in Hesiod.[13] The warrior race sprang from the earth armed and armoured, but without parents; they were not *born*. This is the myth of autochthony. It might be seen as representing the predominance of the maternal theme, if it were true that *Earth* were a universal substitute for *mother*.The truth is probably the reverse; the important point about the myth of autochthony is that it excludes the parental dialectic. Here we have a myth in which the father–son relationship simply disappears. If we replace this myth in its historical and cultural context, it is tempting to add that the religious contribution of the invaders from the north disappears because it is no longer mediated by the maternal relationship, that what the invaders are expressing by means of this myth is the fact that, unlike the people they dominate, they do not belong to any Mother Earth who can be impregnated, that they are born of themselves. We can see in this configuration an erasure of the female element, a denial of castration, in other words foreclosure. And it is no accident that the foreclosed returns to Oedipus, son of Laius, son of Labdacus, in the truly hallucinatory figure of Jocasta. This is the kind of madness into which rationality plunges us.

And yet this is not the image of Greece that Freud gives in *Moses*. Unlike the Jews, the Greeks are harmonious: 'The pre-eminence given to intellectual labours throughout some two thousand years in the life of the Jewish people has, of course, had its effect. It has helped to check the brutality and the tendency to violence which are apt to appear where the development of muscular strength is the ideal. Harmony in the cultivation (*Ausbildung*) of intellectual and physical activity, such as was achieved by the Greek people, was denied to the Jews (*blieb der Juden versagt*)' (223, 115). Perhaps we are not so far away from Nietzsche's Greeks here. For we can legitimately interpret this assumed harmony between body and mind as the reconciliation of the two principles in art, in which case the Greeks are not the people of the logos, but 'artists'. This interpretation is confirmed by the passage in which Freud, who is looking for analogies capable of explaining the resurgence of the Moses religion after a latency period, turns to Homer for comparisons. Just as the Jews are preparing to reactivate the Moses religion, which has become latent, the Greeks are reviving their past glory in the Homeric epic. The same process applies in both cases: past and forgotten grandeurs and happiness are reconstructed. But the results are divergent. The Greeks turn their past into an epic; the Jews turn theirs into a religion. 'If all that is left of the past are the incomplete and blurred memories which we call tradition, this offers an artist a peculiar attraction *(Anreiz)*, for in that case he is free to fill in gaps in memory according to the desires of his imagination *(Phantasie)* and to picture *(gestalten)* the period he wishes to reproduce according to his intentions' (176; 71). The pleasure principle is given free reign in Homerism, but not in the Moses religion. The former represses, or in other words symbolizes, the instinctual representative; the latter excludes it, and rejects it through foreclosure.

In the same passage, Freud notes that the epic form becomes extinct, and gives way to historical writing (175; 71). The Greek way of reactivation will then eventually lead to science. Freud does not say how this substitution comes about; he simply notes that 'The explanation may be that its determining cause no longer exists. The old material was used up *(aufgearbeitet)* and for all later events historical writing took the place of tradition.' Does the fact that the old material was used up mean that the memories that were to be reactivated had been used up? Or that there was no longer the imagination to fill in the gaps? The meaning of *aufgearbeitet* appears to be that there is nothing left to work, that the material has literally 'finished being worked'.[14] In any case, historiographical science and science itself are born as the epic form dies. In the case of the Jews, the old material will never be used up, science will not be born, but art will not have to die because it has not been born, because the form of reactivation leaves no room for phantasy. The Greeks have the harmony of art, and therefore they will be able to have science, which is also a harmony, even though it is, as we shall see, differently located. The Jews are denied that (Freud uses the verb *versagen*, to refuse and promise, to frustrate). And where does the site of frustration lie, if not with the mother?[15]

Another of Freud's comments has similar implications. Speaking of the constitution of the figure of Christ by Paul of Tarsus, he shows that

it matters little whether this figure is a 'phantasy or the return of a forgotten reality' (*GW* 193; *SE* 87), and that in any case, what is to be
found at this point is the origin of the representation of the hero, of
'the hero who always rebels against his father and kills him in some
shape or other'. Christianity is thus the religion of the son, of
mediation, and will be inscribed in the totemic tradition of reconciliation. In Christianity, 'the murder was not remembered; instead of
it there was a phantasy of its atonement, and for that reason this
phantasy could be hailed as a message of redemption' (*GW* 192; *SE*
86). But, says Freud, the Greeks too have their parricidal son, and
therein lies the true basis for the 'tragic guilt' of the hero of drama. 'It
can scarcely be doubted that the hero and chorus in Greek drama
represent the same rebellious hero and company of brothers' (193; 87).
Are we, then, to classify the Greeks, and the Christians, along with the
savages, the men of reconciliation? And are the Greeks obsessionals,
like the totemists, or psychotics, like the Jews?

We have good reason to hesitate here. The Greeks are our masters in
two senses: masters of *logos*, masters of science and of the desire to
know; masters of *aisthesis*, masters of art, of wish-fulfilment. This is
why Freud is unsure about Oedipus: a dreamer, or an analyst? The
contrast with the Jews therefore brings out this conclusion, which we
will meet again later: true science is mediation, but not at all in the
dialectical sense; it does not simply break with art; it too is part of a
reconciliation. It is because it rejects reconciliation that Judaism
denies itself the scientific solution. And yet, as we shall see, it does promote that solution, and contributes to it by brutally displacing the site
of reconciliation: art and savagery reconcile pleasure and reality,
figure and discourse, in the form of phantasy; science tries to expel all
figuration, and to keep it expelled; it conciliates the thing-presentation
of the object which is so externalized and its word-presentation. And in
its delusion, Judaism both effects and fails to effect this exclusion – as a
result of which we are no longer dealing with representations, and
after which epistemological formalization becomes possible.

Savage; Jew: magic; science (?)

This relation is a complication of the former rather than its expression.
It relates to the Freudian theme of belief in the omnipotence of
thoughts. It means that the word itself can be regarded as an act and
can be proffered with a view to transforming the external world: such
is magic. It can be derived from the image/word pair in the following

manner: it is because magic moves from the word-presentation of the object to its thing-presentation that the word is efficacious. We say *horse*; we signify it within a linguistic system which Freud characterizes as a bound system of cathexis; and a horse appears; we see it; we can designate it in a freely cathected sensorial system. This is the hallucinatory procedure which is described at length in the *Traumdeutung* (ch. VI ¶ C) under the heading of consideration of conditions of representability; this is a form of work which makes it possible to move from the signified to the designated because words are taken literally. Words are not, then, proof against a relapse into images. It happens every night with our dream-thoughts, says Freud: 'This is the weak spot in our psychical organization; and it can be employed to bring back under the dominance of the pleasure principle thought-processes which had already become rational.'[16] Magic is the moment when the secondary process, or articulate thought, is treated as a primary process, as wishful thinking.

It is therefore not enough to contrast image and word; when we use the term 'word' a distinction must be drawn between designation (thing-presentation) and signification (word-presentation). And it should not be believed that the elimination of the former dimension, that of the image, is a guarantee of rationality, on the contrary. At the end of his paper 'The Unconscious'[17] Freud describes the fate that awaits a closed use of language: schizophrenia, a distortion of language in which the word-presentation of the object completely eliminates its thing-presentation, in which there is nothing but a closed system of signifieds. This is certainly not a complete description of the schizophrenic's relationship with words (there is also the question of what Freud terms 'organ speech'[18]). But Freud's formulation does situate what science cannot be: a discourse which is so bound as to be immune to modifications of the referent. He says this forcefully at the beginning of 'Instincts and their Vicissitudes'. It is not the experimental material which science takes as its object that guides ideas; on the contrary, it is only gradually that the system is elaborated, that it acquires definitions of precise concepts; but, adds Freud, that state of precision is in itself an obstacle to the progress of knowledge: 'physics furnishes an excellent illustration of the way in which even "basic concepts" that have been established in the form of definitions are constantly being altered in their content.'[19] But what does this constant alteration mean when it is translated into the terminology of word-presentations and thing-presentations? It means that the thing-presentation has not been eliminated, that the thing has to be kept in sight, that there must be designation as well as signification, and that reference is the element through which disequilibrium constantly enters the system of significations. Science avoids the errors of both the dream-work, which mistakes words for things, and of the schizophrenic who mistakes things for words. Its own linguistic status is that of an intersection of axes. They are the very axes defined by Frege in 1892: *Bedeutung* (reference, designation, thing-presentation of the object) and *Sinn* (meaning, signification, word-presentation of the object).[20]

If, as the work of Freud indicates, 'basic concepts' constantly need to change, to what are we to attribute the need for change? The relationship between discourse and its object is constantly being displaced. And is not continual displacement itself a feature of the primary process, of unbound cathexis? Does this mean that the object of the discourse of science is always linked to the primary process? That when we believe we are studying reality, it is always something that relates to a wish that is being studied, even in the so-called exact sciences? It might be argued that Freud is not arguing along these lines when he contrasts the reality principle and the pleasure principle, when he opposes the god Logos and the gods of pleasure. But this opposition is not univocal (the re-emergence of the id as super-ego is proof of that, and there are many other proofs); reality itself can only be defined negatively, as bad, as un-pleasure. In the *Formulierung* of 1911 Freud makes an important pronouncement about the conciliatory function of art: the 'dissatisfaction which results from the replacement of the pleasure principle by the reality principle is itself part of reality'.[21] It would be a mistake to imagine that reality is a *plenum*; reality is the initial rejected element,[22] but the rejected element bears the mark of lack, and that mark is the *fort* in the famous game. It is because reality is essentially open to the play of cathexis, and is opened up to it through the dimension of lack, through the trace left on it by the primary process, that the relationship between discourse and reality is constantly changing. Reality is the other side, the invisible (in the sense of perception, in Merleau-Ponty's sense; this will become clear later), and the invisible exists only through the wish, through a force sponsored by the No.

It is through its invisible aspect that reality solicits (that is, unsettles) the discourse of science. The latter is the discourse of a true science, of knowledge only if it remains open to this mobile element, only if it keeps an eye on its reference, only if it moves as much as its reference moves. Closure is a false science. Exteriority, the relationship with over there, necessarily comes into play in the idea of the well-placed word, which seems to guide Freud's concept of knowledge. And such is the thing-presentation of the object: the object is represented in its thing mode when it is present not as a signified, but as an opaque presence which both masks and indicates its underside.

Is Judaism, then, the opposite of totemism, just as science is the opposite of magic? This is not explicitly stated, and it cannot be. What is stated is that Moses, whom Freud assumes to have been an Egyptian, introduces the idea of 'a single deity embracing the whole world, who was no less all-loving than all-powerful, who was averse to all ceremonial and all magic and set before men as their highest aim a life in truth and magic' (*GW* 151; *SE* 50). This theme calls for two comments which will reveal something of the complexity of the relationship between Judaism and science.

The first concerns magic; being an expression of the belief in the omnipotence of thoughts it is the 'precursor of our technology' (221; 113); that belief, and magic itself were 'an expression of the pride of mankind in the development of speech *(Sprache)* ... The new realm of intellectuality was opened up, in which ideas, memories and inferences became decisive in contrast to the lower physical activity which had direct perceptions by the sense-organs as its content' (ibid). Magic is therefore not purely a matter of phantasy; it is a mediation between the pleasure ego and the reality ego and just as, as we have said, it introduces the image of the designated into the word, so it announces the binding of presentations into the system of signifieds, of concepts. Judaism seems therefore to be inscribed within this second current, which runs through magic and dominates it; it is not magic which it excludes, but the figurative or regressive misuse of magic; it extends the predominance of discourse, which paved the way for it.

And yet, and this brings me to my second comment, Judaism is not science, and its relationship with totemism is not exhausted by the idea of a gain in intellectuality. This relationship implies a complementary loss, that of mediation. The relationship between words and images is broken to such an extent that not only noble savagery but also true science become impossible. Basically, savage mediation is inscribed under the sign of the maternal, or in other words of the figurative; magic transports this mediation into the order of articulated language itself; science is not a mediation in any strict sense; it is a realization that there is an irremediable gap between the two axes of discourse, between signification and designation; it inhabits this right-angle and moves in accordance with it; this is what Freud calls *Ananke*, which he associates with the logos.

But the Jewish religion eliminates one of these axes, and it is therefore no longer noble savagery; but nor is it a rigorous science. It is a discourse without things. The totemic form relates to the dream-work; the Judaic word relates to schizophrenia. 'In the latter, what becomes the subject of modification by the primary processes are the words themselves in which the preconscious thought was expressed; in dreams what are subject to this modification are not the words, but the thing-presentations to which the words have been taken back.'[23] In totemic religion it is the word-presentations which are lacking; in the Jewish religion it is the thing-presentations. It should not be thought that wishes become conscious by working on words; the most elaborate verbalization may display something unconscious. In schizophrenia the cathexis of the *UCS* is withdrawn.[24] No longer seeing at all, but only listening.

Savage; Jew: visible; invisible

This new opposition is an expanded expression of the first. It contrasts the Jew, the man of the book, with the savage, the man of the idol. It implies at least two pairs of oppositions.

First of all, an opposition between two senses: sight and hearing. The readable is not given to the eye, but to the ear. A text is not situated in nature or in a plastic space, hallucinatory or otherwise. A text has no place, and is truly invisible. It is the trace of a word. It is in its entirety a fact of interlocution, except in that the locutor is absent and that the present interlocutor remains silent and listens. With the text, the spirit is at home, and dwells exclusively within signification. Nonetheless, the opacity of the text that exists is not presumed to result from the absence of the interlocutor; for, in theory, all the equivocity of the text is reducible in and through interlocution. The text is the intelligible and finite presence of an absent locutor (a closed corpus). By moving from eye to ear, Judaism allows humanity to move from the worship of a divinity who shimmers and dances in deep space to a god who is, in theory, presumed to be the subject of a completely audible (intelligible) utterance, but who is not in fact that subject because he is at the moment silent.

It has to be added that this invisibility of God is not an imperfection, an extrinsic accident to which the text and our understanding of the text have fallen victim. It is a fulfilment of the essence of the text, and its essence is that it is not addressed to the eye. The eyes must be closed if the word is to be heard. Thy *eidolon*, oh locutor, will fall prey to my phantasy. Phantasy implies deafness, because it is a wish fulfilled, and because it exists prior to any reality and any word.

We see here the establishment of the essential foundations of Western thought, the foundations which will provide a basis for the most modern idea of rationality. The most modern idea, that of the Platonism of *The Republic* V–VII, that of the Husserl of *Ideen* I, that of the Descartes of *Regulae* III, belongs to a very different system of metaphors of sight. But in Judaism, hearing is dominant. And hearing relates to a metaphysics, at least so long as one presumes that Someone has spoken. Now imagine the listening attitude combined with the Greek position, with a circular grouping entered upon an empty *meson!* He who speaks is no longer an absent locutor, but both a real locutor and a potential listener, and he is subject to the same law (*isonomia*) as he who listens, and so the word can pass between them. This initial characterization breaks completely with the Judaic dimension of the absolute other. Here, there is a basis for a dialogue, but the absolute inequality which prevailed between Job and his Lord has had to be abolished. What is abolished here is the sacred dimension of the text, the dimension of its absence.

But the other aspect of the combination of hearing and the circle is no less interesting: the circular grouping of the interlocutors announces the phantasy of closure, which is the motor behind science. The *isonomoi* turn their backs on the things of this world, on the given. They must construct a lexicon and a syntax, and it is through the language they establish in a 'universally valid' discussion that the 'given' will receive its signification. A challenge to meaning, a demand for signification alone, which is articulated in a discourse. But the challenge to meaning, to the given, means of course the exclusion of sight, the denial of designation, of the spacing which puts an open distance between discourse and that of which it speaks. Listening within a circle; that is what leads to axiomatics and, more generally, to the formalism of a discourse whose reference is never in itself taken as a scientific theme, and which is always struck out because it is taken as given, to scientistic formalism. The same formalism is sometimes imputed to philosophy. Thus, Freud writes at the end of the paper on the unconscious: 'It must be confessed that the expression and content of our philosophizing . . . begins to acquire an unwelcome resemblance to the mode of operation of schizophrenics. We may . . . . attempt a characterization of the schizophrenic's mode of thought by saying that he treats concrete things as though they were abstract.'[25]

Treating concrete things as though they were abstract means closing one's eyes, not of course in the sense of sleeping, as it is when we sleep that we open our eyes, but in the sense of excluding sense information on the grounds that it is suspect. One recalls the dream

Freud had the night before his father's funeral: he read the following inscription on some sort of official placard:

> *Man bittet, die/ein Auge(n) zudrücken*
> (You are requested to close the/an eye(s))[26]

Freud wonders about the ambivalence of the inscription. It is, he thinks, an incomplete condensation; the associated texts remain dissociated. One recalls the death of his father; the other (*ein Auge zudrucken*, literally 'to close an eye', but also 'to wink at', 'to overlook') the fact that some members of the family thought they would be disgraced by such a simple funeral. One is tempted to add, drawing on a rather different interpretation, that once the father is dead, one has to close one's eyes to things if his voice is to be heard, and if he is to be reborn. Begetting a father; that is the origin of science. And we are already in the order of *reading*, of inscription; the eyes are already closed. The West will try to fulfil its wish in this way; not only by hearing the word, but by articulating what is not heard. And in any event by refusing to be deluded by the visible.

The visible and the readable are also opposed in another way, in the same way that site and book are opposed. The sense of place, its 'genius' is itself local: it requires the being-there of colours, values and lines, and they have to be seen if what is is to be known. Existence is not divorced from concept, sensibility is reception, archaic passivity. The book, on the contrary, belongs to no place, its signification is emancipated from the site, and it is in theory transhuman: the universality of the statement. Thus, the man of the book has no land, whereas the savage, as Lévi-Strauss admirably shows in, for example, *La Geste d'Asdiwal*,[27] incorporates the natural (geological, climatic) 'deal' into the play of culture. The wanderings of the Jew express the transcendance of the readable over the visible: 'From that time on, the Holy Writ and intellectual concern with it were what held the scattered people together' (*GW* 223; *SE* 115). It is the link between man and earth that is severed by Judaism. Periodizations know nothing of this revolution; yet it upset the achievements of the neolithic age, and it is not over.

Where can the man from nowhere go to look for an answer to his birth, if not to a mobile inscription, to an intelligible trace left by a lost word which owes nothing to nature? The reader has no land. And so, neolithic sedentarization did not put an end to his wanderings; the fertility and abundance of rich lands, the satisfaction of needs, did not overcome the wish for a sign from the sterile desert in which nothing can be distinguished. This is why we have to wait until we have stopped being peasants, stopped being rooted by the mediation of myth or ritual, debased as they may be, before we can really become Jews or Greeks, men from nowhere who are haunted by an alienation that is different from the alienation of savages, men who are no longer dominated by a presence, but by an absence. The Judaic revolution appealed against a neolithic (counter-)revolution on the part of the peasants: the birth of the men of discourse; but we are appealing against a (counter-)revolution which is Jewish in oriign, and which has become a civilization of non-mediated discourse and power. And we are calling for an unknown revolution.

Savage; Jew: mother; father

We can arrive at this new opposition by one of two paths. One is indicated by Freud: 'Maternity is proved by the evidence of the senses while paternity is a hypothesis, based on an inference and a premiss.' This is why 'this turning *(Wendung)* from the mother to the father points . . . to a victory of intellectuality over sensuality . . . a thought-process in preference to a sense perception' (221; 114). The mother is visible; the father is not. The position of the father presupposes hypothetico-deductive language; it is the model for, or a prefiguration of, all science (which is therefore basically the begetting of a father). The father is a voice not a figure. He is not initially situated in the visible world. Does he belong to its obverse?

We see here the appearance of certain features of the Oedipal configuration, but it is difficult to say if it is that of Freud, that of Judaism or that which psychoanalysis elaborates as a universal triangle. This difficulty is the same as that which arises in *Moses*. This theme of the visible mother and the essentially invisible father has to be related, not only to everything concerning the relationship of seduction between mother and son, but also to Freud's early remark to the effect that desire is born when the breast is related to the figure (silhouette) of the mother, when, that is, it ceases to be an 'element' that exists prior to the division between real and imaginary; and that this attribution, which is contemporary with the loss whereby it is bound up with wishes, requires that the child must see its mother. There is an articulation between the mother and sight: the mother is seen when she is absent; she can therefore be signified because she introduces the one thing that creates visibility for man; an invisible face. This verso, this shadow, is the sensible presence of her *Versangung*, of her withdrawal, and of the child's frustration. And this lack is of course the trace of the father, the attestation that the mother is not omnipotence, the signal of castration. And so we discover, on the basis of the visibility of the mother, which necessarily implies her withdrawal, the invisibility of the Other.

But let us not confuse matters. The withdrawal of the mother, her invisible face, which makes her an object 'over there', is an invisibility which is constitutive of visible reality. The object is over there but, between here and there, there is a continuum in which over there and here can change places thanks to movements and actions. This is the sense-reality, with its immanent transcendence, the maternal reality which Merleau-Ponty wanted to uncover beneath the perceptions articulated in language, and which Levinas rejects as a false transcendence. It is through the transition from continuum to outer limit, through the abolition of incompossibility, through the simultaneous provision of recto and verso that the imaginary is constituted; this is also the position of love, a chiasmus between over there and here, 'space and time made perceptible to the heart'.

The invisibility of the father, on the other hand, is that of the symbolic; it is of a different order to the visible, of the order of discourse, of the transcendental. This at least appears to be what is implied by this first path to the father/mother opposition. And this is what we discover if we take the second path: 'An advance in intellectuality consists in deciding against direct sense-perception in favour of what are known as the higher intellectual processes – that is, memories, reflections and inferences. It consists, for instance, in deciding that paternity is more important than maternity, although it cannot, like the latter, be established by the evidence of the senses, and that for that reason the child should bear his father's name and be his heir. Or it declares that our God is the greatest and mightiest, although he is invisible like a gale of wind or like the soul' (225; 117–118). As we move from sight to hearing, we have a gain in *Geistigkeit*, we move from a mother bound to pleasure to a father who will, as a voice, be the principle behind the understanding of all reality. 'The religion which began with the prohibition against making an image of God develops more and more in the course of the centuries into a religion of instinctual renunciations' (226; 118).

Here, a curious episode takes place. Freud explains the satisfaction that results from instinctual renunciations in terms of the pleasure of obeying the superego, the heir to the father; in the case of the Jewish people, the pleasure of obeying Moses, the representative of the father. But, he adds, we cannot explain the predominance of the father or the historical advance in intellectuality in terms of that pleasure, as it is precisely those phenomena which will constitute the cultural superego specific to the Jewish people and to the West, in other words a superego characterized by the overestimation of the father! We therefore have to note the existence of this phenomenon without being able to explain it (226; 118). What can we say? That *Moses and Monotheism* ends in failure, that the book cannot explain the existence of God? Of course it cannot. Or that God is therefore indeed a transcendental which is irreducible to the stuff of the phantasy which produced it? It is into precisely this crack that Ricoeur inserts the blade of his hermeneutics; this is the crack which he opens up in order to inject faith into what Freud sees as an illness. Ricoeur asks himself Freud's question: 'Why does the father figure have a privilege that the mother figure does not have?' His answer is Freud's answer: 'Its privileged status is no doubt due to its extremely rich symbolic power, in particular its potential for transcendence. In symbolism, the father figures less as a begetter equal to the mother than as the name-giver and the lawgiver . . . The father is an unreality set apart, who, from the outset, is a being of language. Because he is the name-giver, he is the name-problem, as the Hebrews first conceived him. Thus the father figure was bound to have a richer and more articulated destiny than the mother figure.'[28] Here we have something quite Jewish: a blatant overestimation of the father, the position of his invisibility, and his relationship with the word. But why totemists then? How has this sublimation, this transition from maternal phantasy to paternal discourse been effected? 'Symbols', says Ricoeur, 'are fantasies that have been denied and overcome.'[29] The expression is borrowed from *Leonardo da Vinci and a Memory of his Childhood:* 'It is possible that in these figures Leonardo has denied *(verleugnet)* the unhappiness of his erotic life and has triumphed over it in his art *(kunsterlisch uberwunden)* by representing *(darstellt)* the wishes of the boy, infatuated with his mother, as fulfilled in this blissful union of the male and female natures.'[30] Ricoeur sees in this denial of and victory over the archaic the possibility of a movement which promotes 'new meanings by mobilizing old energies which were initially invested in archaic figures', the 'movement of interpretation that is contained in the promotion of meaning',[31] the promise of the truth of faith.

The curious episode was not a curious episode. Does Freud's failure mean that the Father is truly irreducible? I think that, on the contrary, the great difference he establishes between monotheism and totemism, and which he specifies as an advance in intellectuality and at the same time as relapse into mediation can itself be interpreted in analytic terms as the difference between, on the one hand, foreclosure or denial (*Verwerfung, Verleugnung*) and, on the other, repression proper.

(Savage; Jew: repression; foreclosure)

(This opposition is placed in brackets because it is itself foreclosed from Freud's text *Moses and Monotheism*.)

Foreclosure *(Verwerfung)* is a term which is frequently, albeit not systematically, used by Freud to designate an operation of rejection which is distinct from the operation which intervenes in repression. The distinction elaborated by Lacan,[32] and which we will use here, refers to the effects specific to each mode of rejection: the repressed is not excluded from the mental apparatus; it finds its place in the unconscious, and it is so worked upon (displacement, condensation, transposition of both the instinctual representative and its quota of affect) as to be able to enter into the symbolic of the unconscious. In his metapsychological paper on the unconscious Freud shows, as we have said, that repression consists of the withdrawal of cathexis from the word-presentation of the object together with the cathecting of the thing-presentation: the symbolic characteristic of the unconscious is not and must not be articulated like that of discursive language, and if the representative is to be unconscious, it must be both present and and non-representable, present as a figure (as, that is, a form and/or image) and non-representable in words. This theme was already dominant in the *Traumdeutung*: the various modalities of the dreamwork all cooperate to make inaudible a discourse, to make inarticulable a text which is presumed to be that of the dream thoughts; this scrambling consists of a plastic reworking of the text, of its replacement by a scenario. The rejected element is present in the scenario as a visible thing, but it is absent as an audible word. Its visible presence is, nonetheless, not simply an image; it too is arranged according to a certain order, and everything indicates that, after the *Traumdeutung* Freud sees it as a form (phantasy) rather than as a structure (of a language). The repressed is a representative which, having been decathected by the bound system of verbal presentations, is subject to the operations of the primary process, which is deconstructed and reconstructed in accordance with the needs of the form in which that process operates.

From the formal point of view, repression is indissociable from regression. The latter consists of a regressive flow of energy back into the psychic apparatus, and into perceptions, which are then recathected from the outside in an imaginary mode. Verbalization, which is a basic precondition for consciousness, is rendered impossible; the figure (silence) captures the energy; the object appears to be a thing whilst the words to say it are not there. But whilst this figuration is a sort of undoing *(Auflosung)* of the dream thoughts and breaks them down into their material elements, it is also an ordering *(mise en ordre)* and a staging *(mise en scène)*. Deconstruction is not disorder, but the expression of an other order, of an order which language lacks or which lacks language.

Far from excluding the object, repression, insofar as it is regression, includes it in a form, in an order whose rules no longer belong to the geometry of linguistic liaisons, but to the topology of plastic relations. Freud explains the connivance between wish and figure in genetic terms,[33] but it may have more to do with the formal meaning of regression. 'A harking back to older psychical structures', he adds in 1914.[34] Not only its origins or its place are old; for Freud figuration is a less elaborated mode of meaning than discourse. The expression of meaning, as opposed to its presence in an articulated discourse, or signification, can only be situated negatively. Expressed meaning lacks a form of negation which belongs to the preconscious alone;[35] the absence of negation is marked by the mobility of cathexis, and therefore by the mobility of meaning; the negation which is absent from the primary process is the form of negation which forbids *confusion*, or the uninterrupted slide from one zone in a phonetic or semantic field to another, which forbids continuity and which imposes the distinction of the signifier. Signification thus depends upon a tightly organized diacritical space. In that respect structural linguistics is an extension of Freud's intuitions, and in particular of his intuition that the system of verbal traces is one in which energy is saved and bound, as opposed to the unbound 'system' of the primary process. The negation which the primary process lacks is a spacing governed by the laws of structure. Displacement and condensation, the 'characteristic signs' of the primary process, are an expression of the mobile cathexis which reigns there. For Freud, these signs are the opposite of the properties of the secondary process, of the site of the articulate discourse.

If, in repression, the object is not excluded from the psychic system but is included within it as a figure (a thing-representation), we can understand why totemism is the religion of the son: the son is a father who has been suppressed and preserved; we can also understand why it is a religion which uses magic and images; the figure is the archaic form in which the rejected element remains present within the system.

And we can understand, finally, why it is the religion of reconciliation (*Versohnung*); repression supplies two processes with the raw materials for a compromise formation; the two processes express ambivalent wishes concerning the father (identification and murder) and the renunciation of those wishes. The totem meal and communion are, according to Freud, exemplary expressions of the compromise between the two.

Now Judaism excludes the figure, excludes magic, excludes reconciliation, excludes the totem meal; Judaism crudely refuses to admit to parricide. Where in the table of mental aberrations are we to place this religion? It does of course have its obsessional features, but they are not specific to it. It is because it is different that it is important. And the empirical mark of its difference has always been the hatred it inspires: antisemitism. It is, says Freud, 'as though Egypt were taking vengeance once more on the heirs of Akhenaten' (254; 136), as though the men of repression, of possible reconciliation and of phantasy were attacking the chosen people. This vindictiveness and resentment might be briefly expressed as: 'They will not accept it as true that they murdered God, whereas we admit and have been cleansed of that guilt' (ibid). The murder of the *Urvater* is not part of Jewish ceremonial or mythology, even in disguised form. And finally, in the last lines of the book we find Freud's question, which provides us with our starting point: 'A special inquiry would be called for to discover why it has been impossible for the Jews to join in this forward step which was implied, in spite of all its distortions, by the admission of having murdered God' (245–6; 136). A distorted admission is recognizable as a neurotic symptom insofar as it is a compromise formation: the initially ambivalent wish for the father has been obliterated by the work of displacement (of the representative) and of repression (of the affect), and the secondary process also profits from the outcome: rationalization, an economizing on the expenditure of energy. But the Jews have not been able to make the admission contained in the myth. It is not that they admit to having murdered the father without distorting anything: that is the work of science, of Freud as he writes *Moses*; the point is that they will have nothing to do with it, in the sense of having repressed it.

This form of negation, *Verwerfung*, characterizes the psychoses. It exhibits several features which Freud stresses throughout his work.[36]

1 *Detachment from reality* (particularly in *amentia*)   The rejected element is no longer incorporated, via the operations of displacement and condensation, into a formally archaic order which is integrated, self-consistent and internal to the subject. The object of *Verwerfung* is

foreclosed, presentation and affect alike, 'as if the idea had never occurred to the ego at all'.[37] 'The ego breaks away from the incompatible idea, but the latter is inseparably connected with a piece of reality, so that, in so far as the ego achieves this result, it, too, has detached itself wholly or in part from reality.'[38]

2 *Splitting of the ego* (particularly in *amentia*, in fetishism) The detachment from reality can, however, never be complete. 'Even in a state so far removed from the reality of the external world as one of hallucinatory confusion [amentia], one learns from patients after their recovery that at the time in some corner of their mind (as they put it) there was a normal person hidden, who, like a detached spectator, watched the hubbub of illness go past him.'[39] The dream then takes on the opposite function to that which it fulfils in neurosis: it no longer betrays instincts which are misrecognized during the waking life of the neurotic; it states clearly the things that the waking delusions of the neurotic are designed to deny. In psychosis, dreams speak and waking delusions 'dreams'. The ego adopts two independent attitudes at the same time. One takes account of reality, and the other detaches the ego from reality. The ego splits. This is obvious in certain perversions. For example, the ego will on the one hand construct the fetish as a displaced substitute for the woman's penis, in a 'compromise formed with the help of displacement, such as we have been familiar with in dreams',[40] which clearly demonstrates that for Freud the fetish in itself is not evidence of complete foreclosure. Nevertheless its formation rests upon a form of negation which is distinct from repression: 'The creation of the fetish was due to an intention to destroy the evidence for the possibility of castration, so that fear of castration could be avoided'.[41] But this is not all; there are also fetishists 'who have developed the same fear of castration as non-fetishists and react in the same way to it',[42] in other words who repress it. Repression implies the admission that there are beings without a penis, beings who have been castrated. Foreclosure knows nothing of castration. Freud specifies this refusal to know in connection with the Wolf Man: 'He rejected castration . . . in the sense of having repressed it. This really involved no judgment upon the question of its existence, but it was the same as if it did not exist.'[43] The fetishists in question therefore both recognize *and* do not recognize that castration exists. This is what is meant by the splitting of the ego.

Two remarks are called for here. Firstly, we must stress the importance of this second aspect of *Verwerfung*, which is very close to *Verleugnung* (disavowal or denial): the 'reality' from which the ego detaches itself is the lack of a penis. What is foreclosed is castration, or woman. Secondly, foreclosure can never be fully accomplished; even in the perversions, the ego is split in its relations with reality because castration cannot be completely disavowed, because both two axes of rejection traverse the ego, one putting castration outside (the symbolic) and the other putting it 'inside'.

3 *The position of language* (notably in schizophrenia).   Here we have to rely primarily on the *Papers on Metapsychology*. They are of considerable relevance to an interpretation of Judaism.

Consciousness presupposes perception, but it also presupposes word presentations of the object which are bound up with the innervations that permit reality-testing. I perceive the book, I can name it, I can verify its presence through gestural operations (of the *Fort-Da* type). Dreams, like the hallucinations of amentia, presuppose not only that cathexis is withdrawn from the word-presentations of objects, but also that cathexis is withdrawn from the *Pcs* system (elimination of reality testing). Only the thing-presentation of the object remains, and credence can be given to it because reality-testing has been eliminated. That credence can be granted if the energy which regresses through the psychic apparatus finds its way into the *Pcs* system. We can then see what we wish, or at least the scene in which our wishes are enacted.

The only difference Freud makes between dreams and amentia concerns the form of the detachment from reality; in the case of dreams, this is a 'voluntary renunciation' (the fulfilment of a *Pcs* wish to sleep), but in hallucinatory psychosis it results from '"repression"';[44] Freud places the word in inverted commas because this 'repression' does not concern the external world (a perception), but something internal (the drive). The abolition of reality-testing is seen 'more clearly' in psychosis than in dreams. This is, perhaps, because psychosis allows 'unrepressed, fully conscious wishful phantasies' into the system, whereas in dreams cathexis is withdrawn from the *Ucs* because of the wish to sleep; the positions occupied by the *Ucs* must be abandoned because their continued occupation *(Besetzung)* might wake the sleeper or re-introduce reality-testing. We have here an important complement to our earlier opposition: the difference between *Verwerfung* (in hallucinatory psychosis) and *Verdrängung* (in transference neuroses and in dreams) is that in the former the rejected element returns from the outside and that in the latter it returns from the inside, because sleep lowers the general level of cathexis, including that of the unconscious, whereas amentia keeps *Ucs* cathexis intact.

But this is a property of hallucinatory confusion, and not of all psychoses. It is by attempting to situate schizophrenia in relation to dreams that Freud succeeds in isolating the difference between neurosis and psychosis in terms of the respective position of language. Having asserted, in the paper on the unconscious, that the operations carried out on words are the same in dreams and schizophrenia (condensation and displacement), which would suggest that both dreams and schizophrenia treat words as though they were things, he is forced to contrast schizophrenia and the transference neuroses on the basis of the respective importance they give to the word-presentation of the object, and then to suggest a general theory of consciousness. In the transference neuroses, 'what repression denies to the rejected presentation ... is translation into words which shall remain attached to the object',[45] whereas in schizophrenia we have 'the predominance of what has to do with words over what has to do with things'.[46] But is not that predominance the effect of consciousness? 'We now seem to know all at once what the difference is between a conscious and an unconscious presentation ... the conscious presentation comprises the presentation of the thing plus the presentation of the word belonging to it, whilst the unconscious presentation is the presentation of the thing alone.'[47] And this is why schizophrenia poses a problem: 'We might ... expect that the word-presentation, being the preconscious part, would have to sustain the first impact of repression and that it would be totally uncathectable after repression had proceeded so far as the unconscious thing-presentations. This, it is true, is difficult to understand.'[48] The problem, which is of central importance to us in that it forms the nucleus for the latent opposition between Judaism and science in *Moses*, is resolved as follows: schizophrenia's characteristic endeavours to regain 'lost objects' set off on a path that leads to the object via 'the verbal part of it', reach it and then 'find themselves obliged to be content with words instead of things.'[49]

Does this mean giving schizophrenia the same status as dreams, which also treat words as things? On the contrary, in 'A Metapsychological Supplement to the Theory of Dreams', Freud states that: 'In dreams there is a topographical regression; in schizophrenia there is not',[50] whereas in dreams, 'What becomes the subject of modification by the primary process are the words themselves in which the preconscious thought was expressed.'[51] He adds: 'for a dream all operations with words are no more than a preparation for a regression to things.'[52] In schizophrenia, in contrast, there is no topographical regression and no return to images; we remain in the verbal domain, in, that is, the domain of consciousness. Cathexis is even withdrawn from the unconscious and is restored to articulated language. It is language as such which is treated in accordance with the operations of the primary process. In schizophrenia, the figure does not appear, as it does in the hallucinations of amentia or in dreams; the figure is no more than a form diffused across the *articuli* of discourse; it is never an image. This explains the viscosity for schizophrenic discourse; it is a property borrowed from the plastic space of the continuity of the figure, as opposed to the discrete space determined by the intervals of language.[53] Words are indeed treated like things, *but they are so treated insofar as they are signifiers* and not designators, as they are in dreams, where operations consist primarily of putting thing-presentations in the place of word-presentations. In the case of the schizophrenic, it is the unconscious itself which is decathected.

The task of drawing up an accurate clinical picture of the Jewish religion must be left to the clinician, but it seems to me certain that, in terms of Freud's lexicology, it must be classified, not as a neurosis, but as a psychosis. I think that if we classify it in that way we can elucidate a number of points. The following suggestions must be confirmed by detailed research. I have relied upon the work of Bultmann in my reading of archaic Judaism, and my argument is restricted to the difficulties raised by revolutionary movement mentioned earlier. I subsequently found in Emmanuel Levinas's admirable commentary *Quatre Lectures talmudiques*,[54] which provides a direct and uncompromising insight into the spirit of Judaism, a great wealth of information which will, I believe, confirm my hypothesis.

1 *Detachment from reality.*   In primitive Judaism, the theme of 'nature created' is quite absent; God is not the author of a visible world. It is only later that the Book of Genesis is adopted, and it is full of borrowings from the cult of Baal. Symmetrically, man 'is not part of the objective world, but stands over against it . . . ' and the world is 'the field of man's experience, the stage on which his work and destiny are played out.'[55] The Jewish God is not the cause of the totality of that which exists. Speculation as to origins is excluded from Hebraic thought. 'The real space where God rules is history. He makes his work known in the history of Israel.' Bultmann even says that: 'The creation story in Genesis I is not just a piece of speculation, but the first chapter in history.'[56]

The appearance of the theme of history must be linked to detachment from reality. We can understand this link: it is not enough to say that the Jewish man turns away from the visible world in order to devote himself to listening to the Word. It has to be said that the repression of castration in the mediated form of the chthonian religions, which are religions of the eye, gives way to foreclosure. Castration is no longer dialecticalized as a moment of fear or death, or symbolized as a woman, a young man or the earth. In general, the inversion of a position and/or relationship no longer appears to be a solution, or in other words a remission. Jewish thought does away with the great 'slated' relationship, which Lévi-Strauss has shown to be characteristic of myth,[57] and which defines perfectly the essence of the dialectic as a double inversion of terms (a $\rightarrow$ a $-$ 1) and of relations ($f_{a-sb(y)} \rightarrow f_y(a-a)$), with the great configuration of the inverted and reduplicated dipytch which we also find in platonic mythology and, of course, in Christian mythology, and upon which the whole Hegelian dialectic is based. There is no reconciliation to be phantasized (Jewish forgiveness is different from Christian forgiveness), and therefore no *archè* to be constructed as a starting point which the second 'slate' must reflect as a symmetrical point of arrival which is both the same and other. When castration is foreclosed, culpability evades all reconciliation, all mediation with or by reality which is posited as a co-creature, as a witness to the ordeal. This is the price that has to be paid if history is to begin.[58]

Detachment from reality is, then, essentially a detachment from myth, and this confirms the above analyses: neurosis has to be classified as a form of myth, as, that is, a form of integration of libido and reality; but detachment from reality, which has already been identified as one of the features of psychosis, implies that the ego gives up its compromise functions and allies itself with formations of the libido against the outside world. We begin here to see an element which is, I believe, of major importance: *the incompatibility of the position of history with the dialectic.* The dialectic is a 'slated' configuration, and it is a Form or Formula capable of writing any reality and any instinctual representative on its open pages; it contains and compensates for the negative; in other words it symbolically expounds *both* the murder of the father *and* the memory of the crime. The dialectic is the expanded form of the neurotic symptom known as a compromise formation.[59] In so far as they are dialectical forms of thought and practices, Christianity, Hegelianism, and 'marxism' must be numbered amongst the many attempts that have been made to reach a compromise, those (futile) attempts to restore the West from psychosis to neurosis.

But historicity is a product of the Jewish West. This historicity presupposes foreclosure, and the renunciation of compromise, myth and figure, the exclusion of female or filial mediation, a face to face encounter with a faceless other.[60] The immobility of the matrix form in which evil is expiated disappears when historicity arises. And the predominance of the text contributes to the formation of this new dimension.

2 *Predominance of the text.*   Bultmann insists on the specificity of the history of Israel. This is not a speculative historiography which is intended to make us understand what has happened or what is happening. It is oriented towards practice. 'The most important point about Hebrew historiography is that the centre of interest is not politics, as with the Greeks. It is the purpose of God and his moral demands. Thus there is no concern with history as a science, no interest in the forces immanently at work in it. Its real interest is in relating the course of history to its end.'[61]

This property of history relates to the invisibility of the Jewish God. 'Hearing is the means by which God is apprehended . . . hearing is a sense of being encountered, of the distance being abolished, the acknowledgment of a speaker's claim on us.'[62] Bultmann sees this as an index of a refusal to *speculate*, or in other words to see. It seems to me that here we come closer to the heart of foreclosure. It may be possible to 'accept' that God has been killed, in the sense of repressing that fact, when castration itself is accepted; according to Freud's hypothesis, deicide is a response to the terror inspired by the castrating father. But if castration becomes the object of foreclosure, if the fear it inspires is fought, not by staging it (*mise en scène*), but by expelling it from the symbolic (*mise hors symbole*), by a refusal to know that brooks no compromise, then it is impossible to admit to having killed God, and it is as though the murder had never taken place. The people of Israel have nothing to admit to in the matter of the murder of God. How then can deicide be present in their religion? In the form of writing. Hearing is the sense of absence of the dead God. The ear listens to writing. Writing is the word of the dead father.

Now we know that sight is the sense of the oneiric scenario (*mise en scène*) and of phantasy in general, whereas in paranoia and even schizophrenia, hallucinations are addressed to the ear.[63] Psychiatrists seem to be agreed that the sense of hearing is more 'intellectual' and 'more closely bound up with mental processes' than vision; but psychoanalysis teaches us that the predominance of the ear bears witness to the fact that the ego has come under the sway of the id, and has taken the side of the inside against the outside. The advance in intellectuality is not an advance in truth.

3 *Overestimation of the father.* The predominance of the text goes hand in hand with the overestimation of the father: the text lays down the law, its author has passed away; it has the force of a testament. But that is still not the essential link between father and text.

In totemism, ritual has to be thought of as, in a sense, the execution of an order, as an accomplishment, as a realization of the cosmic law. Judaism never finally fulfils the paternal order; 'fulfilment', in the Freudian sense, is refused it. 'Nothing could be less reminiscent of the structure of the "savage" word. In no sense is the Talmud an extension of the "way" of the Bible, even if we do assume that way to be mythical. The Bible supplies symbols, but the Talmud does not fulfil the promise of the Bible in the sense that the New Testament claims to be the fulfilment and continuation of the Old.'[64] Is there not a relationship between this refusal of fulfilment and the written character of the paternal order? But what is that relationship?

It is as though God were holding back the word of acquiescence, deferring the *quitus*, denouncing any purported fulfilment, and were testing even him who might be tempted to believe himself to be righteous. What does he give his people? Nothing, neither a world to conquer, a ritual to observe nor a mediation to bring himself, the Lord, closer to his people. What God gives his people is the fact that he takes them, chooses them for his people. 'Even more puzzling', writes Freud (146; 45), 'is the notion of a god's all at once "choosing" a people, declaring them to be his people and himself to be their god. I believe this is the only instance of its sort in the history of human religions. Ordinarily gods and people are indissolubly linked, they are one from the very beginning of things. No doubt we sometimes hear of a people taking on a different god, but never of a god seeking another people.' Freud uses this 'anomaly' as a pretext to extend his hypothesis: God takes the place of Moses; it was in reality the Egyptian prince who designated the Israelites, the foreigners, his people. Here we encounter the problem with the 'construction' Freud erects on the basis of Judaism, a problem which was deliberately ignored at the beginning of this study and to which I will return later.

God gives no sign and no means of fulfilment. He chooses the Jewish people, not as his heir or as the bearer of his mandate, but as his allocutor: he gives them his word in the sense that he addresses them. What is chosen is not a fulfilment, a place, or an earthly origin, but a discursive position. God gives nothing; he gives his people something to listen to. Such is the covenant. But the discursive position which is so chosen is not that of the present instance of speech. In the experience of interlocution, speech passes from one to another, causing the I and the you to be exchanged for one another. In the Hebrew experience, the exchange does not take place; a radical disequilibrium means that I the people cannot hand back the word to god, and that thou, oh Lord, cannot speak with me; thou hast spoken to me, and thou wilt speak to me, without thy word and my word ever being two similar and interchangeable aspects of a single discourse which is passed from mouth to mouth. And that is the basis for the relation of dominance, or at least of transcendence. The father proclaims the law in the violence of the first words; the sons are guided by them and interpret them.[65]

Writing is therefore as different from savage ritual as absence is from presence, but also as articulated language is from gesture (from dance or rhythm). The domination instituted by Judaism certainly differs from savage domination in that it is not reconcilable, in that God is not representable by any visible 'species', but it can be irreconcilable in the sense of mediation only because it has no need to be reconciled, because this domination is a prior conciliation. *The Lord's choice of his people is the conciliation*; it occurs *before* there is any understanding, any fulfilment, any dialectic. By addressing himself first to his people, if only in words of commandment and anger, or even in threats, God ensures that his people will belong to the covenant, come what may.[66] Writing, or the testamentary word, does not simply mean that the father has withdrawn, as happens in all religions; it means that filiation is not a matter of blood or symbols, that being a son of Jahweh is not a matter of staging and acting out a drama which redeems the cosmic drama to which the father fell victim; it means being an allocutor and having to remain in the position of listener before one has any understanding of what is being said. Here, the son does not eat the father, as he does in the savage form of a Hegelian 'suppression-conservation', or in accordance with the cannibalistic truth of what will become the dialectic.

And nor does he *understand*, in the scientific sense of understanding. When we say that the presence of meaning in Judaism is, insofar as it is writing, the discourse of the absent one, we are contrasting Judaism not only with the presence of meaning that we observe in savage society, but also with that which prevails with the scientific spirit. The son's response does not consist of a remissive operation of the sacrificial type; but this does not mean that it is the fulfilment of an unequivocal word, as a technical fulfilment stemming from the establishment of cosmological laws would be. For Judaism, listening to the law does not mean understanding the meaning of what it establishes. The advance in intellectuality is not a fulfilment of the wish to know; the vicissitude of that instinct too is renounced. Here, one ought to cite the whole of Levinas's second reading, which describes the desire of the West as a wish to know, and the wish to know as an avoidance of responsibility, as a flirtation with the known in which the knowing subject 'never gets his fingers burned': for Judaism, knowledge is temptation, and the wish to know is a temptation to temptation, whereas the righteous relationship to the law is an obligation to reply by doing: 'One accepts the Torah before one knows it . . . Hearing a voice which speaks to you means, *ipso facto*, accepting that you have an obligation to him who speaks . . . The Torah is an order to which the ego is beholden without having to enter into it, an order beyond being and choice . . . The impossibility of escaping God is the "mystery of the angels", the "We will do and we will hear".'[67]

4 *Disavowal* What, then, does the Jewish son want? Israel pays for its pride in having been chosen in constant self-accusations, and worries about its responsibilities. Guilt is an essential feature of the Mosaic religion, together with a feeling of being at fault mingled with the certainty of being preferred. This feeling can also exist in rationalized form, but Freud immediately unmasks it for what it is: a theodicy, *eine willkommene Entschuldung Gottes* (243; 135), an exculpation of God which comes at too opportune a moment: 'Things were going badly for the people; the hopes resting on the favour of God failed in fulfilment; it was not easy to maintain the illusion, loved above all else, of being God's chosen people. If they wished to avoid renouncing that happiness, a sense of guilt on account of their own sinfulness offered a welcome means of exculpating God: They deserved no better than to be punished by him since they had not obeyed his commandments' (134). This 'superficial motivation . . . neatly disguised *(maskierte)*' the true origins of the feeling of being in debt. According to Freud the real debt resulted from the murder of the father in the past; it had to be disguised because 'There was no place in the framework of the religion of Moses for a direct expression of the murderous hatred of the father' (134). A curious comment. It should be observed that this hatred never finds direct expression in any other religion; it never gives rise to anything other than compromise formations. It should in fact be said that it is a formation for which there is no place in the framework of the religion of Moses. Freud does not, however, explain this impossibility; and yet, once more, it is the difference between Judaism and other religions that is at stake.

Self-deprecation is a recognizable trait. Freud identifies it and analyses it in depth in his study of melancholia,[68] and he establishes the connection between this symptom, narcissism and psychosis.[69] 'A leading characteristic of these cases is a cruel self-deprecation of the ego combined with relentless self-criticism and bitter self-reproaches. Analyses have shown that this disparagement and these reproaches apply at bottom to the object and represent the ego's revenge upon it. The shadow of the object has fallen upon the ego . . . The introjection of the object is here unmistakably clear.'[70]

Two points have to be underlined here. On the one hand, it is not even the ego which takes its revenge upon the object, but the 'ideal ego', or in other words the super-ego. And the text to which I refer is one of the first in which Freud establishes that the Super-ego is an agency connected with the id, and that the fulfilment which the ego fails to obtain is obtained in a roundabout or ideal way in the super-ego. And, as Freud says so clearly, in melancholia, the ego is in the place of something else; it is in the place of an object which has been both lost and preserved. We can recognize here the features of cannibalism, but this is a cannibalism *without the symbolic*, for, to adopt the terminology of the first topography, everything happens at the level of the preconscious; this proves that we are in the order (or disorder) of psychosis, and not neurosis. The lost object takes the place of the ego, and it is not recognized for what it is.

We can only answer the question 'What does this son, the Jew want?' by designating the object which Judaism is mourning, and which takes the place of its ego. It is not fortuitous that in *Moses*, Freud should expound his theory of the super-ego at the moment when he has to explain the pleasure that can be derived from instinctual renunciation. A link is then clearly established between instinctual renunciation, listening to the law of the father and wish-fulfilment. In economic terms, the advance in intellectuality means that libidinal energy must be cathected on to the agency that arises out of relations with the father; at the same time, cathexis must be withdrawn from the lost object. The wish can then be fulfilled via identification with the father. But this is not all. The economy of Judaism has a very high narcissistic index, in two senses, and Freud misrecognizes, or cannot but misrecognize, one of those senses. On the one hand, the pleasure of observing the law requires narcissistic identification with the father; and Freud demonstrates this well: 'This happy feeling could only assume the peculiar narcissistic character of pride after the authority has itself become a portion for the ego' (225; 117). In terms of the formation of the Judaic super-ego, we are dealing here with what Freud describes in *Group Psychology and the Analysis of the Ego* as identification with the father, as opposed to the choice of the father as object: 'In the first case one's father is what one would like to *be*, and in the second he is what one would like to *have*.'[71] A first narcissism and a first answer to our question; the Jewish son would like to *be* the father, and that identification constitutes his super-ego.

But this process is replicated in a second operation of introjection and this time it applies to the love-object *insofar as it has been lost*. Here is the model for this operation: 'The object-cathexis proved to have little power of resistance and was brought to an end. But the free libido was not displaced on to another object; it was withdrawn into the ego. There, however, it was not employed in any unspecified way, but served to establish an *identification* of the ego with the abandoned object.'[72] This is still a narcissistic identification in that the object has been 'abandoned'; but the love relation persists. The process of melancholia means that 'a strong fixation to the loved object must have been present; on the other hand, in contradiction to this, the object-cathexis must have had little power of resistance.'[73] We are no longer dealing with the formation of the super-ego through identification with the father; the latter identification is distinct from the identification specific to melancholia in that the characteristic element of *mourning*, of the *loss of the object* is absent. The love relation does not persist. On the basis of this double process of identification, which leads on the one hand to the formation of a super-ego and on the other to that of melancholic ego, we can understand why the Judaic ego is an ego accused, an ego which can never atone for the debt it owes its 'conscience', its father. This ego, which is guilty of never having come to terms with the law, with paternal commandment, *is* the lost object. Everything we have said obliges us to recognize this: the lost object whose shadow falls on the ego, without the ego knowing the source of the darkness in which it is bathed or even knowing that it is bathed in darkness, is the mother.

It remains for us to prove that the rejection of the object in melancholia can take the form of foreclosure. A first index is given by the fact that Freud classifies melancholia as a narcissistic neurosis. That nomenclature has now been abandoned; the disorder tends now to be classified as manic-depressive psychosis. But the main point is that Freud did see that there was a specific difference between it and all the other 'neuroses': the impossibility of transference, or in other words the failure of symbolization itself, and an inability to integrate the given (the analytic situation) into the freeplay of the unconscious.[74]

Second index; Freud always adopts Karl Abraham's thesis about dementia praecox and makes it 'the basis of our attitude to the psychoses':[75] Abraham pronounced the main characteristic of dementia praecox to be that '*in it the libidinal cathexis of objects was lacking. . .*

it is turned back on to the ego and *this reflexive turning back is the source of the megalomania* in dementia praecox.'[76] Not only is melancholia to be classified as a psychosis; the narcissism which is its hallmark appears to be the essential clinical theme in all disorders of this kind.

We can find a third index in the description of male homosexuality which is given in chapter VII of *Group Psychology and the Analysis of the Ego* in order to demonstrate the possible role of identification in psychosis. The young man, says Freud, abandons his original sexual object, his mother: that object is renounced, 'whether entirely or in the sense of being preserved only in the unconscious is a question outside the present discussion'.[77] It is true that he is not discussing foreclosure, but it is clear that this is what is at stake in the distinction between total renunciation and a renunciation which preserves the object in the unconscious. And this total renunciation, this foreclosure, is not incompatible with identification with the ego in melancholia. It is even tempting to say that, on the contrary, in melancholia, the object does indeed take the place of the ego, in other words of the preconscious, and that it is in no sense 'preserved in the unconscious'; it would have to have been totally rejected, rendered absolutely unrecognizable for it to be able to take that place without arousing suspicion.

Here we have a few indices. They allow us to advance the hypothesis that the characteristic features of the Judaic religion, and of the West to the extent that it is a product of that religion, are not to be sought in obsessional neurosis but in psychosis. The nature of the latter must obviously be left indeterminate, as we are not concerned with making a diagnosis but with situating it with a view to elaborating a critique of religion and ideology.

But even by attempting to situate it, we move away from the characterization given by Freud. How are we to understand what appears to me to be a misunderstanding?

Freud's general thesis as to the history of religion can be expressed in a few words, and they form a dramatic sequence: the lawless domination of the *Urvater* over the horde – the murder of the *Urvater* – the establishment of a matriarchal and fraternal totemic religion – the return of the repressed, that is, the return of the father and the re-establishment of monotheism. But why does the repressed return amongst the Jews? Why was it that 'the monotheist idea made such an impression precisely on the Jews?' (195; 88). Freud writes:

> It is possible, I think, to find an answer. Fate had brought the great deed and misdeed of primeval days, the killing of the father,

closer *(naher geruckt)* to the Jewish people by causing them to repeat *(wiederholen)* on the person of Moses, an outstanding father
figure. It was case of 'acting-out' *(agieren)* instead of remembering *(erinnern)*, as happens so often with neurotics during the
work of analysis. To the suggestion that they should remember
... they reacted ... by disavowing their action *(mit der Verleugnung ihrer Aktion)*; they remained halted at the recognition of
the great father (88–9).

The reader will have recognized this *Verleugnung* as the rejection-
without-symbolism which, according to our hypothesis, gives Judaism
its specificity: parricide is disavowed because castration has been
foreclosed; why would one have to kill the father if it were as though
the threat of castration had never existed? How could one kill a father
who made a covenant with his sons at the beginning of history? In the
origins of Judaism, this universal fear took on a different accent; it was
not abolished by a re-conciliation, by a salvation, but by a pre-
conciliation, by a covenant.

Freud's research does not lead him in this direction: he insists, as we
have seen, on the opposition between acting-out and remembering.
Here, we encounter a problematic of repetition which, as we know,
eventually gave rise to a general revision of his theory.[78] Acting-out
was identified at a very early stage,[79] and was seen as a failure to
achieve transference. It stems from a compulsion to repeat, and
constitutes an active discharge. Freud thought that the predominance
of the pleasure principle over the primary process had to be criticized
in the light of such phenomena. Be that as it may, the opposition
between acting-out, or the killing of Moses as a repetition of the killing
of the *Urvater*, and remembering appears to induce a final homology
which, according to Freud's thesis, might be formulated as follows: the
Jew is to the savage, or at least to the Christian, what acting-out is to
remembering.

This formula is of some importance in the context of the thesis
which sees Judaism as an obsessional neurosis. It in fact means that the
difference between it and other religions is signalled by the failure to
reach a compromise. Whereas other religions open up the way for
compromise symptoms in which the memory of the original sin can
find a disguised expression, the famous totem meal being only one
example, the Hebrew religion will tolerate nothing of the kind. The
explanation is, according to Freud, that acting-out occurred, because
only the compulsion to repeat the parricide on the person of Moses
could allow the psychic apparatus to discharge successfully without
reaching a compromise with the preconscious. Freud's entire thesis is

based upon these two points: (1) monotheism is a repetition of the archaic cult of the father; (2) the killing of Moses is 'a recent real repetition of the event' which awakens 'the forgotten memory-trace' (208; 101). We can thus understand why the killing 'becomes an indispensable part of our construction, an important link between the forgotten event of primeval time and its later emergence in the form of the monotheist religions' (196; 89). If Moses had not been compulsively killed, the Jews would be savages like any others. If there had been no acting-out, there would have been a compromise formation.

I hope to have shown that this hypothesis is not correct. It would have been possible to refute it on the basis of historical research, and others have done so. But that leaves intact the question of the difference between Judaism and totemism. And it would mean abandoning the rich material supplied by Freud's text in the name of positivism. In this text, Freud faces up to the thing he had to fear most, the thing that lurked in the basement of his own science: his 'prejudice'. To the extent that this science succeeded in discovering the Oedipus complex, it is clear that it was won in the face of Judaism, which is completely steeped in this law. But it is also clear that it is dependent upon that same religion – and this seems to me to be particularly clear in *Moses* – insofar as the form taken by the defence against castration is not investigated.

In a note added to the *Traumdeutung* in 1909, Freud writes: 'I underestimated the importance of the part played by phantasies in the formation of dreams' because 'I was principally working on my own dreams, which are usually based on discussions and conflicts of thought.'[80] It was the study of hysterical neuroses which revealed the importance of phantasy, and its role as a nucleus for dreams. In 1908, Freud writes that phantasies 'give us the key to an understanding of night-dreams – in which the nucleus of the dream-formation consists of nothing else than complicated day-time phantasies of this kind that have been distorted and are misunderstood by the conscious psychical agency'.[81] As early as 1899 he had apologized for the fact that his own dreams were less rich in 'sensory elements' than those of his patients, explaining this in terms of his inability 'to produce any good example from my own experience of an *infantile* memory producing this kind of result'.[82]

The Interpretation of Dreams does contain an infantile memory, a screen-memory or a phantasy which Serge Leclaire analyses as an expression of one of Freud's specific wishes:[83] the wish to understand wishes. It is this that one day led Freud to analyse the dream of the botanical monograph, the memory of tearing up a picture book which

Jakob Freud had abandoned to his eldest daughter and Sigmund *zur Vernichtung*, for them to destroy.[84] Leclaire believes that he has shown that the book is an analogon of the mother, and that tearing out its pages an analogon of the transgression of the Oedipus. But, he has to add, 'the book will not be frozen like screen-memory, for the very good reason that Freud will write a book about wishes. And that book will say that it is through transgression that wishes are revealed'.[85]

The *but* suggests a different interpretation of the significance of the book, of the coloured plates and of the dreams Freud interprets. The former certainly stands for the mother, but does not tearing out the plates signify the abolition of images, rather than incest?; and, in the light of our earlier oppositions, does it not signify the exclusion of the mother and the disavowal of castration? The *Vernichtung* of the figurative is also a *Verneinung* of the maternal. The illustrations deal with Persia, which, like Egypt, is the land of a mediating religion. The dream has much more to do with Freud's identification with his father (who gave him a Bible) than with any transgression of the law. And it is no doubt in this violent and jubilant identification that we should look for the explanation for Freud's conspicuous lack of phantasies. Tearing out the plates breaks the mediation of the mother; gathering flowers puts an end to 'savage' thought, and to wish-fulfilment. That the paternal law was destroyed that day must be in doubt; it was, rather, the seductive appeal of a mother and its irradiation in vertiginous images. How could Freud's vocation be announced to him in the form of transgression, or in wish-fulfilment? Unlike that of Leonardo, Freud's word was not to find an artistic expression or to be a word of reconciliation. On the contrary, Freud always looked on art, and on Italy, as something that was forbidden him. And does transgression 'reveal' a wish? Is it not, rather, a manifestation of wishes as something concealed, as something whose origins are concealed? Where was the transgression, if he was given the book in order to destroy it? His father ordered that nothing should remain of the plates. Freud will try to speak the language of truth, which stands in the corner between the word-axis of the object and its figure-axis. That position has to be constantly won. Freud does not conquer it in the face of a rich phantasy life, but in the face of a lack of images. What he had to overcome was a word which was already in the place of the word he was looking for, and which resembled it; his wish was disguised in that word, not in images. The figure formations were torn out; their leaves were torn out and they withered. There remained a passion for the book; this passion was a real passion; the verso of an action, of the action of the father. That is what had to be unveiled. The desire for the father could only be unveiled by re-establishing the position of phantasy, of the maternal space of transgression, and, finally, by bringing to light the full Oedipus. The signification-presentation and the designation-presentation could then come into contact with one another at right-angles, in the austerity of truth.

The 'construction' of *Moses* testifies to the fact that it was not possible to establish fully the angle of science in Freud's admirable attempt to psychoanalyse psychoanalysis. The position of Judaism escapes him because of the latent but acute oppositions which innervate his text and which ought to have allowed him to situate the mode of rejecting castration which is specific to the religion of Moses; is it not because Freud himself is a product of that peculiarly Jewish predominance of the father that he failed to recognize these indices as an invitation to elaborate a very different construction? By attempting to 'deprive (*absprechen*) a people of the man whom they take pride in as the greatest of their sons' (103), by making him a foreigner, does not Freud in fact betray the same overestimation of the father, and merely displace it in that he himself takes the place of Moses by constructing him, and by making him his *son*? And at the beginning of this book, he does not simply say that Moses was the greatest of the sons of the Jewish people; he says also that the task of 'deprivation' was not undertaken gladly or carelessly, 'least of all by someone who is himself one of them'. The object of Freud's testament may have been to make Moses the father his own son. The father of his father.

It is in that sense that Freud is truly a Jew who has lost his faith; he tries to be the father, to construct the father. It appears to me that this is the meaning of the preface to the Hebrew translation of *Totem and Taboo*:

> ... An author who is ignorant of the language of holy writ, who is completely estranged from the religion of his fathers – as well as from every other religion – and who cannot take a share in nationalist ideals, but who has never yet repudiated his people, who feels that he is in his essential nature a Jew and who has no desire to alter that nature . If the question were put to him 'Since you have abandoned all these common characteristics of your countrymen, what is there left to you that is Jewish?', he would reply: 'A very great deal, and probably its very essence ... Unprejudiced science cannot remain a stranger to the spirit of the new Jewry.'[86]

Freud departs from Judaism in that the word (the truth) is for him no longer an object to be listened to, but an object to be produced (constructed): writing the book, knowing. He remains loyal to Judaism in that what he wants to construct is still a word, in that for him the truth can be sought only in the manifestation of a text, can only be heard in words.

NOTES

1 The following study takes as its starting point a seminar given by Clemence Ramnoux in 1966-7 on structural and analytic methods of interpreting legends.

2 Cf., *inter alia*, 'Creative Writers and Day-Dreaming' (1908), *SE* IX and 'Formulations on the Two Principles of Mental Functioning' (1911), *SE* XII.

3 Page references to *Moses and Monotheism* refer to: S. Freud, *Gesammelte Werke* (Frankfurt am Main: S. Fisher Verlag, 1962), XVI; S. Freud, *The Standard Edition of the Complete Psychological Works of Sigmund Freud*, ed. James Strachey et al. (London: Hogarth Press, 1953-74), XIII. The reference here is *GW*, p. 220; *SE*, pp. 112-13.

4 'Formulations', p. 219.

5 'Creative Writers', p. 145.

6 Ibid., p. 146.

7 'Formulations', p. 221; cf. *Moses* pp. 204; 97.

8 'The Unconscious', *SE* XIV, p. 202: 'Now . . . we are in a position to state precisely what it is that repression denies to the rejected presentation in the transference neuroses: what it denies to the presentation is translation into words which shall remain attached to the object.'

9 *The Interpretation of Dreams*, *SE* V, p. 493.

10 Ibid., IV, pp. 264-6.

11 Ibid., IV, p. 262.

12 Lille: Bibliothèque de l'université, 1939.

13 Claude Lévi-Strauss, *Structural Anthropology*, tr. Claire Jacobson and Brooke Grunfest Schoepf (Harmondsworth: Penguin, 1972), p. 213f.; J.-P. Vernant, *Mythe et pensée chez les Grecs* (Paris: Maspero, 1965), pp. 19-47 and specially pp. 41-2.

14 Cf. *Leonardo da Vinci and a Memory of his Childhood*, *SE* XI, p. 83. In this essay, which was written in 1910, Freud likens 'the way in which the writing of history originated among the peoples of antiquity' to the construction of a phantasy; the pleasure principle recurs even in this *Schreibung*.

15 Cf. Jacques Lacan, 'La Relation d'object et les structures freudiennes', *Bulletin de psychologie X* (12), 15 May 1957, p. 743.

16 'Formulations', p. 223.

17 'The Unconscious', pp. 199-204.

18 Cf. Gilles Deleuze, 'Le Schizophrène et le mot', *Critique*, September 1968.
19 'Instincts and their Vicissitudes', *SE* XIV, p. 117.
20 Frege, 'Über Sinn und Bedeutung', *Zeitschrift für Philosophie und philosophische Kritik* 100, 1898.
21 'Formulations', p. 224.
22 'Negation', *SE* XIX, pp. 233–9.
23 'A Metapsychological Supplement to the Theory of Dreams', *SE* XIV, p. 229.
24 Ibid., p. 235.
25 'The Unconscious', p. 204.
26 *The Interpretation of Dreams, SE* IV, pp. 317–18.
27 *Annuaire de l'école Pratique des Hautes Etudes*, 1958–9, pp. 8–43.
28 Paul Ricoeur, *Freud and Philosophy: An Essay on Interpretation,* tr. Denis Savage (New Haven and London: Yale University Press, 1970), p. 542.
29 Ibid., p. 543.
30 *Leonardo, SE* XI, pp. 117–18.
31 Ricoeur, pp. 175, 541.
32 Jacques Lacan, 'Introduction au commentaire de Jean Hyppolite sur le *Verneinung* de Freud', *Ecrits* (Paris: Seuil, 1966); 'Réponse au commentaire', ibid.; 'D'une question préliminaire à tout traitement possible de la psychose', ibid., tr. Alan Sheridan, 'On A Question Preliminary to Any Possible Treatment of Psychosis', *Ecrits: A Selection* (London: Tavistock, 1977), pp. 179–225.
33 *The Interpretation of Dreams, SE* V, p. 598: 'The first wishing seems to have been a hallucinatory cathecting of the memory of satisfaction,'
34 Ibid., p. 548.
35 'The Unconscious'; 'Negation'.
36 See Jean Laplanche and J.B. Pontalis, *The Language of Psychoanalysis*, tr. Donald Nicholson–Smith (London: The Hogarth Press and the Institute of Psychoanalysis, 1973), articles on Psychosis, Foreclosure, Denial, Projection and (De)negation.
37 'The Neuro-Psychoses of Defence', *SE* III, p. 58.
38 Ibid., p. 59.
39 'An Outline of Psychoanalysis', *SE* XXIII, pp. 201–2.
40 Ibid., p. 203.
41 Ibid.
42 Ibid.
43 'From the History of an Infantile Neurosis', *SE* XVII, p. 84.
44 'A Metapsychological Supplement', *SE* XIV, p. 234.
45 'The Unconscious', *SE* XIV, p. 202.
46 Ibid., p. 200.
47 Ibid., p. 201.
48 Ibid., p. 203.
49 Ibid., p. 204.
50 'A Metapsychological Supplement', *SE* XIV, p. 229.

51 Ibid., pp. 236-7.

52 Ibid., p. 237.

53 Cf. Deleuze, 'Le Schizophrène'.

54 Paris: Minuit, 1968.

55 Rudolph Bultmann, *Primitive Christianity in its Contemporary Setting,* tr. R.H. Fuller (London: Thames and Hudson, 1956), p. 20.

56 Ibid., pp. 20-1.

57 *Structural Anthropology,* p. 228. This relation is written as $F_x(a)$: $F_y \cong F_x(b)$: $F_{a-1}(y)$.

58 This is how Levinas, *Quatre Lectures talmudiques* (Paris: Editions de Minuit, 1976), p. 90, describes the function of reality in Judaism, and its complete subordination to listening to the Law: 'God did not create without concerning himself with the meaning of his creation. Being has a meaning. The meaning of being, the meaning of creation – this is the realization of the Torah. The world is there so that the ethical order has a chance to exist. The act whereby the Israelites accept the Torah is the act which gives reality a meaning. Rejecting the Torah means reducing being to nothingness.'

59 Cf. J. Gabel, *La Fausse Conscience* (Paris, 1962). Gabel's entire book is based upon the hypothesis that the dialectic is the form of true consciousness (though it is true that he speaks of an 'open' dialectic). This is a Hegelian–Lukàcsian hypothesis dating from the period 1919-22. It is striking to note that, for this author, it is always psychosis, and almost never neurosis, which supplies the model for alienated or reified consciousness.

60 This is a central theme in Levinas, and especially in *Totality and Infinity,* tr. Alphonso Lingis (The Hague: Martinus Nijhof Publishers, 1979). For his comments on forgiveness and remission, or in other words on the dialectic, see his commentary on the 'Yoma' treatise in *Quatre Lectures,* especially pp. 58, 63.

61 Bultmann, p. 22.

62 Ibid., p. 23.

63 Cf. Gabel, p. 212, and the article by C. Schneider (cited as reference 422).

64 Levinas, *Quatre Lectures,* pp. 18-19.

65 Ibid., p. 82. Cf. p. 88: 'The teachings of the Torah cannot reach the human person as the result of a choice; that which has to be received in order to make possible free choice cannot be chosen, except after the event. In the beginning, there was violence. Unless it was a form of consent other than the consent that is given after examining matters . . . Is not revelation precisely a reminder of the consent that preceded freedom and even non-freedom? The freedom that is taught by the Jewish text is a non-freedom which, far from being slavery or infancy, lies beyond freedom.'

66 Cf the 'Chabat' treatise 88a, cited Levinas, p. 68: 'The Israelites are committed to "doing" before they "understand". First doing, then understanding.'

67 Levinas, pp. 91, 104–5, 107, 109.
68 'Mourning and Melancholia,' *SE* XIV; *Group Psychology and the Analysis of the Ego, SE* XVIII.
69 *Introductory Lectures on Psychoanalysis, SE* XXII, p. 154.
70 *Group Psychology, SE* XIV, p. 109.
71 Ibid., p. 106.
72 'Mourning and Melancholia', *SE* XIV, p. 249.
73 Ibid., p. 258.
74 See 'On Narcissism: An Introduction', *SE* XIV and 'Neurosis and Psychosis', *SE* XIX.
75 *Introductory Lectures, SE* XXII, p. 415.
76 Ibid.
77 *Group Psychology, SE* XIV, p. 109.
78 *Beyond the Pleasure Principle, SE* XVIII, especially ch. 4.
79 During the analysis of Dora; see 'Fragment of an Analysis of a Case of Hysteria', *SE* VII, and especially §4.
80 *The Interpretation of Dreams, SE* V, p. 494 n.
81 'Hysterical Phantasies and their Relation to Bisexuality', *SE* IX, pp. 159–60.
82 *The Interpretation of Dreams, SE* V, p. 546.
83 Serge Leclaire, 'A Propos d'un fantasme de Freud: Note sur la transgression', *L'Inconscient*, January–March 1967, pp. 31–55.
84 *The Interpretation of Dreams, SE* IV, p. 172.
85 Leclaire, pp. 53–4.
86 'Preface to the Hebrew Translation of *Totem and Taboo'*, *SE* XIII, p. xv.

Translated by David Macey

5

One of the Things at Stake in Women's Struggles

**In the form of writing, the question of the relations
between men and women is itself caught up in these relations**

It may be that you are forced to be a man from the moment that you write. Maybe writing is a fact of virility. Even if you write as a woman, 'femininely'. Perhaps what we call feminine writing is only a variation on a genre that is masculine and remains so: the essay. It is said that the femininity of writing depends on content. Writing is feminine, for example, if it operates by *seduction* rather than conviction. But the opposition of these two efficacies is itself probably masculine.

To avoid such alternatives, you claim no assignable difference between feminine and masculine, in writing or elsewhere: but this *neutralization* of the question is also very suspect (as when someone says that he's not political, neither on the right nor the left; everyone knows he is on the right).

It is a philosopher who is speaking here about relations between men and women. He is trying to escape what is masculine in the very posing of such a question. However, his flight and his strategies probably remain masculine. He knows that the so-called question of a masculine/feminine opposition, and probably the opposition itself, will only disappear as he *stops philosophizing:* for it exists as opposition only by philosophical (and political) method, that is, by the male way of thinking.

In the midst of these aporias, one is tempted to give his pen over to the antonym of the inquisitive adult male, to *the little girl*. But it is said that, like a savage, she doesn't write. And above all, that like savages, she is herself the creation of her so-called opposite, the sober-minded male, who in reality is also her judge: a creation of the jealousy he feels for something he is forbidden to be.

How intelligence supposedly came to women

The King of Ou says to general Sun-Tse: you who are such a great strategist and who undertake the military training of anyone, take 180 of my women and try to make soldiers of them. Sun-Tse orders them to form two ranks led by the king's two favourites and he teaches them the code of drumbeats: two beats: right face; three beats: left face; four beats: about-face. They laugh and talk instead of obeying. He goes over the lesson several times: giggles, disorder, even as they assure him that they know the code. Fine, he says, you have mutinied; military law calls for death: so you will die. The king is alerted and he forbids Sun-Tse to harm the women, and especially his favourites. Sun-Tse answers: You have charged me with their training, all the rest is my business. And he severs the heads of the two favoured women with his sabre. As soon as the king's favourites are replaced, the exercise begins again: 'and, as though these women had always been soldiers, they become silent and orderly.'[1]

Thus, one way to separate masculine and feminine. *Primo:* virility claims to establish order and femininity is the compulsion to deride order. There is chattering in the gynaeceum and silence among the troops. Contrary to our story, even though comedy may be a masculine genre, it represents the successful stratagem of weakness; comedy makes men laugh like women; the prisoner Rosine makes a fool of Don Bartholo. This is only a momentary concession: Rosine escapes her tutor only to fall under the law of the real master, the Count Almaviva. He who laughs *last*, laughs best: the aimless humour of women will succumb to the learned, socratic, teleological irony of men.

Secundo: the ruse of reason (masculine) differs from the snares of sensitivity (feminine): reason *makes use of* death. Sun-Tse kills a few women who laugh: that is sobriety. Women must know the fear of death and must overcome it if they are to be civilized (that is, if they are to be virilized). If not, they give in and are subjugated (but continue to laugh up their sleeves); or they don't, a few of them are killed: these are the dead soldiers who can become heroes. Slaves are never entirely reliable: truly civilized women are dead women, or men.

Tertio: What is pertinent for distinguishing the sexes is the relation to death: a body that can die, whatever its sexual anatomy, is masculine; a body that does not know that it must disappear is feminine. Men teach women of death, the impossible, the presence of absence. Tragedy is a noble genre because one does not laugh: in fact, it shows that there is nothing to laugh about. No way to play the woman. Sun-Tse defines a rite of passage: the feminine is on the side of the child, youth, and nature; death is the ferryman; he shows the way to language, to order, to the consideration of lack, to meaning, to culture.

Sexual theory and practice of men includes the threat of death: or, sexuality makes no sense without a signifier

When Freud asks: What does a woman desire? as a man, he is suggesting that she desires nothing since she is passive. And when he says, libido is masculine[2] – here he agrees with the spectator of pornographic films who answers when asked why women aren't interested in such spectacles: Women? Have you ever seen them take an interest in sex? 'Women have no sex'[3] – by libido, Freud means not an instinctual process but an intelligible one, because it desires (*to say*) something.[4] For Lacan, the signifier inscribing its effects as unconscious statements is the phallus, the a priori condition of all symbolic function when this function works on sexually determined bodies. The body has no sex before being traversed by 'the defiling of signifier', i.e., the threat of castration, or death, a mark of Oedipal law.

Difference is established here, they say: the little boy supposedly overcomes the threat of castration to resolve the Oedipus complex, and becomes virile, while the little girl becomes feminine by entering the Oedipus complex under the law of castration. The first must identify with the phallus in spite of the father, the other must content herself with receiving it. Sun-Tse seems to be in agreement with this thoroughly masculine version: a woman is become a man; let her confront death, or castration, the law of the signifier. Otherwise, she will always lack the sense of lack. She thinks herself eternal for this reason and is deprived of sexuality as well as the activity constituting the body's language.

Plato's Socrates says nothing else when he claims[5] that Love is born not only of ruse, cleverness, and Resource (*Poros*) but also of Lack (*Penia*) – that one does not love what one loves but loves impregnating it and reproducing itself in order to become immortal; thus he subordinates love to the effect of an absent signifier, the Idea, supreme paradigm which carries bodies beyond themselves. And *he will die* to bear witness to this.[6] The great virile association of war and sexuality (an association found also in Chinese erotic treatises, which are concurrently manuals of strategy) proceeds from this distribution of the symbolic function: virility has its *price*: life; the body can speak only if it can die and each time it knows pleasure, the body risks becoming lawless and speechless once again – capable only of living and laughing. That is why love is for man a struggle in which his virility, that is, culture, is at stake.

Men (Western men, in any case) want to conquer, not love. They have nothing but disdain and irony for the sensual, for odours, sensations, secretions, *laissez-faire*, music; they call 'artists' those among them that consent to these things. But women are the artists. Men feel undone when they love. They prefer prostitutes whose impassivity protects them. A woman's pleasure remains an enigma for them because they have not found the technical means to produce it in a predictable and guaranteed fashion. They prefer the clitoris, which they consider a trustworthy and homologable agent working for them in the adversary's camp. Vaginal penetration consists 'then' in the occupation of this camp; it is likewise a *cursus* followed by the conquered until she reaches the ultimate degree of pleasure, which the man claims to extract from her.

But for women, to 'come' or not, in the sense of having or not having the spasm men *anticipate* on the basis of their own orgasm – this is *not a question* when women love. The question does not arise and the answer is indifferent. But it concerns virility to not want to know this; for it implies a body whose pieces do not 'speak' but 'work' without having to produce a meaning they supposedly lack. If pleasure comes easily without love and love without pleasure, then sexual and affective manoeuvres would have nothing to do with producing meaning – theoretical (Beautiful, True) or physical (orgasmic 'satisfaction').[7]

Masculine imperialism either relegates women to its borders or makes them homologues of men if it educates them

Everything is in place for the imperialism of men: an empty centre where the Voice is heard (God's, the People's – the difference is not important, just the Capital letters), the circle of homosexual warriors in dialogue around the centre,[8] the feminine (women, children, foreigners, slaves) banished outside the confines of the *corpus socians* and attributed only those properties this *corpus* will have nothing to do with: savagery, sensitivity, matter and the kitchen, impulsion, hysteria, silence, maenadic dances, lying, diabolical beauty, ornamentation, lasciviousness, witchcraft and weakness. The masculine corpus attributes active principles to itself – so say Hegel, Freud and all the others:

we must seize the object that *seems* human but which, in fact, must *become* human since it *is* not. Virility's imperialism is warlike and pedagogical; it is all the same: it thinks it has the initiative. It is said that women (and everything feminine) are *reactive*, truly passive, always waiting for the intervention of meaning to become excited, fecondated, cultivated, renewed. Like the Indian and the Arab, they are traitresses whose apparent humanity is always elusive: *rauben, rubare;* they are thieves of humanity.[9]

But if we, men, *cannot resist* wanting to seize such an object, perhaps it is because the Voice at the Virile Centre speaks only of this: the voice speaks only of the Empire's limits (which are women) and we have to struggle ceaselessly with their exteriority. If so, then is not such an object unconsciously endowed with what we call activity? And does not the power to scheme accorded this object betray the secret reversal of our role by theirs? (Is not there a desire on the part of western man to be sodomized by woman?) Is not the outside of the man's theatre the most important, even for men? Doesn't he discover his 'origin' there? And isn't it necessary that this origin be woman: isn't the mother the originary woman? That is, the way the exterior sex is represented in theory: as ground, itself ungrounded, in which meaning is generated? The senseless Being?

Woman could indeed be accepted and honoured by the citizen and the politician as mother, the mother of their sons: for as it happens, she is the indispensable intermediary between them and these sons. The *corpus socians* cannot be reproduced without the belly of women. Male homosexuals honour her, but on the fringes of the Empire. Goddesses of fertility are more orgiastic than civic, and their cult is maintained in Greece by banishing it to the obscurity of the Bacchae; it is eliminated in Rome by Christianity, then sublimated as a cult of Mary. The male Christian Westerner does not pay homage to women but to his own reproductive force, stockpiled in the belly of the virgin and exploited in that of the mother.

As for 'whores', those women who are neither mothers nor virgins, they ought to be conquered, pacified, sanctified, saved: made our equals. Christianity has already posed the question: should woman be educated, and how. Capitalism generalizes the method proposed below: exclusion of women on the basis of homologation, not exile. Capitalism contributes to the destruction of their position within the family enclosure; according to its needs, it even partially integrates their reproductive function by acting indirectly on their propension to procreate and by treating as commodities their products, those famous sons, as well as the bellies that bear them. The education of women consists in the exploitation of feminine natural resources, of *all* these resources by incorporating them into her reproductive cycles.

Capital seems to actualize the ideal of reproduction of men by themselves: 'Mother Earth' disappears,[10] Messieurs Father-Capital and Son-Work consider themselves sufficient for the *corpus sociandum* to reproduce itself without recourse to any external force. Women disappear into the male cycle, integrated either as workers into the production of commodities, or as mothers into the reproduction of labour power, or again, as commodities; themselves (cover-girls, prostitutes of mass-media, hostesses of *human relations*), or even as administrators of capital (managerial functions).

Advantages and disadvantages of the consideration of sexual difference by capitalist society

In any case, women can only be part of modern society if their differences are neutralized. 'Eroticism' today, in this truly popular culture composed of pornography, ladies' magazines and the pill, implies this same homologation. It is regulated by the absolute value of the permanent sexual and affective availability called emancipation, liberation, independence, and opposed to the counter-value of the family and conjugality. Now, this value is the very one that capital imposes on men; and those qualities liberty, availability, mobility, are those that conceal their reduction to the status of labour power. Sexual and affective freedom of women (and men) is a capitalist value, not only because it transforms 'sex' into a commodity easily negotiated on the (masculine) market, but because (as with free labour) differences must be neutralized to come globally under the law of the interchangeable. (Here differences of sex, but also erotic singularities.) This is how, for example, hysteria – the masculine name for feminine exteriority – enters into a recession.[11]

A spectator of pornographic films states the same principle of capitalism: 'What I like about women in porno films is that they are like men; they always want to make love.'[12] Always want to negotiate, to capitalize more 'experience': sexuality of expansion, eroticism of conquest, economy of exchange. A few eighteenth-century libertines suggested something similar; the homologation of the sexes (Sade's women ejaculate 'sperm') considers love in terms of strategies and tactics (Laclos) or even as part of a theory of etiquette (Crebillon *fils*) – in short, treats it as a political relation whose laws are entirely masculine: better to die than suffer. From this perspective, to succeed would be to suffer impassively.[13]

Modern *unisexism* is not entirely bad, however: it offers material for new ruses. All the better that the fable of witches and mothers, those half-natural creatures relegated to the *fringes* of a masculine empire, degenerate. Its decline reveals that the differences constituting sexuality are not defined by a political opposition of *corpus socians* and *corpus sociandum;* rather, they penetrate each so-called 'individual' body, be it anatomically male or female. Freud believed in the destiny of anatomy; contemporary interest in transvestites, homosexuality and sex-change operations demonstrates that such belief is on the wane. That all masculine pleasure is not attributed to the emission or retention of sperm, nor even to the erection; that the so-called feminine 'components' of pleasure (which compose nothing . . .) can freely play on bodies whose armour shields them from death; that activity is not the unhappy lot of masculine bodies: that they no longer assume responsibility for attainment of an ideal orgasmic synchronism – these and many other displacements give hope that the signifier's *imperium* over the masculine body can be undone, and that another sexual space could be substituted, a topology of erotic potentialities; comparable to the one Freud calls (somewhat hypocritically) *polymorphous perversion* in the child.[14]

The 'woman's' body would then disintegrate into a puzzle of potentialities (fertility, passivity, sensitivity, jealousy), none of which would dominate the others. If differences traverse individual bodies rather than opposing a 'woman's' body to 'man's', then those regions 'belonging' to two individuals (or more) would be connected (call the association sadist, masochistic, oblational, tender, obsessed or any other nosographic label – but try to do better!), without prejudging what goes on in other regions of the 'same' bodies.

What happens, then, is commonly called love; that is, there is no longer *anyone*, no superior central identity to control and relate what takes place on these intensified surfaces.

So the question is not to safeguard a difference of sex against a movement towards homologation imposed by capital. The 'difference between the sexes' is no more exempt from masculine imperialism than its opposite; we have seen this. Claiming difference simply says that human beings can be grouped in two categories: those with a penis and those without. Only the first would belong to the *corpus socians*. The women's movement could be tempted to resist the assimilation of women to men by insisting on this difference, by claiming for themselves the intuition, the pathos, the irresponsibility attributed to them, by making them weapons in their insurrection against phallocentrism. The sphere of 'weakness' could conceivably be extended and an anti-masculine world established, to be explored only by the voices, cries, whispers and conspiracies of feminine writing.

But this direction could fail and thereby restore the problem of the form in which it is traditionally posed: masculine imperialism gets along well with nocturnal delirium, pastoral dances, and the consumption of raw animal flesh.[15] For the empire needs a border and these provide such a border. In the face of the 'irrational', the master-warrior-speaker, is reinstated in his pedagogical task: he needs a frontier to conquer and savages to civilize. Let us free him instead from his armour of words and death; let us temper him in a large *patchwork* of affective elements that must be intensified. One should not attack him head-on but wage a guerrilla war of skirmishes and raids in a space and time other than those imposed for millenia by the masculine logos. It is tempting to attribute reversible spaces and paradoxical time to a 'feminine principle'. But this would be too great a concession to the so-called 'male principle' which the 'feminine principle' could only complement. Instead, let us propose this as a kind of theory-fiction. Let us set to work forging fictions rather than hypotheses and theories; this would be the best way for the speaker to become 'feminine' . . . .

The destruction of metalanguages is at stake in the women's struggle

One last remark on this subject which was announced at the beginning of the text. The philosopher, as philosopher, is a secret accomplice of the phallocrat. For philosophy is not just any discipline. It is the search for a constituting order that gives meaning to the world, society and discourse. Philosophy is the West's madness and never ceases to underwrite its quests for knowledge and politics in the name of Truth and the Good. By specifically considering the *question* of men's relationship to women, philosophy (or its contemporary positivist travesties, sociology, anthropology, etc.) sends us in the direction of an *answer*. But this answer will be preceded by the *constitution*, itself a regulated elaboration, of this relationship, and therefore of the terms placed in relation, 'man' and 'woman'. Doctrinal variations, even considerable ones affecting this constitution, are of little importance. What matters is that the question (and the possibility or impossibility of an answer) can be posed only in the *metalanguage* (even impossible, always open) of philosophy. For such a metalanguage is already the language of masculinity in the western, and particularly Greek, sense.

In fact, where do we actually see metalanguage founded? In those communities of free men who speak a Hellenic language, carry arms, worship the same gods and submit themselves to the law of equal political rights for all. These are the communities that have formed the core of the *politeia*[16] at the heart of feudal Greek society. Women are excluded at the outset from such groups (along with children, foreigners, half-breeds, slaves). The authority these groups claim for themselves over society as a whole later allows them to impose a general reorganization on the traditional system of *gènè* – that is, large families.[17] The language spoken there claims to *constitute* society in its entirety. And this remains true even of contemporary revolutionary Assemblies: of the French, American, Bolshevik revolutions. Inasmuch as this discourse concerns femininity (it happens that femininity is forgotten), femininity is already constituted, or remains to be constituted, as one part of the *corpus sociandum* or even as its symbol: passivity. Hence, it is opposed to those political groups that allocate the responsibilities of the *corpus socians* to themselves. The congruence between the constitution of politics as an institution, a specifically masculine order, and the institution of philosophy as a constituting discourse can be established historically. Perhaps virility in the West since then is nothing other than a concern for the constituent.

So by no means can the question of masculine/feminine relations be reduced to a problem of the division of labour at the heart of the social body. The frontier passing between the two sexes does not separate two parts of the same social entity. Not only is it the border where the Empire comes into contact with barbarians, but also the line of demarcation between an empirical given, women, the great unknown, and a transcendent or transcendental order that would give them meaning. The complicity between political phallocracy and philosophical metalanguage is made here: the activity men reserve for themselves arbitrarily as *fact* is posited legally as the *right* to decide meaning. The social groups of distributors, that is, citizens, becomes confused with the principle that there is something like distributive reason, matter upon which this reason is inscribed or written, and that there is a distinction between matter and reason.

When a 'feminist'[18] is reproached for confusing the phallus, symbolic operator of meaning, and the penis, empirical sign of sexual difference, it is admitted without discussion that the metalinguistic order (the symbolic) is distinct from its domain of reference (realities). But if the women's movement has an immense impact equal to that of slaves, colonized peoples, and other 'under-developed' groups, it is that this movement solicits and destroys the (masculine) belief in meta-statements independent of ordinary statements.

All discourse of knowledge depends on a *decision*: namely, that the two statements, *soup is on* and *it is true that the soup is on* do not belong to the same class and should be distinguished. But such a decision cannot itself be proved. In order words, what we call Mentor's 'paradox'[19] cannot be refuted. Simultaneously, the decision constituting the discourse of knowledge, constructing a constituting order, appears as a fact of power and power in fact. If 'reality' lies, it follows that men in all their claims to construct meaning, to speak the Truth, are themselves only a minority in a *patchwork* where it becomes impossible to establish and validly determine any major order.

Deceitful like Eubulides and like realities, women are discovering something that could cause the greatest revolution in the West, something that (masculine) domination has never ceased to stifle: there is no signifier; or else, the class above all classes is just one among many; or again, we Westerners must rework our space-time and all our logic on the basis of non-centralism, non-finality, non-truth. A United Nations vote denounced Zionism as racism, to the great scandal of the West which suddenly found itself in the minority. One day a UN vote will denounce as male sexism the primacy accorded theoretical discourse to the great scandal . . . of us all.

NOTES

1 Sseu-Ma Ts'ien, 'The Life of Sun-Tse', *Mémoires historiques,* in *Treize articles sur l'art de la guerre* by Sun-Tse (Paris: Librairie l'Impensé radical, 1971). Sun-Tse is a *condottierre* and Chinese strategist. It is said that he was active between 512 and 506 BC.

2 *Three Essays on the Theory of Sexuality,* vol. 7, Standard Edition (1905), *Gesammelte Werke* (Frankfurt am Main: S. Fischer Verlag, 1962), V, p. 120 (henceforth *GW*).

3 Survey by G. Sitbon, *Le Nouvel Observateur,* 18 August 1975.

4 *Some Psychological Consequences of the Anatomical Distinction Between the Sexes,* vol. 19, Standard Edition (1925), *GW*, XIV, (tf 130).

5 *The Symposium,* 201d-207a, in *The Collected Dialogues,* ed. Edith Hamilton and Huntington Cairns (Princeton: Princeton University Press, 1963), p. 555.

6 Cf. *Apology of Socrates.*

7 With respect to this, there is complete continuity between, for example, the Reichian conception of sexuality (*The Function of the Orgasm*, 1947) and the Platonic theory of love.

8 Marcel Détienne, 'En Grèce archaïque: géométrie, politique et société', *Annales, Economies, Sociétés, Civilisation* 20, 3 (May–June, 1965).

9 Hélène Cixous, 'Sorties', in *La Jeune Née*, H. Cixous and C. Clément (Paris: 10/18, 1975).

10 An expression of Marx (*Capital*, III, VII, xxv) which protests, moreover, the elimination of Mother/Nature as the source of material wealth in certain interpretations of his theory of labour value. Cf. *Capital*, I, I, 2: *Critique du Programme de Gotha*, I, i.

11 Ilza Veith, *Hysteria, the History of a Disease* (Chicago: University of Chicago Press, 1965).

12 Survey by G. Sitbon, *Le Nouvel Observateur*.

13 A theme articulated in Pierre Klossowski's work on Sade. Cf. *Sade mon prochain* (Paris: Seuil, 1967); *La Monnaie vivante* (Losfeld, 1970).

14 *Drei Abhandlungen* (1905).

15 Cf. E. R. Dodds, *The Greeks and the Irrational* (California: University of California Press, 1959).

16 J.-P. Vernant, *Les Origines de la pensée grecque* (Paris: Presses Universitaires de France, 1962); M. Austin and P. Vidal-Naquet, *Economies et sociétés en Grèce Ancienne* (Paris: A. Colin, 1972).

17 P. Leveque and P. Vidal-Naquet, *Clisthene l'Athenien* (Paris: Les Belles Lettres, 1964).

18 Luce Irigaray, *Speculum. De l'autre femme* (Paris: Editions de Minuit, 1974).

19 Attributed to Eubulides of Megara, a contemporary of Aristotle. According to Cicero, he says: *If you say that you lie and you speak the truth, you lie.* A formulation more resistant to metalogical reduction is: *I am lying.*

*Translated by Deborah J. Clarke
with Winifred Woodhull and John Mowitt*

6

Lessons in Paganism

'I really don't understand. For a start, you seem to be taking an interest in the forthcoming legislative elections in my country, but I know perfectly well that in your view the narratives of the left and the right are, give or take the odd comma, interchangeable, and so are the narratives of big parties in countries with a two-party system. Not so long ago, you yourself were telling me that if the right came to power with a small majority, it would have to adopt more or less socialist policies, and that if the left came to power in similar circumstances, it would have no option but to reach a compromise with the right. And as for your third hypothesis of a major swing to the left, you are well aware of the difficulties that would face any government that came to power under those circumstances. Once the euphoria surrounding the initial social reforms had died down, the owners of capital, the bosses and the bourgeois political class would inevitably use all the means at their disposal to launch an offensive to prevent the Common Programme from being carried out, and the persistent difficulties facing the world economy would provide them with powerful allies. So much so that the government would either have to knuckle under so as to win over some of its opponents – and the Socialist party is obviously in favour of that strategy – or take Draconian social and economic measures, and that is the one thing it would be impossible for it to do. For it to be able to do that, the Communist Party would have to be the major party on the left, and it would also have to have the ability to channel and stoke up the impatient energy of the workers and the poor; but the CP is a minority party and, as for its offensive capacity, you know perfectly well that it was reduced to virtually nothing in order to preserve the balance of world power during the Stalin era, and that it has now been reduced to less than nothing because of the official ban on using all the big words that might intimidate the right and should galvanize its supporters: revolution, dictatorship of the proletariat, internationalism, soviets and so on and so forth. You don't need me to tell you that it would rather take an oppositional stance, if it hasn't already done so, and leave the Socialist party to be beaten by a right-wing coalition or to participate in a centre-left government. You might say that the picture I am painting leaves no room for the unexpected, but there is nothing unexpected to be expected of organizations which are programmed like efficient machines with a 3 per cent margin of tolerance. On the other hand, Everyman might turn out to be unpredictable if he gets tired enough of the production-consumption narrative capital forces him to act out both at work and at home, and angry enough with the left for not enacting the promised scenario, to begin to tell and act out a thousand and one disturbing little stories of his own. You never know. That, and I think we are in agreement on this point, is the only exciting possibility, because it offers the only possibility that something that hasn't already been analysed by some programmer or other might be said and done. Is that why you are interested in the elections?'

'No, but I do find your scenario convincing. But first tell me what else you don't understand.'

'What I don't understand is why you think fit to start giving me what you call "lessons in paganism" at a time when the country is beset with such day-to-day worries and when the outlook is as bleak as I'm painting it. If it weren't so stupid, it would seem intolerably elitist.'

'When I say "pagan", I mean godless. And the reason why we (you, not me) need to be taught a lesson is that we still want justice. That is the point of my instructive story : justice in a godless society.'

'But godlessness has been the norm for a long time now in secular societies, and justice is a commonplace in all the programmes they put forward. I fail to see any difference between your slogan and those put forward by the liberal right and the liberal left.'

'The liberals may well be godless, but they are not very bothered about justice. The left, on the other hand, does want justice, but is still extremely pious. The one new feature of your little electoral battle is that, for the first time in fifty years, most of your country's intellectuals are not prepared to tell and justify even an updated version of the Marxist narrative because they take the view that it has had profoundly unjust effects wherever it has been fully implemented. All I would add to that is that the injustice it generates stems from the very piety it inspires and demands.'

'Are you by any chance in agreement with the anti-Marxist ravings of that handful of new men known as philosophers?[1] You are not being very rational.'

'I disagree with almost all of their arguments, most of which are insultingly naive. But I would say that, whilst the rows they are kicking up and provoking might not be very seemly, they do at least show that your intelligentsia is no longer prepared to be intimidated by the Marxist version of history and politics, and that it is resolved to learn all it can from the injustice and even the horrors it has produced.'

'So basically, you concentrate on the symptoms and ignore the content in this business about Clavel & Co.?[2] But the symptoms themselves are no more than a matter of fashion, the result of a marketing operation.'

'There's no denying that, but there's no point in being scandalized by it either (you have to believe in something before you can be scandalized). It's worth looking because it is a truly commercial power structure which has no qualms about interfering with all kinds of discourses which used to be kept out of the marketplace and confined to the groves of Academe and to schools of political science. Personally, I think neither better nor worse of television than of specialist journals, of academic chairs than of the round-tables organized by chain "bookshops". If we do have to take sides, it has to be on the basis of what is said, not on the basis of form. But in the present case what is said implies forms. You haven't proved your point. Ever since the Industrial Revolution we have enjoyed some very good things in commodity form. Why not ideas? Yes, they are pathetic, but do you really think that the ideas of Merleau-Ponty or Lévi-Strauss, which were not pathetic, were exempt from marketing? And there is no glory to be won in devoting fifteen years of your life to writing, editing, publishing and distributing an avant-garde journal that no one reads, even if it does say all the right things. Some people enjoy doing that, and there is no accounting for tastes. But the principle that obscure means correct is wrong. There are just as many clichés in the dark corners of the library as there are in the high street.'

'But what about fashion?'

'Do you really think that's a pertinent category in the circumstances? Both good and bad can be in fashion. Or out of fashion. Socrates and Protagoras were the target for Aristophanes' mockery, and he put their success down to a ridiculous fad. The recent intellectual history of your country provides countless other examples, both positive and negative. The reason you are attacking fashion is that you believe that anything important is, by definition, always beyond the public of the day, and that great thoughts are always the product of obscurity, if not tradition. You are contrasting the odyssey of Suffering Reason with the instant success of passing fads. And you do so because you persist in believing in the Passion of truth in history. But, given the vagaries of today's fashions, anything goes, both the excellent and the despicable. Our only judge is the judgement we arrive at by ourselves: there is nothing in appearances, which can be modest or showy, to guide us. We might well take the view that our thinkers are pathetic, but let's not blame that on the fact they they are famous.'

'But they are colluding with the right.'

'That's what the left always says when people stop humouring it. And the point about that argument is that it cuts both ways. I don't know if they have links with the right or not, but I do know that both the communists and the fascists used that kind of argument against Daniel Cohn-Bendit; one lot suggested that he was working for the French secret service, the other that he was in the pay of the East German political police. You have to admit that neither claim is a lot of help when it comes to understanding May '68. Of course this is not May '68, but the French intelligentsia's current disenchantment with Marxism cannot be explained in terms of plots like that.'

'So on the whole, you don't really have anything against this crew?'

'They provide a very good example of what's bothering your left-wing intelligentsia.'

'And what might that be?'

'Power.'

'But they spend their days denouncing power and all its works!'

'That's a fairly accurate description of the tenor of what they say. But if you look at the pragmatics of their narratives, you find a perfect but miniaturized power machine.'

'The what of their narratives?'

'Pragmatics. It means all the complicated relations that exist between a speaker and what he is talking about, between the story-teller and his listener, and between the listener and the story told by the story-teller.'

'I don't see what that has to do with power and with our men.'

'You will, but forgive me if I start on a somewhat serious note. The individual who is now talking to you usually refers to himself as "me", and don't forget that when I draw your attention to a few minor political matters and issues in contemporary history, I am merely telling you a story, unfolding a little story of my own. As a preliminary lesson, I would suggest that, rather than asking if that story is more or less true than any other, you should simply note that it exists, that it is the product of an almost invincible power to tell stories that we all share to a greater or lesser extent – I'm no judge of individual cases –

and that it leaves you all the time in the world to tell a very different story about the same historical and political points, should you choose to do so.'

'What do you mean? That you are not convinced by your own story? That just means that you won't make a convincing teacher.'

'No, but it does mean that I would not give what I am about to tell you the status of a scientific narrative.'

'You mean you think it's not true?'

'You can pass it off as a true story and defend it as such, but that isn't why it interests me; it contains an idea about history, and that idea should be pursued much further than I can pursue it here. When I tell my story, I am not acting as a mouthpiece for some universal history. And I make no claim to being a professional theorist, or to be saving the world by reminding it of a lost meaning. Look, let's put it another way, and then we might learn something else: like any story, my story takes other stories as its reference. All stories go like this: "I say that they say" . . . What we are talking about is diegesis . . . '

'Diegesis?'

'The reference of the present narrative, the story that the present narrative message stages "outside" words. So, just remember that the diegesis of my narrative – and yours – is never made up of raw events or facts, that events and facts always come to us by way of the other narratives which our narrative uses as a reference.'

'What! So the Commune, Cronstadt, and Budapest in '56 are just stories! And what about the people who died?'

'The dead aren't dead until the living have recorded their deaths in narratives. Death is a matter of archives. You are dead when stories are told about you, and when only stories are told about you. And you are free to expand the archive as much as you like, by including in it even the most anodyne of documents.'

'And I suppose the bullets that killed the dead are also narratives?'

'Bullets would be nothing without narratives, and if you tell me otherwise, or tell me what you think they are, you are telling me a story, or stories.'

'But a physicist . . . '

' . . . Will tell me stories about steel, an economist stories about arms factories, an artillery man stories about ballistics. Bullets can't talk, but they are references for the stories which prepare them and discuss them, and they are also a great help to narrators who are determined to convince incredulous listeners.'

'Are you saying that a runner in the ten thousand metres, or a resistance fighter who slips under the arch of a bridge with a package of explosives . . . that these bodies in action are recounting something?'

'I would say that they are acting out scenarios that are running through their heads or that they have been told about. They are galvanized into action by the constant interplay between the agency of the narratee (*narrataire*), or the agency where the story is heard, and that of the narrated (*narré*), where it is acted out. They become bullets or events, and they adopt positions by referring to what is being said, has been said or will be said. And they become witnesses to the fact that the stories they are acting out are the best stories, simply because they testify to their accuracy.'

'But that's not the same thing as telling stories.'

'No. Telling stories involves another instance; that of the narrator. But you will admit that having stories told about you (or having had stories told about you, or being about to become the subject of a story) is also an aspect of narrative ability because it involves the agency of the narrated. But let me get to the points I wish to make, if you don't mind. There are two of them, and they are both very simple. The first is, as we have said, and as the picture you were painting just now confirms, that in your country there are now fewer intellectuals than there once were who are prepared to justify the Marxist narrative. Not so long ago, most of them would borrow their form or content from the narrators of that narrative when they had something to say about history, politics or society. They borrowed from its narrators (Marx and the marxoids), its narratees (the workers) or its narrated (heroes who were marxiods and/or workers).

'It's difficult to see how we can go on with the story. What was the happy ending of the story told by the Marxist left? The abolition of injustice. And what news do we hear from the countries where this scenario was obstinately put into practice by the government and officially acted out by thousands of men and women? Thousands of uncomfortable little stories have recently been brought back by Solzhenitsyn's books, by eye-witness accounts from dissidents and by travellers. They breathed a new life into the old narrations of the first unbelievers, the narrations of Souvarine, Serge, Ciliga, Rousset and Scholmer, which no one would listen to when the Stalinist narrative reigned unchallenged. They allow those who are at last willing to lend an ear and their voices to hear and pass on the other histories (authors unknown) which were played out by their narrators as they made them up in Prague in '68, in Budapest in '56, in China in '57, and in Berlin and Poznan in '53. Perhaps this new audience will now be able to make out the stories which were acted out in the Ukraine in 1919–20 and in Cronstadt in 1921, though they may be somewhat muted for those who are used to listening to blaring juke-boxes. The clouds of narrative matter that are flooding into your capital may well be inexhaustible now that they have found receivers who can turn them into new narratives'.

'And what do they tell us?'

'You know as well as I do. They quote from countless eye-witness accounts, compare them with the great Marxist narrative which smothered them for so long because it had a monopoly, and they arrive at this sombre paradox: it was only because its addresses, the workers who were at the same time its heroes, were banned from telling stories that the great narrative could attain the supremacy it once enjoyed; it was only because the masters of the meta-narratives, by which I mean the intellectuals whose role it was to justify the history recounted by Communist Power, could find reasons for gagging the very people whose praises it sang at a time when they were reduced to being no more than its silent reference. And if need be, they would even invoke Reason.'

'And they have reached the conclusion that it no longer works because there are so many mouths that they cannot all be gagged.'

'I wouldn't say that, because it worked for a long time and still works. But to get back to the point; why have the intellectuals fallen out with the left? Because the canonic story has suffered the effects of erosion, if only to a minor extent as yet, and has been eaten away by the thousands of little stories that are reaching us from the countries where it is supposed to be the master. Lefort has quite rightly pointed out that it is because it is a work of literature that *The Gulag Archipelago* is so effective. It is because the book is in effect made up of nothing but scenes and pictures that it stirs the reader's narrative imagination and makes it collude with the narrative imagination of Solzhenitsyn's heroes. The fact that there are so many stories and pictures certainly helps, but the crucial thing is their power: the power of narrative. It's not that we identify with the names of Solzhenitsyn's heroes – no one can ever remember their names – but that they establish a continuity by means of the short scenarios and quick screenplays they fall back upon, even though they are the very things that are banned.'

'But making up scenarios and screenplays is not necessarily a good thing in itself . . . '

'It does seem to be when you do it in a place and time when death-threats are being used to discourage you from doing so.'

'Could you explain why our intellectuals are now more likely to believe the stories of prisoners or rebels than the stories of commissars, whereas the reverse was true for such a long time?'

'They didn't listen to the stories of the commissars themselves, or not really; they listened to the justifications of the theoreticians, to the meta-narratives. Broadly speaking, you know why they have lost some of their impact: there has been a decrease in the number of narratives stamped with the Marxist hallmark, mainly as a result of the split between Moscow and Peking, the political humiliation of the greatest power in the world after its defeat in Vietnam, the recovery of certain Third World regimes thanks to the energy crisis and the shortage of raw materials, the discovery that progress is turning the world into a sterile rubbish dump, the obviously artificial nature of the scientific approach . . . . The net result of all that is that the Manichaeism of the great powers no longer has a stranglehold, that uncomfortable stories can circulate and that neither side can silence them on the grounds that they are playing into the hands of the enemy. But there are enough enemies to go round, and it is not really true to say that stories that annoy your enemies are friendly stories.'

'And speaking less broadly?'

'Take May '68. Try as they might, your intellectuals – be they socialists, French communists, Trotskyists or Maoists – couldn't help but understand what was happening in your country, assuming they were not too stupid: the same process of erosion that we were talking about just now. Thousands of unknown narrators , narratees and actors were beginning to tell stories, listen to stories and act out stories without obtaining permission to do so from anyone. Some of your philosophers may well have gone on writing Old Marxist nonsense, and for a while they may well have gone on denouncing what was happening, but the fact remains that it is thanks to that narrative explosion that their tongues are slightly less furred and that their ears are not quite so blocked with wax as they once were.'

'They may think they've discovered something new, but we've known about it for forty years, and we've been talking about it for thirty. You've said so yourself!'

'True. But knowing is one thing; imagining and stirring the imagination is another. I can think of nothing more depressing than the way in which old men, many of them unqualified to do so, use the lessons of history and their own claims of seniority to denounce anything that their younger colleagues say. History is obviously not an exam in which coming top is the only thing that counts. And I am not just talking about the fact that these stupid protestations of loyalty contain an element of bitterness – the bitterness of authors who have been plagiarized. That's a morbid passion if ever there was one. It's much more serious than that. In the whole world, only sixty of us succeeded in making a fairly radical critique of communist bureaucracy on the basis of the signs – clear and unclear alike – that provided the reference for our narratives. We talked about workers in Poznan, workers' councils in Budapest and dissidents in China but, give or take the odd exception, we were narrators and we were looking for narratees other than ourselves. We were in the position of theoreticians, and that's what we were. We had no choice; almost none of our contemporaries could hear the stories coming out of Poznan, Budapest or Peking, and the stories we told about them therefore found virtually no audience. Let's just say that in your country, and three or four others, the honour of story-tellers was saved. But nowadays, there is no need to translate stories from over there into the genre of theory in order to preserve them and to make them accessible to the audience. Their heroes and their narratees are often the same people, or have at least rubbed shoulders. How can you possibly grumble when the intimate and infinite power of stories is unleashed, even if you do find those who spread them despicable? And if you think their version is worthless, you have only to come up with a different version, rather then sagely trotting out the version you told twenty years ago in very different circumstances. I take the view that theories themselves are concealed narratives, that we should not be taken in by their claims to be valid for all time, that the fact that you once invented a narrative is no excuse for not starting all over again, even if your narrative did look like an unshakeable system, that it is not right to be coherent and immutable, or in other words true to yourself, but that it is right to try to be true to your ability to tell the stories you think you hear in what others are doing and saying. As you can imagine, my views are quite in keeping with our preliminary lesson.'

'But precisely what lessons do you draw from the situation we are discussing?'

'The need to be godless in things political. To take a banal example: four months ago, seven or eight out of ten of your fellow citizens thought that the left would win the legislative elections, but six out of ten thought that that would do nothing to change their lives. That's amazing in a country which believes so strongly in the State. You'll soon end up having as little respect for politicians as your Italian or English neighbours. When public opinion is in this state, it seems to me that we are seeing the Western equivalent to the erosion of the great narrative in the Communist empires. Many left-wing politicians, and even some members of what you call Clavel & Co. put this state of affairs down to disenchantment and depression. They are simply projecting the disappointment they feel because of their need to believe in some major narrative. If you forced me to say in my turn something about this state of opinion, or state of narration, I would say that the increase in the number of uncomfortable little narratives isn't such a bad omen.'

'There's little reason to be optimistic. Think of the horror-stories told by people who have got out of the camps.'

'I can't bring myself to talk about them; we in the West are too fortunate to be able to be true to them. It is because they reflect a stubborn attempt to destroy narrative power that they seem so implacable. The Party-state unrelentingly forces its citizens to tell, hear and act out nothing but its own scenario. The scenario may well change. The important point is that the Party-state is coercive; what it coerces people to do is less important. It is a question of narrative pragmatics, not of signification or interpretation.'

'What does that mean?'

'It means that if you are a citizen of one of these regimes, you are regarded as both the co-author of its narrative and a privileged listener, and that you have to be word-perfect when you are told to act out an episode. You are officially assigned to three positions in the master narrative, and in every aspect of your own life. Your imagination is completely fettered, as a narrator, as a listener and as an actor. If you fail to carry out any of your duties, you lose all your qualities. There is no avoiding it, as it is not within your power to control the meaning of the narrative or that of what you have to listen to or do. Its meaning is beyond the limits of your understanding. Make a mistake on stage, mishear something or make a slip of the tongue when you are telling the story, and you end up in jail. And when you are in jail, no one asks you to recite, act out or listen to scenarios; you have been written out of the scenario, driven off the stage, out of the wings, and even out of the theatre. You are banned from telling stories. And that is devastating.'

'But it doesn't really work; we do get to hear of it. Stories do circulate outside the Party-state, and we happen to be their addressees.'

'It works, and at the same time it doesn't work. Assigning citizens to the three instances of the great narrative is in a sense a way of putting them into solitary confinement. What is a secret affair? Two partners see themselves as the only actors, the only initiators and the only listeners involved in their adventure. Imagine what happens if one of them consents to this exclusivity only because he or she is forced to do so by the other; that gives you a rough picture of the pragmatics that binds the citizen to the totalitarian state. Then imagine what happens if the state is in a position to decide that the citizen has failed to do what was required of him. By withdrawing his consent, he gives away the secret, and the affair is broken off. A prisoner is a citizen who has been released from the contractual secret. He loses the interlocutor and the reference that were forced upon him. He no longer talks about what people are talking about; no one can hear him, and he can hear no one. All he can do now is say that he no longer has anything to say, no one to listen to him, and no more reality to invent. And that is why the stories that reach us from over there are so uncomfortable. It is true that the reason we hear them is that another pragmatics does exist and function; the ghost of a civil society made up of distended circuits and improvised modes of circulation. And what it talks about in the stories it helps to circulate is simply the ability to tell stories. It is elementary in two senses. Firstly, it is fragile, and secondly, the one thing it is concerned with is a basic element in all societies, namely narrative activity. But you can see what resolution and what asceticism is needed if that element is finally to disclose itself and to manifest itself – no matter how feebly – outside the tutelage of the narratives programmed by political institutions. There is no comfort to be drawn from that. It's just that honour has been saved – the honour of fables (*fables*).'

'And that of the weak (*faibles*). What's that got to do with your godlessness?'

'It seems to me that, in both the East and the West, the time has come for societies or, to be more accurate, the elementary civil societies we were just talking about, to manifest their activity. There is absolutely no question of a heroic uprising against the state in some battle to the death, as though their relationship with the state was, and had to be, one of symbolic reversion: "You can only exist if you destroy me. Just try." An encounter which ends only when both partners are either annihilated or dishonoured is all very well in a Hegelian dialectic of spirit or a Maussean drama of primitiveness, but I do not think it true to say that the state and civil society can be compared to partners. If we say that, we are making too many concessions to political Manichaeism. The only way that networks of uncertain and ephemeral stories can gnaw away at the great institutionalized narrative apparatuses is by increasing the number of skirmishes that take place on the sidelines. That's what women who have had abortions, prisoners, conscripts, prostitutes, students and peasants have been doing in your country over the last decade or so. You make up little stories, or even segments of little stories, listen to them, transmit them and act them out when the time is right.'

'Why *little* stories?'

'Because they are short, because they are not extracts from some great history, and because they are difficult to fit into any great history. Remember the problems the Marxist narrative, to name but one, had with the student episode. How could that be fitted into a web of relations of production and class struggle?'

'And there are other worrying subjects: socialist lesbians, communism and prostitution, Marx in the kitchen . . . '

'Not forgetting, at the other extreme, Chirac[3] doing the washing up, the young unemployed man in a period of full employment, and his mate the young employer in a period of high unemployment. And what about the old, or the ownership of the seas, and the shit that gets dumped in them?'

'Or anything else, for that matter. Spreading stories is not an end in itself.'

'No it's not, but at the same time I don't see what other ends there could be. And the reason why the stories can be about anything is that capitalism affects everything. So everything provides a basis for stories. You can see it as a finality without ends: and that, to paraphrase Kant, is the one interest we can pursue without becoming pathological cases.'

'So you're supporting Kant now, are you?'

'If you like, but only the Kant who wrote the third *Critique*. Not the Kant of the concepts and the moral law, but the Kant of the imagination, the one who recovered from the sickness of knowledge and rules and converted to the paganism of art and nature. And you will recall that whilst it might well be righteous, that discourse is not true in the sense that a theory claims to be true, and nor is it a meta-narrative, or even a critical meta-narrative. It is a work of art in itself, a product of the pure will of the imagination.'

'What are you getting at, metic?[4]'

'What I'm getting at is this: it is not exactly advisable to resist the plenum of instituted narratives by taking a stand on the void of a universal principle of discourse. "I think" and "You must" can never authorize anything but a democratic liberal politics, even if I am granted the concession of being able to translate those expressions as "I recount". You want a free, open institution in which society can call itself into question, in which its existence is not defined from the outset as being that of a body and has yet to be defined, an institution which institutes.'

'And I suppose you are in favour of its liquidation?'

'No, but what difference do you see between this Institutor and any great Other or great Signifier? After Hegel's critique of Kant, it no longer has to be proven that if any such principle is made both the a priori condition for instituted freedoms and the expression of an instituting freedom, it, . . . well I wouldn't say that it will give rise to

Terror (but there again, you have seen in your own university the said signifier comes to be translated into an organizational practice of exclusion; I am thinking of a certain school of psychoanalysis), but I would say that it will inevitably inspire us to lift up our souls to some major absence, and will therefore lead to the degradation of reality. It is almost as easy to speak in the name of the void as it is to speak in the name of plenum, and it's also very easy to worship a being, supreme or otherwise, even if that being never reveals itself.'

'That's not dangerous, in any event.'

'Not terribly. There's always an element of piety in a concern for theory, even critical theory; it's as though nothing had happened. What sense is there in saying on the one hand that the fact that the *Gulag Archipelago* is an event – and indeed it is – that it was written by someone who shared every aspect of the life of the people in the camps, talked about nothing else and enjoyed – and God knows he paid for it – a privilege that few writers enjoy in that his heroes were his narrators and in that himself was one of them – and then, on the other hand, building a new transcendental theory of Society versus State?'

'Where's the harm in that?'

'It means blinding ourselves to an insight we have just gained. We have gained a crucial insight: history consists of a swarm of narratives, narratives that are passed on, made up, listened to and acted out; the people does not exist as a subject; it is a mass of thousands of little stories that are at once futile and serious, that are sometimes attracted together to form bigger stories, and which sometimes disintegrate into drifting elements, but which usually hold together well enough to form what we call the culture of a civil society.'

'The *Gulag* book implies all that?'

'You say that it's important that it is a story, a work of literature. Everyone takes that to mean that it is important that it is not a work of theory. So why is it so important? Because Solzhenitsyn passes on stories as he narrates his story. Once again, it is a matter of pragmatics. The functions of the narrator and of what he is talking about (the narrated) are permutable because his companions (the narrated) are his narrator-heroes. And because it is also possible for the narrator to change places with the people he is addressing, with his companions and with us. After all, anyone can tell stories; that is the source of Everyman's strength. Anyone who discusses the *Gulag* is simply using the book as a reference for his own discourse, and using it to make up another narration, his own narration, and addressing readers who may or may not be the same. You will notice that the roles change. It is not simply the form of the narrative that changes; it is also its object. Y talks about Z, Solzhenitsyn talks about Y, and Lefort talks about Solzhenitsyn. This succession of serial stories is admirably commonplace, and it implies no recurrence and no revenue.'

'What about theory?'

'Theory is a form of narration without the transitivity. As you will learn, it surrounds itself with silence. Its reference has to remain silent, or in other words insensate, for it to be worthwhile explaining, for it to be made to speak. Hence the absent great Signifier. And its addressee has to remain silent too; he has to know nothing for it to be worthwhile telling him what the thing is that theory is telling him about. He may sometimes be allowed to speak, or be put in the narrator's position, but that's only to prove that he can recite his lesson correctly. Hence the pedagogic tone, Aristotle knew that; he contrasted the sophistication of didactics with the art of discussion, or dialectics, in which opinions clash, and in which Everyman's little narratives begin to compete. A work of literature can only give rise to dialectics; only concept-freaks turn it into teaching material, into theory. But just as there is no literary theory because there is no literature that can be taught, so Solzhenitsyn and others say that there is no political theory, not even a transcendental theory, because politics is not a subject that can be taught. What happens when you move from a dogma to a critique? You are still within the genre of theory, and your pragmatics remains unchanged. It will change if you move over to narrative.'

'But you are forgetting something. Isn't there something of an analogy between the theoretical model and the *isonomia* of citizens sitting in a circle around a centre which is nothing more than a public place in which they all take turns in proposing a decision or a law . . . the old Greek model of democracy, with a transcendental void in the middle? If you abandon the theoretical model, you abandon the democratic model, and you throw the door wide open to tyranny.'

'No, to paganism. What we need is a politics which is both godless and just. It will not be found in this pious organization. And besides, your description is a bowdlerized description, and, as you well know, women, children, metics, slaves, foreigners and dissidents were not allowed to take part. We want a politics based upon narratives, which are social elements, and not upon knowledge, where the *viri* are in their element.'

'Be reasonable; you know perfectly well that there is no country in which civil society consists of the swarm of narrative matter you are describing. Even pagan societies have institutions.'

'Let me follow my train of thought for a moment. *Pagus* was used to refer to the frontier region on the edge of towns. *Pagus* gave us *pays*. It is not the same as *heim* or *home*, meaning habitat or shelter; it refers to regions or countries which, whilst they are not necessarily uncultivated, are not exactly where you would go for a stroll. You don't feel at home there. You do not expect to discover the truth there; but you do meet lots of entities who are liable to undergo metamorphoses, to tell lies, and to become jealous or angry: passible gods.'

'Even so, they had to be honoured. Cults did exist. That wasn't godlessness.'

'It certainly wasn't without its cults, or its culture. As for the prevailing godlessness, you have to look at Plato: it horrified him. He was well aware of how the pagans honoured their gods. They came to terms with them by way of counter-plots, offerings, promises, and little marriage contracts that gave rise to complicitous ceremonies. The atmosphere was one of humour and fear.'

'How did they address them, if they were not pious?'

'In the same way that they talked to one another, by using words that were openly intended to deceive, openly duplicitous. They talked in order to produce certain effects, not in order to profess the truth, to uncover an uncovering or to confess their guilt.'

'Explain and discuss.'

'Gorgias said that in tragic art, it was more upright to seduce than not to seduce, that it was wiser to be seduced than not to be seduced. The Greek for "seduce" is *apatan*. Imagine a world in which justice (and justness) consists primarily of treating speech as an art, in which the discourse of truth is an unknown vulgarity. What does Gorgias's unjust man want? To be right. He would have the whole *pagus* in stitches. He ought to visit the schools of Paris to promote his new mode of speech – theory – and to try to make people forget what they know in the borderlands, namely that it is a late addition to the arts of speech, a literary genre like any other, and a stratagem which has never caught on except amongst the gentry. And what about the addressee, Gorgias's mad listener?; just look at him: he does not want to be caught out; he too desires the truth, words that do not set traps for him, thoughts that have not been transcribed, and he discredits discourses in which he thinks he sees an element of pretence as ideology and motley. For a misanthropist, he shows a distinct lack of wisdom! And he's a misogynist and a misotheriac into the bargain!'

'A what?'

'Someone who hates wild animals. Someone who is suspicious, credulous about suspicion. Pagans never ask whether a narrative conforms to its object; they know that references are organized by words, and that the gods do not guarantee them because their word is no more to be trusted than the word of a man. Rhetoric and hunting keep them busy enough, no one has the last word, and there is no coup de grace.'

'Why the gods then?'

'Just to make sure. They always call their gods "the strongest", because they know that they have the upper hand when it comes to cunning; the gods are more passible than men, not less so; they are no more righteous, but they are more inhuman. They enjoy the advantage of being infinitely protean, and it may be that that makes them immortal. Even so, they still have to be seduced, and it is possible to gain the upper hand, for a moment.'

'Only for a moment?'

'For a good moment, a moment of good.'

'That's cold comfort. But tell me . . . how do you relate this pastoral to your . . . narrative pragmatics?'

'A pagan god, for instance, is an effective narrator. You hear a story you are being told; it makes you laugh, cry or think, it inspires you to do something, to undertake a certain action, to put off making a decision, or to tell yourself a story. The narrator forces you into one or another of the narrative instances; he makes you a listener, an actor or a story-teller. That is where his superior strength lies; he manipulates you like a sorcerer; that is your weakness; you are dependent upon him; you have to get by with the stories he tells you and makes up for you.'

'So we are condemned to react? That's a gloomy philosophy'.

'No, to reply.'

'What's the difference?'

'Reacting means insulting someone who insults you. Replying means you triumph when someone insults you.'

'That's just a bad play on words.'

'But an excellent language game. Your partner-adversary makes you see things one way; you make him see them another way. If you cannot work out how to bring about that displacement, you are not replying; you are reacting. So we're back to narrative pragmatics. If you are the narrator, the narratee or the narrated of a story in which you are implicated, you become dependent upon that story. And we are in fact always under some influence or other; we have always already been told something, and we have always already been spoken. We are weak, and the gods exist because we didn't win. So how can you defend your honour as a pagan? If, for example, you make yourself your adversary's narrated, you act out the role he assigns you, just as Diana turned herself into a deer to make it easier for her assiduous hunter to hunt her down. And having allayed the suspicions of your narrator-hunter, having made him believe in the reality of his tale by acting it out, both you and Diana gently lure him into the trap you have set. Once he is caught, it is his turn to be the narrated of your story. That's one reply and, as you can see, it has to do with the permutation of the roles of narrator and narrated. There are thousands of others, and I leave you to imagine what they are.'

'Don't pagans know anything about reactivity?'

'Oh yes, and they are afraid of it because they know it condemns them to defeat. Listen to what happened to Arachne, who was happy just to react. She challenged Pallas at tapestry-making. The goddess took up the challenge, and used her loom to weave a rich picture of the metamorphoses the gods inflicted on mortals to punish them for being too clever. With equal skill, Arachne portrayed the metamorphoses the gods underwent so shamelessly in order to take advantage of the human victims of their passions. The pictures were of equal merit, but not the weavers. The Lydian girl's tapestry told the gods they were liars; the goddess's tapestry said "We are stronger". And, exasperated at having met her match, she turned her rival into a spider, thus adding a new episode to the tapestry's theme. Arachne fought badly, and simply reacted. She took the same theme as Pallas (the metamorphoses) and made accusations, but she did not displace the object of the narrative and seduced no one. She would have been wiser to allow herself to be seduced.'

'Your gods have an easy time of it! Always the strongest . . . '

'Don't you believe it. Don't forget the pragmatics that governs these fables: these are stories told by men who know that the gods can hear them, and they flatter them by letting them have the last word. But at the pragmatic level, one can never be sure that they do have the last word or that anything is ever settled; after all, arachnids have not been spinning their webs in vain for the last two or three thousand years. There is no reason to be optimistic, but nor is there any reason to be pessimistic. And still less is there any reason to be pious. That's what horrified Plato about paganism; according to him, it is the worst form of godlessness.'

'Are there other forms?'

'He is quite prepared to accept that you might not believe in the existence of the gods, particularly if you are young, provided that you are naturally virtuous and respect the political laws. Provided that you are a disciple, in short. He would, I should imagine, have forgiven someone like Protagoras.'

'Why Protagoras?'

'Protagoras said that he was in no position to know if the gods existed or not, or to know what they might look like. He was, or so they say, accused of not believing in the gods, and they threatened to put him on trial, like Socrates.'

'But he thought it advisable to flee. I am willing to bet that you find his flight more pagan than the ironic courage with which Socrates faced his judges.'

'Of course I do. But in any case, it seems to me that Protagoras was not so much a pagan as an early example of godless Platonism; a short spell in the sophronistery would have been enough to set him back on the straight and narrow.'

'What is a sophronistery?'

'A house of correction where a new sense of prudence and moderation is instilled into convicts. A school for indoctrination and re-education. The second sort of godlessness is more serious; thinking that the gods are indifferent to men. This is more serious because it implies denying their perfection. One may as well say that a great architect only takes an overall view of his building and has no interest in the small cornerstones and keystones that hold it up. But the most godless form of godlessness consists of behaving as though the gods were euparamythomenic.'

'Meaning easily misled by fables.'

'And as though their indulgence had to be bought with offerings and prayers. What, says Plato, dogs would refuse to be corrupted by wolves which offered to share the flock they were guarding. And you are saying that the gods are corruptible! You are saying that they are like steersmen who accept bribes to take their boats off course, or jockeys who can be bribed to hold back their mounts. These unbelievers are godless in two senses: their lust for gain knows no limits, and they are convinced that their gifts will make the gods turn a blind eye to their greed. They are pastmasters at flattery and at cajolery, wheedlers (I am quoting, I am quoting), bad masters; they are soothsayers, sorcerers, tyrants, rhetors, warlords, initiates and, of course, sophists. Liars. Putting them to death twice would not be enough to make them pay for their infamy, according to Aristides.'

'What more can be done to punish them, my dear chap? Do you want them to die three deaths? Do you want to spit in their mouths?'

'They will be interned in the desmostery, the central prison. They will see no one. The judges will decide what food rations they should get, and these will be brought to them by slaves. When they die, their bodies will be cast outside the city walls and left unburied (I am quoting, but these punishments are severe enough, aren't they?).

Where you establish the penitentiary is up to you: Kolyma, Dachau, Cologne-Ossendorf.'

'There is nothing new about attacking Plato on the grounds that he is a totalitarian, Grotius was attacking Plato and rehabilitating the sophists centuries ago. Allow me to draw your attention to more modern and more pressing matters. I still say that your *pagus* is nothing but a daydream; that the civil society into which you want to insert your pragmatics of cunning stories is not an amorphous milieu, that it is already a complicated set of stable narrative circuits, and that, particularly in our countries, it is simply puerile to back society against the state when we know full well that society tends to subordinate all its institutions to the needs of the circulation of capital, and that capital colludes with political bodies. The master of our narratives is not some pagan god; our master is capital. Capital makes us tell, listen to and act out the great story of its reproduction, and the positions we occupy in the instances of its narrative are predetermined. And you dream of little stories fighting a guerrilla war on a terrain where strict financial controls operate!'

'That was the other point I wanted to make. You are perfectly right, and that is why our leftists are not wrong to attack the newcomers. The newcomers think they are attacking all forms of power, but they have a remarkable talent for overlooking the power under which we live. Of course it does not have the crude features that make the totalitarian apparatus so easily recognizable. It is subtle. It does not just stamp out little stories; it also asks for them. It does not automatically send innovators into exile; it sometimes grants them patents and subsidies. It selects its narrators on financial grounds, but it also encourages the spread of narratees and narrateds. And whilst it is true that it puts us under house arrest in its narrative instances, it is also true that it requires us to change places.'

'But you do accept that, to use your jargon, there is such a thing as the great narrative of capital, and that all our narratives, great and small, are tied up with it?'

'Of course I do. After all, we are talking about power. But this is a godless power, and its narrative is about everything and nothing. I'm not saying that capital is pagan; it has its one god (money), its mass (discharging debts), its grace ordinary and extraordinary (profit and super-profits), its elect and its damned. So it is obviously not a *pagus*. But it is godless. Whereas a bishop, a general in your army or a secretary of the Communist Party is, in theory, someone who has heard a certain narrative, but not the first subject of its enunciation, the owner of capital is not the narrator of only one story. Depending on how much capital you own, you can make people listen to, tell and act out any story. If you don't succeed, it must be because the story you are investing has already been told by someone else, or because they told it better. And for their part, the owners of labour power are, asymmetrically, in the same narrative position: in theory, they are not bound to observe or play out any particular story, as is a specialist artisan, a member of a church or a political militant. The only problem is that, although neither capitalists nor workers are assigned to particular stories, they are assigned to narrative instances. This is a pragmatic point, not a semantic point. Capitalism is so godless that it has no respect for any one story, and its power is such that there is only one exception to the rule: it does care about the narrative which tells how narratives are told, listened to and acted out.'

'I don't understand.'

'I am talking about the canonical story which attaches such value to the autonomous activity of the narrator, and which subordinates the activities of the narratee and the narrated to it.'

'I don't understand.'

'Take the case of Clavel & Co. It operates in the political theory sector. It looks for a figure comparable with that of the tyrants, but also with their enemies, the rebels and the revolutionaries, because, it claims, there is nothing to choose between them. The new figure is known by a variety of names: the rebel, the pleb, Socrates, Jesus or Fantasio.'

'Noble uncertainty as a sign of real research?'

'Exactly. And having said that, suppose Clavie produces a book; he recounts what Jessie told him, and what he told Jessie. A certain Levie[5] publishes it. That makes two narratives: Jessie is the narrator of the first, and Clavie is his narratee.'

'And who is the narrated?'

'I don't know what Jessie told Clavie; to be angelic, perhaps . . .[6]'

'What about the second narrative?'

'That is the narrative Clavie recounts to his reader, and its reference is the story of the narrative Jessie told Clavie. As the narratives progress, Jessie moves from the position of narrator to that of narrated, and Clavie moves from that of narratee to narrator.'

'What have power and capital to do with all this?'

'Nothing. You hear something, pass it on to a third party, and give your sources. You may or may not alter it, as the case may be. It's as simple as that.'

'And then?'

'What becomes of the third party? Let's call him Dessie. He tells his

tale to a fourth party: Sollie. Oh, yes. Dessie tells Sollie that in his book
Clavie told him what Jessie told Clavie. That's the third narrative, to
simplify matters. And what does Sollie do? He may simply tell his girlfriend what Clavie told him about what Jessie told Clavie. If he does, a
fourth narrative is grafted on to the third, just as the third was grafted
on to the second and just as the second was grafted on to the first. Now
we have a serial assembly process.'

'You mean that in such cases the narratee pole of one narrative is
always linked to the narrator pole of the next by a name, but that the
name that was in the narrator instance in the first one, moves to the
narrated instance in the second?'

'Precisely. And, as you might expect, one of the effects of the
assembly process is that there is a diminishing level of fidelity to the
first narrative and that the first name becomes forgotten. That does not
necessarily have to happen, but it probably will, and if you want to prevent it happening, you have to take a lot of precautions, such as
preserving the letter of the first narrative and that can only be done
with great difficulty. But that is a different matter. To get back to our
fourth man: telling her what he has read about Dessie telling how
Clavie received a visitation from Jessie might not be the only thing
Sollie gets up to with his girlfriend.'

'What else might he be doing?'

'To restrict the argument to narrative possibilities, he might pretend
that it wasn't Dessie who told him about Clavie's book; he might talk
about it with his girlfriend as though he had read it himself, and that
may or may not be true. He misses out a link in the chain. He tells
Clavie's story. He and Clavie form a series, just like Clavie and Dessie,
but Sollie and Dessie do not form a series: they are in parallel.'

'You mean that both narratives – Dessie's and Sollie's – were
assembled together further up the line but in the same narrative
instance? And that that narrative instance was Clavie because both
Dessie and Sollie are now his narratees?'

'Yes.'

'And that further down the line, the narratives constructed by
Dessie and Sollie both have the same narratee?'

'Yes.'

'But who is he?'

'The first thing that has to be said is that two parallel narratives can
be completely different, as different as a yoghurt-maker and an electric
blanket, even though they were assembled in parallel.'

'They are not quite that different, since at least one name figures in
both their respective diegeses: Clavie.'

'You've just answered your own question.'

'The question about the narratee further down the line?'

'Yes.'

'How come?'

'Suppose the singular effect we have just noted in the case of Sollie is reproduced in the case of Sollie's narratee – let's call him Nemie. According to our hypothesis, Nemie will assemble his narrative in parallel with those of Sollie and Dessie, and rather than telling a distant cousin what Sollie says about what Clavie says he heard from Jessie, he will tell him the story of Clavie's story. A new segment has been added to our parallel assembly line. But, and this is the really interesting bit, the series you would expect to take shape around Sollie (Sollie as narrator and Nemie as narratee, then Nemie as narrator and his distant cousin as narratee, second cousin as narrator, etc.), with all the concomitant displacements that implies at the level of the narrated (Clavie's story as reference for the story Sollie told Nemie, then Sollie's story as reference for his cousin's story and so on) . . . well, that series does not in fact take shape. And the explanation for that is that according to our hypothesis, a new potential narrator always skips a segment up the line in the series and takes the place of the narrator whose narratee he was a moment ago, rather than using that narrator as the narrated of the narrative of which he has to become the narratee. So, the one thing that Dessie, Sollie, Nemie and their successors, and we can assume that they are their peers, have in common is that they all talk about Clavie's story. As the stories progress, his is the only name by which we can identify them: they are Claveans, but only at the level of the narrated. Each of them may well say the opposite of what everyone else is saying about Clavie's story, and their opinions may well clash. That does not matter; it simply proves the point that a narrator who talks about Clavie's story, even if he does turn it into a story that is completely different from that told by the others, only exists thanks to the name of Clavie. And the same goes for his peers. (The name of the narrated is not the only means by which parity – or parallels – can be established; we will look at one example later.) That is the narratee instance you were looking for. It is a set made up of Clavie's readers. I call it the set of first readers, because even the 37,827th reader in a chain of "they say that Clavie said that Jessie . . ." immediately takes up the same position as Dessie who was, according to our hypothesis, the first narratee. And given that the narratee instance of Dessie's story is simply the Dessie set (by which I mean Dessie and his peers) there is no reason why Clavie's story should disappear as the chronology of "they say" unfolds, and nor is there any reason why his name should disappear from one story to the next, as would happen if all the narrators and narratees were assembled in series.'

'You say that it is Clavie's name that is perpetuated in this way; but I would argue that the same is true of Jessie's message, and that Clavie is merely his first apostle.'

'So it would seem.'

'On the other hand, if it were true that the stories of Clavie and his successors were assembled in series rather than in parallel, and if the name of Clavie (or Jessie) was therefore liable to be forgotten with the passage of time, it would still be true to say that his story would still provide the impetus behind and the basis for a series, even if it does become anonymous, and that Clavie (or Jessie) would still have the same power over the set. It seems to me that the differences between the two assembly processes are negligible.'

'There's a vast difference between them, but you have to be shrewd to see it. It is the difference between might and power, between paganism and piety. The reason why a name does not disappear in a parallel assembly process is that it is passed on from one "they say" to the next; one of the functions of all these narratives is to reiterate the name of the referent, and to omit that of the intercessor. For example; Dessie's name is omitted when Sollie is speaking. No matter what they say, all the stories must relate to the story told by Clavie-Jessie, and, no matter how disparate they may be, they can do that adequately enough by mentioning their names. With the serial assembly system, the trademark stamped on the stories disappears, or at least does not necessarily have to be there. And in fact there is no reason why the flow of stories has to be explained in terms of an initial and identifiable impetus, as you are suggesting. If you give it an origin, you are simply telling a story which takes as its reference another story. No doubt it did all take place in the past, but your story has to be told in the present tense. The series, together with the artificiality of the references, constantly undercuts the overweening pretensions of origins. And it is in that sense that its godlessness is truly pagan. But with a parallel assembly line, the income that is paid in arrears to the initial name or names allows piety to take wing, and power to exert pressure.'

'How does that come about?'

'I once asked a physicist friend who suffered as a result of having made a name for himself during the May '68 events why clouds of matter gave rise to a system. His answer was that, firstly, you should never ask why and that, secondly, if you want to imagine how, you have to look at the effect of relations of order. I got much the same answer from a musician friend when I asked him why and how series of noises come to be combined in accordance with the rules of harmony and composition. Let's just say that the reason why sequences of stories come to be organized in parallel, just as particles combine to form bodies and sounds combine to form melodies, is that neither the properties of bodies, the notes of a scale or proper names are easily forgotten.'

'Is that a sin?'

'I don't know the meaning of the word. It's more a matter of tempo; do you like the rhythm that material, sonic or narrative elements beat out in the same way that a wave beats the surface of the sea and consigns it to oblivion in the form of a swell, or would you rather that something remained, come what may? Would you rather tell a story in such a way that it is remembered and never forgotten, or in such a way that it makes something happen? Anamnesiac teleology, or a finality without ends?'

'In any event, Clavie does not want us to forget Jessie.'

'Or him. But I think that it is because they are a language form in which it is possible to love time for its power to forget that those who have no names, and peoples and children like stories, that they tell them in song and dance. That is why they do not set themselves up as subjects and retain almost nothing of the so-called lessons of history; cultures are made up of stories that are assembled in series. The inspiration behind theoretical discourses, on the other hand, is the refrain that we have to stop forgetting the Good, God, Being, Labour, the Unconscious, Time. The precept behind theory, or at least classical theory, is the need to struggle against oblivion; that is why we can say that it too is a meta-narrative: a narrative about remembering stories. But even that meta-narrative is forced to forget something; it forgets that it is a narrative. That is the tribute it pays to time.'

'I still don't see how your fable about Clavie helps me to understand why capitalism meddles in the Clavel & Co. business.'

'It doesn't meddle; the group's stories tended to be assembled in parallel, and they can therefore be capitalized.'

'How does that come about?'

'Take an example at random. Clavie writes a book, Gluckie writes a book, Jardrie writes a book and Benie writes a book.'

'Nothing unusual about that.'

'Levie publishes all of them.'[7]

'My God, it's what they call a collection.'

'Indeed it is, but in a small way it's also the beginning of a parallel assembly process.'

'I fail to see what acts as the initial narrative.'

'You're right. In this case the parallel is not established by using the name of the first narrator, who becomes the narrated of the later stories, as a hallmark. It is the name of the vehicle which serves as a hallmark. That's the name that recurs from one book to the next.'

'All right, but what does that matter?'

'It matters a great deal when narrative vehicles ("supports") are in competition with one another, but let's leave that on one side. Suppose that Clavie becomes what we are calling the first reader of Jardrie's book, Benie the first reader of Clavie's book and Gluckie the first reader of Benie's book.'

'When you talk about first readers you mean that each of the first lot will talk about each of the second lot in such a way that subsequent readers react as though they themselves were the first readers.'

'Right. But, on top of that, the first readers are not content with giving an oral account of what there is in these books, and they too publish in their turn.'

'How do they do that?'

'Levie takes care of that. He's in a position to do so.'

'You're assuming that he has unlimited powers.'

'No, I'm not; as it happens, I'm simply describing how things stand. Now imagine a second round in which the series of "they say" is distributed like this: Gluckie reviews Clavie's book, Clavie reviews Jardrie's book, and Jardrie reviews Benie's book. What do you think will happen?'

'People will laugh.'

'That's good for business. Laughter sells books, and that way, they get read.'

'But what gets read?'

'To cut a long story short ... It's not hard to see that if we saturate the possible combinations – and only four factorials are involved – and if we also assume that each of the articles refers not only to the book it describes, but also to at least one other article, a reader who stumbles across any term in any series of combinations stands little chance of escaping the other three terms. And, given that our present fable involves four terms, the parallel would have been established when the second series was published.'

'How come?'

'The names of the authors of the books are the same as those of the first readers, or as those of the authors of the articles. Each author is the next author's reader, and each reader is an author who is read by the other readers. Each frontline narrator is a second-line narratee, and each frontline narratee (each first reader) is a second-line narrator. The set of narrators (authors) and the set of narratees (first readers) are identical, and that identity forms the "narrated" set. As you can see, what I call the auto-effect is more pronounced than it was in my original fable, where there was only one initial narrative (by Clavie-Jessie) and where the addressee set, which did not include Clavie himself, was made up solely of first readers (the Dessies) and owed its unity to the name of the hero of the stories told by the narrators in that set. The unifying name was applied only to the "narrated" instance. In our present fable, there are several initial narratives and four unifying names, and it is because they all permutate around the three narrative instances that they can celebrate the pious rites of commemoration and income-generation. They permutate two by two (Narratee/narrator; Narratee/narrated; Narrator/narrated), provided that the same name never appears in the same position in both series.'

'Why does that proviso matter?'

'That is what limits the expansion of the permutations to factorials; any series parallel to the first is excluded if the same name appears in the same position in both, because it would be indecent for Benie to be Benie's narratee and for him to begin to narrate what Benie told him as a first narrator.'

'Is decency a property of such systems?'

'I was joking; of course it isn't. But if the auto-effect were restricted to cases in which narrator, narratee and narrated all had the same name, we would have to adopt a different hypothesis – that of a secret autobiography. And that is scarcely a capitalist pragmatics.'

'And what's capitalist about your four-part fable?'

'The element of public autographography. Who is capitalism's addressee? The capitalist who invests. And the book's? The author who writes it. What is the connection between the two? They both have the same name.'

'So we're talking about autobiography?'

'No. Under capitalism, there have to be at least two commodities: the commodity X buys from Y, and the commodity Y buys from X. X and Y are both buyers and sellers. Similarly, there must be two narrative-commodities; the book is one and the review is the other. And there have to be two different names; an author's name and a reader's name.'

'So both the man who writes the article and the man who writes the book are two-headed capitalists who, because they invest by exchanging two commodities and make a profit, are at once narrators and narratees.'

'Precisely. And, as we have said, it's just like trade: the particular nature of the commodities in question is of no importance. What is important is the fact that they can be exchanged. And the fact that they are no more than "outward" forms of capital; narratives are no more than "outward" forms of narrative reproduction.'

'And what is Levie's role in all this?'

'Money capital. He lends the author the wherewithal to publish a book, the reader the wherewithal to publish his review, and he puts them in a position to be able to strike a deal; in other words, he gets both of them read by getting one to read the other and getting one to write for the other.'

'What about surplus-value?'

'Let's leave it at that. We can't deal with surplus-value here, as that would mean going into the circulation time of capital, capital as an advance on narration, and narrative as capital-income.'

'But just where does your metaphor get us? Is capital a narratics (*narratique*), or is it the other way around?'

'Have it your own way. That's why this is not a metaphor, but a parallel set of . . . two little stories.'

'What are you criticizing Clavel & Co. for? Having turned their theoretical narratives into commodities?'

'For having reproduced power when they put them into circulation, and at the same time using them to curse power.'

'You object to that?'

'Yes, in the same way that La Boétie objected to the One, the only difference being that their One is semantically important and pragmatically unimportant. *Mutatis mutandis*, I am saying the same things about them that certain very shrewd old comrades wrote about the uprisings in Guyana; the uprisings were the peasants' answer to the arrival of the king's salt-tax gatherers in 1548, shortly before La Boétie told Montaigne the story which, if Butor is to be believed, became the central but hidden theme in his own stories. The rebels and the men of no property wanted nothing to do with the novelty of royal taxes, and not only because they had their own ideas about how money should circulate. They also had their own ideas as to how stories should be put together. They wanted their tongues, their ears and their bodies, which were their three narratives instances, to go on being able to assemble infinite series of narratives, just as they had been able to in their own cultures, to produce revenue for a name. "Peasant" means "pagan" . . . and we are pagans. What is new is that there is something behind the men of Clavel & Co.: the money narrative, which collects the tax on theoretical discourses.'

'But they claim to be dissidents; they support good causes.'

'Luther was a dissident too, but he used to dine with the bourgeois and the princes, and he sold out the peasants. Your men often dine out with the media. I'm telling you once again that you should take more notice of postures and less notice of significations. The funny thing about narrative pragmatics is that it uses power's networks to spread horror stories about power. The networks we are talking about here may well be on a small scale, but they are homogeneous with the bigger ones.'

'But you make a distinction between totalitarian and capitalist powers. Why do you say that the power that caught our new men out belongs to the capitalist camp?'

'Capitalism is pretty well indifferent to the content of the stories it allows to circulate, but it is not indifferent to the form of their pragmatic. The money-narrative is its canonical story because it combines two properties. Firstly, it tells us that we can tell any stories we like, but it also tells us that authors must reap the profits on their narratives. That first property is godless, if you compare it with the narrative political powers demand.'

'But its second property is very much a matter of power.'

'Yes, but let's see why. The money-narrative presupposes a first narrator, an author, an entrepreneur and a subject. He tells us that he has not heard the story he is telling from anyone else. Those who listen to it and execute it do not change it (or so he imagines); they are the scenario's spectator-actors, but he is in sole charge. So much that they think it fair to pay him tribute for the so-called use they make of his argument.'

'So-called?'

'Stories can never be used up.'

'I can see what tribute you are thinking about when it comes to production. But when it comes to narration?'

'It's just like any other tribute; in order to pay narrative tribute, you hand over part of your narrative ability to someone who is supposedly the first narrator. You find yourself deprived of your narration, but he seems to be its master and possessor. You will notice that you are not being asked to recite the scenario well, but that you are being asked to learn it and act it out carefully. It is because you have been prevented from making up stories that the story you are acting out can revert to its first narrator, and that it can recur down all the narrative generations.'

'I can quite see how your description applies to the Clavie apparatus. Its operator is a so-called "first reader", who will not allow narration to be organized in free series. But I don't see how that apparatus differs from the pragmatics that are forced on us by totalitarian Party-states.'

'They order you to take up three narrative positions because you are a citizen or a militant. You are the narratee of the political narrative; it is intended for you: they govern for the people. You are its narrated; you act it out: this is the government of the people. But in theory you are also its narrator: the people is governed by the people. In fact it is this narrative, and this narrative alone, that you are required to tell, as a free narrator, to all applicants for citizenship or for Party membership, to children, candidate members, and delinquents alike. And they in their turn will recite it when they reach adulthood, achieve real political awareness or repent fully. As I've already told you, the power of capital does not require such recitations because it precludes the possibility of moving from the position of narratee–narrated to that of narrator; it reserves that position for itself, without any hypocrisy.'

'So there is an element of religion in capitalism: the exclusive worship of the narrative entrepreneur.'

'Obviously. But be careful not to be fooled by the exorbitant privileges it grants the narrator. He is privileged in two ways, perhaps even in contradictory fashion.

'Firstly, he has the privilege of having an income; the narrator enjoys the authority conferred upon him by the fact that his name reoccurs in the narratives of subsequent narrators, as we saw in the example of the first addressees of the Clavie story. But he also derives his authority from the fact that they say he was the primary autonomous force behind the narrative of which he is reputedly the author, and which others learn and act out. He is not simply the end stop in a circuit of narration; he is regarded as the prime mover who set it in motion.'

'But there's no such thing. Stories are not the product of some subjective talent for narration which sets them in motion. Stories tell themselves; they are by definition mobile, and their narrators are no more than one of the paths along which they travel.'

'I couldn't have put it better myself. But a belief in the author's creativity can take on a certain consistency thanks to the parallel assembly system. Respect for the story's beneficiary leads to the worship of his initiative. That's one aspect of the auto-effect. And it is true that you cannot be a narrative entrepreneur unless you seem to have invented some new story, or a different product. That is not something that is required of the supposed narrators of the totalitarian narrative. On the contrary. That is why the totalitarian narrative discourages emulation and suppresses narrative power by sending it to sleep and, should it resist, by deporting it. With capital's canonical narrative, it is the other way around; whilst it remains true to the income principle, it spreads the story that, for a narrator, a narrative is an opportunity to make a profit, not because of what it narrates (its narrated), but to the extent that it differs from the narrated vehiculed by the other narratives that are in circulation.'

'I'm beginning to see your point, but I'm not too clear about the relationship between what you are saying now and the distinction you make between serial and parallel assembly.'

'In a serial assembly process, the names of the narrators gradually fade from one narrative generation to the next; and so does the name of the shifting narrated.'

'Yes. You can only become part of a series if your narrative says something about your narrated that is not said in the narrative he recounts to you, even if he was your narrator only a moment ago.'

'Exactly, if only because his name is that of the narrator of the previous narrative, and that of the narrated of the next narrative.'

'But when we were talking about the Clavel & Co. fable, didn't you say that the narratives of the first readers could differ, and that that was of little importance? But they were in parallel, not in series.'

'I would now say that they have to be different, and that that is not unimportant. The variants are in fact proof that we are in a capitalist apparatus and not a totalitarian apparatus. And the fact that the narratives are different does not mean that they weren't assembled in parallel. In fact that is the classic solution in this system. It suffices that the narrated have a name in common (Clavie; that takes care of the revenue function), and that their respective narrators (first readers) speak in their own names, which takes care of the initiative function. If these two conditions are met, both narrative generations can enjoy the twofold privilege of the so-called subject of the enunciation. And you can see how, because they are different, narrative segments require the freedom of the series, but are at the same time assembled in parallel.'

'And what's your answer to that?'

'There are two lessons to be learned: putting narratives into series, and forgetting names. I say "forget names" because names are rather like the gods of the late Roman Empire and the great political upheavals of our time: there are rather too many of them. It's not out of some desire for anonymity.'

'Are you suggesting that we should deal with the narratives of both left and right in the same way?'

'Yes. We should reply to their respective narrative pragmatics. You can't really attack one and leave the other alone; that would be a poor strategy.'

'You are looking for a valid and complete strategy?'

'There isn't one. The most valid strategy is the most prudent strategy, and prudence is a matter of seizing opportunities. Fronts are not continuous, you know. Fifteen years ago one of your fellow citizens told me that in the space of a single year he had helped to form a CGT branch in a little factory in a village, whilst his criticisms and initiatives caused an upheaval in the same union's apparatus in a big company in a neighbouring town. And you are in a better position than I to know that, during the Algerian war, it was perfectly possible both to carry suitcases for the FLN and to criticize the military-bureaucratic power that it was likely to establish after independence. All that is only inconsistent if you believe in the universal narrative. But histories and policies are like cultures; they are their own references, and they determine their own enemies. It may sometimes be possible to unite or even combine efforts and effects, and to both recount and implement particular narratives, but it goes against reason, and reason is pagan, to totalize them on any lasting basis.'

'In praise of opportunism?'

'Of seizing opportunities. Opportunity is the mistress of those who have no masters, the weapon of those who have no arms, and the strength of the weak, amen. It is not simply a contemporary and unexpected relationship between powerful established narrative apparatuses and the interference of a strange little history, a minor history which momentarily nonplusses them. So, alternate between harassing the State and harassing capital. Attack them by attacking their pragmatics. And if it is at all possible to do so, use one to attack the other.'

'How can we do that?'

'You know very well: use laws and institutions against the abuses committed by entrepreneurs, organize tenants' associations, shopfloor struggles, ecological campaigns ... And use the opposite argument, and the right to be an entrepreneur, when it is a matter of checkmating some dangerous state monopoly: set up pirate radio stations, invent unorthodox teaching methods (as at dear old Vincennes), try to unionize soldiers or prostitutes ... '

'You won't win any lasting victories.'

'I don't expect to. We have to take our time.'

'You won't scare them.'

'If they are self-confident and laugh at us, so much the better. That is the only way stratagems work.'

'One final point. Why do you attach such extraordinary importance to narratics?'

'We live in societies in which the question of the social bond is being raised. The issue of power is merely one aspect of that question. And you will find that, even before you answer that question, you have assumed the existence of that bond by giving an answer. What does a question mean to you? It is an interrogative utterance with you as its addressee. And what is that utterance? A narrative which expects you to tell it to the end. By beginning to answer the question of the social bond, or even by repeating the answer, you are continuing an unfinished narrative, or ensuring that it never ends. And in doing so, you realize the bond in question, because you are now the narrator. Previously, you were being asked questions. You were a narratee, and your questioner, whom you assume to be society (and were it not for society, you wouldn't give a damn), is now the object of your narrative. The pragmatics of your answer gives an answer even before you answer the question. Or at least that is the story I would tell in response to your question.'

'I'm beginning to see what you mean when you say you are godless. But what about your justice?'

'It cannot be expressed in a formula or a canonic law. It is a perspective.'

'What perspective?'

'Destroy narrative monopolies, both as exclusive themes (of parties) and as exclusive pragmatics (exclusive to parties and markets). Take away the privileges the narrator has granted himself. Prove that there is as much power – and not less power – in listening, if you are a narratee, and in acting, if you are the narrated (and let the fools believe that you are singing the praises of servitude when you do so).'

'Isn't that self-management *(autogestion)*?'

'Not at all. That is the auto-effect run riot: totalitarian power is insinuated into every body, and the meta-narrative of capital is seen as the canonic narrative. We should be struggling to include meta-narratives, theories and doctrines, and especially political doctrines, in narratives. The intelligentsia's function should not be to tell the truth and save the world, but to will the power to play out, listen to and tell stories. That power is so universal that it would be impossible to deprive the people of it without then answering back. If you want an authority, that is the only place you will find it. Justice means willing it.'

NOTES

1 Editor's note: The philosophers in question here are the so-called *Nouveaux Philosophes*.

2 Editor's note: The reference here is to the philosopher Maurice Clavel who was associated with the *Nouveaux Philosophes*.

3 Editor's note: Jacques Chirac, the Lord Mayor of Paris and the leading Gaullist. It should not be forgotten that Lyotard's entire text can be read as a political intervention concerning as much the world in which a possible Socialist electoral victory was on the agenda, as it does that of philosophy and publishing.

4 Translator's note: Metic: resident alien in a Greek city, enjoying certain of the privileges of citizenship. Lyotard plays on *métèque*, which derives from the Greek, but which is used in popular French as a term of racist abuse: 'wop', 'wog'.

5 Editor's note: Here and elsewhere in the text Lyotard plays with the names of the *Nouveaux Philosophes* and their associates. The code is as follows: Levie is Bernard-Henri Lévy, Clavie is Maurice Clavel, Sollie is Philippe Sollers, Nemie is Philippe Nemo, Gluckie is André Glucksman, Jessie is Christian Jambert, etc.

6 Translator's note: The reference is to Guy Lardeau and Christian Jambert, *L'Ange* (Paris: Grasset, 1976).

7 Editor's note: Lyotard is referring to the series 'Figures' that was edited by Bernard-Henri Lévy and published by Grasset. It was the series that presented many of the major works by the *Nouveaux Philosophes*.

Translated by David Macey

7

Beyond Representation[*]

Ehrenzweig's book, his second and his last, becomes accessible in French[1] at a moment when there is a general awareness of a crisis in psychoanalysis. It is not a matter of fashion but rather of an authoritative questioning and doubting that bear on some of the categories of psychoanalytic theory and practice. This book, far from answering such questions, can only open them further, displace old questions and pose new ones, and thus increase the disruption. Indeed it is in order to provoke this that we have chosen to present first a central theme of the book but one that is little developed: a critique of the notion of 'applied psychoanalysis'. Ehrenzweig himself never defined the orientation of his work in this way, not because he failed to understand its thrust but because he felt that the thing criticized holds back and even consumes the one who criticizes, as Sodom petrified Lot's wife. He believed it more important to assert what is in fact the case than to deny that things work as others claim or have claimed. This is the artistic point of view. We, however, shall briefly risk the ungenerous mode that he eschewed.

For the epistemologist, the notion of 'application' in an expression such as 'applied psychoanalysis' is simply flabby. It would seem to imply that a body of theory, more or less rigorously formulated, can be applied without modification to a set of data or to a field of study (in this case, works of art) different from that for which it was constructed (the set of psycho-neurotic symptoms and abnormal psychic phenomena). If this were so, the two domains would be indistinguishable; if they are not, then the attempt at application requires modifications that, however trivial, make that body of theory different from what it was in its first 'state'.

---

[*] This essay was first published as a preface by Jean-François Lyotard to *L'Ordre Caché de l'Art* by Anton Ehrenzweig, Editions Gallimard 1974.

However, if Freud, his collaborators and his successors have not hesitated to 'apply psychoanalysis' to works of art, it must be because in the absence of other reasons there were powerful drives that motivated a confusion of domains. Let us leave aside the imperialistic ambitions of the adepts of a new method or of the mandarins of established psychoanalysis that lead both (but what a difference between, say, Reik and Schneider!) to annex the domain of art to the realm of symptoms, to arrogate to themselves the privilege of analysing diagnostically the artistic process and even the works or artists themselves. With Freud (or Reik) we are dealing with something different; we are at the very least dealing with what Jean Starobinski has recently demonstrated: the infiltration of clinical thought by tragic themes drawn from Greek and Elizabethan drama, particularly from *Oedipus Rex* and *Hamlet*. These themes help to shape, not so much in a directly thematic way but rather as models of a pattern of relations, the central ideas of the relationship between the self and desire (the Oedipal triangle repressed in *Hamlet*) and the therapeutic function (catharsis). Such interpenetration is already problematic, in that the privileged role granted to these themes leaves unspecified the *scope* that they may legitimately be granted; and yet we are still dealing with explicit themes. We must go a step further and grasp the fact that Freud's belief in or effective acceptance of the Sophoclean and Shakespearian scenarios is first of all a belief in the theatrical space where these scenarios are acted out, the space of theatrical representation, and in the scenography that constitutes and defines this space.

It has already been recognized that, compared with the other arts, the theatre enjoys a privileged status in Freudian thought and practice. Freud himself not only admits this; on at least one occasion he appears to offer justification for it. In a short paper of 1905–6 entitled 'Psychopathic Characters on the Stage' he sketches the genesis of psychoanalysis in terms of the problem of guilt and expiation: the sacrifice designed to mollify the Gods is the parent form; Greek tragedy, itself derived, as Freud believed, from the sacrifice of the goat, gives birth to socio-political drama and then to individual (psychological) drama, of which psychoanalysis is the offspring. This genealogy not only reveals the extent to which, by Freud's own admission, the psychoanalytic relationship is organized like a ritual sacrifice; it also suggests the identity of the various spaces in which sacrifice takes place: temple, theatre, the chambers of politics and doctors' surgeries – all *disreal* spaces, as Laplanche and Pontalis might call them: autonomous spaces no longer subject to the laws of so-called reality, regions where desire can play in all its ambivalence, spaces where for the 'proper objects' of desire are substituted accepted *images,* which are assumed to be not fictions but authentic libidinal products that have simply been exempted from the censorship imposed by the reality principle. The analogy continually drawn between artistic creation and dream or fantasy, as in 'The Relation of the Poet to Day-Dreaming' (1908), reflects the same tendency. Despite protestations that psychoanalysis is not qualified to penetrate the secret of artistic creation, we can see perfectly well that the treatment inflicted upon Leonardo da Vinci's *Holy Family,* for example, is precisely identical to the treatment that would be applied to the story of a dream recounted on the analyst's couch.

No doubt one can say that Freud always maintained between dream or fantasy and the work of art a distinction that seemed to him to be sufficient to preserve between their respective statuses a qualitative difference, in which can be located the bribe or 'pleasure premium': the formal qualities of the work of art are said to have the specific function of disarming any censorship of content. Ehrenzweig observed in *The Psychoanalysis of Artistic Vision and Hearing*[2] that Freud's best analysis of works of art is in *Jokes and their Relation to the Unconscious,* because only there does he concentrate on the formal operations that produce the object – in this case, the joke. However, Ehrenzweig adds, the pleasure afforded by the form does not anticipate and give access to that of the content, but follows or accompanies it. This is not a negligible shift. It implies, among other things, that this pleasure premium does not function as the discharge of a fee that allows one to enter the disreal space of the libido and to find free pleasure there. Above all it entails a corresponding shift in the function of form: no longer does it have essentially, not to say exclusively, the role that Freud assigns to it of quieting pre-conscious censorship. (According to Freud's thesis the pleasure premium functions in the same way as *sleep* does in the theory of dreams: the latter also has the role of lowering defences and thus conspires with the process of secondary elaboration.) This new role of form should allow us to extend the set of works of art to include those whose formal organization is not necessarily harmonious, does not respect the supposed demands of the secondary processes, and, far from quieting censorship, may provoke it. But we know how far the aesthetic corpus to which Freud refers was restricted to classicism, even academicism, especially in the non-literary arts; how far this Viennese was able to ignore the music of Schoenberg and his school; and how far this modernist in psychoanalysis was able to neglect all contemporary modernism in painting (Hofmannsthal, for example, testifies that a Van Gogh exhibition was held in Vienna in the last years of the nineteenth century). For Freud painting meant Italy, that is to say something like Egypt, a country of amnesia, a libidinal space.

This confidence in the hypnotic function of artistic form generally led applied psychoanalysis to neglect the conscious or unconscious choice and organization of the formal constituents of works, although it is scarcely a secret that here rather than in the 'subject' (when there is one) is where real artistic activity takes place. The method of free-floating or equally poised attention should, however, have led to this aspect, and indeed we find such a case in Freud's approach to Michelangelo's *Moses*. But generally, and even here, such attention serves only as a point of departure and soon gives way to a more reassuring, totally reductive method: a *reading of affects,* as it were, to which the details noted at the outset serve only as a kind of release mechanism. Thus one falls into, or risks falling into, a procedure that, if it is not quite as crude as applying a prefabricated code of symbols to the work (sexual symbols, of course!), is never more subtle than a semiotic analysis, which is also characterized by the restricted nature of its corpus and its inability to experience and identify effects of the energy released by formal constituents. In this methodological nihilism, which transforms entities of language, painting or music into signs or groups that *stand for* something else, and therefore treats the material and its organization as a surface to be penetrated, one finds the same prejudice: the notion that works of art have a substitutive or vicarious function. They are there only in place of a missing object, as the accepted formula has it; and they are there only *because* the object is missing.

An account of the economy of works of art that was cast in libidinal terms (but should we still, in this case, continue to speak of *works?*) would have as its central presupposition the affirmative character of works: they are not in place of anything; they do not *stand for* but stand; that is to say, they function through their material and its organization. Their subject is nothing other than a possible formal organization (not an inevitable or necessary organization); and it conceals no content, no libidinal secret of the work, whose force lies entirely in its surface. There is only surface. Freud himself even formulated in *Beyond the Pleasure Principle* the project of an economy of aesthetics: 'These cases and situations which have an increase in pleasure as their final output could form the object of esthetics conceived as an economy.'[3] But it is not by chance that, instead of summing up with the firm proposal that would be required, this sentence is subordinate to the famous analysis of the child's game of *fort-da*. Within the perspective that interests us this latter analysis is a dead-end. It testifies to the continuing power of the theatrical schema in Freud's unconscious epistemological assumptions, but it ought to have been nothing less than a demonstration (at least attempted, even if it proved impossible) that the theatrical schema can be deduced from the economy of drives. It ought to have answered the question of how the libidinal surface, swept by the drives of Eros and Thanatos, can give rise to an illusion of volume, a three-dimensional space, divided into stage and house, allurement and reality. How can the film on which move the drives of the primary process (which, as Freud has taught us, know no limit, no negation) turn back on itself and become a space of disjunction, uniting an inside and an outside: that is to say, a space that is both conceptual and representational?

It is clear that for Freud the roll of film is something like a work of art because it is a sign, because it replaces something (the mother) for someone (the child). But for the student of the libidinal economy this function of image or sign is not pertinent because it presupposes what one must try to produce by a theoretical argument: negativity. To say that the child acts out in his suffering the pain caused by his mother's absence is to take suddenly as given all the components of the theatrical space: an actor-spectator (the child for himself), an object-sign (the roll of film), a memory (the presence of an absence), a final cause or goal (catharsis). In short one immediately gives in to the demands of the order of representation (which is secondary), without allowing oneself to be concerned at all with the principle that one had oneself so cleverly established: if it is indeed true that the primary processes know no negation, then in the economy of drives there is not, nor can there ever be, an absence of *the* mother, or especially an absence of *mother* (as absent object); nor will there ever be a person to suffer from absence. Pleasure and pain, or enjoyment, must thus be conceived as purely affirmative; one can have no recourse to the easy epistemological solution of 'the lack', which is a major concession to Judeo-Platonic theology. This is to say, among other things, that we must deal in some other way with the place and role of representations (*Vorstellungsrepräsentanz*) in relation to drives; not as substitutes concealing objects or the goals of drives, but as concentrations of libidinal energy on the surfaces of the visible and the articulable – surfaces that are themselves part of the endless and anonymous film of primary drives.

In this perspective works would not be treated as images; we should not distinguish between their form and their libidinal content; we should understand that their power to please resides wholly in the formal labour that produces them on the one hand and in the work of various kinds that they stimulate on the other. We should stop relegating them to this special space of the disreal that artists more appropriately call a cultural ghetto; we should grant them the same reality as what we call reality and the same seriousness as . . . say, psychoanalytic discourse, for example. The relationship between this discourse and the domain of art would be overturned: not simply inverted so as to secure for art some kind of revenge on analysis, but shifted so that the division between what appertains to truth on the one hand and what belongs to beauty or pleasure on the other would be abolished and it would become clear that in both cases, on both sides, we are dealing with transformations of libidinal energy and with devices governing these transformations – none of which, neither devices nor transformations, could be privileged and labelled as more profound than another, since they are all on the surface. Understanding will no longer be a matter of establishing an ultimate libidinal content (be it even a lack, the effect of an empty signifier) but rather of identifying, in all its ineffectual delicacy and complexity, the *device* by which the energy of drives is guided, blocked, freed, exhausted or stored up – in short, channelled into extreme intensities. And precisely the same holds for the device of the psychoanalytic relationship itself as for the devices required by a hyperrealistic painting or by a piece of serial music.

Ehrenzweig's works are decisive contributions to a libidinal aesthetic of this kind. In noting some of its major aspects we should give full weight to his repeated affirmation, already central to *The Psychoanalysis of Artistic Vision and Hearing,* that the primary processes are not chaotic or disordered in themselves; that it is only their encounter with the rigid structures of secondary organization that produces an effect of disorder; and that the primary operation *par excellence* is *scanning,* a free sweep of energy or attention. Freud often outlined, while declaring that they were beyond the grasp of direct description, the characteristic features of primary processes: no negation, no modalization, no logical connections, no temporal distribution, and consequently the undifferentiated nature of the world of drives, which resists discursive definition through its opacity,[4] its 'Egyptian' obliqueness,[5] its simultaneity,[6] and its paratopic nature.[7] But for Freud these metaphorical indications serve above all as methodological warnings; they indicate that the most basic structures of thought are powerless before the space-time of libidinal drives, and they therefore work to justify procedures as paradoxical as 'surface listening', as free-floating attention, as an approach through the unusual or through free association, and in general to encourage the analyst to remain passively receptive to all the material offered by the analysand – although, as Freud's own practice shows, this passivity does not exclude bold interventions but is rather an instance of that 'negative capability' that Keats recommended in his famous letter on the poet-chameleon.

Ehrenzweig offers a positive description of the primary processes – as syncretic, 'sweeping', holistic and undifferentiated – whereas articulated secondary structures, which are not only the forms of understanding, as Kant would say, but the forms of feeling as well, require analytical discussion, a focus on parts, a breakdown and differentiation of their components. In an earlier investigation he had offered an excellent approximate analysis of unconscious perception, of the way in which the periphery of the visual field is grasped. Using Monks's work on visual fixation in linear systems, Bates's investigation of the eye's unconscious tendency towards peripheral vision, and Frankl's study of Cézanne's system of colours, he had treated Cézanne's works as the summary of partial instantaneous views 'prior to' the focusing and differentiation required for good form and colour (required, in other words, for a realism of recognizable objects). These views are 'prior' by right only, since in fact it is the pre-conscious ordered vision that first presents itself, and Cézanne's eye, so intensely fixed on the motif, resists this 'already known' order with an immobility whose function recalls that of hallucinatory drugs.

These analyses and others helped to deny Freud's pessimistic account.[8] One can no longer say that the deformations or distortions of Cézanne's pictorial space (for that was how Ehrenzweig then labelled them) were negative *metaphors* for those of a primary space-time; the former are positive versions of the latter; or the latter are the same as the former. Nevertheless, there was still a negative element in the descriptions, which could be noted even in the prefixes attached to words that were then used to designate the properties and operations of this space. In his later book, however, Ehrenzweig goes further: he tries to eliminate even the function of disruption (what he had previously called 'baffling'), which now he considers to be not a primary feature but a kind of undertow effect produced when the waves of libidinal drives meet the rigid secondary structures. In this way he not only advances further than ever before in the direction of an affirmative aesthetic economy; he also opens the way to further discussion of a problem that is central to any psychoanalytic study of works of art: that of the relationship between works and symptoms, between the artist and the neurotic or the psychotic.

Freud left his successors a contribution to this discussion that is already a major problem in its own right: the notion of sublimation. If we discuss this notion in terms of the object or goals of drives it simply represents an enigma, the enigma of culture itself: how can the sexual give rise to painting? What distinguishes an obsessional programme, for example, from the amazing set of ordered constraints that a painter imposes on himself? The differences in the objects and goals of drives are totally insufficient to set apart works of art from the products of neurosis or psychosis, especially if the latter also involve, as Freud showed in his *Metapsychology,* all kinds of inversions, reversals and displacements. Can one imagine that the clinical portrait offered by President Schreber's paranoia would be easier to deduce from the order of libidinal drives than the work of Michelangelo?

Freud, as we know, never fully elaborated the notion of sublimation, but he did leave several valuable suggestions, outlined in terms of an economy rather than in terms of objects, and it is these that Ehrenzweig develops, even if he does not refer to them. In the *Introductory Lectures on Psychoanalysis* (1917)[9] the ability to sublimate is associated with a certain laxness (*Lockerheit*), a laxity in repression that normally ends conflict. This suggests that the economy or system of sublimation is not to be sought in the realm of libidinal investment or concentration: if repression is malleable it is because the counter-investments of repression are relatively minor, and use little energy, because the drives themselves are relatively unconcentrated and erratic. As for escaping neurosis, 'everything depends', Freud writes, 'on the *amount* of unemployed libidinal energy that can be kept in a suspended state [*in Schwebe*].' Confirmation of the importance of this floating reserve comes in the discussion of displacement potential (*Verschiebbarkeit*) in *The Ego and the Id* (1923):[10] economically speaking, sublimation is above all an availability of unbound, displaceable energy. It is uninvested potential. We find no model for this disposition in the clinical description of diseases, and for good reason. At a pinch, perversion might serve, but it would have to be extended to the notion of 'polymorphous perversion', which Freud used in 1905 to describe infant sexuality. Unlike masochism or fetishism, which are later described as blockages that deny certain libidinal givens, polymorphous perversion is not inalterably concentrated on any particular object of satisfaction, but sweeps in a random way over the range of possibilities offered by the body as erotic object. But the fact that sublimation is left outside the realm of clinical description should not serve as pretext for a return of the ego, as ego psychology would have it in this as in other cases. What is the artist? A powerful ego, it replies, who can 'control the primary process', who 'dominates' it, who reverses to the benefit of consciousness the relationship between primary and secondary as it obtains in dream work.[11]

Ehrenzweig takes a very different line; he continues to develop the notion of displacement potential under other names: the artist is rather someone with little ego, with few defences, and with a large available reserve of energy. Such a statement has nothing to do with the psychology of the artist, or even art – unless we give to the term 'psychology' the scope that Nietzsche granted it. It even goes beyond the references to specific investigations that delimit and directly support – perhaps too directly – Ehrenzweig's analysis: references to Kleinian psychoanalysis and especially to this school's theory of objects. We cannot discuss here the specific claims: that in creative work a so-called schizoid phase consists of the fragmentary projection of unbearable material (phantasms, partial threatening objects); that it is followed by a manic phase that scans the projected fragments and unifies them in an unconscious syncretism that is that of uncontrolled and undifferentiated integration; that in a third, depressive phase of secondary elaboration the surface ego, frightened by what it perceives as chaos, attempts to insert or introject the materials into secondary structures so as to make them into a work. Let us simply note two reservations about this theory. This dramatization is predicated upon an opposition between interior and exterior, that is to say, upon the schema of scenic representation. The fundamental operations are called projection and introjection, and the central question is that of constituting an object: good object or bad object? This is, of course, the Kleinian conceptual framework, and if it escapes the platitudes of ego psychoanalysis it is perhaps too ready to accept the theatrical schema; it allows one to assume that any displacement of energy is necessarily destined to organize itself (either actively or passively) round the relation to the object. It thus risks making unintelligible within its own terms the power of displacement and its ability to avoid definitive fixation on or investment in an object. When Ehrenzweig, somewhat the prisoner of his Kleinian schema, attempts to describe the artist's relation to his work as a 'good' object relation, as a dialogue, he shows us, despite himself, how restrictive this clinical mode of analysis can be when we are trying to understand artistic production. For the truth is that for the artist his relation to the work is not dialogue but an encounter, in the sense of *tuchè*, not capitalization but indifference to the object produced. This leads to our second objection, which we shall simply state thus: this conceptual framework centred on the object is inextricably linked with the fastidiously edifying, almost

Hegelian character of this whole dialectic, as is further shown by Ehrenzweig's declaration of allegiance to the most moral of myths: the myth of the dying god, which underlies almost all western thought, religious or not, and which is the foundation on which Hegel constructed his reconciliatory monument.

This, however, is neither Ehrenzweig's particular contribution nor the essence of his position. Rather, following Winnicot and Marion Milner, he emphasizes that the laxity of the artist begins by lowering the barriers that in theory separate exterior from interior reality. This gives prominence to the notion of a single libidinal surface without thickness or limits, which does not exist prior to what might be inscribed there by pen, brush, noise or voice, but is produced by the operations that transform affective intensities into colours, sounds, sentences. The artistic body extends beyond the body of the artist and beyond any body closed in on itself in its supposed three-dimensional identity. Freud said that there is communication within the unconscious or between one unconscious and another. There is nothing paradoxical in this if by communication we mean the transmission of intensities into new intensities, and if we recognize that as it occurs such transmission produces its own medium: the heterogeneous surface that includes skins, organs, streets, walls, canvases, instruments.

As for the question of symptoms, Ehrenzweig goes so far as to propose a major correction of the Kleinian thesis of schizophrenic anxiety. Whereas Melanie Klein and her students attribute it to the oral fear of dependence on the mother's breast, Ehrenzweig replies: on the contrary, think of the psychotic in relation to the artist. It is the absence of the undifferentiated, so powerfully present in the case of the artist; it is the absence of the region of contact, as Bion says, or of the undecidability between the phantasm and the structures of the secondary processes; it is the absence of the region of scanning, which leads the schizophrenic (in the clinical sense, of course) to cling to his surface faculties, to strengthen their resistance against the pressure of unconscious phantasms, and thus to produce his characteristic plastic space.[12] And thus in order to clarify the enigma of sublimation we need not have recourse to the repressions of some super-ego; the 'structural repression' suffices – repression that bears not on the content but on the very organization of material, and of which Freud speaks in a letter to Fleiss. What suffices, in fact, is the shift in our approach to the problem more than the structural repression: the problem of art that is insoluble in terms of a topic is literally dissolved when conceived in terms of an economy.

It is this region of contact, this laxist libidinal space or region of free displacement potential that is always at work in art, or at least in true artistic initiative. For Ehrenzweig art is perhaps always initiative, and this is a complementary shift brought about in the artistic field by his approach. The power of the written, the painted, the played, is proportional to its originality. 'First editions' have an inestimable and incomparable power: after that we have mannerism, formulae. The notion of the 'first time' is not naive, but it is a concept that cannot be thought out or thought through, and it should provoke some hesitation in theoreticians when they encounter it. It is the categorial equivalent of what alone is crucial in the economy of affects: the encounter. The thesis of first editions, first versions, far from being foolish, compels the reader, if he is willing to go as far as it will lead him, to abandon the safe harbour offered to the mind by the category of 'works of art' or of signs in general, and to recognize as truly artistic nothing but *initiatives* or *events*, in whatever domain they may occur. Of course here Ehrenzweig is moving towards Nietzsche, but this destructive, dissolving approach is also that of contemporary artists, for whom, as for Ehrenzweig, there is a necessary affinity between the artistic object, the displacement potential of libidinal energy, the encountering of unexpected forms, and finally the ephemeral and unique character of the emotional power produced by this encounter. Nothing could do more to confirm the economic approach sketched by Ehrenzweig than its convergence and interpenetration with the artistic experience itself: one does not psychoanalyse painters or musicians, or their works; one espouses the metamorphoses, produced in their workrooms, of the libidinal into the pictorial or the musical.

There are other strands to this aesthetic of affirmation: the notion that absence, the lack that Freud noted in the production of jokes and that Ehrenzweig locates in any artistic creation, is 'a full absence'; the idea that the 'white' of abstraction is in fact composed, in art as well as in science, of a rich chromatism of undifferentiated images; the notion, related to Klee's and Boulez's work (and sufficient to repel any accusation of romanticizing the primary process), that one must deploy the most subtle and sophisticated conceptual apparatus in order to release the potential intensities that sound and colour conceal, and that have been censored by the tradition of focused and analytical thought. On every page of Ehrenzweig's work one senses the steadiness of his approach to the problem of the unconscious, the wealth and delicacy of his psychoanalytic documentation, and the breadth of his experience of art.

Finally, we should discuss the philosophy of art history, to which, as in his earlier book, Ehrenzweig grants a crucial role. We can only mention it, although one ought to compare carefully the schema of the final chapters in *The Psychoanalysis of Artistic Vision and Hearing*, which make contemporary art the final stage in a growing libidinal withdrawal, with the hypothesis, offered in *The Hidden Order of Art*, of periodic alternation between the poles of realism and abstraction. Suffice it to indicate here the two directions in which we think Ehrenzweig's historical remarks ought to be pursued. First, there is the importance of abandoning notions of continuity, of sequential linkage, of influences, not only between one culture, school or artist and another, but between artistic institutions and their social contexts. Ehrenzweig says somewhere that the idea of causality is nothing but the echo in consciousness of the pathos of guilt. If it is true that art is an initiating event, then a 'history' freed of guilt would be a surface like that of the Egypt of distractions such as Freud imagined it,[13] where all forms would be simultaneously present to one another, or even within one another, and where, consequently, at any 'period' as determined by secondary chronology there could be found a large number of completely different, 'anachronistic' and incompatible musical or pictorial objects, and transformational linkages running in all directions. The history of art would be a historical or historiated surface, itself scanned, undifferentiated, syncretic at every point. A (non-hidden) order would be introduced only by the blocking and channelling devices that at one point assure the predominance of the water-colour scene with its transparent perspective, at another exclude any distortion of a visual scene, or at yet another, impose the chromatic scale and equal temperament on any object that seeks to enter the domain of music, and so on. Moreover, at any period there is available a wide array of such devices; and there can be no question of attempting, through some sort of 'explanation', to reduce the arbitrariness of this array, for that arbitrariness is the counterpart of, or perhaps only another word for, artistic initiative.

The other line of investigation, closely tied to this, would be to take seriously what Ehrenzweig asserts more firmly here than previously: that *all art is flat*, as it were, pellicular, like a film. Each initiative, each event consists of extending the boundaries that circumscribe the play of metamorphosis, of placing over emptiness a bit of libidinal space that can become a new extension of the single-surfaced tape or film. An economy of aesthetics must describe every form in terms of its contribution to the patchwork of this tape, to the space of scanning. This contribution is not important as disruption, nor even as criticism – both of which are secondary effects – but as peculiarity, as non-reducible difference. If disruption and criticism were to be related to conscious or pre-conscious processes and thus to repressive functions themselves, it would be because they involve the simultaneous grasp of the old and the new, of the criticized and the critique, which is to say a synthesis following an analysis, a conjunction of what is disjoined. And thus the space in which criticism and disruption take place would still be the theatrical space, but in fact the artistic never moves in this space. Let us take the least favourable case:[14] the producer or director, like the perspectivist of the *Quattrocento* or of the seventeenth century in France, is not, as one might suppose, the inventor of depths, an illusionist, but a projective geometrician, a mind convinced that if one can create the three-dimensional on a canvas it is because the world is flat, because there exists only the infinite set of transformations, of which art or science is one. The three-dimensional space of the theatrical (and of criticism, and of deconstruction and of 'knowledge') is itself also, therefore, one of the adventures that befalls the libidinal skin.

NOTES

1 In a translation by Francine Lacoue-Labarthe and Claire Nancy that is all the more remarkable in that Ehrenzweig's language is difficult in itself and he died before he could complete the revision of the text.
2 Ehrenzweig, *The Psychoanalysis of Artistic Vision and Hearing* (London: Sheldon Press, 1975).
3 *Beyond the Pleasure Principle, The Standard Edition of the Complete Psychological Works of Sigmund Freud*, ed. James Strachey et al. (London: Hogarth Press, 1953–74), XVIII, end of §11 (henceforth *SE*).
4 *New Introductory Lectures in Psychoanalysis*, *SE* XX.
5 *From the History of an Infantile Neurosis* (Wolf-Man), *SE* XVII.
6 *Instincts and their Vicissitudes*, *SE* XIV.
7 *Civilisation and its Discontents*, *SE* XXI.
8 For example: 'There are negative characteristics [the atemporality of primary processes] which can only be made meaningful by comparison with unconscious mental processes' (*Beyond the Pleasure Principle*); or: 'The little we know [of the Id] has, moreover, a negative character and can only be described in context with the Ego' (*New Introductory Lectures*).
9 *New Introductory Lectures*, *SE* XVI.
10 *The Ego and the Id, SE* XVI.

168 *Beyond representation*

11 E Kris, *Psychoanalytic Explorations in Art* (New York: Schocken, 1967), p. 25; cf. p. 302.
12 So it is claimed. Unlike Ehrenzweig, we have some doubts on the matter. See M. Thévoz's study, *Louis Soutter* (Lausanne and Zurich, 1974).
13 G. Lascault, 'L'Egypte des égarements', *Critique,* 260 (January 1960).
14 Ehrenzweig, *Hidden Order.*

Translated by Jonathan Culler

8

Acinema

The nihilism of convened, conventional movements

Cinematography is the inscription of movement, a writing with movement, a writing with movements – all kinds of movements: for example, in the film shot, those of the actors and other moving objects, those of lights, colours, frame and lens; in the film sequence, all of these again plus the cuts and splices of editing; for the film as a whole, those of the final script and the spatio-temporal synthesis of the narration (*découpage*). And over or through all these movements are those of the sound and words coming together with them.

Thus there is a crowd (nonetheless a countable crowd) of elements in motion, a throng of possible moving bodies which are candidates for inscription on film. Learning the techniques of film-making involves knowing how to eliminate a large number of these possible movements. It seems that image, sequence and film must be constituted at the price of these exclusions.

Here arise two questions that are really quite naive considering the deliberations of contemporary cine-critics: *which* movements and moving bodies are these? Why is it necessary to select, sort out and exclude them?

If no movements are picked out we will accept what is fortuitous, dirty, confused, unsteady, unclear, poorly framed, overexposed . . . For example, suppose you are working on a shot in video, a shot, say, of a gorgeous head of hair à la Renoir; upon viewing it you find that something has come undone: all of a sudden, swamps, outlines of incongruous islands and cliff edges appear, lurching forth before your startled eyes. A scene from elsewhere, representing nothing identifiable, has been added, a scene not related to the logic of your shot, an undecidable scene, worthless even as an insertion because it will not be repeated and taken up again later. So you cut it out.

We are not demanding a raw cinema, like Dubuffet demanded an *art brut*. We are hardly about to form a club dedicated to the saving of rushes and the rehabilitation of clipped footage. And yet . . . We observe that if the mistake is eliminated it is because of its incongruity, and in order to protect the order of the whole (shot and/or sequence and/or film) while banning the intensity it carries. And the order of the whole has its sole object in the functioning of the cinema: that there be order in the movements, that the movements be made in order, that they make order. Writing with movements – cinematography – is thus conceived and practised as an incessant organizing of movements following the rules of representation for spatial localization, those of narration for the instantiation of language, and those of the form 'film music' for the soundtrack. The so-called impression of reality is a real oppression of orders.

This oppression consists of the enforcement of a nihilism of movements. No movement, arising from any field, is given to the eye-ear of the spectator for what it is: a simple *sterile difference* in an audio-visual field. Instead, every movement put forward *sends back* to something else, is inscribed as a plus or minus on the ledger book which is the film, *is valuable* because it *returns* to something else, because it is thus potential return and profit. The only genuine movement with which the cinema is written is that of value. The law of value (in so-called 'political' economy) states that the *object*, in this case the movement, is valuable only insofar as it is exchangeable against other objects and in terms of equal quantities of a definable unity (for example, in quantities of money). Therefore, to be valuable the object must move: proceed from other objects ('production' in the narrow sense) and disappear, but on the condition that its disappearance *makes room for still other objects* (consumption). Such a process is not sterile, but productive; it is production in the widest sense.

Pyrotechnics

Let us be certain to distinguish this process from sterile motion. A match once struck is consumed. If you use the match to light the gas that heats the water for the coffee which keeps you alert on your way to work, the consumption is not sterile, for it is a movement belonging to the circuit of capital: merchandise-match $\rightarrow$ merchandise-labour power $\rightarrow$ money-wages $\rightarrow$ merchandise-match. But when a child strikes the match-head *to see* what happens – just for the fun of it – he enjoys the movement itself, the changing colours, the light flashing at the height of the blaze, the death of the tiny piece of wood, the hissing of the tiny flame. He enjoys these sterile differences leading nowhere, these uncompensated losses; what the physicist calls the dissipation of energy.

Intense enjoyment and sexual pleasure (*la jouissance*), insofar as they give rise to perversion and not solely to propagation, are distinguished by this sterility. At the end of *Beyond the Pleasure Principle* Freud cites them as an example of the combination of the life and death instincts. But he is thinking of pleasure obtained through the channels of 'normal' genital sexuality: all *jouissance*, including that giving rise to a hysterical attack or contrariwise, to a perverse scenario, contains the lethal component, but normal pleasure hides it in a movement of return, genital sexuality. Normal genital sexuality leads to childbirth, and the child is the *return* of, or on, its movement. But the motion of pleasure as such, split from the motion of the propagation of the species, would be (whether genital or sexual or neither) that motion which in going beyond the point of no return spills the libidinal forces outside the whole, at the expense of the whole (at the price of the ruin and disintegration of this whole).

In lighting the match the child enjoys this diversion (*détournement*, a word dear to Klossowski) that misspends energy. He produces, in his own movement, a simulacrum of pleasure in its so-called 'death-instinct' component. Thus if he is assuredly an artist by producing a simulacrum, he is one most of all because this simulacrum is not an object of worth valued for another object. It is not composed with these other objects, compensated for by them, enclosed in a whole ordered by constitutive laws (in a structured group, for example). On the contrary, it is essential that the entire erotic force invested in the simulacrum be promoted, raised, displayed and burned in vain. It is thus that Adorno said the only truly great art is the making of fireworks: pyrotechnics would simulate perfectly the sterile consumption of energies in *jouissance*. Joyce grants this privileged position to fireworks in the beach sequence in *Ulysses*. A simulacrum, understood in the sense Klossowski gives it, should not be conceived primarily as belonging to the category of representation, like the representations which imitate pleasure; rather, it is to be conceived as a kinetic problematic, as the paradoxical product of the disorder of the drives, as a composite of decompositions.

The discussion of cinema and representational–narrative art in general begins at this point. Two directions are open to the conception (and production) of an object, and in particular, a cinematographic object, conforming to the pyrotechnical imperative. These two seemingly contradictory currents appear to be those attracting whatever is intense in painting today. It is possible that they are also at work in the truly active forms of experimental and underground cinema.

These two poles are immobility and excessive movement. In letting itself be drawn towards these antipodes the cinema insensibly ceases to be an ordering force; it produces true, that is, vain, simulacrums, blissful intensities, instead of productive/consumable objects.

The movement of return

Let us back up a bit. What do these movements of return or returned movements have to do with the representational and narrative form of the commercial cinema? We emphasize just how wretched it is to answer this question in terms of a simple superstructural function of an industry, the cinema, the products of which, films, would lull the public consciousness by means of doses of ideology. If film direction is a directing and ordering of movements it is not so by being propaganda (benefiting the bourgeoisie some would say, and the bureaucracy, others would add), but by being a propagation. Just as the libido must renounce its perverse overflow to propagate the species through a normal genital sexuality allowing the constitution of a 'sexual body' having that sole end, so the film produced by an artist working in capitalist industry (and all known industry is now capitalist) springs from the effort to eliminate aberrant movements, useless expenditures, differences of pure consumption. This film is composed like a unified and propagating body, a fecund and assembled whole transmitting instead of losing what it carries. The diegesis locks together the synthesis of movements in the temporal order; perspectivist representation does so in the spatial order.

Now, what are these syntheses but the arranging of the cinematographic material following the figure of *return*? We are not only speaking of the requirement of profitability imposed upon the artist by the producer, but also of the formal requirements that the artist weighs upon his material. All so-called good form implies the return of sameness, the folding back of diversity upon an identical unity. In painting this may be a plastic rhyme or an equilibrium of colours; in music, the resolution of dissonance by the dominant chord; in architecture, a proportion. Repetition, the principle of not only the metric but even of the rhythmic, if taken in the narrow sense as the repetition of the same (same colour, line, angle, chord), is the work of Eros and Apollo disciplining the movements, limiting them to the norms of tolerance characteristic of the system or whole in consideration.

It was an error to accredit Freud with the discovery of the very motion of the drives. Because Freud, in *Beyond the Pleasure Principle* takes great care to dissociate the repetition of the same, which signals the regime of the life instincts, from the repetition of the other, which can only be other to the first-named repetition. These death drives are just outside the regime delimited by the body or whole considered, and therefore it is impossible to discern *what* is returning, when returning with these drives is the intensity of extreme *jouissance* and danger that they carry. To the point that it must be asked if indeed any repetition is involved at all, if on the contrary something different returns at each instance, if the *eternal return* of these sterile explosions of libidinal discharge should not be conceived in a wholly different time-space than that of the repetition of the same, as their impossible copresence. Assuredly we find here the insufficience of *thought*, which must necessarily pass through that sameness which is the concept.

Cinematic movements generally follow the figure of return, that is, of the repetition and propagation of sameness. The scenario or plot, an intrigue and its solution, achieves the same resolution of dissonance as the sonata form in music; its movement of return organizes the affective charges linked to the filmic 'signifieds', both connotative and denotative, as Metz would say. In this regard all endings are happy endings, just by being endings, for even if a film finishes with a murder, this too can serve as a final resolution of dissonance. The affective charges carried by every type of cinematographic and filmic 'signifier' (lens, framing, cuts, lighting, shooting, etc.) are submitted to the same law of a return of the same after a semblance of difference; a difference that is nothing, in fact, but a detour.

The instance of identification

This rule, where it applies, operates principally, we have said, in the form of exclusions and effacements. The exclusion of certain movements is such that the professional filmmakers are not even aware of them; effacements, on the other hand, cannot fail to be noticed by them because a large part of their activity consists of them. Now these effacements and exclusions form the very operation of film directing. In eliminating, before and/or after the shooting, any extreme glare, for example, the director and cameraman condemn the image of film to the sacred task of making itself recognizable to the eye. The image must cast the object or set of objects as the double of a situation that from then on will be supposed real. The image is representational because recognizable, because it addresses itself to the eye's *memory*, to fixed references or identification, references known, but in the sense of 'well-known', that is, familiar and established. These references are identity measuring the returning and return of movements. They form the instance or group of instances connecting and making them take the form of cycles. Thus all sorts of gaps, jolts, postponements, losses and confusions can occur, but they no longer act as real diversions or wasteful drifts; when the final count is made they turn out to be nothing but beneficial detours. It is precisely through the return to the ends of identification that cinematographic form, understood as the synthesis of good movement, is articulated following the cyclical organization of capital.

One example chosen from among thousands: in *Joe* (a film built entirely upon the impression of reality) the movement is drastically altered twice: the first time when the father beats to death the hippie who lives with his daughter; the second, when 'mopping up' a hippie commune he unwittingly guns down his own daughter. This last sequence ends with a freeze-frame shot of the bust and face of the daughter who is struck down in full movement. In the first murder we see a hail of fists falling upon the face of the defenceless hippie who quickly loses consciousness. These two effects, the one an immobilization, the other an excess of mobility, are obtained by waiving the rules of representation which demand real motion recorded and projected at 24 frames per second. As a result we could expect a strong affective charge to accompany them, since this greater or lesser perversion of the realistic rhythm responds to the organic rhythm of the intense emotions evoked. And it is indeed produced, but to the benefit, nevertheless, of the filmic totality, and thus, all told, to the benefit of order; both arrhythmies are produced not in some aberrant fashion but at the culminating points in the tragedy of the impossible father/ daughter incest underlying the scenario. So while they may upset representational order, clouding for a few seconds the celluloid's necessary transparency (which is that order's condition), these two affective charges do not fail to suit the narrative order. On the contrary, they mark it with a beautiful melodic curve, the first accelerated murder finding its resolution in the second immobilized murder.

Thus the memory to which films address themselves is *nothing* in itself, just as capital is nothing but an instance of capitalization; it is an instance, a set of empty instances which in no way operate through their content; *good* form, *good* lighting, *good* editing, *good* sound mixing are not good because they conform to perceptual or social reality, but because they are a priori scenographic *operators* which on the contrary determine the objects to be recorded on the screen and in 'reality'.

Directing: putting in, and out of, scene

Film direction is not an artistic activity; it is a general process touching all fields of activity, a profoundly unconscious process of separation, exclusion and effacement. In other words, direction is simultaneously executed on two planes, with this being its most enigmatic aspect. On the one hand, this task consists of separating reality on one side and a play space on the other (a 'real' or an 'unreal' – that which is in the camera's lens): to direct is to institute this limit, this frame, to circumscribe the region of de-responsibility at the heart of a whole which *ideo facto* is posed as responsible (we will call it *nature*, for example, or *society* or *final instance*). Thus is established between the two regions a relation of representation or doubling accompanied necessarily by a relative devaluation of the scene's realities, now only representative of the realities of reality. But on the other hand, and inseparably, in order for the function of representation to be fulfilled, the activity of directing (a placing in and out of scene, as we have just said) must also be an activity which unifies all the movements, those on *both sides* of the frame's limit, imposing here *and* there, in 'reality' just as in the real (*reel*), the *same norms*, the same ordering of all drives, excluding obliterating, effacing them *no less off* the scene than on. The references imposed on the filmic object are imposed just as necessarily on all objects outside the film. Direction first divides – along the axis of representation – and due to the theatrical limit – a reality and its double, and this disjunction constitutes an obvious repression. But also, beyond this representational disjunction and in a 'pre-theatrical' economic order, it eliminates *all impulsional movement, real or unreal, which will not lend itself to reduplication,* all movement which would escape identification, recognition and the mnesic fixation. Considered from the angle of this primordial function of an exclusion spreading to the exterior as well as to the interior of the cinematographic playground, film direction acts always as a factor of *libidinal normalization,* and does so independently of all 'content' be it as 'violent' as might seem. This normalization consists of the exclusion from the scene of whatever cannot be folded back upon the body of the film, and outside the scene, upon the social body.

The *film*, strange formation reputed to be normal, is no more normal than the *society* or the *organism*. All of these so-called objects are the result of the imposition and hope for an accomplished totality. They are supposed to realize the reasonable goal *par excellence*, the subordination of all partial drives, all sterile and divergent movements to the unity of an organic body. The film is the organic body of cinematographic movements. It is the *ecclesia* of images: just as politics is that of the partial social organs. This is why direction, a technique of exclusions and effacements, a political activity *par excellence*, and political activity, which is direction *par excellence*, are the religion of the modern irreligion, the ecclesiastic of the secular. The central problem for both is not the representational arrangement and its accompanying question, that of knowing how and what to represent and the definition of good or true representation; the fundamental problem is the exclusion and foreclosure of all that is judged unrepresentable because non-recurrent.

Thus film acts as the orthopedic mirror analysed by Lacan in 1949 as constitutive of the imaginary subject of *object a;* that we are dealing with the social body in no way alters its function. But the real problem, missed by Lacan due to his Hegelianism, is to know why the drives spread about the polymorphous body *must have* an object where they can unite. That the imperative of unification is given as hypothesis in a philosophy of 'consciousness' is betrayed by the very term 'consciousness', but for a 'thought' of the unconscious (of which the form related most to pyrotechnics would be the economy sketched here and there in Freud's writings), the question of the production of unity, even an imaginary unity, can no longer fail to be posed in all its opacity. We will no longer have to pretend to understand how the subject's unity is constituted from his image in the mirror. We will have to ask ourselves how and why the *specular wall* in general, and thus the cinema screen in particular, can become a privileged place for the libidinal cathexis; why and how the drives come to take their place on the film (*pellicule*, or *petite peau*), opposing it to themselves as the place of their inscription, and what is more, as the support that the filmic operation in all its aspects will efface. A libidinal economy of the cinema should theoretically construct the operators which exclude aberrations from the social and organic bodies and channel the drives into this apparatus. It is not clear that narcissism or masochism are the proper operators: they carry a tone of subjectivity (of the theory of Self) that is probably still much too strong.

The tableau vivant

The acinema, we have said, would be situated at the two poles of the cinema taken as a writing of movements: thus, extreme immobilization and extreme mobilization. It is only for *thought* that these two modes are incompatible. In a libidinal economy they are, on the contrary, necessarily associated; stupefaction, terror, anger, hate, pleasure – all the intensities – are always displacements in place. We should read the term *emotion* as a *motion* moving towards its own exhaustion, an immobilizing motion, an immobilized mobilization. The representational arts offer two symmetrical examples of these intensities, one where immobility appears: the tableau vivant; another where agitation appears: lyric abstraction.

Presently there exists in Sweden an institution called the *posering*, a name derived from the *pose* solicited by portrait photographers: young girls rent their services to these special houses, services which consist of assuming, clothed or unclothed, the poses desired by the client. It is against the rules of these houses (which are not houses of prostitution) for the clients to touch the models in any way. We would say that this institution is made to order for the phantasmatic of Klossowski, knowing as we do the importance he accords to the tableau vivant as the near perfect simulacrum of fantasy in all its paradoxical intensity. But it must be seen how the paradox is distributed in this case: the immobilization seems to touch only the erotic object while the subject is found overtaken by the liveliest agitation.

But things are probably not as simple as they might seem. Rather, we must understand this arrangement as a demarcation on both sides, that of model and client, of the regions of extreme erotic intensification, a demarcation performed by one of them, the client whose integrity reputedly remains intact. We see the proximity such a formulation has to the Sadean problematic of *jouissance*. We must note, given what concerns us here, that the tableau vivant in general, if it holds a certain libidinal potential, does so because it brings the theatrical and economic orders into communication; because it uses 'whole persons' as detached erotic regions to which the spectator's impulses are connected. (We must be suspicious of summing this up too quickly as a simple voyeurism.) We must sense the price, beyond price, as Klossowski admirably explains, that the organic body, the pretended unity of the pretended subject, must pay so that the pleasure will burst forth in its irreversible sterility. This is the same price that the cinema should pay if it goes to the first of its extremes, immobilization: because this latter (which is not simple immobility) means that it would be necessary to endlessly undo the conventional syntheses that normally all cinematographic movements proliferate. Instead of good, unifying and reasonable forms proposed for identification, the image would give rise to the most intense agitation through its fascinating paralysis. We could already find many underground and experimental films illustrating this direction of immobilization. Here we should begin the discussion of a matter of singular importance: if you read Sade or Klossowski, the paradox of immobilization is seen to be clearly distributed along the representational axis. The object, the victim, the prostitute, takes the pose, offering his or her self as a detached region, but *at the same time giving way and humiliating this whole person*. The allusion to this latter is an indispensable factor in the intensification since it indicates the inestimable price of diverting the drives in order to achieve perverse pleasure. Thus representation is essential to this fantasmatic; that is, it is essential that the spectator be offered instances of identification, recognizable forms, all in all, matter for the memory: for it is at the price, we repeat, of going beyond this and disfiguring the order of propagation that the intense emotion is felt. It follows that the simulacrum's support, be it in the writer's descriptive syntax, the film of Pierre Zucca whose photographs illustrate (?) Klossowski's *La Monnaie Vivante*, the paper on which Klossowski himself sketches – it follows that the support itself must not submit to any noticeable perversion in order that the perversion attack only what is supported, the representation of the victim: the support is held in insensibility or unconsciousness. From here springs Klossowski's active militancy in favour of representational plastics and his anathema for abstract painting.

Abstraction

But what occurs if, on the contrary, it is the support itself that is touched by perverse hands? Then the film, movements, lightings, and focus refuse to produce the recognizable image of a victim or immobile model, taking on themselves the price of agitation and libidinal expense and leaving it no longer to the fantasized body. All lyric abstraction in painting maintains such a shift. It implies a polarization no longer towards the immobility of the model but towards the mobility of the support. This mobility is quite the contrary of cinematographic movement; it arises from any process which undoes the beautiful forms suggested by this latter, from any process which to a greater or lesser degree works on and distorts these forms. It blocks the synthesis of identification and thwarts the mnesic instances. It can thus go far towards achieving an *ataxy* of the iconic constituents, but this is still to be understood as a mobilization of the support. This way of frustrating the beautiful movement *by means of the support* must not be confused with that working through a paralysing attack on the victim who serves as motif. The model is no longer needed, for the relation to the body of the client-spectator is completely displaced.

How is *jouissance* instantiated by a large canvas by Pollock or Rothko or by a study by Richter, Baruchello or Eggeling? If there is no longer a reference to the loss of the unified body due to the model's immobilization and its diversion to the ends of partial discharge, just how inestimable must be the disposition the client-spectator can have; the represented ceases to be the libidinal object while the screen itself, in all its most formal aspects, takes its place. The film strip is no longer abolished (made transparent) for the benefit of this or that flesh, for it offers itself as the flesh posing itself. But from what unified body is it torn so that the spectator may enjoy, so that it seems to him to be beyond all price? Before the minute thrills which hem the contact regions adjoining the chromatic sands of a Rothko canvas, or before the almost imperceptible movements of the little objects or organs of Pol Bury, it is at the price of renouncing his own bodily totality and the synthesis of movements making it exist that the spectator experiences intense pleasure: these objects demand the paralysis not of the object-model but of the 'subject'-client, the decomposition of his own organism. The channels of passage and libidinal discharge are restricted to very small partial regions (eye-cortex), and almost the whole body is neutralized in a tension blocking all escape of drives from passages other than those necessary to the detection of very fine differences. It is the same, although following other modalities, with the effects of the excess of movement in Pollock's paintings or with Thompson's manipulation of the lens. Abstract cinema, like abstract painting, in rendering the support opaque reverses the arrangement, making the client a victim. It is the same again though differently in the almost imperceptible movements of the No Theatre.

The question, which must be recognized as being crucial to our time because it is that of the staging of scene and society, follows: is it necessary for the victim to be in the scene for the pleasure to be intense? If the victim is the client, if in the scene is only film screen, canvas, the support, do we lose to this arrangement all the intensity of the sterile discharge? And if so, must we then renounce the hope of finishing with the illusion, not only the cinematographic illusion but also the social and political illusions? Are they not really illusions then? Or is believing so the illusion? Must the return of extreme intensities be founded on at least this empty permanence, on the phantom of the organic body or subject which is the proper noun, and at the same time that they cannot really accomplish this unity? This foundation, this love, how does it differ from that anchorage in nothing which founds capital?

NOTE

These reflections would not have been possible without the practical and theoretical work accomplished for several years by and with Dominique Avron, Claudine Eizykman and Guy Fihman.

Translated by Paisley N. Livingston

9

Philosophy and Painting in the Age of Their Experimentation: Contribution to an Idea of Postmodernity

I imagine you are asking for my system on the arts today, and how it compares with those of my colleagues. I quake, feeling that I've been caught, since I don't have anything worthy of being called a system, and I know only a little about two or three of them, just enough to know they hardly constitute a system: the Freudian reading of the arts, the Marxist reading, and the semiotic reading. Perhaps what we should do is change the idea that has been dressed up with the name 'system'.

By wanting something systematic we believe we are real contemporaries of the 'system theory' age and the age of the virtue of performativity. Do you have something to say about the arts? Let's look at how you say it, at the set of language-based operators you use to work on your material, the works of art. And let's look at your results. That's the system being asked for: the set of word tools that are applied to given aspects of music, painting, film, words, and other things, and that produce a work of words – commentary. The time is past when we can plant ourselves in front of a Vernet and sigh along with Diderot, 'How beautiful, grand, varied, noble, wise, harmonious, rigorously coloured this is!'[1] Don't think we don't regret it. We are philosophers though, and it's not for us to lay down how you should understand what artists do. Recently in France, philosophers have made enough of an incursion into art to prove pretty irritating to critics, gallery directors, curators, and occasionally artists;[2] so it is futile now for us and those like us to flaunt pretended innocence in front of works of art. If something systematic is what is wanted, doesn't the fault lie with those philosophers who, by getting involved in commentary on art, transformed it into something of a theoretical treatise and dared the specialists to do the same?

This is only an illusion though. If you look just a little closer you will see that when the philosophers you have in mind decided to talk about the arts, it was not in order to explain works or interpret them. They wanted even less to make them fit into a system or build a system based on them. What then was their purpose? I'm not quite sure, and this is what we must try to grasp. But in any case these philosophers have had almost no part in the request for a system, except inadvertently. More often than not, they have purposely thwarted it as best they could. The request emanates instead from a new stratum: the managerial staff of the art professions, the reading engineers, the maintenance crews for the big explanatory machines patented under the name of Ideology, Fantasy, Structure. The less unscrupulous of these specialists have stopped at what offers resistance in the work, seems to be badly coded, badly ciphered, in a word, really deceptive because it cannot be converted easily into system words. To explain the works' elusiveness, these specialists have worked out a system for the necessity of these asystematic zones. Homage is paid indirectly, by using terms like the symbolic, the Other, the text.

This is the way philosophers enter the stage of 'criticism', by way of this gap through which the work escapes being converted into meaning. The work is evasive? That's what they like. Isn't the commentary machine working very well? Does a given work make it malfunction? This is a good sign, indicating that the work cannot be transformed wholesale into signification, that its destination is uncertain and its relevance with respect to certain systematic features is undecidable.

But doesn't this quite simply amount to re-establishing the ineffable in aesthetics? 'How beautiful, grand, etc.'? Now, we should know that the exclamatory and the vocative are outmoded games or figures, that the genres in which they were accepted are completely out-of-date today, namely the ode, dithyramb, entreaty, and address; we should know that the progress of 'philosophy' according to Diderot,[3] of history according to Nietzsche,[4] and of industrial society according to Benjamin,[5] stifles style's verve, exhausts artists' energy, and tarnishes the works' aura. And we should know that we're supposed to mourn this loss. We no longer converse with works of art, says Benjamin, or at least they no longer return our gaze when we look at them,[6] which shows just how deep-seated the crisis of perception is. You may think this crisis is over, but hasn't it got even worse? Forty years after Benjamin's diagnosis, isn't there a crisis of communication in which today's works are relegated to the limits of not only the visible but also the intelligible? Wasn't this turn for the worse really the cause for the request for a system, the request being quite simply to understand apparently senseless works?

Things could be put this way. But let's go back a bit to Diderot's vocative. When he exclaims, 'O nature, how great you are! O nature, how imposing, majestic, and beautiful you are!',[7] he is actually speaking to nature, he believes himself able to speak to it. Is he crazy? Is this the eloquence that Bataille referred to when he said that eloquence ended with Manet?[8] Does Diderot believe that nature is a person endowed with language, a goddess? And is this where we differ from him, in the fact that for us, spectacles of nature and of the arts are objects to be made into systems, and for him they are to be adored?

We should pay attention to Diderot's style. In the same 1767 *Salon*, while discussing Vernet's painting, he describes Vernet's landscapes without any warning as natural sites he is passing through in the company of a tutor-abbot, his two young pupils, and two servants carrying picnic baskets; he also relates to Grimm the conversations he had with this abbot and with himself concerning nature, the sublime, art, worldliness and politics, all the while scaling these pretend mountains and setting out on these lakes painted with oils. What is Diderot doing with this contrivance, which prefigures the manner of *Jacques the Fatalist*? He leads one to confuse, or rather to make permutable, reality and fiction, history and narrative, as they used to say, diegesis and metadiegesis as Gérard Genette calls it.[9] In other words he leads one to treat the interlocutor we are told about (the abbot) the same way as the interlocutor to whom 'Diderot' speaks (Grimm, the reader); he leads one to situate in the same realm, both the story's hero, the actor of assumed reality, the object of narration (*he*, the abbot) and this narrative's addressee, the spectator of this reality, the listener of this story (*you*, reader). The two scenes, the one involving Vernet's painting, where the dialogue with the abbot occurs, and the one involving Diderot's text, where the philosopher's address to his reader occurs (and perhaps where the present commentary is taking place), are thus placed on a par. They are not mixed together, but they are also not hierarchized, neither of them entitled to be called exclusively real or exclusively fictional.

Under such conditions even the *I* is subject to the principle of permutability. By staging himself in his own name during these conversations with the abbot which pepper their meandering strolls through Vernet's landscapes, Diderot, too, ends up on the side of third persons and nature.

Another consequence of this style is that you and I, Diderot's readers, can also be counted among his characters. According to the reciprocity of the principle whereby his hero, the abbot of the 1767 *Salon*, becomes his interlocutor, he has only to speak to us and thereby make us his addressees for it to become reasonable, due to this mechanism, to assume that we can just as well be counted among his heroes.

This same principle is applied, even though the effect seems extremely paradoxical, when the philosopher, having described a corner of a Vernet painting as if it were a real landscape, turns with amazement to the painter and urges him to begin drawing. 'Vernet, my friend, take up your pencils and enrich your portfolio as quickly as you can with this group of women.'[10]

There is no eloquence in this style. Eloquence is the rhetoric of the irreversible. It is not *I* speaking, but rather what *I* speak about that speaks through me. This rhetoric is based also on a movement of substitution: the referent of my discourse is, in a way, the latter's addressor. 'Nature' is speaking, if you wish. Fine, but this style can go no further. It must not be implied that the inverse is possible, that I and also *you*, the addressee, can occupy the place of referent; there must be no suggestion that instead of being destined exclusively to speaking and listening to the evanescent meaning of being, our phrases might be the referent of other phrases, our works the referent of other works, our names the referent of other names, and that we might be written just as much as we are writers. Eloquence is a manner of speaking or writing that suggests the permutation's irreversibility: it, the divine, speaks in me, never do I speak in it. The univocal movement in which the referent is called to occupy the place of the addressor seems inevitable, if what is at stake is speaking truthfully. This seems to be the only way to attest to the faithfulness of what is said to what is.

If, like Diderot, you accept the reversal, if you show that what is can present itself 'in person' only because it is presented in this mode or according to this voice, as the referent of another 'poem' which also has its addressor and addressee, if you show that these interlocutors in turn are never original but are instead themselves the possible characters of one or more games that are played out on other stages and related by and to other interlocutors, and, finally, if you state that nothing is off-stage or that what is off-stage is a component of the stage, and that no eye can know all theatres at once, then in your rhetoric the words occupying the various instances will have to be able to switch among these instances. Thus the addressee of your work will be led to call *being* or *nature* not this instance that is assumed to speak through your work, but the very circle of metamorphoses your work displays and of which it is an episode.

Diderot's manner is made up of these movements of permutation. What is spoken about can indeed begin to speak and address itself to whomever is speaking. There can be no eloquence in this, and the effect is always, as Schlegel wrote regarding Diderot's style, one of 'impudence' and an 'incomparable impertinence'.[11] Why? Because the referent has no monopoly on the *I*, or, inversely, because what speaks has no privilege to speak the being of the referent. The *I* position is occupied by a succession of proper nouns, as is the case with two other instances, that of the referent and the addressee. Allow me to call this metamorphic manner *satire*.[12]

What is really important is not even the impertinence Schlegel mentions. 'More than once,' he writes, '[Diderot] surprised nature in a charming state of undress, sometimes he also saw her relieve herself.'[13] Whether or not in satire nature shows her rear is not the most interesting thing for the philosopher, rightly or wrongly. What is interesting is first of all that nature shows something and hence that it addresses itself to us, and second that nature shows us not one, but many things. And so it is very hard for us to know what it wants to signify to us; it is as if nature were unaware of us. Nature never says to the artist, 'that's the way to show it,' or to the critic, 'that's the right commentary,' or to the philosopher, 'you've got it, speak for me.'

Nature is a 'site' machine, to use Diderot's term; we would call it a 'situation' machine, just as Horace Vernet or a *Salon* exhibition is a picture machine. Unlike the systematic or scientific thinker, the philosopher is interested in this machine not because its products repeat themselves as equivalencies (multiple copies), but because they repeat themselves as events (singularities, originals). Nature is judged to be artistic when it is not induced by laziness to produce regularities, when the series of its 'tableaux' does not form continuous calculable curves that can be ascribed to divine providence, to divine proportion, to the universality of structure and taste, that authorize us to 'read' its works. In satire there is greater artfulness if the theatres aren't alike, if in passing from one to another the 'author' is not constricted by the necessity of a unity that lies in wait for him like his sepulchre, so that instead of conquering his identity through working, he dissipates it. Rather than foster in the addressee a lamentable turning back to self or in the commentator the morbid jubilation of having proved with examples that his system 'works' in every case, he instead breaks his discourse, and those to whom it is directed, into the discipline of incommensurables, which is the discipline of the infinite.

Are we to take this nice speech to mean that this is the present situation of the arts and commentary on them, that nothing has changed since Diderot? Do you think that the pages of Diderot's *Essay on Painting* devoted to divinities made flesh and flesh made divinities – I can't quote them, just go read them, you know: 'The poet consecrated Thetis's two beautiful feet, and these feet were true to life, Venus's ravishing bosom, and this bosom was true to life, etc.'; you know the passage that ends with, 'In the tribute of admiration that they [the Ancients] paid to beauty, there was some strange mixture of dissoluteness and devotion'[14] – well, do you think this praise of paganism, this indulgence for an art that 'had an effect on nature itself' and could be said to turn reality into theatre, can still be applied at the present time? Isn't it to be feared that nothing could be less present-day than this paganism, in this the age of systems, telecommunications, and profitability matrixes?

As you know, one can debate a lot about what is contemporary and what is not. As far as I'm concerned paganism can be extended to include even time: there is no one single time; a society (or a soul) is not synchronous with itself, nor is a sector of society, or an institution like art, or even (if this still has any reality today) a segment of the institution like sculpture or film. There are only parachronisms all around; it is the observer's timepiece that judges what is present-day, just as in the universe, except that one wonders what in human history, and especially in the history of the arts, functions as the speed of light.

One must account for the fact that certain descriptions from the 1767 *Salon,* despite the genre's obsolescence, are more current than certain axioms from Kandinsky's *Point, Line, Plane,* dated 1926; certain aspects of Duchamp's *Bride,* which has already passed fifty, are fresher than the latest Balthus. According to my timepiece, at least. By this I mean, without wanting to impose my own time, that examples of parachrony such as these are possible and are possible for everyone. Thus we must admit a multiplicity of current times, which necessarily gives rise to paradox.

Now, if today's art works can be identified and commented on, it is at the price of the paganism or the satire that deifies the multiple to the point of including even the computation of time. Reread the text Kojève wrote for Kandinsky which, chronologically speaking, isn't all that old.[15] It is a model of what is not present-day. Figurative painting is put into four classes, all of which are declared to be abstract, and all subjective, since figures are taken from nature by the subject, the painter. With the water-colour of 1910,[16] however, Kojève maintains that an objective and concrete type of painting is born which draws nothing from nature, which reproduces nothing. This type of painting is an object that possesses its own self-sufficiency and does not derive it from its model. Thus it is itself nature. Kojève can go on to conclude that this is '*total* painting, as opposed to *abstract* and *subjective* [read figurative] painting, which is necessarily *fragmentary*.' This is obviously the Hegelian speaking, a man of the nineteenth century, because he believes in a univocal, albeit complex movement of natural, cultural, and spiritual realities towards their perfect elucidation. He is seeking to persuade you that with Kandinsky, the art of painting, by abandoning representation, passes from the subjective to the objective, and from the part to the whole, and that it is passing through a moment in its development as decisive as the one that brought about the transition from Kantian subjective criticism to Hegel's absolute idealism. I am saying that this way of placing things in perspective is out-of-date, even though it is of today and aims at extolling what is currently most up-to-date.

If our French philosophers take some interest in these aspects of art, it is to the extent that they come looking for this experience of the perceptible, or rather these experiments on the perceptible, which help them pursue their own experiments on philosophical language. Merleau-Ponty certainly would not have been a great commentator on Cézanne if 'Cézanne's doubt' hadn't been his own. As for Diderot, he off-handedly places the philosopher's task under the authority of the dictum of *Ut pictura poesis*. 'I have got into the habit of arranging my figures in my head as if they were on canvas; it may be that I transfer them there, and that I am looking at a huge wall when I write.' This is how he excuses his connivance with the works of his friends, Greuze, Lagrenée, and Chardin.[17] Thus commentary will be made to conform to figures, and figural work will take place in language analogous to what painters do on canvas.[18]

There is a name for this successfully completed work – 'the most beautiful colour in the world', and 'unctuous white, even, without being either pale or matte', a 'mixture of red and blue that transpires imperceptibly', 'blood and life that make the colourist lose heart'. It must be rendered if you are to have anything more than 'a simple and limited little technique, which among ourselves we call a protocol'. In a word, the flower of chromatics is called 'flesh', and if Chardin's limitations are taken for nature itself, 'it is because he makes flesh whenever he wants', even with peaches and grapes.[19]

I am not saying that Merleau-Ponty was looking at a huge wall when he wrote *The Eye and the Mind*, or that the 'flesh' he attempts to describe in the feline prose of *The Visible and the Invisible*, the silent spoken word dwelling in the chiasma of the perceptible, has anything to do with the rears and bosoms of Greuze that Diderot hallucinated while writing. Merleau-Ponty implies as much when he says, 'This flesh that one sees and one touches [when the body clasps another body] is not all there is to flesh, nor this massive corporality all there is to the body.'[20] But how can one keep from seeing that with the chiasma of the perceptible, the reversibility of the seer and that which is seen, of the speaker and that which is spoken, of the thinker and that which is thought, he pursues the same shift of positions that gives our satire its style?

'It is first of all by the world that I am seen or thought.' The seer is seen while he sees, and thus there is vision in things. If the philosopher's phrases never stop beginning anew and folding back on themselves, leaving nothing, certainly not concepts, in his reader's mind, only the trail of a passing, it is because the philosopher's phrases must themselves make it perceptible in their form that they are a work. As a work these phrases seek out another work (that of the artist), and are displayed before other works (those of commentaries) which in turn seek them out. Actaeon can pursue Artemis only being pursued; painting looks at you, music hears you, etc. The three positions of sensing and of using language – *who, about whom,* and *to whom* – must be able to be occupied by the same word: I who am speaking, but also *I* am the one to whom *one* is speaking, and someone about whom *one* is speaking.

You're protesting, raising the objection that Merleau-Ponty is no satirist (even though his model, Proust, was not too bad a one). Yet just reread the following passage from 'The Intertwining – The Chiasma' and you'll see that in attempting to say what kind of speech it is that he calls 'operative', he designates the very reversibility of language-based instances we have just mentioned as one of satire's basic traits. 'As the visible takes hold of the look which has unveiled it and which forms a part of it,' he writes, ' . . . no locutor speaks without making himself in advance allocutary, *be it only for himself;* because with one sole gesture he closes the circuit of his relation to himself and that of his relation to the others and, with this same stroke, also sets himself up as *delocutary,* speech of which one speaks: he offers himself and offers every word to a universal Word.'[21]

No, I assure you that the following argument can be put forth without too much paradox: there is a double requirement for satire. On the one hand there must be the reversibility of what is visible with what sees, of what can be said with what speaks. This establishes the isomorphism of the one group with the other. On the other hand, there must be a lack of referentiality for the whole set of experiences, an impossibility of making them topographically contingent and synchronous, a necessity for the contingency of points of view and/or speech, or the infiniteness of the system of stages. This twofold requirement governs 'the prose of the world' no less than it does 'satire', and it finds its double basis in the experience of the arts, which are polytheistic.

Here I'll admit my disadvantage and grant you that Merleau-Ponty fails in the satirical task, and it is because he remains monotheistic. Once again a matter of style. Even if the Treatise assumes the modern form of the Meditation or the Inquiry, it is a genre and nothing but a genre, unable to match the multiplicity it treats. With satire, however, you have free rein, and according to the occasion you can turn pedagogical, dissertational, narrative, conversational, lyrical, epic, or dry as an auditor at the Government Accounting Office; and so you can give yourself the means to enjoy the most heterogeneous of experimentations, to have them be enjoyed, and to be enjoyed by them. In satire, genres are mixed because the persons speaking are varied, and each speaks according to his or her own genre. The Treatise, how-ever, is a genre that incites arrogance, and the arrogance of philo-sophers is metaphysics. Merleau-Ponty, one of the least arrogant of philosophers, still is unable to say that the eye's relation to the visible, which is the relation of Being to itself in its primordial 'enfolding', finds expression in Cézanne or Giacometti, without immediately devalorizing other experimentations, such as Marey's, the cubists', or Duchamp's.[22] He does so because they are unaware, he believes, of 'the paradoxical arrangement', the dischrony of elements as they relate to the whole, which alone, according to Rodin whom the philosopher follows here, can restore the being of movement or being as movement. This peculiar intolerance causes Merleau-Ponty to mis-judge experiments on the perceptible and the speakable in works that require the commentator to exert just as strong a pressure on language as the pressure exerted by a Cézanne. Such inflexibility in the name of Being . . . . But being didn't choose Cézanne to express itself, now did it? Nor Merleau-Ponty, nor anyone. Don't try to re-establish these ponderous elections, poetic institution, Heideggerian preaching. 'Being' chose Rameau's Nephew – in other words, everyone and no one, a late water-colour of Mont Sainte Victoire, but also a certain photograph of a hand touching a mouth taken by Man Ray around 1930.[23] This bypasses the banalities the philosophers of the decline of the *aura* or of the institution of being have managed to peddle concerning photographic art.[24]

You're wondering what connection these reflections could have with the situation of the arts and their commentary, in this the beginning of the eighties, since you're convinced of their obsolescence. Here's my answer. Take the catalogue of a fairly important international exhibition, Documenta 5 for instance, which isn't recent but was strong enough to remain in people's minds. Then tell me whether the arts today – not even including music, dance, theatre, and film (which were not represented at Krefeld), to say nothing of literature – whether the current plastic arts do not by themselves form a world according to the previously mentioned twofold requirement. Don't they form both a satire through the immense diversity of the genres, and at the same time a field where the whole point is always to try out whether that situation, that event, that hole in the ground, that wrapping of a building, those pebbles placed on the gound, that cut made on a body, that illustrated diary of a schizophrenic, those *trompe l'oeil* sculptures, and all the rest – whether that too says something to us. The powers of sensing and phrasing are being probed on the limits of what is possible, and thus the domain of the perceptible-sensing and the speakable-speaking is being extended. Experiments are made. This is our postmodernity's entire vocation, and commentary has infinite possibilities open to it.

Today's art consists in exploring things unsayable and things invisible. Strange machines are assembled, where what we didn't have the idea of saying or the matter to feel can make itself heard and experienced. The diversity of artistic 'propositions' is dizzying. What philosopher can control it from above and unify it? Yet it is through this dispersion that today's art is the equal of being as the power of things possible, or the equal of language as the power of plays.

It should not be said that each of these experimentations is merely a subjective perspective on a Being that is its single totality or its single kingdom, and that Leibniz after all expressed the truth of perspectivism in metaphysical discourse.[25] The unity of what is involved in each artistic proposition today is included in the proposition itself in its singularity; no one singularity is more 'subjective' than another, since none of them has the privilege of objectivity. These essays, like these phrases, are made 'within being' and not before its eyes. Each work presents a micro-universe; each time, being is nothing but each one of these presentations.

No one knows what 'language' Being understands, which it speaks, or to which it can be referred. No one even knows whether there is only one Being or many, and whether there is only one language of Being or many. The arrogance of the philosophical Treatise, implicit in its form, is saying at least, 'There is one single Being'. This arrogance increases when it asserts, 'And it speaks only one language'.

It is fulfilled by assuming, 'I am going to speak it to you'. But what do innumerable artists do? They are careful not to make pronouncements on the matter. Instead they essay. And so through them we glimpse the importance that must be given to the Essay. Being or beings do not reveal themselves; they present tiny universes with each work. They essay and make micrologies that babble, huff and puff, and are envious of one another. And these essays together constitute satire.

The possibility of a classical aesthetics is called into question once again. What such an aesthetics requires is an architectonics of the faculties, or a logic of the concrete universal, be it only an idea of Nature as a priori.[26] But these must be invariants occurring as a rule. Now, the only invariable criterion with which today's work complies is whether or not some untried possibility of sensation or language is revealed in the work, something still without rules. Aesthetics becomes a paraesthetics, and commentary a paralogy, just as the work is a parapoetics. Being or beings only let themselves be tempted indirectly, seduced, like the gods.

This leads to experimentation, which is poles apart from experience. Remember the words of Benjamin: 'The replacement of the older narration by information, of information by sensation, reflects the increasing atrophy of experience.'[27] What would he have to say today about the works of music, photography, film, and video, but also painting or dance, theatre, and literature, that explicitly take the usable information unit in the relevant sensorial field as their experimentational material, striving to construct syntaxes as scarcely 'human' as possible!

I see no decline in this at all, except that of an aesthetics stemming from Hegel, for whom what was at stake was indeed 'experience' in the sense of a passion of the spirit traversing perceptible forms in order to arrive at the total expression of self in the discourse of the philosopher. This is an aesthetics grounded on the 'absolute' genre of the speculative narrative, on the form of finality, and on metaphysical arrogance. 'It is not the object of the story,' Benjamin wrote, 'to convey a happening *per se*, which is the purpose of information; rather it embeds it in the life of the storyteller in order to pass it on as experience to those listening.'[28] It can indeed be said that there is no longer any experience in this sense, which is that of the Phenomenology of Spirit. Today what subject would the great metaphysical narrative tell about? Would it be the odyssey, and for what narratee? The direction artistic research is taking consists precisely in producing with experimentations something that does not give rise to this sort of experience and in which it is not essential that a subject objectivize its suffering and know it as meaning. Adorno sees this mutation much more clearly than Benjamin (thirty years later, to be sure), and he discerns the sort of peril the postmodern work incurs. 'The real reason for the risk of all these works of art [today] is not their contingent element, instead it is the fact that all of them have to follow the will-o'-the-wisp of their immanent objectivity with no guarantee that the productive forces, the artist's mind and his technical process, will be equal to this objectivity.' At least the transition to experimentation is not immediately rejected here as an aestheticism that blocks out the sombre obviousness of the end of history and experience after Hegel. 'What can be called the seriousness of art,' Adorno adds, 'without any musty idealism, is the pathos of objectivity which presents the contingent individual with something more and something other than he is in his historically necessary insufficiency.'[29]

The break with the thought of decline is not complete, however. Adorno has to restrict experimentation's effect. Its 'seriousness' must also be a manner of maintaining art 'outside suffering', in a state of relative irresponsibility. This judgement shows that an aesthetics of the passion of meaning still persists even in the very intuition of the 'pathos of objectivity', which was announced by the satire of micrological presentations.

In Milwaukee, I remember, there was a meeting on performance in postmodern culture organized by Michel Benamou. Raymond Federman had made his contribution, which was an audio-visual montage of eleven texts, each marked by the suspension of meaning, deported, orphaned, refugee, stateless.[30] John Cage, who was with us there, stood up afterwards and, with uncharacteristic vehemence, withdrew his support from the work, protesting that, despite its clever deconstructive apparatus, it remained dedicated to expressing the lack of meaning for a subject. In short it was modern, in other words, romantic. The gap between the pathos of objectivity and the passion of meaning depends on very small details. Even the project of Benjamin's *The Arcades,* or Adorno's 'micrologies' is probably not enough to maintain this gap.[31]

Perhaps the passion of meaning 'must' continue to dwell in works, and so Hegel must continue to outlive himself in them. Who can decide that such is surely the case, or whether the opposite is? But we must come to a decision. It is not the same thing to stress invariants, the persistence of the nostalgia of meaning and romanticism in contemporary works, as it is to emphasize the minuscule but immense conversion that causes them to cease bearing the responsibility of continuing speculative metaphysics and be answerable to an ontology and a politics that are satirical. If you side with the second course, the first judges you to be ignorant and frivolous, not very up on the traps of representation. But be that as it may, we still want, and the question is: What do we want of art today? Well, for it to experiment, to stop being only modern. By saying this, we're experimenting.

And what do we want of philosophy? For it to analyse these experimentations by means of reflexive experimentations. Thus philosophy heads not towards the unity of meaning or the unity of being, not towards transcendence, but towards multiplicity and the incommensurability of works. A philosophical task doubtless exists, which is to reflect according to opacity.

One more remark. Why say satirical 'politics'? Because what is tried in each artistic proposition and in the satire they make up collectively is also social being. You multiply manners of speaking and sensing, but how will you communicate? The contemporary artist knows that this difficulty in communicating happens. Along with Baudelaire he tries to transform it into experience.[32] Cézanne, who conveniently legitim-ated his experimentations by calling them innate 'sensations', appears to have given up the idea already. Sounding like one of Zola's heroes, he repeats and accepts the undermining of consensus that his work instigates and reflects when he writes to his son just before his death, 'Connections (*relations*) can help us slip in, but sooner or later the public can tell that it's being hoodwinked.'[33]

How can generalized satire and the social bond be made compatible? This question anticipates the possibility of a satirical 'politics'.

NOTES

1 Denis Diderot, *Salon de 1767*, in *Oeuvres complètes*, 15 vols (Paris: Club Français du Livre, 1970), VII, p. 140.
2 Presentation by Catherine Millet at the symposium *Critica O*, Montecatini, May 1978.
3 Diderot, VII, p. 165.
4 Friedrich Nietzsche, *Thoughts Out of Season; On the Future of Our Educational Institutions.*
5 Walter Benjamin, 'On Some Motifs in Baudelaire' (1939), in *Illumina-tions*, tr. Harry Zorn (New York: Harcourt, Brace and World, 1968), pp. 157–202.
6 Benjamin, p. 189.
7 Diderot, VII, p. 163.
8 Georges Bataille, 'La Destruction du sujet', in *Manet* (Geneva: Skira, 1955).
9 Gérard Genette, *Figures III* (Paris: Seuil, 1972).

10 Diderot, VII, pp. 146–7.
11 Friedrich Schlegel, *Fragments* (*Athenaeum*, 1978), French tr. P. Lacoue-Labarthe and J.-L. Nancy in *L'Absolu littéraire* (Paris: Seuil, 1979), fragments 189 and 201, pp. 123 and 125–6.
12 This is the Latin sense of a saturation of genres in the same work. The magical power of the imprecation which has been attributed from the beginning to Archilochus is not unrelated, in my view, to the permutations of words in pragmatic instances. See Robert C. Elliot, *The Power of Satire: Magic, Ritual, and Art,* 3rd edn (Princeton: Princeton University Press, 1972).
13 Schlegel, fragment 201, *L'Absolu,* p. 126.
14 Diderot, *Essai sur la peinture,* VI, pp. 284–5.
15 Alexandre Kojève, 'Pourquoi concret' (1936), in Vasili Kandinsky, *Ecrits complets* (Paris: Denoël, 1970), II, pp. 395–400. See the discussion of Kandinsky's 'concrete period' by Michel Conil Lacoste, *Kandinsky* (Paris: Flammarion, 1979), pp. 81–91.
16 'Untitled — First abstraction' in the Grohmann catalogue. The work is at the Musée National d' Art Moderne (Beaubourg). The question of its date is analysed by Michel Conil Lacoste, pp. 46–51.
17 Diderot, *Salon de 1767,* VII, p. 105.
18 The sense of figural here is that of its use in Jean-François Lyotard, *Discours, Figure* (Paris: Klincksieck, 1971).
19 Diderot, VII, p. 105ff.
20 Maurice Merleau-Ponty, *The Visible and the Invisible,* tr. Alphonso Lingis (Evanston: Northwestern University Press, 1968), p. 144.
21 Ibid., p. 154.
22 *The Eye and the Mind,* in *The Primacy of Perception* (Evanston: Northwestern University Press), p. 185.
23 Reproduced in Man Ray, *Photographs (1920–1934)* (New York: East River Press, 1975), p. 42.
24 Especially Benjamin's 'On Some Motifs in Baudelaire', pp. 188–9 (more so than in the 'Petite histoire de la photographie', which was written earlier); and Merleau-Ponty, *The Eye,* pp. 185–8.
25 This is Vincent Descombe's argument in *Le Même et l'autre: Quarante-cinq ans de philosophie française (1933–1978)* (Paris: Minuit, 1979), pp. 219–21.
26 On the heretofore unfulfilled request for universality in aesthetics, see Theodor W. Adorno, *Frühe Einleitung* (1970), French tr. by Marc Jimenez and Eliane Kaufholz, *Autour de la théorie esthétique: Paralipomena, introduction première* (Paris: Klincksieck, 1976), pp. 109–45. The situation can be summarized in two sentences: 'No theory, not even aesthetic theory, can do without elements of universality' (p. 119); and 'The universal is the scandal of art' (p. 134).
27 Benjamin, 'On Some Motifs', p. 161.
28 Ibid.

29 Adorno, *Aesthetische Theorie* (1970), French tr. Marc Jimenez, *Théorie esthétique* (Paris: Klincksieck, 1974), p. 58.
30 Raymond Federman, 'Voices Within Voices', in Michel Benamou and C. Caramello, eds, *Performance in Postmodern Culture* (Milwaukee and Madison: Center for Twentieth-Century Studies and Coda Press, 1977), pp. 159–98.
31 'Introduction première', p. 143; *Negative Dialectics* (1966), tr. E.B. Ashton (New York: Seabury Press, 1973).
32 'This,' wrote Benjamin, 'would be a peak achievement of the intellect. It would turn the incident into a moment that has been lived (*Erlebnis*).' 'On Some Motifs', p. 165.
33 Paul Cézanne, *Correspondance,* ed. J. Rewald (Paris: Grasset, 1937), p. 283 (letter to his son, 12 August 1906). The word *'relations'* should be understood in the sense of forms of support by powerful persons.

Translated by Mária Minich Brewer and Daniel Brewer

10

The Sublime and the Avant-Garde*

I

In 1950–1, Barnett Baruch Newman painted a canvas measuring 2.42 m by 5.42 m which he called *Vir Heroicus Sublimis*. In the early sixties he entitled his first three sculptures *Here I, Here II, Here III*. Another painting was called *Not Over There, Here*, two paintings were called *Now*, and two others were entitled *Be*. In December 1948, Newman wrote an essay entitled *The Sublime is Now*.

How is one to understand the sublime, or let us say provisionally, the object of a sublime experience, as a 'here and now'? Quite to the contrary, isn't it essential to this feeling that it alludes to something which can't be shown, or presented (as Kant said, *dargestellt*)? In a short unfinished text dating from late 1949, *Prologue for a New Aesthetic*, Newman wrote that in his painting, he was not concerned with a 'manipulation of space nor with the image, but with a sensation of time'. He added that by this he did not mean time laden with feelings of nostalgia, or drama, or references and history, the usual subjects of painting. After this denial (*dénégation*) the text stops short.

So, what kind of time was Newman concerned with, what 'now' did he have in mind? Thomas Hess, his friend and commentator, felt justified in writing that Newman's time was the *Makom* or the *Hamakom* of Hebraic tradition – the *there*, the site, the place, which is one of the names given by the Torah to the Lord, the Unnameable. I do not know enough about *Makom* to know whether this was what

* This text was first published in *Art Forum*, 22, part 8 (April 1984), pp. 36–43, in a translation by Lisa Liebmann, which is reproduced with kind permission. Alterations were made to the French text by Jean-François Lyotard when he gave the paper in Cambridge in March 1984, and these have been translated by Geoff Bennington and Marian Hobson and incorporated into the translation.

Newman had in mind. But then again, who does know enough about *Now?* Newman can certainly not have been thinking of the 'present instant', the one that tries to hold itself between the future and the past, and gets devoured by them. This 'now' is one of the temporal 'ecstasies' that has been analysed since Augustine's day and since Edmund Husserl, according to a line of thought that has attempted to constitute time on the basis of consciousness. Newman's *now* which is no more than *now* is a stranger to consciousness and cannot be constituted by it. Rather, it is what dismantles consciousness, what deposes consciousness, it is what consciousness cannot formulate, and even what consciousness forgets in order to constitute itself. What we do not manage to formulate is that something happens, *dass etwas geschieht.* Or rather, and more simply, that it happens . . . *dass es geschieht.* Not a major event in the media sense, not even a small event. Just an occurrence.

This isn't a matter of sense or reality bearing upon *what* happens or *what* this might mean. Before asking questions about what it is and about its significance, before the *quid,* it must 'first' so to speak 'happen', *quod.* That it happens 'precedes', so to speak, the question pertaining to what happens. Or rather, the question precedes itself, because 'that it happens' is the question relevant as event, and it 'then' pertains to the event that has just happened. The event happens as a question mark 'before' happening as a question. *It happens* is rather 'in the first place' *is it happening, is this it, is it possible?* Only 'then' is any mark determined by the questioning: is this or that happening, is it this or something else, is it possible that this or that?

An event, an occurrence – what Martin Heidegger called *ein Ereignis* – is infinitely simple, but this simplicity can only be approached through a state of privation. That which we call thought must be disarmed. There is a tradition and an institution of philosophy, of painting, of politics, of literature. These 'disciplines' also have a future in the form of Schools, of programmes, projects, and 'trends'. Thought works over what is received, it seeks to reflect on it and overcome it. It seeks to determine what has already been thought, written, painted, or socialized in order to determine what hasn't been. We know this process well, it is our daily bread. It is the bread of war, soldiers' biscuit. But this agitation, in the most noble sense of the word (agitation is the word Kant gives to the activity of the mind that has judgement and exercises it), this agitation is only possible if something remains to be determined, something that hasn't yet been determined. One can strive to determine this something by setting up a system, a theory, a programme or a project – and indeed one has to, all the while anticipating that something. One can also inquire about the remainder, and allow the indeterminate to appear as a question mark.

What all intellectual disciplines and institutions presuppose is that not everything has been said, written down or recorded, that words already heard or pronounced are not the last words. 'After' a sentence, 'after' a colour, comes another sentence, another colour. One doesn't know which, but one thinks one knows if one relies on the rules that permit one sentence to link up with another, one colour with another, rules preserved in precisely those institutions of the past and future that I mentioned. The School, the programme, the project – all proclaim that after this sentence comes that sentence, or at least that kind of sentence is mandatory, that one kind of sentence is permitted, while another is forbidden. This holds true for painting as much as for the other activities of thought. After one pictorial work, another is necessary, permitted, or forbidden. After one colour, this other colour; after this line, that one. There isn't an enormous difference between an avant-garde manifesto and a curriculum at the Ecole des Beaux Arts, if one considers them in the light of this relationship to time. Both are options with respect to what they feel is a good thing to happen subsequently. But both also forget the possibility of nothing happening, of words, colours, forms or sounds not coming; of this sentence being the last, of bread not coming daily. This is the misery that the painter faces with a plastic surface, of the musician with the acoustic surface, the misery the thinker faces with a desert of thought, and so on. Not only faced with the empty canvas or the empty page, at the 'beginning' of the work, but every time something has to be waited for, and thus forms a question at every point of questioning (*point d'interrogation*), at every 'and what now?'

The possibility of nothing happening is often associated with a feeling of anxiety, a term with strong connotations in modern philosophies of existence and of the unconscious. It gives to waiting, if we really mean waiting, a predominantly negative value. But suspense can also be accompanied by pleasure, for instance pleasure in welcoming the unknown, and even by joy, to speak like Baruch Spinoza, the joy obtained by the intensification of being that the event brings with it. This is probably a contradictory feeling. It is at the very least a sign, the question mark itself, the way in which *it happens* is withheld and announced: *Is it happening?* The question can be modulated in any tone. But the mark of the question is 'now', *now* like the feeling that nothing might happen: the nothingness now.

Between the seventeenth and eighteenth centuries in Europe this contradictory feeling – pleasure and pain, joy and anxiety, exaltation and depression – was christened or re-christened by the name of the *sublime*. It is around this name that the destiny of classical poetics was hazarded and lost; it is in this name that aesthetics asserted its critical rights over art, and that romanticism, in other words, modernity, triumphed.

It remains to the art historian to explain how the word sublime reappeared in the language of a Jewish painter from New York during the forties. The word sublime is common currency today in colloquial French to suggest surprise and admiration, somewhat like America's 'great', but the idea connoted by it has belonged (for at least two centuries) to the most rigorous kind of reflection on art. Newman is not unaware of the aesthetic and philosophical stakes with which the word *sublime* is involved. He read Edmund Burke's *Inquiry* and criticized what he saw as Burke's over 'surrealist' description of the sublime work. Which is as much as to say that, conversely, Newman judged surrealism to be over-reliant on a pre-romantic or romantic approach to indeterminacy. Thus, when he seeks sublimity in the here and now he breaks with the eloquence of romantic art but he does not reject its fundamental task, that of bearing pictorial or otherwise expressive witness to the inexpressible. The inexpressible does not reside in an over there, in another words, or another time, but in this: in that (something) happens. In the determination of pictorial art, the indeterminate, the 'it happens' is the paint, the picture. The paint, the picture as occurrence or event, is not expressible, and it is to this that it has to witness.

To be true to this displacement in which consists perhaps the whole of the difference between romanticism and the 'modern' avant-garde, one would have to read *The Sublime is Now* not as *The Sublime is Now* but as *Now the Sublime is Like This*. Not elsewhere, not up there or over there, not earlier or later, not once upon a time. But as here, now, it happens that, . . . and it's this painting. Here and now there is this painting, rather than nothing, and that's what is sublime. Letting-go of all grasping intelligence and of its power, disarming it, recognizing that this occurrence of painting was not necessary and is scarcely foreseeable, a privation in the face of *Is it happening?* guarding the occurrence 'before' any defence, any illustration, and any commentary, guarding before being on one's guard, before 'looking' (*regarder*) under the aegis of *now*, this is the rigour of the avant-garde. In the determination of literary art this requirement with respect to the *Is it happening?* found one of its most rigorous realizations in Gertrude Stein's *How to Write*. It's still the sublime in the sense that Burke and Kant described and yet it isn't their sublime any more.

II

I have said that the contradictory feeling with which indeterminacy is both announced and missed was what was at stake in reflection on art from the end of the seventeenth to the end of the eighteenth centuries. The sublime is perhaps the only mode of artistic sensibility to characterize the modern. Paradoxically, it was introduced to literary discussion and vigorously defended by the French writer who has been classified in literary history as one of the most dogged advocates of ancient classicism. In 1674 Boileau published his *Art Poètique,* but he also published *Du Sublime,* his translation or transcription from the *Peri tou hupsou.* It is a treatise, or rather an essay, attributed to a certain Longinus about whose identity there has long been confusion, and whose life we now estimate as having begun towards the end of the first century of our era. The author was a rhetorician. Basically, he taught those oratorical devices with which a speaker can persuade or move (depending on the genre) his audience. The didactics of rhetoric had been traditional since Aristotle, Cicero, and Quintilian. They were linked to the republican institution; one had to know how to speak before assemblies and tribunals.

One might expect that Longinus' text would invoke the maxims and advice transmitted by this tradition by perpetuating the didactic form of *technè rhetorikè.* But surprisingly, the sublime, the indeterminate – were destabilizing the text's didactic intention. I cannot analyse this uncertainty here. Boileau himself and numerous other commentators, especially Fénélon, were aware of it and concluded that the sublime could only be discussed in sublime style. Longinus certainly tried to define sublimity in discourse, writing that it was unforgettable, irresistible, and most important, thought-provoking – '*il y a à partir d'elle beaucoup de réflexion*' (*hou polle anatheoresis*) (from the sublime springs a lot of reflection). He also tried to locate sources for the sublime in the ethos of rhetoric, in its pathos, in its techniques: figures of speech, diction, enunciation, composition. He sought in this way to bend himself to the rules of the genre of the 'treatise' (whether of rhetoric or poetics, or politics) destined to be model for practitioners.

However, when it comes to the sublime, major obstacles get in the way of a regular exposition of rhetorical or poetic principles. There is, for example, wrote Longinus, a sublimity of thought sometimes recognizable in speech by its extreme simplicity of turn of phrase, at the precise point where the high character of the speaker makes one expect greater solemnity. It sometimes even takes the form of outright silence. I don't mind if this simplicity, this silence, is taken to be yet another rhetorical figure. But it must be granted that it constitutes the most indeterminate of figures. What can remain of rhetoric (or of poetics) when the rhetorician in Boileau's translation announces that to attain the sublime effect 'there is no better figure of speech than one which is completely hidden, that which we do not even recognize as a figure of speech?' Must we admit that there are techniques for hiding figures, that there are figures for the erasure of figures? How do we distinguish between a hidden figure and what is not a figure? And what is it, if it isn't a figure? And what about this, which seems to be a major blow to didactics: when it is sublime, discourse accommodates defects, lack of taste, and formal imperfections. Plato's style, for example, is full of bombast and bloated strained comparisons. Plato, in short, is a mannerist, or a baroque writer compared to Lysias, and so is Sophocles compared to an Ion or Pindar compared to a Bacchylides. The fact remains that, like those first named, he is sublime, whereas the second ones are merely perfect. Shortcomings in technique are therefore trifling matters if they are the price to be paid for 'true grandeur'. Grandeur in speech is true when it bears witness to the incommensurability between thought and the real world.

Is it Boileau's transcription that suggests this analogy, or is it the influence of early Christianity on Longinus? The fact that grandeur of spirit is not of this world cannot but suggest Pascal's hierarchy of orders. The kind of perfection that can be demanded in the domain of *technè* isn't necessarily a desirable attribute when it comes to sublime feeling. Longinus even goes so far as to propose inversions of reputedly natural and rational syntax as examples of sublime effect. As for Boileau, in the preface he wrote in 1674 for Longinus' text, in still further addenda made in 1683 and 1701 and also in the *Xth Réflexion* published in 1710 after his death he makes final the previous tentative break with the classical institution of *technè*. The sublime, he says, cannot be taught, and didactics are thus powerless in this respect; the sublime is not linked to rules that can be determined through poetics; the sublime only requires that the reader or listener have conceptual range, taste, and the ability 'to sense what everyone senses first'. Boileau therefore takes the same stand as Père Bouhours, when in 1671 the latter declared that beauty demands more than just a respect for rules, that it requires a further 'je ne sais quoi', also called *genius* or something 'incomprehensible and inexplicable', a 'gift from God', a fundamentally 'hidden' phenomenon that can be recognized only by its effects on the addressee. And in the polemic that set him against Pierre-Daniel Huet, over the issue of whether the Bible's *Fiat Lux, et Lux fuit* is sublime, as Longinus thought it was, Boileau refers to the opinion of the Messieurs de Port Royal and in particular to Silvestre de Saci: the Jansenists are masters when it comes to matters of hidden meaning, of eloquent silence, of feeling that transcends all reason and finally of openness to the *Is it happening?*

At stake in these poetic-theological debates is the status of works of art. Are they copies of some ideal model? Can reflection on the more 'perfect' examples yield rules of formation that determine their success in achieving what they want, that is, persuasiveness and pleasure? Can understanding suffice for this kind of reflection? By meditating on the theme of sublimity and of indeterminacy, meditation about works of art imposes a major change on *technè* and the institutions linked to it – Academies, Schools, masters and disciples, taste, the enlightened public made up of princes and courtiers. It is the very destination or destiny of works which is being questioned. The predominance of the idea of *technè* placed works under a multiple regulation, that of the model taught in the studios, Schools, and Academies, that of the taste shared by the aristocratic public, that of a purposiveness of art, which was to illustrate the glory of a name, divine or human, to which was linked the perfection of some cardinal virtue or other. The idea of the sublime disrupts this harmony. Let us magnify the features of – this disruption. Under Diderot's pen, *technè* becomes '*le petit technique*' (mere trivial technique). The artist ceases to be guided by a culture which made of him the sender and master of a message of glory: he becomes, insofar as he is a genius, the involuntary addressee of an inspiration come to him from an 'I know not what'. The public no longer judges according to the criteria of a taste ruled by the tradition of shared pleasure: individuals unknown to the artist (the 'people') read books, go through the galleries of the Salons, crowd into the theatres and the public concerts, they are prey to unforeseeable feelings: they are shocked, admiring, scornful, indifferent. The question is not that of pleasing them by leading them to identify with a name and to participate in the glorification of its virtue, but that of surprising them. 'The sublime', writes Boileau, 'is not strictly speaking something which is proven or demonstrated, but a marvel, which seizes one, strikes one, and makes one feel.' The very imperfections, the distortions of taste, even ugliness, have their share in the shock-effect. Art does not imitate nature, it creates a world apart, *eine Zwischenwelt*, as Paul Klee will say, *eine Nebenwelt*, one might say, in which the monstrous and the formless have their rights because they can be sublime.

You will (I hope) excuse such a simplification of the transformation which takes place with the modern development of the idea of the sublime. The trace of it could be found before modern times, in Medieval aesthetics – that of the Victorines for example. In any case, it explains why reflection on art should no longer bear essentially on the 'sender' instance/agency of works, but on the 'addressee' instance. And under the name 'genius' the latter instance is situated, not only on the side of the public, but also on the side of the artist, a feeling which he does not master. Henceforth it seems right to analyse the ways in which the subject is affected, its ways of receiving and experiencing feelings, its ways of judging works. This is how aesthetics, the analysis of the addressee's feelings, comes to supplant poetics and rhetoric, which are didactic forms, of and by the understanding, intended for the artist as sender. No longer 'How does one make a work of art?', but 'What is it to experience an affect proper to art?'. And indeterminacy returns, even within the analysis of this last question.

III

Baumgarten published his *Aesthetica,* the first aesthetics, in 1750. Kant will say of this work simply that it was based on an error. Baumgarten confuses judgement, in its determinant usage, when the understanding organizes phenomena according to categories, with judgement in its reflexive usage when, in the form of feeling, it relates to the indeterminate relationship between the faculties of the judging subject. Baumgarten's aesthetics remains dependent on a conceptually determined relationship to the work of art. The sense of beauty is for Kant, on the contrary, kindled by a free harmony between the function of images and the function of concepts occasioned by an object of art or nature. The aesthetics of the sublime is still more indeterminate: a pleasure mixed with pain, a pleasure that comes from pain. In the event of an absolutely large object – the desert, a mountain, a pyramid – or one that is absolutely powerful – a storm at sea, an erupting volcano – which like all absolutes can only be thought, without any sensible/sensory intuition, as an Idea of reason, the faculty of presentation, the imagination, fails to provide a representation corresponding to this Idea. This failure of expression gives rise to a pain, a kind of cleavage within the subject between what can be conceived and what can be imagined or presented. But this pain in turn engenders a pleasure, in fact a double pleasure: the impotence of the imagination attests *a contrario* to an imagination striving to figure even that which cannot be figured, and that imagination thus aims to harmonize its object with that of reason – and that furthermore the inadequacy of the images is a negative sign of the immense power of ideas. This dislocation of the faculties among themselves gives rise to the extreme tension (Kant calls it agitation) that characterizes the pathos of the sublime, as opposed to the calm feeling of beauty. At the edge of the break, infinity, or the absoluteness of the Idea can be revealed in what Kant calls a negative presentation, or even a non-presentation. He cites the Jewish law banning images as an eminent example of negative presentation: optical pleasure when reduced to near nothingness promotes an infinite contemplation of infinity. Even before romantic art had freed itself from classical and baroque figuration, the door had thus been opened to inquiries pointing towards abstract and Minimal art. Avant-gardism is thus present in germ in the Kantian aesthetic of the sublime. However, the art whose effects are analysed in that aesthetics is, of course, essentially made up of attempts to represent sublime objects. And the question of time, of the *Is it happening?*, does not form part – at least not explicitly – of Kant's problematic.

I do, however, believe that question to be at the centre of Edmund Burke's *Philosophical Inquiry into the Origin of our Ideas of the Sublime and Beautiful,* published in 1757. Kant may well reject Burke's thesis as empiricism and physiologism, he may well borrow from Burke the analysis of the characterizing contradiction of the feeling of the sublime, but he strips Burke's aesthetic of what I consider to be its major stake – to show that the sublime is kindled by the threat of nothing further happening. Beauty gives a positive pleasure. But there is another kind of pleasure that is bound to a passion stronger than satisfaction, and that is pain and impending death. In pain the body affects the soul. But the soul can also affect the body as though it were experiencing some externally induced pain, by the sole means of representations that are unconsciously associated with painful situation. This entirely spiritual passion, in Burke's lexicon, is called terror. Terrors are linked to privation: privation of light, terror of darkness; privation of others, terror of solitude; privation of language, terror of silence; privation of objects, terror of emptiness; privation of life, terror of death. What is terrifying is that the *It happens that* does not happen, that it stops happening.

Burke wrote that for this terror to mingle with pleasure and with it to produce the feeling of the sublime, it is also necessary that the terror-causing threat be suspended, kept at bay, held back. This suspense, this lessening of a threat or a danger, provokes a kind of pleasure that is certainly not that of a positive satisfaction, but is, rather, that of relief. This is still a privation, but it is privation at one remove:

the soul is deprived of the threat of being deprived of light, language, life. Burke distinguishes this pleasure of secondary privation from positive pleasures, and he baptizes it with the name *delight*.

Here then is an account of the sublime feeling: a very big, very powerful object threatens to deprive the soul of any 'it happens', strikes it with 'astonishment' (at lower intensities the soul is seized with admiration, veneration, respect). The soul is thus dumb, immobilized, as good as dead. Art, by distancing this menace, procures a pleasure of relief, of delight. Thanks to art, the soul is returned to the agitated zone between life and death, and this agitation is its health and its life. For Burke, the sublime was no longer a matter of elevation (the category by which Aristotle defined tragedy), but a matter of intensification.

Another of Burke's observations merits attention because it heralds the possibility of emancipating works of art from the classical rule of imitation. In the long debate over the relative merits of painting and poetry, Burke sides with poetry. Painting is doomed to imitate models, and to figurative representations of them. But if the object of art is to create intense feelings in the addressee of works, figuration by means of images is a limiting constraint on the power of emotive expression since it works by recognition. In the arts of language, particularly in poetry, and particularly in poetry which Burke considered to be not a genre with rules, but the field where certain researches into language have free rein, the power to move is free from the verisimilitudes of figuration. 'What does one do when one wants to represent an angel in a painting? One paints a beautiful young man with wings: but will painting ever provide anything as great as the addition of this one word – the Angel of the *Lord*? and how does one go about painting, with equal strength of feeling, the words "A universe of death" where ends the journey of the fallen angels in Milton's *Paradise Lost*?'

Words enjoy several privileges when it comes to expressing feelings: they are themselves charged with passionate connotations; they can evoke matters of the soul without having to consider whether they are visible; finally, Burke adds, 'It is in our power to effect with words combinations that would be impossible by any other means.' The arts, whatever their materials, pressed forward by the aesthetics of the sublime in search of intense effects, can and must give up the imitation of models that are merely beautiful, and try out surprising, strange, shocking combinations. Shock is, *par excellence*, the evidence of (something) *happening*, rather than nothing, suspended privation.

Burke's analyses can easily, as you will have guessed, be resumed and elaborated in a Freudian-Lacanian problematic (as Pierre

Kaufman and Baldine Saint-Girons have done). But I recall them in a different spirit, the one my subject – the avant-garde – demands. I have tried to suggest that at the dawn of romanticism, *Burke's* elaboration of the aesthetics of the sublime, and to a lesser degree *Kant's*, *outlined a world of possibilities for artistic experiments in which the avant-gardes would later trace out their paths.* There are in general no direct influences, no empirically observable connections. Manet, Cézanne, Braque, and Picasso probably did not read Kant or Burke. It is more a matter of an irreversible deviation in the destination of art, a deviation affecting all the valencies of the artistic condition. The artist attempts combinations allowing the event. The art-lover does not experience a simple pleasure, or derive some ethical benefit from his contact with art, but expects an intensification of his conceptual and emotional capacity, an ambivalent enjoyment. Intensity is associated with an ontological dislocation. The art object no longer bends itself to models, but tries to present the fact that there is an unpresentable; it no longer imitates nature, but is, in Burke, the actualization of a figure potentially there in language. The social community no longer recognizes itself in art objects, but ignores them, rejects them as incomprehensible, and only later allows the intellectual avant-garde to preserve them in museums as the traces of offensives that bear witness to the power, and the privation, of the spirit.

IV

With the advent of the aesthetics of the sublime, the stake of art in the nineteenth and twentieth centuries was to be the witness to the fact that there is indeterminacy. For painting, the paradox that Burke signalled in his observations on the power of words is, that such testimony can only be achieved in a determined fashion. Support, frame, line, colour, space, the figure – were to remain, in romantic art, subject to the constraint of representation. But this contradiction of end and means had, as early as Manet and Cézanne, the effect of casting doubt on certain rules that had determined, since the Quattrocento, the representation of the figure in space and the organization of colours and values. Reading Cézanne's correspondence, one understands that his *oeuvre* was not that of a talented painter finding his 'style', but that of an artist attempting to respond to the question: what is a painting? His work had at stake to inscribe on the supporting canvas only those 'colouristic sensations', those 'little sensations' that of themselves, according to Cézanne's hypothesis, constitute the entire pictorial existence of objects, fruit, mountain, face, flower, without consideration of either history or 'subject', or line, or space, or even light. These elementary sensations are hidden in ordinary perception which remains under the hegemony of habitual or classical ways of looking. They are only accessible to the painter, and can therefore only be re-established by him, at the expense of an interior ascesis that rids perceptual and mental fields of prejudices inscribed even in vision itself. If the viewer does not submit to a complementary ascesis, the painting will remain senseless and impenetrable to him. The painter must not hesitate to run the risk of being taken to be a mere dauber. 'One paints for very few people', writes Cézanne. Recognition from the regulatory institutions of painting – Academy, salons, criticism, taste – is of little importance compared to the judgement made by the painter-researcher and his peers on the success obtained by the work of art in relation to what is really at stake: to make seen what makes one see, and not what is visible.

Maurice Merleau-Ponty elaborated on what he rightly called 'Cézanne's doubt' as though what was at stake for the painter was indeed to grasp and render perception at its birth – perception 'before' perception. I would say: colour in its occurrence, the wonder that 'it happens' ('it', something: colour), at least to the eye. There is some credulity on the part of the phenomenologist in this trust he places in the 'originary' value of Cézanne's 'little sensations'. The painter himself, who often complained of their inadequacy, wrote that they were 'abstractions', that 'they did not suffice for covering the canvas'. But why should it be necessary to cover the canvas? Is it forbidden to be abstract?

The doubt which gnaws at the avant-gardes did not stop with Cézanne's 'colouristic sensations' as though they were indubitable, and, for that matter, no more did it stop with the abstractions they heralded. The task of having to bear witness to the indeterminate carries away, one after another, the barriers set up by the writings of theorists and by the manifestos of the painters themselves. A formalist definition of the pictorial object, such as that proposed in 1961 by Clement Greenberg when confronted with American 'post-plastic' abstraction, was soon overturned by the current of Minimalism. Do we have to have stretchers so that the canvas is taut? No. What about colours? Malevitch's black square on white had already answered this question in 1915. Is an object necessary? Body art and happenings went about proving that it is not. A space, at least, a space in which to display, as Duchamp's 'fountain' still suggested? Daniel Buren's work testifies to the fact that even this is subject to doubt.

Whether or not they belong to the current that art history calls Minimalism or Arte Povera, the investigations of the avant-gardes question one by one the constituents one might have thought 'elementary' or at the 'origin' of the art of painting. They operate *ex minimis*. One would have to confront the demand for rigour that animates them with the principle sketched out by Adorno at the end of *Negative Dialectics,* and that controls the writing of his *Aesthetic Theory*: the thought that 'accompanies metaphysics in its fall', he said, can only proceed in terms of 'micrologies'.

Micrology is not just metaphysics in crumbs, any more than Newman's painting is Delacroix in scraps. Micrology inscribes the occurrence of a thought as the unthought that remains to be thought in the decline of 'great' philosophical thought. The avant-gardist attempt inscribes the occurrence of a sensory now as what cannot be presented and which remains to be presented in the decline of great representational painting. Like micrology, the avant-garde is not concerned with what happens to the 'subject', but with: 'Does it happen?', with privation. This is the sense in which it still belongs to the aesthetics of the sublime.

In asking questions of the *It happens* that the work of art is, avant-garde art abandons the role of identification that the work previously played in relation to the community of addressees. Even when conceived, as it was by Kant, as a *de jure* horizon or presumption rather than a *de facto* reality, a *sensus communis* (which, moreover, Kant refers to only when writing about beauty, not the sublime) does not manage to achieve stability when it comes to interrogative works of art. It barely coalesces, too late, when these works, deposited in museums, are considered part of the community heritage and are made available for its culture and pleasure. And even here, they must be objects, or they must tolerate objectification, for example through photography.

In this situation of isolation and misunderstanding, avant-garde art is vulnerable and subject to repression. It seems only to aggravate the identity-crisis that communities went through during the long 'depression' that lasted from the thirties until the end of 'reconstruction' in the mid-fifties. It is impossible here even to suggest how the Party-states born of fear faced with the 'Who are we?', and the anxiety of the void, tried to convert this fear or anxiety into hatred of the avant-gardes. Hildegarde Brenner's study of artistic policy under Nazism, or the films of Hans-Jurgen Sylberberg do not merely analyse these repressive manoeuvres. They also explain how neo-romantic, neo-classical and symbolic forms imposed by the cultural commissars and collaborationist artists – painters and musicians especially – had to block the negative dialectic of the 'Is it happening?', by translating and betraying the question as a waiting for some fabulous subject or identity: 'Is the pure people coming?', 'Is the Führer coming?', 'Is Siegfried coming?'. The aesthetics of the sublime, thus neutralized and converted into a politics of myth, was able to come and build its architectures of human 'formations' on the Zeppelin Feld in Nürnberg.

Thanks to the 'crisis of overcapitalization' that most of today's so-called highly developed societies are going through, another attack on the avant-gardes is coming to light. The threat exerted against the avant-garde search for the artwork event, against attempts to welcome the *now*, no longer requires Party-states to be effective. It proceeds 'directly' out of market economics. The correlation between this and the aesthetics of the sublime is ambiguous, even perverse. The latter, no doubt, has been and continues to be a reaction against the matter-of-fact positivism and the calculated realism that governs the former, as writers on art such as Stendhal, Baudelaire, Mallarmé, Apollinaire and Breton all emphasize.

Yet there is a kind of collusion between capital and the avant-garde. The force of scepticism and even of destruction that capitalism has brought into play, and that Marx never ceased analysing and identifying, in some way encourages among artists a mistrust of established rules and a willingness to experiment with means of expression, with styles, with ever-new materials. There is something of the sublime in capitalist economy. It is not academic, it is not physiocratic, it admits of no nature. It is, in a sense, an economy regulated by an Idea – infinite wealth or power. It does not manage to present any example from reality to verify this Idea. In making science subordinate to itself through technologies, especially those of language, it only succeeds, on the contrary, in making reality increasingly ungraspable, subject to doubt, unsteady.

The experience of the human subject – individual and collective – and the aura that surrounds this experience, are being dissolved into the calculation of profitability, the satisfaction of needs, self-affirmation through success. Even the virtually theological depth of the worker's condition, and of work, that marked the socialist and union movements for over a century, is becoming devalorized, as work becomes a control and manipulation of information. These observations are banal, but what merits attention is the disappearance of the temporal continuum through which the experience of generations used to be transmitted. The availability of information is becoming the only criterion of social importance. Now information is by definition a short-lived element. As soon as it is transmitted and shared, it ceases to be information, it becomes an environmental given, and 'all is said', we 'know'. It is put into the machine memory. The length of time it occupies is, so to speak, instantaneous. Between two pieces of information, 'nothing happens', by definition. A confusion thereby becomes possible, between what is of interest to information and the director, and what is the question of the avant-gardes, between what happens – the new – and the 'Is it happening?', the *now*.

It is understandable that the art-market, subject like all markets to the rule of the new, can exert a kind of seduction on artists. This attraction is not due to corruption alone. It exerts itself thanks to a confusion between innovation and the *Ereignis,* a confusion maintained by the temporality specific to contemporary capitalism. 'Strong' information, if one can call it that, exists in inverse proportion to the meaning that can be attributed to it in the code available to its receiver. It is like 'noise'. It is easy for the public and for artists, advised by intermediaries – the diffusers of cultural merchandise – to draw from this observation the principle that a work of art is avant-garde in direct proportion to the extent that it is stripped of meaning. Is it not then like an event?

It is still necessary that its absurdity does not discourage buyers, just as the innovation introduced into a commodity must allow itself to be approached, appreciated and purchased by the consumers. The secret of an artistic success, like that of a commercial success, resides in the balance between what is surprising and what is 'well-known', between information and code. This is how innovation in art operates: one re-uses formulae confirmed by previous success, one throws them off balance by combining them with other, in principle incompatible, formulae, by amalgamations, quotations, ornamentations, pastiche. One can go as far as kitsch or the grotesque. One flatters the 'taste' of a public that can have no taste, and the eclecticism or a sensibility enfeebled by the multiplication of available forms and objects. In this way one thinks that one is expressing the spirit of the times, whereas one is merely reflecting the spirit of the market. Sublimity is no longer in art, but in speculation on art.

The enigma of the 'Is it happening?' is not dissolved for all this, nor is the task of painting, that there is something which is not determinable, the 'There is' (*ll y a*) itself, out of date. The occurrence, the *Ereignis,* has nothing to do with the *petit frisson,* the cheap thrill, the profitable pathos, that accompanies an innovation. Hidden in the cynicism of innovation is certainly the despair that nothing further will happen. But innovating means to behave as though lots of things happened, and to make them happen. Through innovation, the will affirms its hegemony over time. It thus conforms to the metaphysics of capital, which is a technology of time. The innovation 'works'. The question mark of the 'Is it happening?' stops. With the occurrence, the will is defeated. The avant-gardist task remains that of undoing the presumption of the mind with respect to time. The sublime feeling is the name of this privation.

11

Scapeland

Cast down the walls. Breach and breathe. Inhalation. BREATH, inside and outside. This concerns the thorax. The muscular walls of the rib-cage, of the defences of the thorax, exposed to the winds. Your breath has been set free, not taken away. An understatement: mouth to mouth contact with distance, as though with an infinity of air. And because the walls are down, there is no swelling.

Vesania or 'systematic' madness: 'The soul is transferred to a quite different standpoint, so to speak, and from it sees all objects differently. It is displaced from the *sensorium communi* that is required for the unity of (animal) *life*, to a point far removed from it (hence the word *Verrückung*) – just as a mountainous landscape sketched from an aerial perspective calls forth a quite different judgement when it is viewed from the plain.'[1] Conversely, for the bird, the rat that dwells on the plain must also be systematically mad, a landscape-artist, an other alienated, an other estranged. Breathing and breaching the walls of the cage are not, then, the main point. For the bird, the mole's myopic tunnels would mean distance, and would be a landscape which abolishes limits. A burrow in which it is impossible to see anything, impossible to breathe. No one element (an aura, a breeze) is privileged over any other. There would appear to be a landscape whenever the mind is transported from one sensible matter to another, but retains the sensorial organization appropriate to the first, or at least a memory of it. The earth seen from the moon for a terrestial. The countryside for the townsman; the city for the farmer. ESTRANGEMENT (*dépaysement*) would appear to be a precondition for landscape.

A stretch of road lined with poplars at midday, made strange by the light of a full summer moon a few years ago at about eleven at night when Mars was in conjunction with Venus. Baruchello calls me from Rome to ask if I've seen the wonderful sky. Theatrical lighting engineers understand LIGHT's function in painting a landscape. So do the Impressionists. And Rembrandt, when it comes to shadows.

Losing oneself in a world of sound. Hearing breaks down the defences of the harmonic and melodic ear, and becomes aware of TIMBRE alone. And then we have the landscape of Beethoven's late quartets.

Infinity: inexhaustible resources are required if there is to be any landscape. 'A palace is not worth living in if you know its every room', writes Lampedusa. A burrow is like that palace; habitable because it is UNINHABITABLE.

The opposite of a place. If place is cognate with destination. See Aristotle, Landscape as a place without a DESTINY. Apply J.-L. Déotte's argument about works of art to the object known as 'landscape'; when they are hung in a museum, works of art are stripped of their destination (be it mythical, religious or political). They are exhibited in their visible presence, here and now. A cove, a mountain lake, a canal in the metropolis can be hung short of any destination, human or divine, and left there. When they are hung in this way, their 'condition' is impalpable, unanswerable. The grey that drifts over the sea after a storm. It is not that you get lost in them, but that their meanings are lost. Foreign capitals visited for the first time. The darkness of all the Rembrandts in the Metropolitan Museum in New York dazzles you as soon as you enter the room. A very long time ago when I was very small; the port of Amsterdam; rails and points encrusted into the cobbles on the quayside; the mist lit from behind by the rising sun like a gauze, and through it I watch the elephantine liners and freighters ruminating, as though they had been stabled in a thousand docks.

Deserts, mountains and plains, ruins, oceans and skies enjoy a privileged status in landscape painting, rather as though they were by definition without any destiny. And they are therefore disconcerting (*dépaysant*). This exclusivity is not to be trusted. Meaning soon gives its orphans a new destination (if only for love of landscape). No, landscape has no elective place in these non-places. But the absence of place threatens them, just as it threatens any possible place. Indeterminacy exercises a gentle violence over the determinate, so as to make it give up its QUOD. And it is not I, nor anyone, who begets this non-place.

A sumptuous banister of ebony, smooth to the touch, decorated with Jugendstyl flowers, winding up continuously and without any visible joints to the fourth floor of a block in East Berlin, a block that stands on a boulevard lined by two avenues of bare black trees – it is January – and which is flanked by other blocks in the same style; the streetlights do little to ward off the gathering darkness; deserted, out of the way, and lonely; we are going to visit a colleague and to take him some banned books. That banister has all it takes to make it a non-place as we climb the stairs. And the feeling of strangeness persists over the coffee and cakes in the bottle-green apartment where the lamps are turned down low, and where our voices are low, but violent. The unreality of landscapes as the saying goes. For a brief moment they unmask themselves as CLANDESTINE. And basically, you never see them again. Try as you may. It is always the unknown room in the palace. The corridor in *If It Die* . . . , or in the burrow.

The face, but not the countenance, is a landscape, several landscapes. A photograph of Beckett at eighty. An entire land parched with drought, the flesh defied. And in the wrinkles, in the creases where the pupils flash with anger, a cheerful incredulity. So the mummy is still alive. Just. The network of cracks and furrows represents so many weak points; misery has entered them, infiltrated them and has been welcomed. Waiting for rain.

MYOPIA has one advantage. Always the possibility of two distances; with or without glasses. As though the ear could filter a landscape of sound in two ways. Albertine's cheek as I draw near to kiss it. The smoothness of the forbidden beach is transubstantiated into oily granules. The crystals are too convex, and if I touch the skin they make it echo with astereognostic, chromatic timbre. These landscapes of the flesh are the limits within which you can walk. You never reach the end. Draw back. 'A quite different judgement.'

It is the same with teeth. Landscapes could be classified in terms of how easily they can be nibbled, BITTEN. It would take a bite of tungsten steel to savour the frozen flesh of the lakes of Minnesota in the bitter cold or the Rimouski shore in winter. Given that we don't have that bite, that different judgement, we draw back. But as we do so, we still evoke that impracticable ordeal.

The walls will never be really cast down. Hence the melancholia of all landscapes. We owe them a debt. They immediately demand the deflagration of the mind, and they obtain it immediately. Without it, they would be places, not landscapes. And yet the mind never burns enough.

It is a question of MATTER. Matter is that element in the datum which has no destiny. Forms domesticate it, make it consumable. Especially visual perspectives, and modes and scales of sound. Forms of sensibility which have come under the control of the understanding without difficulty. Things are less clear when it comes to their lower sisters who smell, drink in and touch. For a beautiful visual landscape, walking without any goal, strolling, and the desire to wander simply authorize a transfer of material powers to scents, to the tactile quality of the ground, of walls, of plants. Your foot savours the morbidezza of the mossy heathland and the undergrowth which flank and contradict the sharp stones of the path. In New York, the cars hurtle down Forty-third Street towards Soho, crossing the ruts that criss-cross the street in every direction, their back ends bobbing up and down like badly moored rubber boats. They make the ground ring with the hollow sound of a percussion instrument; their tyres make the noise of suckers being pulled off the road. So many untamable states of matter.

It used to be said that landscapes – *pagus,* those borderlands where matter offers itself up in a raw state before being tamed – were wild because they were, in Northern Europe, always forests. FORIS, outside. Beyond the pale, beyond the cultivated land, beyond the realm of form. Estrangement procures an inner feeling of being outside thanks to an intimist exoticism. States of mind are states of spiritual matter. Suspended between two mental intrigues. See Rimbaud. Beside himself.

Whether or not you 'like' a landscape is unimportant. It does not ask you for your opinion. If it is there, your opinion counts as nothing. A landscape leaves the mind DESOLATE. It makes lymph (the soul) flow, not blood. You do not associate. No more synthesis. It doesn't follow on. Leave it for later. You pray to heaven, to provide for you in your wretchedness. The wretchedness of a soul rubbed raw by the tide-race of matter.

A lonely traveller, a lonely walker. It is not only that conversation, even conversations with yourself, and the intrigue of desires and understanding have to be silenced. As in a temple, a TEMPLUM, a neutralized space-time where it is certain that something – but what? – might perhaps happen. (What I mean is that this 'templation' is the price that has to be paid so that even the cacophony of the Place de la République can become a landscape at 5.30 p.m. on a winter's day, when it is choked with thousands of jammed vehicles.) Not only solitude, but the disconcertment of the powers, and therefore the defences, of the mind. Not alone with oneself, but behind oneself. The self is left behind, sloughed off, definitely too conventional, too sure of itself and over-arrogant in the way it puts things into scale. It is tempting to speak, yet again, of what Cézanne calls 'little sensations'. Inner desolation.

There are a thousand ways of obtaining this surrender. Feasting or fasting, tobacco, grass, *farniente,* overwork. But it always requires something that is TOO . . . (if only too little). In order to have a feel for landscape you have to lose your feeling of place. A place is natural, a crossroads for the kingdoms and for homo sapiens. The mineral, vegetable and animal kingdoms are ordered by knowledge, and knowledge takes to them quite spontaneously. They are made, selected for one another. But a landscape is an excess of presence. My *savoir-vivre* is not enough. A glimpse of the inhuman, and/or of an unclean non-world (*l' immonde*). Is this still a form of order, a different form of order, as Kant suggests in his vesania? A displacement of the vanishing point? A vanishing of a standpoint, rather.

We should describe, succeed in describing. Find a rhythm for the sentences, choose the words on the basis of their specific deviation from phonetic and lexical habits, rework conventional syntax. Get closer to singularity, to the ephemeral. But perhaps it is impossible to describe with any spiritual accuracy, with any accuracy of the soul (I will not even speak of feelings) without recounting how, where and when it happened. Without supplying a framework. For it is at this point, one might think, that landscape's power to dissolve really makes itself felt in the sense that it interrupts narratives. If that is the case, we are not looking for a lexical or phonetic opposition, but for an opposition between two genres, between telling and showing, and they are different tenses. But the opposition is therefore not an opposition. Mind finds its poise, its repose in narrative activity. What I mean is this: it establishes, despite the most intriguing artifices, its persistence, its grip, and its hold on time. It makes time pass, even fly, but it also holds it back, turns it back, makes it curl into spirals, makes it escape itself and catch up with itself. Whereas as landscape simply seizes it. What we call description is no more than a literary procedure which puts mental activity on a par with its narrative stance, and difference is reduced to the *shifting* of temporal indicators (pronouns, verbal tenses, adverbs, etc.). An operationalist reduction of what is 'in reality' (?) an ontological abyss. I am not saying that it has no pertinence; how could we capture the breath of wind that sweeps the mind into the void when the landscape arrives, if not in the texture of the written word? But despite, or beneath, this conscientious approach, we must bear in mind that telling and 'showing' are not two mental positions, or that, if they are, it is only because we forget that they are incommensurate, that showing (the landscape) is already of the order of a reprise or a takeover, that the mind draws itself up when it draws a landscape, but that the landscape has 'already' drawn its forces up against the mind, and that in drawing them up, it has broken and deposed the mind (as one deposes a sovereign), made it vomit itself up towards the nothingness of being-there. In description, writing tries to meet the challenge of being equal to its momentary absence. Not only is it always too late (nostalgia); words themselves are outrageously cumbersome, that is, at once too wretched and arrogant to designate the super-plenitude of this void state (melancholia; we will always owe landscape a debt; impossible mourning). Poetry arises out of this understanding of wretchedness; otherwise it is merely a staging (*mise en scène*) and a mobilization (*mise en oeuvre*) of the powers of language. It is the writing (*écriture*) of the impossible description; DESCRIPTURE (*décriture*). And the difference between describing and recounting should not be confused with deferring, which is the fate that awaits the mind when it tries to grasp itself through logic, theory of knowledge or of literature, narrative or essays. It is matter as landscape that is at stake in poetic descripture, and not the forms in which it can be inscribed. Poetry tries not to tame the forms which form language, not to procure the inscription which retains the event of the landscape. It tries to slip by before its withdrawal.

We therefore have to correct ourselves again, constantly: it is not estrangement which procures landscape. It is the other way around. And the estrangement that landscape procures does not result from the transfer of a sensorial organization into an other sensorium, such as the transfer of the fragrance of scents into the flagrance of colours or into the light of timbres. This estrangement is absolute; it is the implosion of forms themselves, and forms are mind. A landscape is a mark, and it (but not the mark it makes and leaves) should be thought of, not as an inscription, but as the erasure of a support. If anything remains, it is an absence which stands as a sign of a horrifying presence in which mind fails and misses its aim. Fails, not because it was looking for itself and did not find itself, but (we are forced to fall back on comparisons) in the sense that one can say that one missed one's footing and fell, or that one's legs gave way, as one sits on a bench, watching a window which is lit up but empty.

A baby must see its MOTHER's face as a landscape. Not because its mouth, fingers, and gaze move over it as it blindly grasps and sucks, smiles, cries and whimpers. Nor because it is 'in symbiosis' with her, as the saying goes. Too much activity on the one hand, too much connivance on the other. We should assume, rather, that the face is indescribable for the baby. It will have forgotten it, because it will not have been inscribed. If there is an element of the 'too' involved, it is because there is too much of a mark, rather too much support. The first act in the 'deferred action' Freud tried to elaborate. But he was too much of a psychologist. This mother is a mother who is a timbre 'before' it sounds, who is there before the coordinates of sound, before destiny.

Anyone who asks me, 'Where does your landscape take place?' is prescribing me a topography and a chronography of the mark that is landscape. And yet it is clear that landscapes do not come together to make up a history and a geography. They do not make up anything; they scarcely come together at all. Can it even be claimed that they have a family likeness? But although its boundaries are indefinable (how far does kinship extend?; the institution decides), a family is localized (its members live under the same roof), articulated (in terms of categories: father, daughter, maternal cousin, etc.) and may be hierarchically organized (a family tree) around an arbitrarily chosen centre (the *ego*). It is not the same with landscapes; they may display no likeness, may date from different epochs, and so on. It is said that they are the product of an imaginary space-time. I think that they have nothing to do with the imagination in the normal sense of the word (which includes Lacan's sense), or with even a free synthesis of forms. Where and when they happen is not signalled. They are half seen, half touched, and they blind and anaesthetize. A plaint of matter (of the soul), about the nets in which the mind incarcerates it.

It is only 'after' it has been a landscape, but also while it is still a landscape, that the face is covered over by a countenance and uncovers the countenance. The INNOCENCE of walking in it is forgotten. Prescriptions begin to come and go between you and me. The law takes a grip on the gaze, the nose, the face, the forehead, the joints between the maxillaries and the parietal bones, and the cervical supports of the cranium. Features have to be deciphered, read and understood like ideographs. Only the hair, and the light that emanates from the skin escape its discipline. The law sends signals across what was once a landscape, between its remains; indignation, supplication, distress, welcome, disgust, abandon. It says: Come, Wait, You cannot, Listen, I beg you, Go, Get out. When tragedy steps on to the stage of the passions and of debts, it empties the landscape. And yet, if you ever happen to be in love, really in love, the vista of the face continues to grip you even as you bow to the law that emanates from the countenance. And that is why you no longer know where you are. Too innocent for love if you experience only a defeat due to the excess of presence; too cunning if you only try to obey its peremptoriness. What comes from the other in love is no mere demand. In obedience to the imperative of dependency, and even without the beloved knowing it, the nothingness of the landscape that is his/her face wreaks a very different desolation on your mind. You are no longer simply its hostage, but its lost traveller.

NOTE

1 Kant, *Anthropology from a Pragmatic Point of View*, tr. Mary J. Gregor (The Hague: Martinus Nijhoff, 1974) 54, 4.

Translated by David Macey

12

Anamnesis of the Visible, or Candour*

I imagine a man withdrawing (*qu'un homme se retire*). When the man who withdraws is a painter, something happens to representation.

Withdrawal, *ritratto*, portrait. On 7 September 1983, he draws an *Autoritratto*. On 14 August, he paints it. As we were saying, he combines his withdrawal (*se retire*) with drawing (*tirer*) his own portrait. He takes off (*tire*) or withdraws (*retire*) his mask, and holds it out to us. A tragedian's mask, and it does in fact look like him. He folds his face in his hands. He says that the hands are from an eighteenth-century engraving, that they are the hands of an actor. When he takes off his mask, is it only to reveal another mask? Is this merely a moment within the perpetual motion of a masquerade? I think not. I think that this withdrawal is a move towards candour. As though he were trying to clear the visible. This unbalanced body, which is losing its slipper in the same way that one loses one's illusions, or that Oedipus loses his eyes, appears to be rushing towards a candour of vision, towards an other vision.

As he withdraws, Adami's stage becomes even barer. The ambiguities of line of the period of the metamorphoses, which had to be discussed with reference to Ovid and Apuleius, disappear. Especially the bosomy line which we can still see wrapping itself around the feet under *La Tavolá*, around the little temple in the rucksack in *Ascension*, the trophy standing on the Beidermeier piano in *Medea*, the woman's thigh in *Incantesimo del lago* and the hat in *Omphallos*. In defiance of all known etymology, I would like to associate this bosomy line, which curves (*girare*), with gestation, earth (*gè*) with shelter and with lying down (*gite, gésir*). The hope of being wrapped in some lethean, matricial garment, which may perhaps be the inspiration behind love-play, fades on the shores of the 'disenchanted lake'. The archaeological duel, the whirlwind dance of prey and predator, which hollows out

---

* This essay was originally published in the *Catalogue ADAMI*, Editions du Centre Georges Pompidou, Paris, December 1985.

Valerio Adami, *Medea/Biedermeier Zimmer*, 1984, acrylic on canvas, 198 ×
146 cm, Galerie Lelong, Paris, © ADAGP, Paris, DACS, London, 1989.

Valerio Adami, *La Tavolá*, 1984, acrylic on canvas, 198 × 146 cm, Galerie Lelong, Paris, © ADAGP, Paris, DACS, London, 1989.

the navel of tragedy, but without which there can be no possible knowledge of the other ... all that ceases. A man seems to be dedicating himself to solitude and to his past, to an inquiry into his solitary memory, of which he knows nothing. He is entering, one might say, into self-recollection, quite naked, as one goes into holy orders. By which I mean to say that he is stripping himself of our collective imagery. There are few actors on the new stage he has set up. Often only one figure in the centre, working, working through.

Those who like their paintings rich will say that this is an impoverishment. That there is only one character does impose certain limitations on the narrative. The point is not to construct a self-portrait, or a self-anything. The point is to be alone, to be less likely, that is, to be distracted by any intrigue, even with oneself. No intrigue, or almost none. Perhaps even the opposite of an intrigue: disintriguing, or disintricating. No clutter. The point seems to be to construct a landscape, a backdrop without a stage. We move from narrative to description. He points out that there are no landscapes in classical Italian painting. (Is he also attempting an anamnesis of that painting, of which he is a product?) The thread of the narrative is broken, its knots undone. Any landscape appears to indicate a denouement. Or at least the denouement or unknotting of the line that represents the drama. He is looking for the line which announces that denouement. It is horizontal and parallel rather than coiling, gestural and gesticulative. The stakes are higher before the drama than during it. And that would seem to be the denouement he is seeking: the point that exists before there are any knots. The landscape where the knots of history will be tied, where history will build to a climax. A primal landscape. On the shores of the disenchanted lake, a woman awaits the storm. He evokes Poussin: sumptuous landscapes, and a miniaturized plot which is marginalized, out of focus. The satirical stage engulfing the tragic stage, criticizing it.

The withdrawal that I sense, that I am trying to grasp, also speaks the language of colour. The stage lighting is paler now; the light is washed out or too chilly, pale and bloodless, as it should be when it is time to play down activity and passion, and to reflect. The visible is shot through by a light which, if it were translated into sound would be a murmur, the clicking of a rosary, a tender substance, water lapping against a boat as you push it out with your foot into a grey lake at twilight. Dawn and dusk. The painter goes to seek his repose at the point where time becomes open space. As he walks away, he crosses the parallel lines of the landscape's legible score, and the only visible trace of his withdrawal is the gentle lapping of the water on our shoreline. The light whose only source is the violins at the end of *Die Verklärte Nacht*, of Schoenberg's transfigured night.

The importance given to colour detracts from the draughtsmanship. He certainly does not neglect draughtsmanship; he would be incapable of doing so. But he can 'criticize' it, as he puts it. Transferring a sketch to canvas and translating it into colour necessarily involves 'criticism'. This uncompromising draughtsman's line moves by itself, smoothly imposing its presence as though it were emerging from the paper itself. The sheet of paper is like the rectangle of a train window when you are sitting with your back to the engine: the landscape moves away from you, escapes from you, he says, closes in on itself and becomes impenetrably blurred. The coloured canvas based on the same sketch inverts the movement. You are facing the engine, the landscape comes towards you and is restored to time and place by the grace of light, something of which the severity of line knows nothing. Colour is both the withdrawal of line (*le retrait du trait*), its 'critique', and its elucidation. Tones that are midway between night and day bathe both the figure and the landscape, and give us access to the soul.

When he is drawing, he says, he begins with the foreground, and leaves the line to organize the background, the context. First the knot of the intrigue, then the stage on which it is acted out. When he is painting, it is the other way around; he first blocks in the landscape, the sky and the background, and it is only when the painting is complete that he introduces the actor.

The women are reclining, and have no faces. And yet are they not the obligatory subject-matter of all painting? And is not this painting yet another testimony to the curse of separation and to the search for redemption in fiction? What else is there to paint, even if one paints abstracts, but the flesh, and the knowledge which puts an end to the woes of 'each to his own'? There can be no work of art if the seer and the seen do not hold one another in an embrace, if the immanence of one for the other is not manifested and glorified, if the visual organization does not make us feel that our gaze has been seen and that the object is watching. And is not the purpose of painting – even when it is withdrawn, even at its haughtiest, its most reserved or its most modest – to tame the savagery of the thing, to make it submit to the visible, and at the same time to make our usual gaze submit to its savagery? By pursuing and intensifying the spontaneous intercourse that takes place between vision and its objects? We thought we knew how to see; works of art teach us that we were blind. Just as a woman can sometimes teach a man. (Yes, but such a woman never appears on stage; such a body is never desirable. An apparition, a denuding (*dénuement*) which is always veiled, which does not ask to be unveiled. A body from a time when there were no genders, a woman from a time when there was no difference.) He thought he knew how to feel and judge, but she revealed his insensitivity. Abandon the attempt to hold in the present (*maintenance*), let go your hold. Form does not belong to you, but to matter. Give in to resipiscence. Give me your eyes, your ears, your tact. You can only touch me if I can touch you. This denuding is a preliminary to consciousness and painting, but does it not persist in the very movement that leads to solitude? Is there really any great difference between turning in upon oneself and turning to the other? Isn't it more a matter of a mutation within a community? A transition from a community of intrigue to a community from a time when there was no drama, no knots and no laps? From history to pre-historicity?

Hands hanging free: the hands of Ariadne in *Thésée*, the left hand of the faun in *Early Morning*. The hand of resipiscence, which says, 'I give up. I have surrendered my weapons, my concepts; come and see.' A hand lying horizontal, holding nothing. The hollow palm of surrender is a refutation of its obverse, of the aspect which appears when the hand grasps the object, suddenly clasps it, captures it, measures it and violates it. The hidden side to it, the hollow palm that is usually concealed by the gestures of intrigue. Intriguing means not opening your hand, holding things in the present (*maintenance*). A hand is like an eye; in order to seize something, it closes, takes aim, focuses, grasps. When it is open wide, extended, fingers spread, it reveals its susceptibility, the vacant gaze that awaits the caress it promises. When it is in recline, it has already received. It has already both admitted and denied the crime, the drama and the intrigue of its poignant closure. It has freed the gaze from the grip of the present.

Withdrawal as anamnesis of the visible: this could mean painting or drawing a hand in a position in which it can neither paint nor draw as it can grasp neither a pencil, a brush nor a theme. The resipiscence which is being enunciated is at odds with the mode and the rigour of its enunciation. The paradox of saying 'I am no longer one of you', but saying so by going on painting. Being active, in order to signify passivity. How is Adami's taste for order, for, in a word, rigour, which he also refers to as clarity, compatible with this denouement? This work, this *Durcharbeitung* is usually accomplished at great cost, with great effort, at the cost of the suffering caused by reopening scars with such sharp precision. The enigma, for the hand of a painter, of wishing to be involuntary.

The precision required for this is not that of the ruler or of mensuration, nor that of a project. It is feeling which guides the scalpel. Neither the will nor the understanding. Nor yet emotion, which is too still, too subjective. The *I* which uses painting to say 'I am no longer one of you; I am going away' also asks what *we* is, and may perhaps be evoking an other community. After all, his visual rigour is not subjective; it is a matter of feeling. Feeling, or rather sentiment, is not a matter for the ego; it is matter taking on a form, and its hold is neither active nor passive, as it exists before the act and before subjectification. Affinity rather than precision. By moving through the intrigue, by reaching a point in advance of any intrigue, he may be moving towards candour.

At the beginning of 1985, he stopped dating his canvases. The erasure of dates means that we can no longer periodize the evolution of his *oeuvre*. Today's period will never be a period, an act within the unfolding of the action which will have been his life, or his life in painting, an hour within a tragic day, a knot in the complexity of the intrigue. An other time erupts into chronology, and submerges it. A diluvian rain washes away the uncertainties of the passions.

The women who recline here display their backs and their buttocks, but hide their faces. *Grottesco, Reclining Nude, Sunset.* It is as though he had gone into mourning. As though he were mourning the scene of conflict, the metamorphoses, intrigues and intrications, the Olympus where plots are hatched and where squabbles take place, the sumptuous tributes that the drawings and the paintings of recent years paid to separation and to love, to knowledge. Could it be that he has taken his leave of tragedy, for the sake of the tranquil pleasures of 'wisdom', of a well-tempered melancholy?

He asks me if I know Ferdinand Hodler. In 1908, the 55-year-old symbolist and decorative painter met Valentine Godé-Darel. They fell in love, and in 1913 she gave him a daughter. On 26 January 1915, she died of cancer in a clinic in Lausanne. During her interminable death-agony, Hodler took the train from Geneva to Lausanne every day and drew her as she lay on her death bed. The result was a series of over 200 pitiless drawings and paintings. The edifying style lasted only for the duration of the ordeal. What is more important, and this may show us what it means to be withdrawn, as he sat in the dying woman's room, Hodler also painted the lake. He had been painting Lake Geneva for fifteen years; it was his Montagne Sainte-Victoire. And the death of his wife revolutionized his style as a landscape painter too.

Hodler held to the doctrine of horizontal parallelism, and applied it by painting heavy lines across his canvases. The same principle still governs his views of the lake, but it is no longer applied by the use of line; it springs forth, wells up and stems from chromatics alone. There are two wonderful *Sunsets*, one painted the day before Valentine died, the other painted the day after she died. Adami says that they anticipate Rothko. Colour wells up as Hodler mourns the line which accompanies and works upon the end of the intrigue. I am not saying that this is always the case, as there are no rules. (And yet a similar change came over Klee in Tunis, when the golden moon was revealed to him. Like a femininity dating from a time when there were no women.) As for Adami, something similar happens, I think, in the later paintings, where colour produces a surface by laying down parallel horizontal bands, the mortal remains of an intrigue. Does this form of mourning free him from the volubility of line? Does colour undo knots? To make way for 'wisdom'? Or for childhood? Or does it hatch a new intrigue, build a new stage?

My question is this: what question is Adami asking in his later work?

Foolish as it may seem, let me give a brief periodization. The paintings of the 1960s are a hateful exhibition and enumeration of the objects which Consumerism carves out of bodies and souls; they denounce a plot against grace. This catalogue of alienations is followed by the Album of the Baffled Mind; in the 1970s he paints portraits of the thinkers, writers and politicians of the modernist renaissance, those who were massacred by the Terrors of the 1930s. By about 1980 he is simply painting memories of love, offerings to an impossible union, ex-votoes to the metamorphoses of desire, monuments to separation and death. If it is true that he is now withdrawing, to what memory is Adami dedicating his work? To what lost time and space are line and colour devoted when the painter leaves the world? When the hand no longer grasps anything. What is a painting when it is not inspired by desire? What is a painting in which nothing is at stake? Is death a painter?

No longer being in the world may not mean death. There may be several ways of being in the world, and several kinds of world. And the painter's way of being may not be exactly the way of intrigue and desire. If the work is to exist, he may have the opposite way, or an other way. Such as feeling, feeling as being in the world, withdrawing from desire and all its workings. And what if there were no relationship between desiring and feeling? Or at least no causal or purposive relationship, such as the relationship Freud postulates between pleasure and wish-fulfilment? Suppose there were a feeling, a specifically aesthetic feeling, that existed independently of motive, tendency and fulfilment. And what if it were more than independent?

What if it were prior? A susceptibility which was already there, before there was any intrigue. And what if that prior affinity were the object of Adami's present anamnesis? An affinity which is not the subject of a painting, but which makes painting possible. Its condition of existence.

It is as though he had said: 'Turn away'. Either an order or a hypothesis. Turn away, full stop. Turn away in order to see, and to be seen. Or as though he had said: 'Turn away; I am not building a memorial to you, but to a presence which your presence hides'. Turn away, in order that presence might be. There is no presence. It comes too late. But I would like to present you with the fact that presence did once exist. Just as the dying Valentine set free landscape, the childhood of the visible. I would like to present the presentation. It will be presented; it will have been present, and that is why I can present it. Belatedly. Like the childhood of what will be represented: you, as seen by me. Withdraw, not so that I may desire you and wish to be as one with you to the death, but in order that in your absence, and thanks to your absence, there may come into being a memory of what made your presence and our scene possible.

This painting certainly still remembers. But this is not the art of the past, of exposure. It is, rather, the art of exposition, of expounding and not of holding in the present. An open-handed art. There is no attempt to see again, or to reveal anew something which was once seen but which is no more. There is no memory of images. By reproducing a lost object, which means producing an image of it, the imagination merely reproduces separation and amnesia. 'And here at last', writes Barthes in his *Discours amoureux*, 'is a definition of the image, of all images: the image is that from which I am excluded.' '*I*' is to be understood as meaning 'subject of and to the visible'. The repetition of the visible, its re-presentation, is and repeats the banishment of that subject.

It is believed that once there was, in the present, a stage: action, drama, characters, conflict, intrigue. Scene one, blow one. All the rest was simply a representation, a repetition. But the fact that the scene was, and is, staged is not shown on stage. On stage, we had misrecognition and tragic destinies, exceptions, and what Barthes calls exclusions. The stage and the intrigue that was played out on it were not the product of some primal trick, a blow of fate, a throw of the dice, a harsh blow, a dirty trick or some primal crime. Given that all these blows and tricks were and can be represented, there must already have been a stage. The stage was set by a scenogenic or even scenographic pincer movement, by a trick which cannot have been an event for the hero as it was that trick which constituted him as being subject to forgetfulness and misrecognition, made him a subject of desire and images, made him a will to know; and it constituted us as his spectators. Of course he felt nothing, saw nothing and knew nothing. He was born of it, immediately deceived, put on stage, represented and personified, like one of the legendary Giants. It was this trick that gave birth to scenes and images. Because he was tricked in this way, the young Oedipus could not see the trick that was played on him when he was cast for his part either. Always too late for that moment, condemned to living and reliving a childhood he could not recover, or have.

In his Metamorphoses, Adami depicts great scenes from the Intrigue of Antiquity. We are still acting them out. Nowadays we would say that he is attempting their anamnesis. He is trying to accomplish that trick, rather than to re-present the legendary first trick. Deferred action (*l'après-coup*) is not a repetition of some first trick or act (*coup*). The trace that was first traced in the soul of the hysterical Emma was inscribed outside presence, without any subjective emotion, explains Freud (even though he still believed in the reality of the primal scene in 1895). It was a turning point, a *Wendung* rather than a trick. A trick played by circumstance, in the circumstances, an about (*circum*) turn. But it was not meant to take anyone in, and no one took that turning. A trick that misfired. A repetition or a rehearsal, in the theatrical sense, but not one which repeated a scene; it simply staged it, expounded it, and is still expounding it. An exposition.

That is why the scene, the 'second trick' or the intrigue requires anamnesis, and not an identificatory fixative memorization which tries to go beyond it. We attempt in vain to cognize, in the sense of recognizing, because there was no first thing, or cause, and no initial scene. No object. What can consciousness grasp when the trick has been played on it so gently, so smoothly. It is the pain of the present, plague and doubt which warn us too late that a destiny has been sealed, that a deferred action is about to take place. The pain now suggests that a wrong was done. It demands a commentary, a cause, but it is mistaken, for the beginning is part of the plot, and so is the wish for a beginning and the wish to have done with the beginning. Oedipus.

Pain does at least trace a line of return, a line of flight to an already. It institutes childhood as the moment when the trick was played unnoticed, even if it does give it the lustre of the first scene. It traces the horizon for the formation, the shaping of a soul shaped before any concept or object existed, and it is always there, and always allows us to see. Childhood, the space-time of presentation or exposition, is the lost

Valerio Adami, *L'incantesimo del lago*, 12.1.84–12.7.84, acrylic on canvas, 196 × 260 cm, Galerie Lelong, Paris, © ADAGP, Paris, DACS, London, 1989.

landscape for which the represented cries out in its pain, and which it will always fail to recognize.

Extension and plasticity. A strong, thick, ample line. Powerful feet, hands and necks. The unusually stocky proportions of the bodies. He evokes those of Luca Signorelli, the sturdiness of the Romagna. I think of Piero. Their sturdiness is accentuated by his habit – though it is less pronounced than it once was – of dovetailing one part of an object into another, as though he were working in marquetry: the pointed neck thrusting into the hollow of the collar-bone in *Incantesimo del lago*, or the edge of the boat biting into the tibia, and replicated by the stomach of the dead duck. The joints reveal a highly complicated anatomy, something to be touched rather than seen, that gives the visual work of art a musculature which appears to operate beyond or before visible appearances. And the majesty with which he deploys dimensions. The backgrounds come from afar to pay homage to the pensive figure. Painting, he says, depicts scenes of thought. I think of Fuseli; he corrects me: Blake. He speaks of tactility, of air and of wind. A breeze caresses the buttocks of the figure in *Clear Midnight*. Currents flow, as visible to the eye as they would be tangible to an inert hand in running water. The gaze is drawn into the flesh of things and left in suspense. By the use of horizontals, muted colours, by the central solitude of the figure, by the gestures of abandonment. As for the viewer, his desire to participate, to step on to the stage, to share the suffering is held in abeyance, reined back, reflected back to him. A seduction thwarted.

Anamnesis of the *visible*? We know (more or less) what is meant by anamnesis of the unconscious, of fantasy, of hallucination, of a symptom or a dream. But of the visible? Is it anything more than a vague analogy? The anamnesis of a patient in analysis is at least a mat-ter of language; that of the working painter remains, we may assume, in the realm of vision. Can we use figures and colours to go back to the childhood of vision, to the active circumstance which we rediscover in the visible, just as we can use verbalization on a couch and free association to undo obsessional images, recurrent dreams, ritualistic behaviour, slips of the tongue and parapraxes by naming their lost origins? If so, Adami's purpose, even if it is anamnesis, would relate only to an analysis of his own fantasies, and not to an analysis of our vision. It is conceivable that the unconscious, or in other words the persona, might be the offspring of a trick played on identity and on the community by the gods, or by the Other. But what *Wendung* could possibly give rise to the visible? What crime, what incest produces this bastard?

Or shall we speak of ontological difference, of the reversal whereby Being, like Adami's women, allows us to see, receive and conceive only its back, and shows us nothing but 'existents' (*étants*), represented objects which have been abandoned by presence? Of the trick whereby the presentation itself is hidden from the eye, from the mind? In that case, the existent is not an image in Barthes's sense of the word. The subject of vision is not a lost, panicked soul. On the contrary, the field of the visible, the world, is, by its very constitution, transitive through and through. Woven like a network of ever-possible, incessant transactions between here and over there, between him or you and me. Stretched between a thousand positions which any existent, myself included, can occupy for an instant. Of course we cannot presume to see everything, or to have seen everything, as there are innumerable positions, and as it is impossible to totalize the field. But we can rest assured that all points of view are, in theory, visible points, that the immanence of the seer to the field of the visible is the lot of any seer. Insofar as it is a field, the visible is the opposite of the image; it does not exclude the seer, but disjoints him. Chiasmus, as Merleau-Ponty used to say.

In that sense, singularity is not merely compatible with a sort of potential universality; it demands it. Otherwise, the visible would not be visible; it would be hallucinated. A *we*, or at least a *one* is required for, by and with the visible. 'Those who are awake (vigilant) share a single, common world', writes Heraclitus, 'but every sleeper falls back upon his own idiom' (*eis ton idion apostrephesthai*). The analogy between the unconscious and the visible no longer holds when it encounters the caesura which *idion* introduces into the *koinon*, against this 'apostrophe', this turning away. Each man turns his back on the others.

This scission is the trick which generates the unconscious, the blinded hero. No such trick presides over the birth of the visible, which is, by its very constitution, universal, far removed from any heroism, anonymous, and which can be shared in its perpetual availability. What could the childhood of vision be? An oracle, or a curse laid upon it even before anything was seen, condemning it to the misrecognition that generates sight as blindness?

Philosophy tells us that the visible is deceptive. But it deceives all of *us* at once, and the concept of any science that exists independently of the percept and the gaze must take account of the extent of the deception. It may then be possible to correct the 'misrecognition' that has been attributed to vision's immanence within the field; and it is indeed corrected by the introduction of measurement and calculation, or by intellectual education. Yet it is still incorrigible, as it is corrected in an order which is not its own, within a system of ideas, whereas its order, the immanence of views is, or so we may assume, disavowed, unauthorized as appearance. Even so, sight still makes the setting sun look bigger.

The *logos* may well criticize the delight of seeing; it cannot do away with it. Indeed, it needs to see, because vision provides an irresistible model of unanimity. When it comes to making a judgement of existence, the visible has a sort of irreproachably modest rectitude, a probity of its own. A candour. It does not preclude ambiguity or error, but it always includes the promise of correction. The flesh is transitive, but the unconscious is exclusive. How, indeed why, can we attempt the anamnesis of something which has not been and is not taken away? Which is still proffered to us?

(*En lisant*) *l'Hyperion de Hölderlin*. In the last of his *Remarks on Oedipus*, Hölderlin points out what is so different about Sophocles' tragedy: '*der kategorischen Umkher*', the categorical reversal, God categorically ceasing to address his law to man. In the poem entitled *Dichterberuf* ('the poet's vocation'), this withdrawal is referred to as *Gottes Fehl*, God's fault, defaillancy or absence. In the *Remarks* he speaks of God's 'infidelity'. Oedipus was tricked and cast in his role by the oracle, but he was also abandoned. Not only to a self which was not a self, nor doomed to wander as was Hyperion; his abandonment is the basis on which a stage will be built for the intrigue to be played out. But even when he 'knows' that his abandoned destiny has been fulfilled and known, that the set has been struck, he is still abandoned. He will not die of it, he will encounter another form of abandonment, openly, candidly: the categorical reversal that takes place when the tragedy is over. At Colonus, Oedipus fulfils the destiny of man who no longer has a destiny. He leads a life without any intrigue. Being there for nothing. 'At the extreme limits of pain', writes Hölderlin 'there remains nothing but the conditions of time or of space.' At the extreme limits of the plot, there remains nothing but the presentation, the candour of the here and now, as revealed by the absence of God. A withdrawal which does no doubt still bear the mark of that absence, but which offers itself up to what is there in a deserted landscape. An aesthetic born of a poetics, a tragedy which has become impossible.

The visibility of the stage of intrigue (the image) is deposed and given over (?) to the field of the visible, to the aesthetic. Could description be a product of the absence of narration; could candour be a product of a clarification (a desperate clarification?), which is itself due to the infidelity of God (or of destiny or desire)? Could that be the anamnesis that is in play in these works?

'For the moment I have again sought refuge with Kant, as I always do when I can no longer tolerate myself.' Beaufret cites the admission Hölderlin made to Neuffer in his introduction to an ethical reading (ethical in the sense of Kant's second *Critique*) of the *Remarks on Oedipus*, and, more specifically, of the problematic of the defaillancy of God. I too would like my reading of Adami's withdrawal to take refuge behind the intrepidity of Kant's thought. But I prefer the aesthetic Kant of the third *Critique*.

I can only outline that reading here; the stakes are too high for me to develop it. But I can at least indicate that the withdrawal, or perhaps the anamnesis, which hovers over these powerfully reserved canvases, does clear the field of visibility itself, the abandoned flesh upon which the modern aesthetic has elaborated the pure and 'simple' spatio-temporal conditions of beauty.

Kant's analysis of the beautiful is inscribed under the aegis of the faculty of 'reflective' judgement, which takes a case and tries to discover its 'law' or, as we would now put it, its meaning. When it is transcribed into the topography of the faculties of the soul, this capacity is known as the feeling of pleasure and pain. The question of the beautiful is posed, and divorced from knowledge and morality: the aesthetic approach refuses both to resort to determination by the concept (to structure, semiotic systems, socio- or psycho-genetic explanation, or to theory in general), and to locate the aesthetic 'object' (if we can use such an expression; aesthetics of course has no object) in a process of will or a domain of desire. No concessions are made to Burke, whose aesthetic is polarized around an anthropology of needs, or – to anticipate – to Freud, for whom pleasure of any kind, even aesthetic pleasure, is inevitably a form of wish-fulfilment. In matters of beauty, the metaphysics of energy is stripped of its authority, as is the metaphysics of the concept (the matheme).

It is because it is not bound up with the fulfilment of any need or wish that aesthetic pleasure is independent of all interest; it is because, unlike a judgement of knowledge, it does not have to be validated by any formal condition or by some agreement between the partners involved with the work of art, that it can be universal and necessary without the mediation of concepts. Do not confuse the rules and the issue of the true, be it cognitive, speculative or even merely logical, or those of the good, be it empirical, utilitarian or ethical, with the rules and issues of the beautiful; their differences of opinion are irre-missible, even though it is possible, even desirable, for them to encroach on one another.

We think we know these theses; they form, so they say, Kant's 'theory' of the beautiful which, as Kant himself tries to convince us, unifies the system and heals its scars. We have difficulty in seeing, and we fail to see, that the third *Critique*, and especially the *Analytic of the Beautiful*, consists of an anamnesis which is slow, laborious, and often clumsy but still admirable, and which tries to recapture the childhood of a thought dedicated to the world. That minimum of thought, that minimal thought, so to speak, is known as the faculty of presentation, *das Vermögen der Darstellung*, or imagination. *Dar-stellung, Nun-stellung*, the position of the (in the) here and now. Far from resulting in a system, the analysis of taste forces the critique to do more than break down the *I think* into faculties (thinking the truth in one manner, and justice in another, in accordance with heterogeneous rules), and to exhume a plural state of thought, or perhaps another faculty, which is the childhood of all the other faculties and which still gives them credit, and a world that exists prior to knowledge and will, which is not even a world, but rather a 'field': *ein Feld*.

In the third moment of the *Analytic of the Beautiful*, Kant's negative criteria of pleasure without interest and universality without concepts, give way to a positive analysis: the finality without ends of the judgement of taste resides in a content, and that content is form. The form which governs taste is not the form *of* the object; it is not a pure universal form of feeling, or an empty time-space; and nor is it the more specific form of the schema which, by introducing order into the material datum, prepares it for determination by the concept in cognition. It is a free form which 'floats' over (or under) objects. Its beauty is immediately present for the subject, like the delight, the joy we feel in our souls when we apprehend a direct affinity between a form and our 'inner' receptiveness. There is no boundary to be crossed between an object and a subject existing in a mode of respective closure, but an instantaneous openness. Landscapes have no need of exposition; they exist as states of the soul.

Before it prepares the schema of number, time is a musical rhythm that exists as a free form. Before a triangle prepares the space of geometry, it is a free-floating drawing, a monogram. Before judgement determines the object in accordance with its law, it is reflective; it is in the grip of the case (this particular form). And before it is used to discover the concept, or reason (which has no role to play in aesthetic matters), the case is judged on the basis of feeling. Before thought determines objects, it is gripped by free forms which it does not initially objectify. Susceptibility to forms is a constituent element of the sensibility which creates sentiment, and not a world. If the faculty of judgement is the preserve of the understanding alone, then form is a prejudgement.

There is therefore meaning in donation, in the imaginative *Darstellung*. And that meaning is feeling. It relates to form. Donation is a matter of form. In terms of transcendental logic, form is the ultimate example of reciprocal causality: each part exists only in terms of the whole, and conversely. It requires a judgement of inclusive disjunction: an angle or an interval can be cognized in isolation, but a quadrangle or a melody exists in terms of an immediate synthesis with other angles, other intervals. The whole distributes the parts.

Inclusive disjunction is Kant's term for the immanence of the sensible. Form is simply the field, flesh and mode of its donation, a presentation which presents, which is not noticed, but which is felt. When the painter withdraws from the world, turns his gaze away from the intrigue and from motion, he abandons himself to forms, opens his hand to them.

In the fourth moment of the *Analytic of the Beautiful*, it is stipulated that this free conformity has nothing to do with the laws of association. A break with Hume, a shot across Freud's bows. The associative imagination is merely reproductive, subject to knots of association, to intrication. In the judgement of taste, the imagination is 'productive' and exerts 'an activity of its own (as originator of arbitrary forms of possible intuitions)'. Kant uses the term 'arbitrary'. (Perhaps this is what I insist on calling experimental. In my view, the responsibility for the experimental lies with the avant-gardes. I say that because I have been criticized for doing so. By experimenting with forms, the avant-gardes explore our common sensibility.)

Question: if forms, far from being an objective given, are freely produced by everyone, how can it be claimed that the feeling or judgement that 'this is beautiful' has a universal value, as Kant argues? Yet it is the very fate of art that is at stake in this claim. Unless it has a universal value, art is merely empirically agreeable, and the feeling that it procures must be as incommunicable as a predilection for a scent. Do not the arbitrary and the spontaneous imprison form in an idiolect which cannot be communicated to others? The return of Heraclitus' apostrophe. The destruction of the hope that there might be an aesthetic community. Towards which *we* is Adami withdrawing?

I have yet to say it, but we know that Kant sees the feeling of delight or aesthetic pleasure as resulting from a conformity between the imagination (of presentation) and the understanding (of cognition). Not between specific sense data and a specific concept, but between the imaginable and the conceivable. Form has the same place as the schema (but what place? what sight? and defined by what topography?). It is a prior order immanent within the 'given', the here and now. When truth is at stake, the schema anticipates the conceptual rule by giving the datum a preliminary grooming before knowledge grasps it (diachrony prefigures the ordinal series of numbers and

clocks). When beauty is at stake, this compatibility between receiving/
seeing (*recevoir, voir*) and conceiving is not achieved. Form signals it
and accomplishes it in the mode of aesthetic pleasure (diachrony is the
pleasure of rhythm). (Once again, Freud is refuted in advance: the
pleasure of the beautiful is the pleasure of unfulfilment, 'the pleasure
of mere reflection', writes Kant.)

(It should be noted in passing that the demand for a free interplay
between the understanding and a presentation is an indication that
candour implies rigour rather than expressivity. Adami's hostility
towards expressionisms. Forms no more come from inside than they
come from outside. They date from before that division. The inside
merely produces knots of associations, the intransitive. The outside
produces only objects, appearances which can already be used to
produce regularities. Forms as apparitions formed and produced of
their own volition. It is rigour which keeps open and free the
impossible location of forms.)

If the feeling that something is beautiful does have a claim to
universality, it is because aesthetic pleasure, or the very specific
sensation, occasioned by a form, that there is free affinity between the
presentability and conceivability, is a reflective revelation of the
conditions of all knowledge: a possible affinity between concept and
datum. If thinking in accordance with the true, or cognizing, lies
within the ability of 'ordinary sound understanding', then thinking in
accordance with the beautiful, or feeling, must also be communicable.

It must be. But we will never be able to prove that it is. It is reasonable to assume the existence of the *sensus communalis* which founds
the sentimental *we* of art. It would be insane to demonstrate it. A scientific community exists *de jure* because proof has to be supplied if a
judgement of knowledge is to be recognized as true. Argumentation
must have taken place; the *we* of science is that place, the concept. But
the *we* which feels that this is beautiful cannot and must not be
instituted on the basis of a conviction. It cannot be instituted at all, and
must not be instituted. Every individual aesthetic judgement demands
that the feeling must be shared, and at the same time insists that it can
only be promised (the expression is Kant's) that it will be shared.

The enigma of pleasing forms: in theory they can be shared, but
they are never shared. The tension between those who share in the
beautiful is immediate, and it means that they are at once friends and
alone. A *de jure* promise of communality.

We share a love of works of art. But there are no determinable conditions for membership of our community. Nor can conditions be
imposed upon works to ensure that they deserve our love. There are
many houses in the mansion of the beautiful. Who can predict a given

form will inspire a feeling of delight in one of us, will trigger the signal that there is a great affinity between our power to imagine and our capacity to interpret?

Sketch all possible forms, all possible compositions (including disjunctive compositions), using the various given elements that have already been compounded in the sensible world (by the schema). Someone will find them beautiful, and everyone will then assume them to be beautiful, if someone experiences pure pleasure, a pleasure independent of all intrigues, upon encountering them. Space-time unfolds its possibilities freely, and even though the understanding has not succeeded in imposing its law upon them, it will admit that they are not alien to it. Neither chaos, nor rationality. Neither the logic of desire nor the logic of the concept. Space and time made tangible to the heart, as Proust has it, but also exciting for the mind.

Catharsis. The form the artist presents may well result from a trick played on him by the gods, and it may well have been knit together in fantasy. And yet this reclusive, bad childhood, the childhood of the repetitive image and of the exception, can procure an honest pleasure which can in theory be communicated to all, if the manner of its shaping, the arrangement of space-time created for its presentation, gives endless food for thought. If it is steeped in the good childhood of minimal thought.

Towards which community is Adami withdrawing? The sentimental *we* demanded and promised by aesthetics is an Idea. It cannot be shown. It marks the limits of an anamnesis of the visible, of the sensible. If it is possible to imagine its consistency, we have to imagine it as being that of the flesh, of the field. 'By the name *sensus communis*', writes Kant, 'is to be understood the idea of a *public* sense (*eine gemeinschaftlichen Sinnes*), i.e. a critical faculty which in its reflective act takes account (*a priori*) of the mode of representation of every one else.' This is how feeling escapes a singular, disastrous and idiolectal fate. This is how it escapes the apostrophe. Kant adds: 'This is accomplished by weighing the judgement, not so much with actual, as with the merely possible, judgements of others.'

An abstract comparison or argument, as in the sciences? According to Kant, that seems to be the case only because of the expressions we use to speak of it. We have to imagine a comparison which does not compare, a transition from my appreciation to yours without any mediation, without any *tertium comparationis*, a transition which is possible because it is immediate. And the field of the visible provides the model for this silent exchange because it is made up of an implicit toing and froing between this and that, here and there, now and then, you and me. As with the visible, the silent exchange demanded by the beautiful never ends, because it can never be concluded. It is merely a promise of unanimity. Just as we never cease to see, we never cease to know if and how any given form pleases us, if it gives us the pleasure of a *jouissance* bound up with a phantasmatic, idiolectal matrix, or the pleasure that is independent of empirical interests and finalities, the pleasure which results from a harmonious freeplay between the imagination and the understanding. Am I seeing, or am I dreaming? Hallucinating, or sharing? My madness, or our meaning?

This consensus of feeling, this consent, is in abeyance, but it is *there* in abeyance. Just as, in the represented, the presentation is in abeyance, but *there* in abeyance. *There* is the only way we can put it. *There* does not refer to a site within the visible: it is the visible. As he withdraws, a man, a painter, listens to the call of this spatio-temporal childhood. And now (*maintenant*), a woman appears on stage, holding out her hand (*main-tenant*). She is the wife-woman of all men; she turns towards you, turns upon you all her power to intrigue and to suspect, and asks: 'Are you sure that we are innocent of all intrigue as we strive towards candour? That we can be free of desire and knowledge? That Valentine might not have to die and that God might not have to be unfaithful if your here and now is to be revealed to be Hodler's last resort? *Time . . . resort . . .* aren't they words from a denouement; don't they indicate that you still hope – and strive – for a disintrication, and isn't the intrigue a matter of will? Do you think you will have done with the ruses of desire quite so easily? Aren't you being caught out if you think you can turn to aesthetic immediacy, to the immediacy of feeling? Doesn't your very art show signs of belonging to history? To the history of the West, which merely repeats the oracle, the lie, and their fulfilment? Is it possible for the desert of space-time not to be repeopled with characters and plots, for scenography not to weave scenes?'

'Yes, it is. Please, I beg you, don't turn my anamnesis into an ideology, a false truth and a false rule for life. The will pursues its research in ethics; the understanding and reason pursue theirs in knowledge. Art does not take place. Above all, not that. Its place, its own place, cannot be localized on other stages, on those of desire and knowledge, of the desire to know and of the knowledge of desire. Keep it away from them and their bustling activity.'

'Art for art's sake?'

'No, there's no *for*, because there is no finality, and no fulfilment. Merely the prodigious power of presentations.'

Translated by David Macey

_____

13

Newman: The Instant

The angel

A distinction should be made between the time it takes the painter to
paint the picture (time of 'production'), the time required to look at
and understand the work (time of 'consumption'), the time to which
the work refers (a moment, a scene, a situation, a sequence of events:
the time of the diegetic referent, of the story told by the picture), the
time it takes to reach the viewer once it has been created (the time of
circulation) and finally, perhaps, the time the painting *is*. This
principle, childish as its ambitions may be, should allow us to isolate
different 'sites of time'.

What distinguishes the work of Newman from the corpus of the
'avant-gardes', and especially from that of American 'abstract expressionism' is not the fact that it is obsessed with the question of time
– an obsession shared by many painters – but the fact that it gives an
unexpected answer to that question: its answer is that time is the
picture itself.

One acceptable way to locate and deploy this paradox is to compare
Newman's site of time with that which governs two great works by
Duchamp. *The Large Glass* and *Etant donnés* refer to events, to the
'stripping bare' of the Bride, and to the discovery of the obscene body.
The event of femininity and the scandal of 'the opposite sex' are one
and the same. Held back in the glass, the event has yet to occur; in the
thicket, and in the judas-hold, the scandal has already occurred. The
two works are two ways of representing the anachronism of the gaze
with regard to the event of stripping bare. The 'subject' of the painting
is that instant itself, the flash of light which dazzles the eye, an
epiphany. But, according to Duchamp, the occurrence of 'femininity'
cannot be taken into account *within* the time of the gaze of 'virility'.

It follows that the time it takes to 'consume' (experience, comment
upon) these works is, so to speak, infinite: it is taken up by a search for

apparition itself (the term is Duchamp's), and 'stripping bare' is the sacrilegious and sacred analogon of apparition. Apparition means that something that is other occurs. How can the other be figuratively represented? It would have to be identified, but that is contradictory. Duchamp organized the space of the *Bride* according to the principle of 'not yet' and that of *Etant donnés* according to that of 'no longer'. Anyone who looks at the Glass is waiting for Godot; the viewer pursues a fugitive Albertine behind the door of *Etant donnés*. These two works by Duchamp act as a hinge between Proust's impassioned anamnesis and Beckett's parody of looking to the future.

The purpose of a painting by Newman is not to show that duration is in excess of consciousness, but to be the occurrence, the moment which has arrived. There are two differences between Newman and Duchamp, one 'poetic', so to speak, and the other thematic. Duchamp's theme is related, however distantly, to a genre: that of *Vanitas*; Newman's belongs to the Annunciations, the Epiphanies. But the gap between the two plastic poetics is wider than that. A painting by Newman is an angel. It announces nothing; it is in itself an annunciation. Duchamp's great pieces are a plastic gamble, an attempt to outwit the gaze (and the mind) because he is trying to give an analogical representation of how time outwits consciousness. But Newman is not representing a non-representable annunciation; he allows it to present itself.

The time taken to 'consume' a painting by Newman is quite different from the time demanded by Duchamp's great works. One never finishes recounting *The Large Glass* and *Etant donnés*. The Bride is enveloped in the story, or stories, induced by the strange names sketched on the scraps of paper of the Boxes, etched on the glass, represented by commentators. In the instructions provided for the installation of *Etant donnés* narrativity is held back and almost disappears, but it governs the very space of the obscene creche. It tells the story of a nativity. And the baroque nature of the materials demands many a story.

A canvas by Newman draws a contrast between stories and its plastic nudity. Everything is there – dimensions, colours, lines – but there are no allusions. So much so that it is a problem for the commentator. What can one say that is not given? It is not difficult to describe, but the description is as flat as a paraphrase. The best gloss consists of the question: what can one say? Or of the exclamation 'Ah'. Of surprise: 'Look at that.' So many expressions of a feeling which does have a name in the modern aesthetic tradition (and in the work of Newman): the sublime. It is a feeling of 'there' (Voilà). There is almost nothing to 'consume', or if there is, I do not know what it is. One cannot consume an occurrence, but merely its meaning. The feeling of the instant is instantaneous.

Obligation

Newman's attempt to break with the space *vedute* affects its 'pragmatic' foundation. He is no longer a painter-prince, an 'I' who displays his glory (or poverty in the case of Duchamp) to a third party (including himself, of course) in accordance with the 'communication structure' which founded classical modernity. Duchamp works on this structure as best he can, notably by researching multidimensional space and all sorts of 'hinges'. His work as a whole is inscribed in the great temporal hinge between too early/too late. It is always a matter of 'too much', which is an index of poverty, whereas glory, like Cartesian *générosité* requires respectability. And yet Duchamp is working on a pictorial plastic message which is transmitted from a sender, the painter, to a receiver, the public, and which deals with a referent, a diegesis which the public has difficulty in seeing, but which it is called upon to try to see by the myriad ruses and paradoxes contrived by the painter. The eye explores under the regime of *Guess*.

Newman's space is no longer triadic in the sense of being organized around a sender, a receiver and a referent. The message 'speaks' of nothing; it emanates from no one. It is not Newman who is speaking, or who is using painting to show us something. The message (the painting) is the messenger; it 'says': '*Here I am*', in other words, '*I am yours*' or '*Be mine*'. Two non-substitutable agencies, which exist only in the urgency of the here and now: me, you. The referent (what the painting 'talks about') and the sender (its 'author') have no pertinence, not even a negative pertinence or an allusion to an impossible presence. The message is the presentation, but it presents nothing; it is, that is, presence. This 'pragmatic' organization is much closer to an ethics than to any aesthetics or poetics. Newman is concerned with giving colour, line or rhythm the force of an obligation within a face to face relationship, in the second person, and his model cannot be *Look at this (over there)*; it must be *Look at me* or, to be more accurate, *Listen to me*. For obligation is a modality of time rather than of space and its organ is the ear rather than the eye. Newman thus takes to extremes the refutation of the distinguo introduced by Lessing's *Laocoon*, a refutation which has of course been the central concern of avant-garde research since, say, Delaunay or Malevitch.

Subject-matter

Subject-matter is not, however, eliminated from Newman's painting in any strict sense. In a monologue entitled *The Plasmic Image* (1943–5), Newman stresses the importance of subject-matter in painting. In the absence of subject-matter, he writes, painting becomes 'ornamental'. Moribund as it may be, surrealism has to be given credit for having maintained the need for subject-matter, and for thus preventing the new generation of American painters (Rothko, Gottlieb, Gorky, Pollock, Baziotes) from being seduced by the empty abstraction to which the European schools succumbed after 1910.

If we accept the views of Thomas B. Hess, the 'subject-matter' of Newman's work is 'artistic creation' itself, a symbol of Creation itself, of the Creation story of *Genesis*. One might agree insofar as one can accept that there is a mystery or at least an enigma. In the same monologue Newman writes: 'The subject matter of creation is chaos.' The titles of many of his paintings suggest that they should be interpreted in terms of a (paradoxical) idea of *beginning*. Like a flash of lightning in the darkness or a line on an empty surface, the Word separates, divides, institutes a difference, makes tangible because of that difference, minimal though it may be, and therefore inaugurates a sensible world. This beginning is an antinomy. It takes place in the world as its initial difference, as the beginning of its history. It does not belong to this world because it begets it, it falls from a prehistory, or from an a-history. The paradox is that of performance, or occurrence. Occurrence is the instant which 'happens', which 'comes' unexpectedly but which, once it is there, takes its place in the network of what has happened. Any instant can be the beginning, provided that it is grasped in terms of its *quod* rather than its *quid*. Without this flash, there would be nothing, or there would be chaos. The flash (like the instant) is always there, and never there. The world never stops beginning. For Newman, creation is not an act performed by someone; it is what happens (this) in the midst of the indeterminate.

If, then, there is any 'subject-matter', it is immediacy. It happens here and now. What (*quid*) happens comes later. The beginning is that there is . . . (*quod*); the world, what there is.

Duchamp took as his subject-matter the imperceptibility of the instant, which he tried to represent by using spatial artifices. From *Onement I* (1948) onwards, Newman's work ceases to refer, as though through a screen, to a history which is situated on the other side, even if that history were as stripped down and as supremely symbolic as is, for Duchamp, the discovery, invention or vision of the other (sex). Take the sequence of 'early' paintings (in which Newman becomes Newman), that come after *Onement I: Galaxy, Abraham, The Name, Onement II* (1949), *Joshua, The Name II, Vir Heroicus Sublimis* (1950-1) or the series of five *Untitled* paintings (1950), which ends with *The Wild*, and each of which measures between one and two metres in height and four to five centimetres in breadth; we can see that these works do not 'recount' any event, that they do not refer figuratively to scenes taken from narratives known to the viewer, or which he can reconstitute. No doubt they do symbolize events, as their titles suggest. And to a certain extent the titles do lend credence to Hess's Kabbalistic commentaries, as does Newman's known interest in reading the Torah and the Talmud. Yet Hess himself admits that Newman never used his paintings to transmit a message to the viewer, and never illustrated an idea or painted an allegory. Any commentary must be guided by the principle that these works are non-figurative, even in a symbolic sense.

If we examine only the plastic presentation which offers itself to our gaze without the help of the connotations suggested by the titles, we feel not only that we are being held back from giving any interpretation, but that we are being held back from deciphering the painting itself; identifying it on the basis of line, colour, rhythm, format, scale, materials (medium and pigment), and support seems to be easy, almost immediate. It obviously hides no technical secrets, no cleverness that might delay the understanding of our gaze, or that might therefore arouse our curiosity. It is neither seductive nor equivocal; it is clear, 'direct', open and 'poor'.

It has to be admitted that none of these canvases, even if it does belong to a series, has any purpose other than to be a visual event in itself (and this is also true, if not more so, of the fourteen *Stations* of 1958-66). The time of what is recounted (the flash of the knife raised against Isaac) and the time taken to recount that time (the corresponding verses of Genesis) cease to be dissociated. They are condensed into the plastic (linear, chromatic, rhythmic) instant that *is* the painting. Hess would say that the painting rises up (*se dresse*), like the appeal from the Lord that stays the hand of Abraham. One might say that, but one might also say in more sober terms that it arises, just as an occurrence arises. The picture presents the presentation, being offers itself up in the here and now. No one, and especially not Newman, makes me see it in the sense of recounting or interpreting what I see. I (the viewer) am no more than an ear open to the sound which comes to it from out of the silence; the painting is that sound, an accord. Arising (*se dresser*), which is a constant theme in Newman, must be understood in the sense of pricking up one's ears (*dresser son oreille*), of listening.

The sublime

The work of Newman belongs to the aesthetic of the sublime, which Boileau introduced via his translation of Longinus, which was slowly elaborated from the end of the eighteenth century onwards in Europe, of which Kant and Burke were the most scrupulous analysts, and which the German idealism of Fichte and Hegel in particular subsumed – thereby misrecognizing it – under the principle that all thought and all reality forms a system. Newman had read Burke. He found him 'a bit surrealist' (cf. the Monologue entitled *The Sublime is Now*). And yet in his own way Burke put his finger on an essential feature of Newman's project.

Delight, or the negative pleasure which in contradictory, almost neurotic fashion, characterizes the feeling of the sublime, arises from the removal of the threat of pain. Certain 'objects' and certain 'sensations' are pregnant with a threat to our self-preservation, and Burke refers to that threat as *terror*: shadows, solitude, silence, and the approach of death may be 'terrible' in that they announce that the gaze, the other, language or life will soon be extinguished. One feels that it is possible that soon nothing more will take place. What is sublime is the feeling that something will happen, despite everything, within this threatening void, that something will take 'place' and will announce that everything is not over. That place is mere 'here', the most minimal occurrence.

Now Burke attributes to *poetry*, or to what we would now call writing, the twofold and thwarted finality of inspiring terror (or threatening that language will cease, as we would put it) and of meeting the challenge posed by this failure of the word by provoking or accepting the advent of an 'unheard of' phrase. He deems painting incapable of fulfilling this sublime office in its own order. Literature is free to combine words and to experiment with sentences; it has within it an unlimited power, the power of language in all its sufficiency, but in Burke's view the art of painting is hampered by the constraints of figurative representation. With a simple expression like 'The Angel of the Lord', he writes, the poet opens up an infinite number of associations for the mind; no painted image can equal that treasure; it can never be in excess of what the eye can recognize.

We know that surrealist painting tries to get around this inadequacy. It includes the infinite in its compositions. Figurative elements, which are at least defined if not always recognizable, are arranged together in paradoxical fashion (the model is the dream-work). This 'solution' is, however, still vulnerable to Burke's objection that painting has no potential for sublimity: residual fragments of 'perceptive reality' are simply being assembled in a different manner. And Newman finds Burke 'a bit surrealist' because, as a painter, he sees only too well that this condemnation can only apply to an art which insists upon representing, upon making recognizable.

In his *Critique of Aesthetic Judgement* Kant outlines, rapidly and almost without realizing it, another solution to the problem of sublime painting. One cannot, he writes, represent the power of infinite might or absolute magnitude within space and time because they are pure Ideas. But one can at least allude to them, or 'evoke' them by means of what he baptizes a 'negative presentation'. As an example of this paradox of a representation which represents nothing, Kant cites the Mosaic law which forbids the making of graven images. This is only an indication, but it prefigures the minimalist and abstractionist solutions painting will use to try to escape the figurative prison.

For Newman, the escape does not take the form of transgressing the limits established for figurative space by Renaissance and Baroque art, but of reducing the event-bound time (*temps événementiel*) in which the legendary or historical scene took place to a presentation of the pictorial object itself. It is chromatic matter alone, and its relationship with the material (the canvas, which is sometimes left unprimed) and the lay-out (scale, format, proportions), which must inspire the wonderful surprise, the wonder that there should be something rather than nothing. Chaos threatens, but the flash of the tzimtzum, the zip, takes places, divides the shadows, breaks down the light into colours like a prism, and arranges them across the surface like a universe. Newman said that he was primarily a draughtsman. There is something holy about line in itself.

Place

'My paintings are concerned neither with the manipulation of space nor with the image, but with the sensation of time,' writes Newman in *Prologue for a New Aesthetic*, an unfinished monologue dating from 1949. He adds: 'Not the *sense* of time, which has been the underlying subject matter of painting, which involves feelings of nostalgia or high drama; it is always associative and historical . . .' The manuscript of the *Prologue* breaks off here. But some earlier lines allow us to elaborate further on the time in question.

Newman describes how, in August 1949, he visited the mounds built by the Miami Indians in south-west Ohio, and the Indian fortifications at Newark, Ohio. 'Standing before the Miamisburg mound – surrounded by these simple walls of mud – I was confounded by the absoluteness of the sensation, by their self-evident simplicity.' In a subsequent conversation with Hess, he comments on the event of the sacred site. 'Looking at the site you feel, Here I am, *here* . . . and out beyond there (beyond the limits of the site) there is chaos, nature, rivers, landscapes . . . but here you get a sense of your own presence . . . I became involved with the idea of making the viewer present: the idea that "Man is present".' Hess compares this statement with the text written by Newman in 1963 to introduce a maquette for a synagogue which he designed and built together with Robert Murray for the Recent American Synagogue Architecture exhibition. The synagogue is a 'perfect' subject for the architect; he is not constrained by any spatial organization except in so far as he is required to reinstate as best he can the commandment: 'Know before whom you stand.'

> 'It is a place, Makom, where each man may be called up to stand before the Torah to read his portion . . . My purpose is to create a place, not an environment; to deny the contemplation of the objects of ritual . . . Here in this synagogue, each man sits, private and secluded in the dugouts, waiting to be called, not to ascend a stage, but to go up to the mound where, under the tension of that "Tzim-tzum" that created light and the world, he can experience a total sense of his own personality before the Torah and His Name.'

On both the sketches and the plan, the place where the Torah is read is inscribed 'mound'.

This condensation of Indian space and Jewish space has its source and its end in an attempt to capture 'presence'. Presence is the instant which interrupts the chaos of history and which recalls, or simply calls out that 'there is', even before that which is is has any signification. It is permissible to call this idea 'mystical', given that it does concern the mystery of being. But being is not meaning. If Newman is to be believed, being procures 'personality' a 'total meaning' by revealing itself instantaneously. An unfortunate expression, in two senses. It so happens that neither signification, totality or personality are at stake.

Those instances come 'after' something has happened, and they do so in order to be situate within that something. *Makom* means place, but that 'place' is also the Biblical name for the Lord. It has to be understood in the sense of 'taking place', in the sense of 'advent'.

Passion

In 1966 Newman exhibited the fourteen *Stations of the Cross* at the Guggenheim. He gave them the subtitle: *Lama Sabachthani*, the cry of despair uttered by Jesus on the cross: *My God, why hast thou forsaken me?* In a text written to accompany the exhibition, Newman writes: 'This question that has no answer has been with us so long – since Jesus – since Abraham – the original question.' This is the Hebrew version of the Passion: the conciliation of existence (and therefore of death) and signification does not take place. We are still waiting for the Messiah who will bring meaning. The only response to the question of the abandoned that has ever been heard is not *'Know why'*, but *Be*. Newman entitled a canvas *Be* and in 1970, the year in which he died, he reworked it as *Be I (Second Version)*. A second canvas, which was entitled *Resurrection* by the dealer who exhibited it in New York in 1962, was shown together with the *Stations* at the Guggenheim in 1966 under the title *Be II* (it was begun in 1961). In Hess's book, the reproduction of this work bears the legend *First Station, Be II*.

It has to be understood that *Be* is not concerned with the resurrection in the sense of the Christian mystery, but with the recurrence of a prescription emanating from silence or from the void, and which perpetuates the passion by reiterating it from its beginnings. When we have been abandoned by meaning, the artist has a professional duty to bear witness that *there is*, to respond to the order to be. The painting becomes evidence, and it is fitting that it should not offer anything that has to be deciphered, still less interpreted. Hence the use of flat tints, of non-modulated colours and then the so-called elementary colours of *Who's Afraid of Red Yellow and Blue?* (1966–7). The question mark of the title is that in *'Is it happening?'*, and the *afraid* must, I think, be taken as an allusion to Burke's terror, to the terror that surrounds the event, the relief that *there is*.

Being announces itself in the imperative. Art is not a genre defined in terms of an end (the pleasure of the addressee), and still less is it a game whose rules have to be discovered; it accomplishes an ontological task, that is, a 'chronological task'. It accomplishes it without completing it. It must constantly begin to testify anew to the occurrence by letting the occurrence be. In Newman's first sculptures of 1963–6, which are entitled *Here I, Here II,* and *Here III* and in the *Broken Obelisk* he completed in 1961, we find so many three-dimensional versions of the zip which strikes through all the paintings in a rectilinear slash, ineluctably, but never in the same place. In Newman verticality does not simply connote elation, or being torn away from a land that has been abandoned and from non-meaning. It does not merely rise up; it descends like a thunderbolt. The tip of the inverted obelisk touches the apex of the pyramid, 'just as' the finger of God touches that of Adam on the ceiling of the Sistine Chapel. The work rises up *(se dresse)* in an instant, but the flash of the instant strikes it like a minimal command: *Be.*[1]

NOTE

1 I will break off this study here. A lot remains to be said. In the meantime, it is time to state my debt to the memory of Thomas B. Hess for his *Barnett Newman* (New York: Museum of Modern Art, 1971), which is the source for all direct quotations from Newman.

Translated by David Macey

14

The Story of Ruth

Prague, Vienna

Kafka: German among the Czechs, Jew among the Germans. And among the Jews, not Jewish enough, as he writes to his father: 'Your Judaism was completely exhausted while you entrusted it to my hands.' Through her parents, Ruth comes from the Jewish community of Prague. They flee to Vienna between the two wars when she was three months old. Freud is still there. They speak the German of this ex-micro-aristocracy of business. A language which is not of the people, Czech, nor of the culture and the political, German. Frynta says that with this language 'one could name and designate things, but not express them'. A language of realistic accountants. A logic that defies interpretation. Deleuze and Guattari define the language, literary strategy of Kafka: 'Since the vocabulary is dried up, make it vibrate in intensity. Put a purely intensifying use of the language in opposition to all symbolic, or even significative, or simply signifying usage.' They say: this is Joyce or Beckett in English. I'm not so sure about Joyce. Rather, this would be Gertrude Stein. But that other Jewish woman who is Ruth and who recognizes herself in Kafka is not a writer. But there is certainly anguish and the resolution of the anguish of not being able, or not knowing how, 'to speak' in the vocation of painting. The words are missing. Certainly colours and lines for their own part can be just as disposable as sentences, on the condition that they belong to a living culture. Countryside and city landscapes, illumination, reliefs, fauna and flora, paintings hung in family houses and churches, railway-station posters, images in school books, not to mention the customary models in the tradition of the art school and workshops, all provide a sort of plastic language to the young artist. But as in literature, the modern resolve (the arrogance) in painting is to unleash hostilities against these received 'languages'. Cézanne has nothing to do with Corot or Pissaro. What a sad advantage one must have in modern creation not to have conquered a heritage of language! But also what incertitude of position. Ruth asks herself and always will ask herself not only who she is, but what she does and how to put it. The *Portraits,* as well as many other works before the *Portraits*, originate from this blind spot on her retina, from a paralysis of language, from a Babeling. It will be necessary to make this understandable to the French, a nation spaciously established on the lands restored to it by its Revolution a long time ago and whose taste in art is just as slow to develop and to dissolve as is soil to change from rotation: the exile who paints among them is the witness of something almost inaccessible to country people – that since the past half-century history consists of the loss of history. 'One could say,' writes Frynta, 'that Prague had no present just before the First World War. Everything related to the past and to the future. Everyone had to construct his or her own present in the midst of an assault of questions posed from all sides by facts and myths.' When the past and future no longer consist of certainties and plans, but of questions, the present is contained in the question mark, and history is the storm of what occurs. The discontinuities of material, of genre and tone in Ruth's work foil definition: expressionist gouaches of the sixties, neo-realist photometallic sculptures and montages of the seventies, photo-drawings (minus-ism) of the later seventies and eighties. Do they truly form *a* work, she asks herself? Incidentally, is the synagogue named Vieille-Neuve in Prague truly a single synagogue? Is a face truly *a* face?

Oxford

There is no single line for constructing faces. I am not entering into the precise description of the fabrication of *Mirrorical Return.* Butor and Sicard have done it successfully. One knows that frontal and/or profile photography is torn to pieces. The missing fragment is sometimes recovered through pencil (in the *Otages*). Inversely, what remains of the photograph must be seen as a fragment coming to fill a gap in the drawing. The face is exhibited in the incompleteness of its two looks. There is certainly an intention, she says, to critique the 'affidavit' provided by the photographic portrait. But with or without intention, there is also a critique of the eloquence of the well-drawn portrait. The result of the combat between the two techniques, the classical artistic and the modern industrial, remains uncertain. But I return to the line. The parts in pencil are drawn speck by speck. Sicard and Butor speak of the 'thread' to which these specks belong: are they specks of paper, of the photo, or of the face itself? Incertitude also reigns here. Photographic enlargement (making itself more apparent in *Otages*) reveals the discontinuity of luminous impacts. Bundles of photons attack the surface of the face and create its relief, its bas-relief, like a lunar landscape. Connecting the bit of photograph to a beaded cardboard drawing, the artist transmits the granulation of support as that of light. One mixes with the other in the guise of pores of the skin. The faces are landscapes of small craters created by light or by woman. It is said to be a sculptor's drawing. That was not exactly what Rodin or Michelangelo would have done. One should say rather that it's a sculpture in which there are no traits but relief. However the relief is obtained by varying the density of pin-pointed elements, without a cast. The medium, pencil, is not ruined, displayed, but distributed like shavings. No more covered than linear. This distribution of specks of shadow provides, says Ruth, the rhythm of the face's respiration, the breath of its pulsations. The woman ventilates the interior of heads first by ripping open their envelopes, but most of all, by meticulously piercing their surfaces. Or, rather, there isn't a surface to perforate; the gaps between pieces are what constitute the surfaces, what simulate them. In ignoring the bidimensional, the volume begets itself from the point. The result is that even in the most absent face, Lidner, in the most haggard, Beuys, in the most suspicious, Tinguely, in the most melancholic, Xenakis, this technique of evil eyed pin-pricks, far from subjugating the victim to a destiny, unleashes in the victim a free energy to speak (to whom?) with a thousand small mouths, to listen with a thousand ears, and a bliss to be-there completely open. That is, then, how females (*elles*) love us, why they don't require us to be pretty like advertisements, smooth as the baby bottoms of soap opera. In ravaging us, they reveal us, men, to this pointillist and hairsplitting activity. They transform for us our barriers of composed, impregnable countenance into leaves of St John's wort. How well they pierce us. And it is thus that we can be animated. It was at Oxford during the bombardments that Arthur Segal, the Jewish artist in exile from Nazi Berlin whose works we saw in the Paris-Berlin exhibition, taught painting to the young woman from Prague. He forbade lineament.

New York

Gertrude Stein: 'Most of the time we see only a portion of the person with us, the other parts are hidden either by a hat or clothes or by light or shadow. Every one is accustomed to completing the whole entirely by memory. But when Picasso saw a single eye, the other ceased to exist for him.' She adds: 'He was right ... painters have nothing to do with reconstructions or memory; they only have to do with visible things.' Painters of the twentieth century. Picasso is a painter of the twentieth century. Gertrude Stein is probably not a writer of the twentieth century. But writers often speak about painters they have *understood*, therefore with delay, as Baudelaire spoke about Delacroix rather than Manet. And me? Is Ruth Francken a painter of the twentieth century? Rather than this twentieth century-and-a-half that begins after Auschwitz and that is not yet the twenty-first? What distinguishes this mini-century, the half-century, is that painting has little to do with the visible and much to do with the past and future, memory and the possible, acknowledgement and estrangement. We of this half-century view Cézanne, Braque and Picasso, the windows of Delaunay, the Improvisations of Kandinsky, the Compositions of Malevitch as expressions of love for the visible world and space. Even Mondrian. This is because they all are anxious to pay honour and homage to the colours and lines which the world offers us, to settle as well as possible the debt of the sensible acquired in life. Even the most severe abstractions of this twentieth century are dedicated to the comprehension and the presentation of what can best satisfy the heavenly donors of the visible. Reread Apollinaire. The elimination of the subject during this period of abstraction finds its justification in the passion for 'material'. Not in the sense of 'material' art, but of the mystery of the colour and form brought forth by nature's womb. From this Cézannian mystery is the world a 'body of flesh'. In this twentieth century-and-a-half, painters are really interested more in time than in space, in history than in nature. Not merely the history of all, but of each. Which gods must be appeased, with what images? After the crimes against humanity, after the sombre drives of the unconscious? With which unknown images can we hope to pay off the debt incurred by cruelty? These questions previously haunted surrealist painting. The sympathetic writing of these painters is not illuminist like that of Apollinaire, but surrealist at least, like that of Breton in New York. With Bataille the idea (or ideology) prevails that painting was originally a ritual of redemption for the crimes perpetrated by men against the life, especially animal life, most similar to them. Abstract expressionism in the United States during the forties inherited this anxiety together with the exiled surrealism and expressionism of Europe. Abstraction indeed was inscribed in the American tradition where it had been reanimated by Mondrian. But the new abstraction bears no resemblance to that of the teens. It does not analyse the components of the sensible but examines the inconsistency of the signifiable and the improbability of the continuous. Ruth immigrates to New York in 1942, she continues her painting studies at the Art Students League, she works as a designer of (fashion) fabrics. She returns to Europe in 1950, at the beginning of the twentieth century-and-a-half. Giving way to the heretical theology of a history whose sense is neither conceivable nor even felt was the grand European tradition received from Arthur Segal at Oxford, consisting of the analysis of sensorial and plastic data and their reconstruction independent of every object, the metaphysics of a world to be taken in and fashioned. *Guernica* was still too orthodox. Gorky, Pollock, Kline, De Kooning, Rothko, even Motherwell made quake on their canvases the pure uncertitude between what is below and above, before and after, in front and behind. When Hans Hofmann asks Pollock if he paints after nature, Pollock responds: 'I am nature'. To this nature, as with the unconscious, history is unknown. I mean: the connection of events. The painting is the event. This is what Newman shows for the first time in New York, the year Ruth leaves. How does the *Now*, the painting, inscribe itself in a temporal order? Painting is in history the way the Jews of Prague were in the Empire: it has lost the ins and outs of its acts.

Barcelona, Venice

She returns to Europe, to France which she traversed as a child fleeing the war. (Was it a war? The end of eyes, tortured 'flesh'.) Is she starting over? But one doesn't start over. Today you see: faces, strong and dilated by the soul, completely rendered happy to be-there by the turn of minuscule caresses of pencil. She says that they are all similar to the *Köpfe*, the Heads, which she painted and lithographed twenty years ago in Berlin. But these heads and the works of the other series of this period, *Corrida, Corps de femme, Pourquoi?, Grandes Têtes, Tête-à-tête*, are made only by gestures of large brush-strokes crushing the paper with heavy tints of black, blue, and sepia gouache. The soul does not expand them, but terror bursts them. This is not abstract expressionist in the American sense. This is not German expressionist. It is informal expressionist, as Tapié says. Enactment more than anamnesis. The theme of the bullfight (*Corrida*) suggests Bataille or Picasso. She says that the horse and bull are a couple, also, like the faces of *Tête-à-tête*, a couple condemned like them. The horse is the victim given to injury and inexplicable death. The bull has skulls in its eyes and sometimes newspaper cuttings in its nostrils, a cross on the snout. This is a free-for-all. Attention is required to distinguish the silhouettes, carried away by hate, anger. A continuation of *Guernica* and *Horreurs de la guerre*. There is a citation of Goya's *Sabbat*.

> The Spanish are perhaps the only Europeans who never have experienced emotion in the face of the reality of things or in the face of the progress of science. The Spanish do not mistrust progress, they have never known the need. When the other European countries still belonged to the nineteenth century, Spain, in its lack of organization, and America, in its excess, were naturally ready to approach the twentieth century.

So writes Gertrude Stein in 1938. Is the Spain of Ruth Francken the same as that of Gertrude Stein? The *Grandes Têtes* are sometimes like the snout of a monstrous animal or sometimes like the impression left by a crucified face on the veil of a Veronica. Painting tries to pay the debt of a monumental defiguration. The informal is not a style, at least it doesn't want to be, it is the state of European history. The newspaper, lodged in the nostrils of animals, exhales the same terror in the direction of an anaesthetized public. The veil, however, announces the mirrorical return, like the coupling of heads in *Tête-à-tête*. I am the witness of the destruction of faces. I repeat on my paper (these are gouaches on paper) the event of this crime. Fear and pity, tragic purgation. A few years previously Ponge commented on the *Otages* disfigured by Fautrier:

> Here is the most important business of the century: the business of the Hostages . . . It is not in the tumult and heat of battle, but in the silence and cold-blood of the *occupations* that they (the disfigurations) had been perpetrated. And what's more, on the hostages; that is to say, on the abused innocents who are left without defence (and first almost without conscience), without complaints, without possible struggle, the weak.

Ponge says that contrary to Picasso 'masculine, leonine, solar, virile member, erection' etc., Fautrier 'represents the feminine and feline side of painting, lunar, mewing,' etc. The *Köpfe* of '64 do not have this lunar weakness, nor the solar force of the friend of Gertrude Stein. There is an uproar of imprecations, hate, terror, and love that babbles. It is Antigone, and Antigone is not 'feminine'. She cries No! to politics, masculine and feminine. Artaud as well. The *Têtes* spit out letters in disorder. These letters sometimes form words. The word *Word, mot,* for example. A flood of phonemes does not make argumentation. Politics do not take it into account. Sir Herbert Read has a politics. He sees the works of Ruth in her Venice studio, and he writes *A Letter to a Young Painter*, published in 1962. The Young Painter is Ruth Francken. He rebukes her. You create neither a painting of sensations nor a painting of form. You seek spontaneity, vitality. But in this manner your work flushes out symbols (archetypal, Jungian), the symbols prevail over the sensations, and your painting lacks the playful grace that Schiller and Nietzsche require of great works. You have style and force, but no form. You are Jewish and German, writes the nice Lord Read, your soul full of desire for death, nihilism, and despair, like Heidegger and Freud. (This is what he writes.) Great work is affirmative. You will become affirmative in establishing your home, the new country you will have found. In the meantime, your fate will be only to stray (like that of Gabo). One is not an artist without sensuality: 'The sensual in art is everything virile, invigorating, and enriching existence.' There he goes again. In the margin of her copy of Read's book, where I read this advice that irritates her, Ruth noted in the margin: 'Male?'! The twentieth century was perhaps male in painting. The twentieth century-and-a-half has decided, finally, not to leave space-time in the hands of men. I hope.

Berlin

There are thus the horrors of the *Köpfe* beneath the tendernesses of the *Portraits*. Well, 'beneath' . . . , I'm not sure. Within, with. In the same way that there is Nazism in, with and beneath our nice everyday life, as Syberberg shows in *Hitler, a film of Germany*. And one cannot again do Matisse with that beneath the skin. One can have nostalgia for Matisse. In 1964, when Ruth arrives in Berlin as a Fellow of the Ford Foundation, she knows that she must be done with American and German expressionism, not in forgetting it, but in fulfilling it. She has a guide in this direction. It is Lindner who is in Paris in 1950. Jew from Nuremberg, he studies painting in Munich well after the fine time of the Blaue Reiter, too late for the grand analytic abstraction. Interned in France in '39 as a German immigrant, like Walter Benjamin. Passage through the Legion. Arriving in New York in '41, too late for abstract expressionism. When in Paris, where he decides to be a painter, he tries his land at *portraits* (he also). Proust, Kant, Verlaine, the academicians. The dead. In the portraits, one senses Picasso, Leger, a realist pencil, predisposed to aura. His direction becomes set forth in New York which he sees and shows as an immigrant, 'my greatest adventure', he says. He is the painter of the closed line, of the impenetrable, of women corseted, gloved, laced by separation, of body-machines, of colours catching the eye all at once. He isn't Pop because the source from which he fetches his plastic themes isn't the commercial advertising of the society of consumption. Maybe sex shops and B-thrillers perhaps. But drawing's authoritarian distribution of plastic space prevails over allusion to the merchandise and its packaging. He remains a European without a country, 'a child of ten or twelve years', who has lost his past, who travels in America, and who collects puppets of despair. 'At bottom, I am interested in the waiting room, the waiting room of life. We are all in a waiting room; we are waiting for death.' German expressionist metaphysics loses its pathos in the rigorous drawing of cubism and achieves its own satire thanks to 'the matter of fact' colours of new daily life. But the work lies in wait neither for this life nor for beautiful form. It interrogates the twentieth century-and-a-half, its time, brutal and without memory. It is an anamnesis of the amnesiac terror hidden by flash. The classicism of drawing and construction denounces the false gaiety of colours in which Pop Art revels. They refuse even the resort to the sublime of chromatic shores, that by which the 'cool' expressionism of Rothko and Newman escapes realism.

In an analogous fashion, the scream of Ruth's *Köpfe* remains here, twenty years later, with and beneath the calm rhythm of the *Portraits*. But by a completely different path, also requiring a long voyage. The pathetic seems to have disappeared from *Mirrorical Return* and *Otages*. It was merely strangled, but here by the discipline acquired from images and industrial objects. Photography and design are the heirs of what is most male in European plastic art, renascent perspectivism, constructivism and Bauhaus, the revolutions of virility. In abandoning painting in 1964, in turning to the fabrication of large photometallic montage and the sumptuous steel and plexiglass sculptures of the sixties and early seventies, Ruth elaborates, perlaborates, the anguish of what has no identity by means of forms and materials which are the 'coldest', the most clearly defined, the most calculable of Occidental intelligence. Lindner entrusted this (Apollonian) task to drawing, Ruth to the optical geometry of cameras and the machinery of automatic lathes, what originates from the 'seeing' line and what makes its rendering by hand useless. The clamour of disembowelled horses in the *Corrida* is drowned out by the drone of cameras, projectors, and studios. I wouldn't say that she confronts the adversary, the identical, the recognizable, the reproducible, the self (which was entirely the project of Nazism, as it is inscribed in the technology of the media and industries), but she becomes familiar with it, she aims to tame it at the same time that she examines her own pathos. She says that she could no longer tolerate expressionist painting, that it was never finished, not only in her own paintings but in those of others, that she wished it would be finished, that it would hold together and contain itself so that one might no longer add anything to the work. I became crazy, I surprised myself by wishing to finish a Rauschenberg. I needed to have a result in hand, I needed to control the work, so that it would be-there, definitive, unchangeable. By virtue of this identification crisis, in the midst of this impatience, an impulse led her to accept a language in common with her contemporaries. Images and industrial objects are the ordinary vehicles of our communication, to the point of becoming ignored by the users. Their 'basic' platitude is in proportion to their vehicular force. This is an impoverished language, like the German of Ruth's parents. But this is not an idiom, not to say an idiolect, as was the gouache on paper and as is every expression loaded with affect. The tenor of silence in *Köpfe*, *Corrida*, *Tête-à-tête* is in proportion to the pathos which the gesture tries to inscribe 'immediately' (she says) on the paper. By way of the grammar and rhetoric of mediating images, the affect undergoes ascesis, it neutralizes and universalizes itself because it allows itself to be known by the recipients of the work. (Perhaps the scissors period, the series of the Anticastrateur (1973-74), deserves credit for this type of plastic circumcision.) As is often the case, the theme seems the opposite, that is, the protest against the 'repression' brutally symbolized by the scissors. But the change in material, manner, and language signifies at the same time that she accepts her position as the recipient of the common tongue of the present time, that she resigns herself to the loss of a 'femininity', of an expressiveness of the unutterable. It seems that she ceases to scream (like Antigone).

Paris

In a letter cited by Adorno, Benjamin writes:

> The saving effect of writing always resides in the secret of language ... In eliminating the unutterable of language, in making it pure like a crystal, one obtains a truly neuter and sober style of writing ... This style and writing, neuter and at the same time highly political, aim to lead to what is refused to speech ...

The intense orientation of speech in the nucleus of the most profound silence results alone in the effect.

Adorno adds that this extreme objectivity, this universalism of neuter language, 'this ontological asceticism of language is the only style that nevertheless permits the expression of the unutterable'. Ruth learns from clean images and polished surfaces that emotion cannot be conveyed simply, that it surrenders only by holding back, through which the sickening concentration of silence, far from being effaced by the means of reproducible communication, leaves its negative trace better than in 'immediate' eloquence (which, of course, is also a rhetoric, but not an alienated one). The photography of *Mirrorical Return* doesn't aim primarily to enter into conflict with drawing and to display its expressive flatness in this conflict. Sufficiently enlarged, it also guides the drawing, it imposes on it the discipline of pointillism, it denies drawing the flair of eloquent line and gesture, it tames the soul. Ruth says that she learned to draw around 1970, following the photographic and sculptural work. The collage-drawings of the series *Partition pour un orchestre* and *Black Bread* are from 1973–76. And she says that she still learns to draw since she will never know how. But the scope of her drawing is not univocal, such as it works in *Mirrorical Return* (and already to a degree in *Partition pour un orchestre*). The pointillist inscription of the respiratory pores that constitute the skin are like a caress inflating the faces and endowing them with a thrust of presence. But there are also lines, at least in *Mirrorical Return*. They function not to shape the face but to frame it (Sartre, Leopold Lindner) or to encompass the profile of the torn photographic fragment (Xenakis, Lyotard). In this way drawing encircles silhouettes. These lines then can be repeated, either on a face by doubling its contour (Beuys, Cage), or the entire length of a Return's 'film' by giving rhythm to the recurrence of the contour across the modified face. This rhythmic value is more perceptible in the latest triptychs (Lyotard, the second Tinguely, the first Beckett, 1982–83) where the melodic line is incessant, since the form of the fragment creates a series from one aspect of a face to another. Drawing, then, does not construct the face, but arranges the melody forming the multiple aspects of the face, in giving the image its rhythm.

The screams of the *Köpfe* are still audible, but are now ordered by the rules of harmony and composition; they follow from the rules. The time of the work has changed. The work is no longer stretched towards and by the event of the scream or the flash. Ruth writes: 'The fragment of torn photo (signifies) this fissure-wound that makes men, in my eyes, so pathetic by what they *have seen*. The fragment of the face torn away here and there from the geometric drawing of its totality is for me the equivalent of a *scream*.' She develops the analogy in justifying herself: 'The act of tearing the photograph will resemble a veritable birth, as in re-birth. The torn placenta, the "primal" scream, the liquid that functions as the developer of photographic printing.' And she concludes: 'The act of tearing the photograph is an act characteristic of woman.' I hear: the scream is from woman, from the disembowelled horse. But now it discovers its harmonics, men are born from it, each being many, but all also forming, as she says elsewhere, a 'people'. I understand this generation of a resonant people as that taking place in Bach's *Musical Offering* or in *Explosante-fixe* of Boulez, and the calculation of drawing is its support. A plastic, logical, or musical figure can sustain an identical transformation (it is transferred as it is), or a reciprocal transformation (which musicians call repetition, the phrase is reversed in relation to the beat as with 'the lobster') or a negative transformation (inversion in relation to the musical pitch) or dual transformation (or correlative: double musical inversion in time and pitch, introduced by Schoenberg). Boulez and Butor apply these transformers to new variables and materials. One finds them again in the triptychs of Ruth, along with others not forming a system, like ablation and engraftment. Two functions of drawing, then, which are both musical, that of Boulezian composition, but also that of the pores, the discontinuous emergence of small orifices that one will permit me to understand, forcing things a bit, like the 'freeing sounds' of Cage or Feldman. (Since what passes through these orifices is neither a scream.) And in the *Otages*, photographic enlargements of part-photo, part-drawing, sometimes touched up once more in pencil, the function of the composition is set aside, with nothing remaining but that of presentation, of the *Darstellung* of Cage, the sweet nudity of small craters of sound or space.

But to be heard melodiously, the harmony of a people of faces and of aspects of faces and fragments of faces needs a time other than that of the event of their presence. It needs a diachrony. I don't mean a succession, since the order of the study of the different triptychs and the different aspects of the face represented in each is of no importance. Instead, I mean a display of duration. It is conveyed by the elongation of the triptychs that relates them to films or comic strips. One could begin them anywhere and traverse them indifferently in the two directions. The display would not have a unique direction. The time taken by the eye to traverse the long cartoons is not fixed by a tape machine or projector. It is more a matter of the time required in order for what is recognizable, the portrait, to give way to alteration, to exfoliation in lightly diverging aspects, allowing what is concealed by its surface to arise from the background, including the irrepresentable of its heraldic emblem, the shit-coloured dust glued to the grey cement of Beckett, the synthetic foam masked by the midnight blue acetate of Sartre, the rusted cast-iron plate of Tinguely.

Kleider machen Leute, Clothes make the man, say the German and the English. To which the French and Italians respond: the habit doesn't make the monk, *Non e l'abito che fa il monacco*. The four languages say the same thing, that is one thing and its opposite. Denial, in both cases. *Mirrorical Return* is born from Ruth's dream about this paradox. What Duchamp called: the paradox of appearance and apparition.

Ios

One asks her: but why only men, and the elite? She is accused of machismo and elitism. I suggest to her that there is something to glean from the relation of woman to fame. (Antigone.) She experiences a night of insomnia before leaving for Ios. A final book, *Labyrinths* by Borges, abandoned ten years ago on her bookcase, is put in her suitcase for summer reading. In Ios she reads the first story, *The Immortal*. It responds, she says, to the above question. Here is how, in my view at least, I reread it in *Aleph* at the same time I studied her letter on this subject, sent from Ios in August 1982.

Mirrorical Return is an expression she attributes to Duchamp, which is correct, but more precisely to designate this article of sluggish hardware: 'a faucet that stops running when one doesn't listen to it', which I cannot verify. The faucet would reflect mirrorically its living image only to the attentive ear. The photographic apparatus lacks an ear, the hand of woman is an ear. The faces belonging to us, the elite, are faucets. Her hand makes them run. She obtains from them what I call above a 'thrust of presence'. We are an elite because we are capable of this pressure and gush. The surrounding vulgarity sneers: you are her *Booz*, it decides, she lets herself be impregnated during your sleep. The psychoanalyst intervenes, suggesting that it is rather a transference, citing the story of Diotima.

But she proceeds in another manner. While stuffing it with her own parenthetical remarks, she cites page 155 of her *Labyrinths*, which is page 129 of my *Aleph*, being the end of the story entitled *Averroes' Search*:

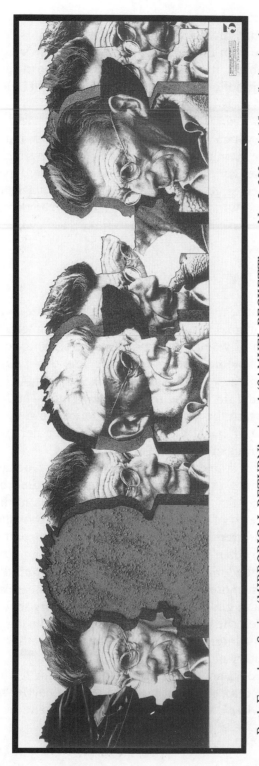

Ruth Francken, Series: 'MIRRORICAL RETURN', triptych 'SAMUEL BECKETT', part No: 3. 200cm × 65cm (ht.) mixed media. Collection: Musée National d'Art Moderne, Centre Georges Pompidou, Paris. Photograph: Adam Rzepka. Reproduced by kind permission of Ruth Francken.

I felt, on the last page (with the last drawing), that my narration (my work) was a symbol of the man (of the woman) I was when I wrote (when I drew) and that, in order to compose that story (in order to do that drawing) I had to become that man (that woman) and that, in order to be that man (or that woman) I had to write this story (make this drawing, this hypothetical portrait), and so on to infinity. ('Averroes' disappeared the minute I ceased to believe in him.)

The relation of the hand-ear of Ruth to the face-faucet of the Portrait is not a hysterical transference, but an identification. The narrator of *Averroes' Search* identifies with his hero once the story is told, after the fact. He wanted to relate the adventure of this 'prisoner of Islamic culture who was never able to know the meaning of the words *tragedy* and *comedy*' which he finds in Aristotle. But the narrator himself, prisoner of Occidental culture, can know nothing or almost nothing of what was Averroes. It is thus precisely that he becomes Averroes, in failing him, as the Arabic fails Greek. Ruth becomes Cage, Lindner, Beckett in failing them as they themselves have missed 'what they have seen' and what they might mean. To repeat, she writes in her letter from Ios: 'Talk about this fissure/wound that makes men, in my eyes, so pathetic by what they *have seen*.' What liquor flows from the faucet? At all events, the same one oozing from the hand-ear of Ruth. This is why she neglects the difference of the sexes and can insert in her citation *woman* where it should be *man*. (If she doesn't make portraits of women, it is because, she says, they don't allow their image to be wounded. Would she herself accept it?)

The letter from Ios recalls a sentence from Bataille that 'a young woman' cited at Cerisy during the conference following the presentation of *Mirrorical Return* in 1982. Bataille writes: 'We communicate only through our wounds.' Relation of Bataille to Duchamp's faucet?

But this is still not the main point of this matter of the scream and the flow. The main point is that the mirrorical return, by awakening of the wounds and exfoliation of history's covering left on the faces, has no ending. This is also what is understood by the reference to *The Immortal* by Borges: 'Among the immortals, on the other hand, every act (and every thought) is the echo of what has preceded it in the past or the faithful conjecture of those who will repeat it in the future to the point of vertigo. There is nothing that does not appear lost between indefatigable mirrors.' Except that Borges adds this, which Ruth does not cite: 'Nothing can happen only once, nothing is preciously precarious.' The narrator of *The Immortal* (interned in Ios), who is also

'Homer', depicts an abandoned and absurd metropolis under the name of the City of Immortals. The Immortals are those Troglodytes who demolished it, rebuilt it as non-sense and deserted it for the miserable opposite shore. They don't speak (since there is no death except by language). Immortality is the non-sense of an infinite repetition without difference, the purely specular. Ruth understands it differently. She writes me that she would like to exhibit the entire *Mirrorical Return* and *Otages* together and that she despairs at seeing them dispersed. One would wander there like in a labyrinth. Huge mirrors would be arranged so that the spectators would unite their faces in virtual space with those of the Portraits. The screams and the summons-responses would resound together in a brouhaha. 'But something will be heard/understood there that I still cannot describe with precision . . . I might say that this labyrinth will be a place where the chant of a beyond-Babel will be born.' Thus she thinks that beyond the cacophony of singular sufferings, even across the irreparable wounds that death (that is language) leaves on the faces, a *philia* makes itself heard, poor in words and invincible. The anguish of death and the solitude of singularities reign over the *Köpfe* of 1964. The *Portraits* of 1983 conserve their contingency, but immortality swells their pores. This is not that of glory, in the mundane sense at least. It is that of a 'people' or a 'family', she writes, which is an elite today only because it announces the republic tomorrow. The mirrorical return is not specular reflection. The society of immortals is not doomed to the repetition of the same, but to the infinite expression of the other. If Ruth lays out a labyrinth of mirrors, it is not for seeing your reflection there, but for wounding your faces and making the juice of alterity flow without end, which requires creation for its manifestation.

Translated by Timothy Murray

15

Analysing Speculative Discourse as Language-Game

The following analysis will appear to be guided by an interference: between Hegel's discourse, which states what speculative language ought to be, and statements (my own) which, in presenting Hegel's discourse as a language-game or discursive genre, determine its rules. This interference appears to be contingent, just as the meeting of two independent series of events is contingent. Indeed, if the two families of statements, those of the object-language (Hegel's speculative discourse), and those of my commentary (the language of the '*ludi sermonis*) are as foreign to each other as are types of events such as the fatigue of a solitary car-driver and the presence of a tree on a bend, it follows that the linking (*enchaînement*) of my statements with those of Hegel is like an accident.

In the Preface to the *Phenomenology of Mind*,[1] this accidental relation is said to characterize predication in positive knowledge. Hegel describes it as follows: on the one hand the *Selbst* (what is in question, the subject of the statement) constitutes the base, *Basis*, an inert support; on the other the contents bearing on it obey an oscillating movement; they do not belong to the *Selbst*, and can be applied to other 'bases', giving rise to other statements. These statements have the form of attributive judgements, and the contents are the predicates. *God is good*, for example, would be a statement pertaining to positive knowledge, which Hegel also calls formalistic thinking (*das Räsonnieren*). What he has in view here is the philosophy of the understanding in the Kantian sense of the word, a philosophy which, according to Hegel, gets stuck on the question of knowing what is the nature of the relation between predicate and subject of a judgement. Conceiving thought, *das begreifende Denken*, does not take as subject the subject of the statement, the *Selbst* in repose, *ein ruhendes Subjekt*, which would support accidents (*das unbewegt die Akzidenzen trägt*); in conceiving or speculative thought, the concept is 'the *Selbst* proper to equivocality. If the terminology were permitted when dealing with speculation, we would say that *aufheben* is an element of the object-language. But it also belongs to the 'metalanguage', if indeed there is one in speculation, and is an important operator of that metalanguage: *to maintain something and bring it to an end* is, in 'conceiving thought' (that is, speculative discourse), the operation which is applied to its object. This object, its referent, is the subject of the statement or judgement in 'formalistic thinking', which is on the side of the 'object-language'. Taken up by the lifting machine, that is *aufgehoben*, the subject of the statement sublates its equivocality: the attribute applied to it by formalistic thinking only expresses one of its meanings. And there is at least one other, in the best cases opposed to the first.

The fact that *aufheben* is at once a term of the 'object-language' and an operator of the speculative 'metalanguage' ought to suffice to prove that this opposition between object-language and metalanguage is not pertinent in the speculative set-up. (It should reveal only the exteriority of *my* analysis with respect to that set-up.) Natural language is already speculative, and the equivocality of its terms is the signal of this; and speculative language is still (and never other than) a natural language, which needs no extrinsic expedient to express itself and link its statements together.[6]

We should place this observation in reserve: we shall come back to it. The relationship between natural and speculative language is itself subject to the rule of equivocality, which is marked at once by the precession and recession of meaning. This rule holds not only inside natural language, and inside speculative language, but between the two. Thanks to the operator of equivocality, the two languages are in a relationship of continuity: the speculative is still the ordinary, the ordinary is already the speculative.

Of course the speculative is distinguished from the natural in that it brings to expression the duplicity of meanings and their unification, which remains undeveloped in natural language. However, the result of their related nature (marked by equivocality) is that even in natural language, the driving force behind the linking of statements also consists in the 'force of the negative', that is in the presence under a single signifier of two signifieds which are in opposition and which 'must' express themselves. The competition of signifieds with a view to finding their signifier is not only the motor of speculative language, but is already, for speculative language, the motor of the ordinary language which is its object. This is why, according to Hegel, the method followed in the system of logic is the only true one (*wahrhafte*): 'it is nothing distinct (*nichts Unterschiedenes*) from its objects and contents; for it is the content itself, the dialectic which the content has in itself, which makes the system advance (moves it onward, *ihn fortbewegt*).'[7]

Equivocality is thus not a state of provisional obscurity, but a state of tension between (at least) two opposing signifieds searching for their signifier. There is an inequality between signifier and signified because at a given moment there are more signifieds to be expressed than signifiers to express them. Yet they *must* be expressed (following the rule of competition for expression). But when they *are* expressed, when they have found their signifiers, a new equivocality *must* inhabit that expression (following the rule of the persistence of equivocality). The equality of signifier and signified is never reached, there is no end to equivocality.

This is why the attributive proposition *cannot* be the right form of expression of signifieds. It must crack under the pressure of this inequality.[8] The statement *God is good* cannot be true, because God can take on many signifieds other than *good*, and *good* can be attributed to many subjects of statements other than *God*. The speculative set-up must destroy (*zerstören*) the 'identical proposition'. The word, overloaded with opposing signifieds, explodes, but the attributive proposition cannot take them all up and express them satisfactorily. A longer discourse is necessary, a sequence of statements (just as a sequence of shots is needed to express the diverse meanings contained in the equivocality of the first).

What are the rules of this discourse? What prescriptions must the statements of this discourse or a sequence of such statements obey in order to be speculative statements?

From an analysis of the first chapter of the *Logic*, on being and nothingness, we draw the following discourse (that is, the following series of statements):

1 When one says *being*, one says nothing determinate, and therefore one says *nothing* (*Nichts*, nothingness): and therefore when one says *nothing*, one also says *being*, since being is nothing. Thus *being* disappears in *nothingness*, and *nothingness* in *being*. The identity of the two terms is born of the reciprocal disappearance of the one into the other: saying *being* or *nothing* is *the same*. This identity is empty. To say *being* or *nothing* is to say nothing; or: *being and nothingness are the same thing*. 'Formalistic thinking' comes to a stop here, on this void.

2 A new speculative rule intervenes and unfreezes the situation: 'Here a proposition is posed which, when examined more closely, has the movement of disappearing through itself. Thus happens to it

the object, represented as *its becoming*', that is 'the concept in the process of moving and taking its determinations back into itself'.

From this point of view, if the analysis to follow has an accidental relationship with the subject of its statements (i.e. the speculative statement), this is because it itself belongs to formalistic thinking and has failed to place the subject properly, in the very movement by which it grasps speculative discourse.

The question here is not without analogy with that of the cinema. The analysis of the Koulechov effect shows that the linking of a second shot with a given shot determines the meaning of the first. If you take the first shot as the *Selbst*, its link with the second is a problem, because many sorts of links are possible, and the actual relation appears to be accidental. That is the case for fixed thought. If on the other hand the *Selbst* is the movement pulling the shots along, then the determination of each comes from a kind of ricochet (a *Zurücknehmen*, a *Gegenstoss*) from the whole. But this whole itself is never given all in one: it is either not yet there, or already no longer there, or both at once (when the film is being projected, or even being made). Thus the speculative subject cannot be assigned once and for all, it is restless, worried, and escapes positive grasp. But at the same time it is without internal contingency, it forms an organism, through a complex relation involving readjustment of the parts onto the state of the whole, and remodelling of the whole according to the ingestion of a given element. Meaning is consequently both ahead of itself and behind itself, anticipating itself in the singular formation, taking itself up again in the 'life of the whole'. This is why the speculative set-up needs the *Doppelsinnigkeit* and the *Zweifelhaftigkeit*: the double sense of element and the whole, and their dubious character.

In the *Aesthetics*,[2] Hegel characterizes the symbol by its 'essentially *zweideutig*' nature: the lion I see on a medal is 'a form and a sensory existence'; is it a symbol? That has to be decided. And if it is, what does it symbolize? What is its *Bedeutung*? That too has to be decided. There are thus two levels of equivocity: (1) sensory or symbol? (2) if the latter, what is its meaning? We can only decide by saying expressly what the sensory form is, and what the meaning is. But then the symbol is destroyed, and the sensory becomes a form which the explicit statement *compares* with the meaning.

In this text from the *Aesthetics*, the equivocality can appear to the reader to be a provisional state of meaning, necessarily bound to disappear as one progresses in clarity, and in particular through the passage from plastic to linguistic expression. Correlatively, this linguistic expression can appear to be subject to the model of predicative judgement: a meaning (a content) is attributed to a subject of a statement (the sensory form of the lion).

But what speculative discourse demands is in no way univocity. There is in Hegel's writings a repeated demand for equivocality to be preserved.[3] There is real joy for the mind in the discovery of the multiplicity of significations of a word in a natural language, and this joy is at its height when these significations are not only different, but opposed (*entgegengesetzt*). Given equal lexical differentiation, a natural language is in Hegel's eyes the more inhabited by 'a speculative spirit' the more terms it has the significations of which are opposed. 'Coming across words of this type can be a true joy for thought.'[4] In such cases, thought finds 'what is at the same time the result of speculation and nonsense for the understanding, that is the reunion of opposites, lexicalized in a still naive way in a single word with opposing significations'.

The German language is privileged from this point of view.[5] Speculative thought is particularly happy with the word *aufheben*. Even more so than with the Latin *tollere*: the affirmative signification of this latter term, which is to raise (*élever*) (the negative signification is to remove (*enlever*)), does not *already* contain a negative weight, as is the case with the German *aufheben*, whose negative signification is to *bring to an end*, but the affirmative to *maintain* (*erhalten*). Now 'it is impossible to maintain an object without removing it from its immediacy, and thereby from an existence open to external influences.' The equivocality of *aufheben* is thus redoubled: first it unites negative and positive in the word itself, but it unites them again (or already) in the word (maintain) which expresses only the affirmative meaning. (It would be possible to discover an equal treasure of equivocality on the side of the negative meaning: *to set a term*.) Far from disappearing when one progresses to comparison, the symbol, in the sense of the *Aesthetics*, proliferates in the elements thus separated out. Equivocality is always maintained, even when one sets a term to it.

So here we have a first requirement, that of safeguarding the equivocalities thus determined. In satisfying it, one is obeying a constitutive rule of the speculative game.

An observation is required here on the subject of *aufheben*. The term is 'perfectly' equivocal because it has two opposing signifieds: and it is thus to be classed with many other words furnished by natural languages. Described in this way, these terms belong to the domain of reference denoted by those speculative statements which deal with (*geschieht an ihm*) what must effectuate (*ausmachen*) its specific content, that is, becoming.'[9] If you say: 'Being and nothingness are the same thing', taking this statement as a judgement, then you get stuck in empty identity because of the form of the attributive proposition. However, it conceals something else, which is not a signified, but an effectuation which traverses it: the movement of the disappearance of being into nothingness and nothingness into being which the above reasoning has just effectuated (no. 1 above). This movement is the 'content proper to' the proposition on being and nothingness. It is already becoming, but we ought not to be able to say so yet.

3 A new speculative rule: this content (the movement of reciprocal disappearance of being and nothingness) is not yet a signified, because it is not expressed in the form of the proposition; it only 'arrives at' the proposition. The proposition *is* the result. It does not *express* the result. A result which is not expressed (*nicht ausgedrückt*) is not a speculative result. We *must* find a signifier to express the content of the proposition, *Being and nothingness are the same thing*. But how are we to proceed with this denomination? If, for example, we say that what the proposition signifies is the *unity* of being and nothingness, then what are we doing? *Wir meinen*, we are giving our opinion. Now according to Hegel, 'the *Meinen* is a form of the subjective, and in this series the subjective does not belong to the presentation.'[10] We must eliminate a signifier introduced subjectively from the outside, a heterogeneous third term which does not appertain to the presentation. 'The third term in which being and nothingness have their residence (*Bestehen*) ought also to take place here, and has taken place here: it is *becoming*.' The signifier which *must* be found in order to unfreeze the empty identity in which formalistic thinking comes to halt is the term which *must* take place in the same *presentation* as the two opposed terms, and form a series (*Reihe*) with them. And we have *already* found it, but in unexpressed form, in the movement presenting their reciprocal disappearance. It has already taken place in this presentation, but has been only effectuated. Its effectuation came before its expression. 'What is truth is neither being nor nothingness, but the fact, not that being and nothingness pass over (*übergehen*) the one into the other, but that they *have* passed over (*übergangen*).'[11] The perfect tense emphasizes the delay of expression with respect to effectuation, but this delay guarantees that the third term (the becoming, the passing over) indeed belongs to the same presentation and is indeed located in the same series. What we have said in trying to understand what being is is that insofar as it is indeterminate it is nothing. We have *effectuated* the becoming-nothing of being. Now we can express this becoming as the unity of being and nothingness.

We have just isolated three rules bearing on the formation and linking of statements. These statements are speculative if they respect these constitutive rules. The rule of equivocality bears on the formation of terms. These terms enter a speculative statement only on the condition of having at least two signifieds (in opposition, if possible, on the model of *aufheben*).

The two other rules concern the linking of statements (and are therefore discursive rules). The rule of immanent derivation prescribes that the two signifieds of the equivocal term should give rise to opposing statements, p and $\bar{p}$, such that, *if p*, then $\bar{p}$, and if $\bar{p}$ then p. (If being is, it is nothing; if nothing is, it is being.)

In proportional logic (formalistic thinking, philosophy of the understanding), this derivation has the form of a reciprocal implication, or in other words, of an equivalence; semantically it is a paradox, or nonsense (*Widersinnige*). (*Not-being is because it is not being*: Aristotle denounces this syllogism, which he attributes to Antisthenes, as a paralogism.) Speculative thought sees here the unity of two signifieds, at least in the process of effectuation (*ausmachen*).

A third rule, that of expression (*ausdrücken*), indicates that the result of the immanent derivation must be expressed in a term designating the movement of effectuation of the unity of two opposed signifieds. This term alone merits the name of result (*Resultät*). Then this term undergoes in its turn its own dissolution in its putting-into-motion, and then in the expression of its equivocality (that is of the internal opposition of its signifieds).

Supposing that the preceding description of the speculative set-up fits, there remains the question of what one is doing when proceeding in this manner.

We have linked with the statements of speculative discourse a series of statements which isolate constitutive rules of speculative statements and sequences of statements. We have thus situated speculative discourse at the instance 'referent' of the discourse analysing it, and we have signified it as being , if not a language-game, then at least as a regulated complex of diverse language-games, a complex which constitutes a discursive genre. The use of terms such as 'constitutive rules' or 'language-game' appears to place the discourse of the analysis sketched here outside speculative discourse: and indeed these terms belong rather to a philosophy of the understanding and to formalistic thinking (like that of 'conditions of possibility'). It is only in such thought that the distinction between a first level of statements (object-language, here speculative discourse) and a second level of statements taking the first as their referents (metalanguage setting out constitutive rules) can have a meaning, since this distinction presupposes that operators (statements presenting empty formal transformations) can be isolated independently of the statements on which they operate and the contents of which are contingent with respect to those operators.

Thus the description would be one of the understanding, whilst what is described is speculative. They are thus in opposition. But opposition is the speculative driving-force *par excellence*. It is easy to show that the analysis of speculative discourse in terms of language-games or of discursive genres, as it has been carried out here, consists in showing the equivocality of speculative discourse, in deriving from it a meaning which is opposed to that it seems to have, and in resolving this opposition in the notion of language-game. And this work is speculative effectuation *par excellence*, and so the passage from speculative discourse to discourse on speculative discourse (in terms of language-games) would itself be speculative, at least as effectuation.

There is thus an equivocality in the relationship between the object (speculative discourse) and the commentary (discourse on the discursive genre). Just when the second thinks it is posing the first outside itself (as a language-game), it opposes itself to the first, and this opposition places them both inside one and the same presentation, in a milieu where they reside together as opposed: movement as concept.

Having admitted this equivocality, are we sure that it gives rise to speculative work, to the work of the concept? Speculative logic is a logic of the infinite. It is *logic* because it is a discourse on discourses about which it says the truth. It does not say the truth in the same way as a theory does, nor even as a description does. It effectuates in itself the truth of the discourses it talks about. This truth consists in nothing other than the patient dissolution of identities of meaning (signifieds); and this dissolution of signifieds has as its result new signifiers (new terms). And so on. There is, in Hegel, a sort of eternal return (without repetition). This is his Heraclitism. It doesn't much matter here what name we give to the force driving this return: it isn't even necessary to metaphorize a force; let us simply say that language wants itself (*le langage se veut lui-même*). But the fact remains that in speculative discourse this force or this will is subject to rules bearing on the linking of one statement to the next, the rules we have described as the rules of the speculative set-up, and notably the rules of immanent derivation and of expression.

Now the dissolution of the speculative involved in the foregoing analysis by the formalistic thinking of language-games *must* (in speculative terms) also dissolve this form. This form is also what Hegel calls the subject. The speculative subject is of course not the subject of the statement, and no more is it the subject of the enunciation, but is the group of rules of equivocity, of derivation and of expression, that is, the concept inasmuch as it is a transformer of meanings: work.

Let us now return to ordinary language. Take a statement (as *token*): ' I can come round to your place' (*je peux passer chez toi*). Every statement presents a universe, with at least four instances (occupied or not); the signified, the referent, the sender (*destinateur*) and the receiver (*destinataire*), and their reciprocal situations. As is the case with most statements, our example copresents several universes. *I can* copresents *I have the capacity* (which in its turn develops into, *I know where you live, I'm not immobilized, I've the time*, etc.). *I can* also copresents, *it is an eventuality* (as opposed to, *it's certain, it's a promise*, etc.). Again, it copresents *I can if you want* (that is, on condition that you say that you want me to, which presupposes that I want to myself).

Many statements (no.2) can be linked with this first, according to the copresented universe they retain: *Your car's been repaired?, You're well again?, I've moved, You're too busy*, for the capacity; or, for the desire, *I'd rather you didn't, With pleasure*, etc. Or again, for several of these values, *Do you think so?*, and others.

What would be the speculative follow-up to the statement 'I can come round to your place'? The one the effectuation of which I have just sketched, by showing its equivocality, developing the opposing meanings, and expressing the results of its dissolution.

But in ordinary language, it is impossible always to be patient over one's reply (*sur le coup*) (this would just about come down to replying *Do you think so?* every time). The statement will in any case be the presentation of *a universe*. It is articulated onto the previous statement by one or the other instance (the sender in *You're the one who said it!*, the receiver in *Who do you think you're talking to?*, and so on); it may or may not belong to the same language-game: the first statement is denotative with modalized assertion, the second can be prescriptive (*All right, come*). The second statement may also be formally derivable from the first (*Have you any news of Chantal?*).

In none of these cases does the linking obey the rules of speculative discourse. Where does this difference, between what Hegel calls the contents (the discourses spoken of by the philosopher) and philosophy (speculative discourse itself), come from? I have supposed, following Gérard Lebrun's indication, that it comes from *impatience*.[12] The second statement does not develop all the universes copresented in the first statement, but retains one, or perhaps none, and neglects the rest. Is this the error of finite logic, the fault of the exclusion of the copresented universes? From the point of view of infinite speculative dissolution, that indeed seems to be the case. But if we say that, then we are simply repeating what philosophers (of understanding and representation) have always said: that ordinary language is badly made, that the common man makes mistakes, that only philosophy tells the truth, and that we have to be patient.

In the impatience of the linkings of ordinary statements, there is perhaps something else (which can perfectly well be stated), which speculative patience misses because it is patience. If this is so, the contingency of these linkings would not be a failing (compared with the fine necessity of speculative discourse). Rather, it would indicate this: that perhaps language wants itself (this would be why one *must* say everything), and in wanting itself it wants the infinite. But the infinite it wants is not that of the diastole and systole of meanings passing through the speculative machine, but that of the inadvertency of *moves* (*coups*).

A statement is a move. A move implies rules for the game, a previous move (the preceding statement), and a looseness in the linkings. It is this last which is excluded by speculative discourse.

NOTES

1 *Phänomenologie des Geistes*, ed. Lasson (Hamburg: Meiner Verlag, 1920), pp. 143ff. (henceforth *PhG*); *Préface de la Phénoménologie de l'Esprit* (Paris: Hyppolite, edn bilingue, Aubier), pp. 148ff.
2 Jubiläumsausgabe, 12, 408.
3 *Wissenschaft der Logik* (Hamburg: Meiner Verlag, 1923), p. 10 (henceforth *WL*); *Enzyklopädie*, §96, Anm.
4 *WL*, p. 10.
5 *WL*, p. 94.
6 'The system is realized in a continuous and pure progression, making no reference to anything beyond itself', *WL*, p. 36.
7 *WL*, p. 36.
8 *PhG*, p. 143.
9 *WL*, p. 76.
10 *WL*, p. 78.
11 *WL*, p. 67.
12 Gérard Lebrun, *La Patience du concept* (Paris: Gallimard, 1968).

Translated by Geoff Bennington

16

Levinas' Logic

The following lines of thought are part of a study that is in progress, aiming to establish that prescriptive statements are not commensurable with denotative ones – or in other words, with descriptive ones. We begin by examining the situation of Levinas' thought in the face of Hegelian persecution. This brings into the centre of reflection the question of commentary and, as will be seen, the confrontation with the second Kantian *Critique*. The reader will see by the end of this essay that the implications and conclusions to which these lines of thought should lead are here treated in very abridged or precipitate manner.

Commentary and persecution

To begin with, this is a discourse that sets a trap for commentary, attracting it and deceiving it. In this course lies a major stake, which is not merely speculative but political. Let us run through the stages of the seduction.

Levinas asks that the absolutely other be made welcome. The rule applies to any commentary on Levinas as well. So, we will take care not to flatten the alterity of his work. We will struggle against assimilations and accommodations. This is the least justice we can do him. Such is the first figure of commentary: the hermeneutic – discourse of good faith.

But good faith is never good enough, or the request for alterity is never satisfied. We will say to ourselves that the best way of answering it is to reinforce the difference between work and commentary. The more, as aliens to Levinas, we speak of Levinas, the more we conform to his precept – and also, the more Levinas will be bound to welcome the commentary. For example, what could be more alien to a Talmudist than a pagan? Second figure; the paradoxical – discourse of ambivalence.

The merest trifle separates it from the third figure (and this trifle means that Levinas dislikes pagans). In the third figure the commentator superadds to the alterity: since you ask for it, he says to Levinas, I will not treat you as my similar, but as my dissimilar; I can do you justice only by mistreating you. Indeed, if in your view to be just is to court alterity, then the only way to be just towards your discourse of justice is to be unjust about it. And what is more, you will have to do me justice, in accordance with your law. So if I say, like Hegel in his *Spirit of Christianity*, that the infinity of your God is the bestiality of your people, that the letter of your writing is your people's stupidity, you and your people will have to say to me: that is just.[1]

Discourse of persecution. It is not even above parodying the persecuted. It will say, for example, '*Do before understanding*';[2] is this not what the commentator is bound to do with this work, if he understands it? This doing, which in this case is a saying (the saying of the commentary), would not deserve its name, according to the very terms of the work under commentary, and would merely be something *said* if it did not *interrupt* what is said in the work, if it were not a word that stands in sharp contrast to it.[3]

What seems to authorize the parody and the persecution is the principle that justice consists in alterity. So the persecutor reasons thus: only alterity is just, the unjust is always the other of the just, and so all that is unjust is just. If the one who suffers the injustice should protest against this sophism, I will declare that he has only its major term to blame, which is none other than his own law. For if the premise states that the rule is alterity, then it necessarily authorizes retortion, enabling the same to be drawn from the other and the other from the same. If this amounts to persecution, it is the fault of the persecuted alone; he suffers only from his own law and refutes himself. Such is the mechanism of the Hegelian description; this phenomenology is ironic by means of its 'I understand you'.

Levinas sometimes tries a riposte against the persecuting commentary by keeping on its own ground. For instance, he attacks Hegelian alterity so as to show that it is only a caprice of identity (and that it consequently cannot be just): 'The *otherwise than being* is couched in a saying which must also unsay itself so as thus to tear away the *otherwise than being* from the said, wherein the *otherwise than being* already begins to signify nothing more than a *being otherwise*.'[4] The absolutely other is not the *other of* a same, *its* other, in the heart of that supreme sameness that is being; it is *other than* being. The just does not relate dialectically to the unjust, because there is no neutral middle ground (except in insomnia) where they might be twisted around, where their mutual opposition might be synchronized.[5] The discourse of the would-be middle ground is presumptuous.

Now this riposte is not irrefutable. And if there is a trap in Levinas' discourse, it consists first of all in tempting its reader to refute this riposte. It seems appropriate to follow the path of this seduction.

The enunciative clause

In order to escape my argumentation, says the persecutor, it is not enough to plead the exclusive disjunction, in a statement such as, for instance, *The entirely other is other than all that is.* All things considered, the mechanism of the refutation is simple enough. Whatever the operator used in the statement, however strongly negative it may be, to use it always 'implies' an assertion in the enunciation. So we could always 'infer' an affirmative expression from a negative expression; we only have to bring into play the enunciative clause. In this way, for example, we can maintain that *nonbeing is,* because we can state that *nonbeing is nonbeing.*[6] The enunciative clause that permits this 'inference' constitutes the unexpressed premise of this argumentation: *All that is said to be, or not to be, something, is.*

The 'implication' in question can be declared a sophism only if it is agreed that it is forbidden to formulate the enunciative assertion in the form of an attributive statement; or in other words, only if the above-mentioned premise is rejected.

But if we are trying to escape from the aporias of positivism and mere propositional logic, it seems inevitable and even desirable to use this premise, and therefore the 'sophism' seems necessary. The enunciative clause is indeed the king-pin, which seems to allow us to derive the 'substance' of statements from the 'subject' of the enunciation, as in the Cartesian meditation on the *Cogito*, or to include the subject in the substance, as in Hegel's phenomenological description. It can be shown that all philosophical discourses, no matter how diverse, make use of this clause, if only in a hidden manner. For the philosopher, to be forbidden this clause as formulated by logicians – by Russell, for example, in the theory of types of statements[7] – would make it impossible to philosophize.

Now Levinas' books abound in such statements. This is obviously true of those texts that thematize the subject of pleasure, in which Levinas describes the constitution of this subject and in which it is methodologically necessary for statements relating to this subject to be proffered, or profferable, by him as well, since in the absence of this

authority the theme could not be validated. Such is the 'phenomenology' of the early books.[8]

We are tempted to object that this validation procedure applies only
to the ego's discourse about itself; that the resulting validity of the
statements merely attests simultaneously to the closure of this discourse in the identity of experience; but that, as soon as we come to the
other great Levinasian theme – the transcendence of the other – we
must not be able to detect the use of the enunciative clause in it. Or
else, if we can manage it, if we can show that the absolutely other is so
only (or is so in any case) in relation to the assertion that maintains the
statement of its exteriority, then we can boast that we have ruined the
essential project of the work. Such is the temptation.

On this point, let us take, somewhat at random, the following
passage from *Totality and Infinity*: 'The interiority assuring separation
must', writes Levinas, ' . . . produce a being that is absolutely closed on
itself, not drawing its isolation dialectically from its opposition to the
Other. And this closure *must not* forbid the exit out of interiority,
in order that exteriority may speak to it, reveal itself to it, in an
unpredictable movement . . .'[9] In this text we find two essential
statements: *The self (soi) does not proceed from the other; the other befalls
the self.* Let us call them respectively $\sim p$, q. Levinas tells us first that if
the self proceeded from the other ($=p$), the other would have no
marvels to reveal to it, and no transcendent occurrence would touch it:

$$\text{If } p, \text{ then } \sim q. \tag{1}$$

This relation can also be expressed by the exclusive disjunction $p \vee q$.

After the second *must*, we are told two things. First (and this is in
fact implied in the context of the book rather than in our passage), con-
firming the preceding relation and verifying the disjunction – that the
miraculous transcendence of the other is conditional upon the closure
of the self:

$$\text{If } \sim p, \text{ then } q. \tag{2}$$

The second is more surprising, although more 'natural'; it is that the
other can befall the self only *in spite* of the latter's self-sufficiency –
which would be expressed as:

$$\text{If } \sim p, \text{ then } \sim q, \tag{3}$$

or: if the self does not proceed from the other, then the other does not
befall the self.

We see how Levinas struggles to escape the Hegelian persecution. Far from the exterior's inverting itself into the interior and the interior into the exterior, as is said of language in the *Phenomenology of Mind*, a group of statements and relations between statements is proposed here that could hold the exteriority of the other and the interiority of the self separate. And yet this group is not greatly different from the group of expressions and relations that could be drawn from Hegel's discourse. In particular, the 'lapsus' constituted by relation (3) juxtaposed with the first two relational expressions puts the Levinasian group very close to what, in Hegel, is called 'contradiction' and *Aufhebung*.

The comparison may seem superficial, but it is less so than it appears. Do we think we have exhausted the connotations of the two *musts* that punctuate this passage by translating them into the form of propositional implication? They express not only the necessity that, in different ways, links those parts of statements, which p and q are: they indicate not only an alethic propositional modality (*It is necessary that . . .*), but also an epistemic propositional modality (*It is certain that . . .*), and above all a modality that is not propositional but 'illocutionary' (directed towards the addressee of the message) and almost 'conversational', all of which makes these *musts* into an appeal from the author to his reader with a view to obtaining his agreement to statements (1), (2), and (3) – *failing which*, this 'conversation', which his reading is, will have to be interrupted.[10] Hence, the 'necessity' expressed by this *must* bears upon the pragmatic nature of Levinas' discourse: if you, the addressee of that discourse, accept p (i.e., that the self proceeds from the other), then you must refuse q (i.e., that the other befalls the self), and you will not be on my side – you will be a Hegelian.

In 'propositional' readings of the *must*, its scope is kept at the level of statements (*énoncés*). But to make a pragmatic, or 'perlocutionary', interpretation of it (i.e., one that relates to the locutory situation that defines the message's relations of addresser/addressee), we are obliged to take into account the act of enunciation (*énonciation*). Thus the enunciative clause comes back into the statements.

And it comes back with its customary effect, which is to make the properties of the statements (in the case of our text, the disjunctive exclusion) almost negligible, in favour of the enunciative assertion. This is something one could observe in comparing the *must* of Levinas with equivalent expressions from the pen of Hegel, such as the famous '*es kommt nach meiner Einsicht . . . alles darauf an, das Wahre nicht als "Substanz", sondern ebenso sehr als "Subjekt" aufzufassen und auszudruecken*',[11] or the equally celebrated '*es ist von dem Absoluten zu sagen, dass es wesentlich "Resultat", dass es erst am "Ende" das ist, was es in Wahrheit ist'*[12] ('According to my way of seeing . . . , everything depends on this, that one apprehends and expresses the true not only as *substance*, but just as much as *subject*', and, 'It must be said of the absolute that it is essentially *result*, that only *in the end* is it what is in truth'). The *musts* contained in these statements seem to have exactly the same connotations as those we have just identified – in particular the connotation that if you, the reader, refuse to say that the absolute is result or that substance is also subject, then our interlocution, or perlocution, ceases. Besides, Hegel does not hesitate to indicate the enunciative clause very strongly with a *'Nach meiner Einsicht'*, an 'I assert that . . . ', a 'constative' that is also, it seems, a 'representative,' an *I wish that. . .* or an *I insist that . . .*[13]

Strictly speaking, then, we are not here dealing with mere assertion, regarded by propositional logics as the zero degree of the enunciative modality, but with more subtle enunciative modalities having perlocutionary application. The pragmatic force of statement elements, such as these *musts*, places Levinas' discourse in the same field as Hegel's. Levinas says, 'The interior and the exterior must be exterior', Hegel says, 'The interior and the exterior must be interior'. Propositionally, the two statements are contraries. But they have the same perlocutionary form: for the discourse of ethics to hold together, the claim for the exteriority of the interior relation is just as necessary as the claim for its interiority is for the discourse of phenomenology. In this respect the two discursive positions are not different.

They have another feature in common: both these enunciative demands, but in fact Levinas' infinitely more than Hegel's, are not formulated as such but are slipped into the statements as modalities that govern their parts (*p* and *q*), and not as enunciative acts that govern the attitudes of the protagonists of philosophical discourse. In both cases they are 'speculative' statements in which the form of the statement (in our example, the *must*) implies the instance of the enunciation while hiding it.[14]

Now if this so, Levinas' statements can be placed on a par with Hegel's only to the detriment of Levinas, because this would imply finally that the exteriority of the other, expressed by the statements *p* and *q* and their relations (1), (2) and (3), even when the author of *Otherwise than Being* declares it to be absolute, can obviously be so only according to the enunciative modality of the 'constative – representative' *must*, that is, only relative to the enunciative clause. And consequently it is in the Hegelian discourse, which explicitly needs this clause to be inserted in order to form statements (since substance must also be subject), that the Levinasian discourse must take its place, as a moment of it.

We will thus have shown that Levinas' riposte against ontology is refutable and that the project of emancipating ethical discourse in relation to the same fails in view of the enunciative clause. And we will have thus completely succumbed to the temptation into which the Levinasian discourse leads those who have not broken with the speculative project.

Levinas himself felt this temptation and succumbed to it, as we know incidentally from the last lines of ' Signature', which concludes *Difficile liberté:*

> It has been possible, since *Totality and Infinity*, to present this relation with the Infinite as irreducible to 'thematisation' . . . Henceforth the ontological language still used in *Totality and Infinity* so as to exclude the purely psychological significance of the analyses put forward, is avoided. And the analyses, themselves, refer not to *experience*, where a subject always thematises what he is equal to, but to *transcendence*, where he answers for what his intentions have not measured.[15]

Prescriptives against denotatives

These last lines indicate to the commentator how he has been trapped: by treating Levinas' discourse as if it were speculative when it is not. The word *speculative* designates not only, as previously understood, a discourse whose statements (badly formed ones, from the logician's point of view) 'imply' its enunciation by whatever aspect you like. Speculative discourse in this sense is opposed to positive *discourse*, that is, one whose conditions of validity are determined by propositional logic, in its own metalanguage. But in a more 'elementary' way, the term *speculative* must be set in opposition to other terms designating other kinds of discourse, such as those of the poet, the politician, the moralist, the pedagogue, and others. This second test leads us to place the speculative on the same side as the positive and opposed to these other genres, as discourses with a denotative function must be placed opposite those with a deontic or aesthetic function. The speculative and the positive alike are in effect kinds of discourse placed under the law of truth: we judge them both as true or false. The problem peculiar to the speculative is to determine in what subgenre of discourse one may describe the criteria of truth or falsity valid for all discourses of the denotative genre; and that is where, as we have said, the enunciative clause intervenes.

The nondenotative genres of discourse, for their part, seem reducible to two, according to Levinas: those placed under the rule of the just/unjust, such as the moral and the political, and those of the writer and the orator, which draw on an 'aesthetic' value. Levinas evinces the greatest suspicion concerning the *discursive arts*, which he regularly characterizes as techniques of seduction.[16] We know that his wager is on the contrary to succeed in placing the deontic genre at the heart of philosophical discourse. This implies in principle that the latter consists in describing not the rules that determine the truth or falsity of statements but those that determine their justice or injustice. Hence it seems that the 'well-formed' expressions that concern Levinas do not need to be well-formed in the terms required by propositional logic. They belong to that group of statements that Aristotle, in a text often commented upon, declares he leaves to one side of the reflections of the logician.[17] In their deep structure, and regardless of their surface forms, properly Levinasian statements are 'imperatives'. If justice becomes the unique concern of philosophical discourse, it is then in the position of having to comment not on descriptions (denotative statements) but on prescriptions.

Now to comment on a prescription poses a difficult problem. Take for example an order like *Close the door*. The commentary on this order is not an order but a description. The prescriptive statement gives place to a denotative one.

In the terms of the pragmatics of communication, the commentator is the addressee of a first-order message (here the order) and comes to place himself in the position of addresser of a second-order message having the first message as its reference, while a new addressee (the reader of the commentary, for example) comes to carry out the role previously held by the commentator in relation to the first message. When the initial message is denotative, the commentary, being denotative as well, keeps its own discourse in the same genre as the one on which it comments. But when the initial message is prescriptive, it seems inevitable that the commentary, being denotative, displaces the message's own genre. By taking the order *Close the door* as the object of his discourse, the commentator (whether he is a linguist, a logician, or a philosopher) substitutes for this order an autonym[18] of the sentence or of part of the sentence or, in other words, the name of the proposition.[19]

This substitution, which is the rule of the metalanguage of commentary, may have but little consequence when the object-statement is denotative, since its validity in the matter of truth is not *necessarily* disturbed (even if it should happen to be) by the fact that it becomes an 'image' of itself in the metalanguage. But one could not be so confident when a prescriptive expression is involved; for an order does not ask to be commented on – that is, understood – but to be executed. Or perhaps: not only understood but also executed. Now the commentator, whatever turn of phrase he uses, does not go and close the door but asks, for example, how it is possible for the statement to produce an act instead of (or as well as) its intellection.[20] And in so doing he necessarily transforms the natural-language expression *Close the door*, which is 'immediately' prescriptive, into a metalinguistic 'image' of the expression.

The difference, and it is an immense one, is disturbing because the two expressions can be strictly identical. But the one, which belongs to the natural language (except when the latter makes use of autonyms) 'expects' to be executed, whereas in the other, which is merely the reference level of the commentary, the executive is a sense that it connotes. The second expression may be the object of various transcriptions. It is either reported: *He said to close the door.* Or quoted: *He said, 'Close the door.'* Or symbolized: $O(p)$, which reads, 'It is obligatory that p' where p is, according to some, a well-formed expression of propositional logic[21] (in this case a statement like *the door is closed*), or, according to others, a proposition root[22], which here means roughly 'the closing of the door by you'. Or else it is symbolized in a perhaps more refined way: $Nx'\ Oy\alpha'$, which would read, 'x has ruled: y must do α', where x is the order-giver, y the receiver, and α the action of closing the door.[23]

But no matter how diverse the possible 'images' of the order in the commentator's discourse may be (and there are many others), all these transcriptions have in common that they neutralize the executive force of the order. This neutralization is the index of a modification in the constraints that weigh on the addressee. In making himself a commentator, the addressee becomes an addresser: he has understood/ heard a discourse, and he utters a second discourse having the first as its reference. The addressee of an order, on the contrary, does not have to come and occupy the position of an addresser. He has only to 'cause to exist' the *reference* of the order that he received: to close the door.

Two observations. That it is a question of reference and not of signification in statements of this type is indicated by the use of the deictic: *the door* is understood as *the door of which I am speaking and which you know; this door here* (with the force of *ille*). To avoid the problems raised by the deictic and the reference, we will here be content to note that what gives the definite article its deictic force in this statement is the perlocutionary situation: the current relationship between the addresser and the addressee of the order is what permits both parties alike to dismiss another interpretation of the article *the*, for example, its force of generality.

Is it the same for all prescriptive statements? That is a question to be discussed. It seems certain, in any case, that at least a subset of the set of these statements obeys this rule of perlocutionary force. Statements of a code applicable to a definite circumstance generally appear to escape the rule: the 'legislator' is not a current addresser. But precisely the current addresser (policeman, magistrate, etc.), who we say is 'applying' the statement of the code to the case being considered, is in fact bound to show, by the reasons adduced for his judgement (and if possible in contradiction to the addressee of that decision, who by definition has 'his own word' to say about it), that the perlocutionary situation in which they are placed is truly one of those to which the statement of the code makes reference. His order is thus not executive, so long as the statement of his order does not receive its unambiguous force from the situation in which it is uttered, that is, so long as it is not indicated as executable. This is a property we can verify for all pragmatic situations where the message is imperative, for example, in agonistic situations (military, athletic, dialectic): the order is executive only to the extent that it makes reference to the current situation.

This first observation is trivially obvious. Yet it has an important counterpart. *Close the door* does not only make reference to *this door here*, but to a state of this door that does *not yet* exist. It is in this way that the addressee of the order 'makes the reference exist': he produces a state of affairs. But it is also in this way that, once it is executed, the order loses all executive force, supposing that we repeat it as it is: we can *no longer* close a closed door. If we were to judge the value of an order according to its *conformity* to its reference, we would find ourselves faced with a difficulty that is peculiar to this genre of statement: such statements are never true in the sense of conforming to that of which they speak, for they either anticipate it when the reference is not correct, or they must not be correct when the reference is.[24]

Let us be content with this vague formulation and draw from it an important consequence: that the time put into play in the pragmatic of commands is not only 'punctual' in that it takes its ephemeral origin from the perlocutionary situation, but also that this time occasions paradoxes, at least according to the truth functions used in propositional logic, notably that of noncontradiction ($pV \sim p$), in that from this point of view to assert p (*the door is closed*) is always false at the moment when the order ($O(p)$: 'it is obligatory that p') is given.

This temporal property is not the least of the reasons that would incline us to think that the operators of 'Aristotelian' propositional logic do not enable us to judge the value of prescriptive statements. More than any others, these seem to require a 'Diodorean' or suchlike logic, which introduces into the calculation of predicates and of propositions a time variable t that allows us to specify whether the proposition or reference being considered is true (or false) at the instant (now, n) of its enunciation, or before or after that instant. This relativization has significant effects on the logical calculation of propositions, and it is shown elsewhere that many classical 'paradoxes' arise from it.[25] But here there is more at stake: if we want to situate commentaries on the scale (or on the lack of scale) demanded by Levinas, it is into the logic of prescriptive statements, not descriptive ones, that we must introduce the temporal variable. You may well imagine that the results will be all the more surprising.

For the present, let us merely show for one text of Levinas' that the two observations we have just made about the singular validity of prescriptive statements, according to the perlocutionary situation and the moment of their enunciation, are not alien to his work. It is a simple, and at the same time scandalous, text: for it declares that God himself, the number one enunciator by all accounts (though it is doubtful whether Levinas would agree with this title), is not concerned to, nor has no power to, calculate his orders as a function of situations anterior or posterior to, or independent of, the instant of giving them; and that accordingly there does not exist a tribunal (or stock exchange) of history where all acts (or shares) would be offset against one another with a view to liquidating debts. 'Driven out of Abraham's house, Hagar and Ishmael wander in the desert. Their supply of water is finished; God opens the eyes of Hagar, who notices a well where she can give her dying son drink.'[26] So far, nothing abnormal – we would expect no less from a god who is also goodness itself.[27]

Yet this generosity arouses the concern and reproof of the heavenly counsellors, the angels, who practise a rather unexpected Hegelianism, looking farther than the ends of their noses, calculating, thinking of world history: 'The angels protest to God: "wilt Thou give water to him who will later make Israel suffer?" ' and God in his defence invokes the time of ethics and singular situations: ' "What matters the end of history," says the Eternal One. "I judge each for what he is and not for what he will become." ' What each one *is* is what he alone is at the moment I am speaking to you.

It is not suggested that God judges without a criterion, nor that he has no criterion – although thought that ignores inference is perforce

closely related to scepticism.[28] Some things must be refused, at least; so
there must be a sign by which to recognize them, and it should be injustice.[29] But blood is not always a sign of injustice; injustice is not
always and only the shedding of blood.[30] Ishmael will shed innocent
blood: then he is unjust. But at the moment when God is speaking, he
is dying of thirst; then he is suffering injustice. Injustice cannot be
detected by any constant signs; on the contrary, to have recourse to the
constancy of would-be clear signs, to the articles of the code, to
established institutions, recourse to the *letter* as that which allows the
just to be separated from the unjust – that is unjust. The criterion
'exists' but cannot be the object of omnitemporal descriptive statements. If it is grasped, it is not understood; it is grasped in the
command received 'before' it is understood, before it can be repeated
by the addressee of the order, before it can give rise to commentary. It
is grasped as beyond the appearance, as trace.[31]

We can see what is at stake in this question of commentary: the
status to be given to the relations between prescriptive and descriptive
statements, and hence between ethics and propositional logic; this is
also the tension proper to Levinas' work, which aims at nothing less
than raising above tautology the expressions of obligation, of forbidding, of permission – that is, that entire region of the language where
demands, pleas, orders, wishes, prohibitions, and so on are formulated.
It aims at freeing the criterion of validity of 'orders', that is, the
criterion of their justice, from any justification by truth functions.

An expression like *Welcome the alien*,[32] for example, must be able to
be valid, not because it can be inferred from statements previously
admitted, not because it conforms to older statements, but by the sole
fact that it is *an order having in itself its own authority*. Hence it is in
some sense an *order of an order*.[33] In this refusal to infer normative
statements lies, in particular, the considerable importance attached by
Levinas to the idea of *an-archy*.[34] Likewise, it is from such a refusal
that his attacks on ontology – not only Heidegger's but also Spinoza's,
for example,[35] draw their vigour: ontology is, after all, merely another
word for the metalanguage that is applied to descriptive statements.

It is interesting to translate this repudiation of the *archè* and of being
into pragmatic terms. In the order of the perlocutionary situation, it
corresponds to the decision not to conduct a discourse having as its reference and model a prior discourse, even an enigmatic one, given by
no matter whom. The hatred of the *neutral* constantly evinced by
Levinas[36] is not directed at the unnameable in general, nor even at an
unnameable that is presumed to speak, but at an unnameable that is
assumed to be both speaking and spoken: that unnameable *of which* I
speak or, to use the autonym familiar to philosophers, *of which* the *I*

speaks and of which it (or I) speak(s) in order to say that it (this un-nameable) speaks in its (or my) place, that is, in the place of the *I*, or of me. This aims at that constraint proper to the discourse of truth functions, which lets the enunciator attest the authenticity of his statement only if he assumes that what he is talking about is also what speaks through his mouth:[37] only if he assumes that the subject, which he is, is also (and is no less) the substance of which he speaks. The neutral that Levinas hates is precisely this substance assumed to be subject in the discourse of ontology. Whether this substance be called 'being' and the discourse resting on it 'ontology' rather than 'metaphysics' is of scant importance when it is a matter of thinking exteriority as 'marvel'.[38]

The pragmatic reason for hating the neutral is that its assumption implies that the philosopher, the addressee of the message from the unnameable, comes and places himself in the position of addresser, in order to proffer his commentary from the same place as the assumed first addresser, the unnameable itself. In this replacement, ethics necessarily dissolves. Prescriptions drawn from ontology will be inferred from statements relative to the unnameable and assumed to have issued from it. It matters little whether they are true or false; what matters is that the imperatives of ethics will be judged good or bad only by their conformity with these statements, according to the rules of propositional logic. Now, that is enough in Levinas' eyes to make ethics pass under the jurisdiction of the true – a Western obsession – and succumb.

In this subordination of prescriptives to denotatives, the executive force of the former is lost, and so is the type of validity peculiar to them. To put it another way, this subordination has the effect of transforming all orders into metalinguistic 'images' of themselves and each of the terms composing them into an autonym of itself. In ontological ethics we can no longer understand *Welcome the alien* but *the/Welcome the alien/of Levinas*,[39] that is, a proposition transcribed into the metalanguage that speaks of the same proposition placed in the natural language. By this fact alone it passes under the legislation of truth functions and loses the remarkable properties that it had in the natural language, notably those we observed pertaining to perlocutionary situation, time, and execution.

Levinas and Kant: the Kantian '*Widersinnige*'

Levinas' concern to safeguard the specificity of prescriptive discourse seems closely akin to the care with which Kant, in the second *Critique*, makes the principles of practical reason independent of those of theoretical reason.

After recounting the episode of Ishmael's great thirst, Levinas adds: 'For human consciousness has the right to judge a world ripe at every moment for judgement, before the end of history and independently of that end.'[40] This world, he says, is 'peopled with persons'. If it can be judged at every instant with no consideration of teleology or strategy or even of empirical context, it is because the power to judge not only inhabits it but constitutes it. This power is intact on principle and is not subject to any alteration deriving from situational factors; no alienation could be invoked to excuse or pardon bad judgements.[41]

This faculty of commanding and obeying in complete freedom, regardless of the circumstances, cannot fail to remind us of the autonomy of the will that is for Kant 'the unique principle of all moral laws and the duties which conform to them'.[42] The author of *Otherwise than Being* seems to agree with the author of the *Critique of Practical Reason* that in order for the principle of the will to be moral, it cannot be inferred from statements describing the empirical context, whether psychological, social, or historical, and that it cannot be justified by the various 'interests' of which it is made up. Such statements, which would be denotative, would inevitably explain the act as the effect of causes and would thereby take away its specificity: that it is an uncaused cause. It is owing to this specificity that the act is not a phenomenon, not the object of a science of what is, but the expression of a noumenal freedom – and not apprehensible by any sensory intuition.

Yet this assimilation, however tempting, must be rejected. Practical reason is not an-archy. In Levinas' eyes, the specificity of prescriptive statements is not, and cannot be, sufficiently assured by the Kantian procedure. The reason for his mistrust is contained in a sentence that will serve as our guide: 'There is no point in formally distinguishing will from understanding, will from reason, when you decide at once to consider as good will only the will which adheres to clear ideas, or which makes decisions only out of respect for the universal.'[43] Although Descartes is a target here no less than Kant, we will restrict our cross-examination of the logic of the prescriptive to the latter.

The obstacle to logical justification posed by the prescriptive is the object 'Of the Deduction of the Principles of Pure Practical Reason' in the first chapter of the 'Analytic of Pure Practical Reason'.[44] How can we deduce the moral law (the prescriptive statement) without making it lose its specificity? Although in the case of statements of theoretical reason, which are denotative, we cannot deduce the principles that govern their formation speculatively on the basis of 'a priori sources of knowledge', we can at least have recourse to that *Surrogat*,[45] that expedient, which is experience/experiment – which on the whole, other things being equal, proceeds in the same way as does the logician of the sciences who extracts, from the denotative statements given in the corpus that serves as his reference, the axioms (in the modern sense) that these statements presuppose. We know that for Kant, as a reader of Hume, the chief among these axioms is causality.

The relation between the statement of these axioms in the metalanguage of the Deduction and the object language, which is the discourse of the sciences, is isomorphic to the relation linking the language of science to the 'givens' of experiment/experience. The isomorphism of the two relations in no way contradicts the fact that the first derives from the transcendental level and the second from the empirical level. On the contrary, it is this isomorphism that allows Kant to declare that the deduction of principles, which cannot be done directly 'from the sources', uses experience/experiment as a *Surrogat*. It follows that this metalanguage – the discourse of the deduction of scientific principles and especially of causality – remains isomorphic, on its own level, to the object language that is its reference. This isomorphism is what makes the metalanguage possible. Without it, and without the above-mentioned 'sources', how could the principles of theoretical reason, notably causality, be determined?

For the language of prescriptions, this isomorphism between the metalanguage of deduction and the object language, whose principles it must extract, fails. Prescriptive statements, far from being governed like denotatives by axioms such as causality, are themselves the causes of acts that they engender. This pure causality, or spontaneity of the moral law (i.e., the prescriptive statement *par excellence*), is not a fact of experience, since everything given in experience is governed by the infinite sequences of causes and effects, and since the cause of such-and-such is necessarily also thought of as the effect of so-and-so. Hence, there is an insurmountable allomorphism between the metalanguage of deduction, even considered as the establishment of axioms governing an object language, and the object language that is the prescriptive statement. This is why Kant asserts, concerning the deduction of the practical principle, that 'one cannot hope to succeed as well as with the principles of pure theoretical understanding'.[46] He even exposes the failure of the practical deduction with a sort of satisfaction when he writes: 'No deduction, no effort of reason whether theoretical, speculative, or aided by experience can prove the objective reality of moral law; even if one were willing to renounce apodictic certainty, this reality could not be confirmed by experience and thus proved *a posteriori.*' But he adds at once (and this seems to be the source of his satisfaction): 'And nevertheless it sustains itself by itself.'[47]

Must we then abandon any attempt to deduce prescriptive statements? Here the Kantian analysis takes a strange turn (which is what Levinas' thought breaks with), for while Kant is pleased to recognize the impossibility of deducing the practical principle, that is, of deducing a metalanguage bearing upon prescriptives, he still maintains its functioning but inverts its direction (*sens*): 'Instead of this deduction, sought in vain, of the moral principle, one finds something other and entirely paradoxical' ('*etwas anderes aber und ganz widersinnisches*').[48] One finds something *widersinnig*, a deduction that proceeds in the reverse direction to the one that was sought. The metalanguage that is Kant's transcendental discourse had to try to draw the principle of prescriptive statements (i.e., the moral law) from an object language (having as its model some experience or other). As we have just seen, if it had succeeded in doing so it would have been at the cost of abolishing the principle. It is therefore by failing that it succeeds.

This failure, however, does not do away with the possibility of the metalanguage; it inverts its direction, at the cost of modifying its object. What can still be deduced, in the absence of the law, is freedom. This deduction is made on the basis of the law. Thus, in the new deduction the law is placed not as a conclusion, as a statement extracted by the metalanguage from the object language, but as a premise, as a statement in the object language, about which the metalanguage infers that it presupposes a statement bearing on freedom. This is the reversal of direction: 'This moral principle itself serves inversely as a principle for deducing an inscrutable (*unerforschlichen*) power . . ., I mean the power of freedom . . .'[49]

It follows that freedom is not expressed in any statement in the natural language, but can only be the object of a metastatement in the commentary. In contrast, the law or prescriptive statement is an expression in the natural language that cannot have a place in the metalanguage. The *Thou shalt* is 'felt' by the empirical subject, the *Thou canst* is constructed by the philosopher in the transcendental language: empirically it remains unfathomable.

Apparently Levinas has no objection to this distribution – on the contrary, it corresponds to one of the most important themes of his work, the priority of the seizing (or dispossession) by the *Do* of the content of the order (*Do this*, or *that*) from any understanding, that is, from any commentary, which is necessarily denotative.[50]

We may even be tempted to assimilate the place he assigns to freedom to the one that Kant reserves for it: does not the author of the *Critique*, by giving the expression about freedom the status of an inferred proposition in the metalanguage of practical reason, encourage the suspicion that moves Levinas to relegate freedom to the status of a second-order, inferior infatuation of the ego?[51]

Yet it is with respect to this hinge between law and freedom that the difference bursts out: a difference that is all the more profound because the two thoughts are related. Both, in effect, place the law in the domain constituted by the object language of their own commentary, and both recognize that this object domain is not that of experience. Kant proposes to 'call consciousness of the fundamental law a fact (*Faktum*) of reason.'[52] In this *Faktum*, 'pure reason manifests itself as really practical in us'; but for that very reason this 'absolutely inexplicable' fact (*'ein schlechterdings . . . unerklaerliches Faktum'*)[53] is rather a sort of fact, a quasi-fact. Kant explains that the reality of pure will is 'given *a priori* in the moral law as if by a fact' (*'gleichsam durch ein Faktum gegeben'*).[54] 'As if by a fact', not 'by a fact'. This fact is only a quasi-fact, since the determination of will by the prescription of law is not empirical and may never be established as a simple fact by means of a commentary, whose denotative model would be the deduction of the principles of theoretical reason.

This fact of prescription is so far removed from what a fact in the empirical sense is, so little capable of being subsumed under a concept that, once deduced, would permit us to fix its place in a moral experience, that Kant, in comparing it to sensory experience, calls it an idea: 'The moral law transports us, in an ideal manner (*der Idee nach*) into a nature where pure reason, if it were accompanied by a physical power in proportion to itself, would produce the sovereign good.'[55] The reference domain circumscribed by the quasi-experience of the *Thou shalt* is not nature, but 'a supra-sensible nature', whose 'idea serves as a model for the determinations of our will'.[56] Moral experience is not an experience; the *Thou shalt* is not received in the realm of the sensible like something given in that realm. Yet it is received – that is why it can be called a fact; but it is received in the ideal.

Here again, Levinas would apparently not need to change anything, Levinas who tirelessly devotes himself to dissociating what belongs to the experience of the ego (material to be enjoyed or given a denotative commentary, within the limits we have stated) from what arises out of an untestable making-present of the other, by which is opened up a world of responsibilities transcending the world of enjoyment, although its effects are determined there.[57] Kant for his part, pursuing the theme of the *Faktum-Idee* right to its ultimate implications, concludes with that 'marvel'[58] provided by moral law, which is, as in Levinas, the presence of transcendence: if the 'fact' of the *Thou shalt* circumscribes an ideal nature (it is nevertheless efficient since it gives rise to those effects that are the acts that correspond to it – Levinas' 're-sponsibilities'), it follows 'that reason is itself through ideas an efficient cause in the field of experience', and that 'its transcendent use' is thus, thanks to the *Faktum* of moral law, 'changed into an immanent use'.[59] Reason remains transcendent when it aims to circumscribe in its commentary the essence of empirical nature; but this transcendence is what assures its immanence when, in the form of the prescriptive, it constitutes ideal nature.

Now it is precisely there, on the question of efficiency, that Levinas must turn his back on the Kant of the second *Critique*.

Logical analysis of the Kantian statement of moral law

Causality is indeed the axis upon which Kant makes the deduction of the practical principle operate in reverse. Let us try to demonstrate this briefly. The prescriptive statement *Thou shalt* cannot be deduced: it is a sort of fact (as the scientific statement is for the critique of theoretical reason). The question asked of this 'fact' by the *Critique* is not 'How does this kind of statement find objects to which it may be applied?' (the critical question bearing on the theoretical use of reason).[60] It is rather: 'Strictly speaking, how can this statement prescribe?' Now to prescribe (and here is the axis) is 'to be a cause without objects'.[61] The question that the *Critique* asks of the denotative statement is the question of the causality of objects upon representations: the classical question of truth or reference, in short. But when the object of commentary is the prescriptive statement, the *Critique must* invert the direction of the causality.[62] This is the inversion of direction.

All the rest – the deduction, properly speaking – comes in conse-quence of this reversal, which is stated in the exposition of the principle of practical reason. For if prescription *must* be the cause of objects, it cannot receive its power of efficiency from any object given in experience. In this way all hypothetical imperatives are eliminated. And the only answer left to the question, How does the law prescribe? is 'by an "immediate", "transcendent", "unintelligible", "inscrutable" power.' This transcendent power is freedom, which is none other than pure reason itself, acting as a practical cause.

It seems that the properties able to qualify its power can be applied, just as they are, to the 'other side of the face', which in the other, according to Levinas, commands us to act. Yet no one should be more hostile than the author of *Otherwise than Being* to this deduction of freedom, even when it is an inverted deduction: he would not fail to see therein the return of the denotative, and this in the very procedure by which the *Critique of Practical Reason* seeks to exclude it. This return is indeed effected in the form of the reversal of the Deduction, and first of all in the reversal of causality. In inverting the direction of causality, Kant believes he is emancipating will from experience. But the inversion leaves the concept itself, that of causality, intact, and nothing of this is inverted except the relation of order among the elements that it puts together (synthesizes). Kant justifies himself for this throughout the section that follows the Deduction, entitled 'Of the Right of Pure Reason, in its Practical Usage, to an Extension which is not Possible for it in Speculative Usage'.[63] What is more, he there calls openly for the inverted (i.e., noumenal) use that is made of causality in the second *Critique*.

Kant writes: 'We are not satisfied with applying this concept [causality] to the objects of experience', and further, 'We want to make use of it for things in themselves.'[64] Now we are authorized to do so by the *Critique* of speculative reason itself which, in making this concept a principle of understanding and not as Hume claimed a *habitus*, a general appearance, born of experience, endowed it with a transcendental status. That this a priori cannot be valid outside its application to the givens of experience is the rule of knowledge. However, 'it maintains a different relationship with the faculty of desiring',[65] an inverse relationship whereby the effect is not received from a phenomenal cause but produced by an unconditioned cause. What authorizes the *Widersinnige* of causality (and of Deduction) is, in short, that the same concept of cause is put to two contrary uses, the one in knowing, the other in desiring.

What follows from this as regards statements? That the form of a denotative statement must not be fundamentally different from that of a prescriptive statement. The former effects the synthesis of two phenomena under the category of cause, while the latter effects the synthesis of an agent and an act under the same category (i.e., of cause). Admittedly the agent is noumenal, and the act is not given; these features are registered in the imperative aspect taken by the moral law. But it is simple to show that the main function of the statement of the law is to maintain the imperative within the limits of the indicative, that is, to subordinate the 'inverted' mode of causality in desire to its direct mode in knowledge, or in other words to identify the predication that denotes a given 'nature' with the predication that prescribes an ideal 'nature'. Let us try to expose the denotative form concealed by the categorical imperative.

The fundamental law of practical reason is enunciated thus: 'Act in such a way that the maxim of your will can always be valid as the principle of a universal legislation also' ('*Handle so, dass die Maxime deines Willens jederzeit zugleich als Prinzip einer allgemeinen Gesetzgebung gelten koenne*').[66] This statement can be analysed initially into two parts: *Act*, and *In such a way that . . . Act* can be rewritten as *Do something*, which in turn may be understood as (i) *Thou shalt*, the pure prescriptive, *It is obligatory that . . .*; (ii) *To do something*, which as we have seen may be taken either as a well-formed expression in propositional logic, *A thing of some kind is done*, or else as a proposition root, *The doing of something* (by you). In Von Wright's notation,[67] this part would be expressed $O(p)$, where O is the operator of obligation and p the proposition being considered.

But it must not be forgotten that the moral law must not determine the will except by its 'form', and that the 'matter' to be found in it (e.g., a motive (*Triebfeder*))[68] could not operate in it as a cause, except by falling back into the phenomenal and the infinite chain of causalities. It follows that the expression p must present some remarkable properties.

These appear easily if we rewrite the expression in the notation of Alchourrón and Kalinowski:[69] $O(p)$ is written $Oy\alpha$, which reads, 'y must accomplish α'. Let it be agreed that y here designates the particular (or singular?) addressee of the order, named '*Thou*'. The order would have the developed expression $\exists y(Oy\alpha)$ and the signification 'There is at least one y and this y must accomplish α'.

But especially since the aim is to write a prescription that does not determine the 'matter' of the action to be accomplished, it is not appropriate in the expression $Oy\alpha$ to substitute for α, which designates a determined action, a symbol ζ, which will designate the action not determined by itself, the unspecified action, which is the target of the Kantian law – or a variable of an unknown action. The first part of the statement of the law is thus written $Oy\zeta$ and reads, 'Accomplish an undetermined action'.

To move on to the second part of the statement of the law: 'That the maxim of your will can always be valid as the principle of a universal legislation also.' It indicates that the maxim of the will that motivates the action (by itself the action is a matter of indifference) is equally formulable as a universal norm. The maxim of the action is none other than $Oy\zeta$. According to the chosen convention, the fact that a prescription should be valid as a norm (or as the principle of a law) is written $Nx'-'$, which is read, 'x has ruled: -', where x designates an agent and N a norm function that presents as a norm the expression placed in inverted commas on its right.

This operator is not to be confused with the one designated by the symbol O, 'It is obligatory that . . . ' The latter belongs to deontic logic, or the logic of prescriptions, while the operator marked N derives from the logic of norms. An expression such as $Nx'Oy\alpha'$ reads, 'There is a norm decreed by x which declares: y must accomplish α.' This reading brings out that the function N is descriptive; it denotes the fact that the expression placed on its right is a norm whereas the function O is prescriptive, indicating that the action α must be accomplished by y.

It can be seen that the expression $Nx'-'$ is to the expression $Oy\alpha$ as a metastatement is to a statement in the object language. The inverted commas around $Oy\alpha$ in the statement of the norm attest that the statement of the prescription is here a quotation made by x, and that the reader, the addressee of the complete message, is dealing with the 'image' of the deontic statement in the metalanguage of norms. These observations refer back to those made above[70] on the subject of the neutralization of the prescriptive in the metalanguage that comments on it: the commentary that concerns us consists in declaring that the prescription is a norm.

It is in this metalanguage of norms that, according to Kant, the maxim of a particular action can be declared the principle of a universal legislation. The obligation $Oy\zeta$, obligation for a particular subject y to accomplish the indifferent action ζ, is taken as the object of a meta-assertion, which declares it a universal norm. The one who can declare it such is any subject whatever. Thus, x in $Nx'-'$ symbolizes here an agent which has the universal quantifier, and this is developed as $\forall x(Nx'-')$.

We can now write the second part of the statement of the law, still agreeing, however, to ignore for a moment the operation that links it to the first part, which Kant enunciates as *in such a way that*. Isolated then, this part is expressed, *The maxim of your will can always also be valid as the principle of a universal legislation.* The 'maxim of your will' is the norm enunciating that the act is obligatory for the agent. Let us recall that the act in question was posited in the first part of the statement as an indeterminate act. Finally, if this norm is only subjective, the subject who enunciates it as such is the same as the one who makes for himself an obligation to act as he does. The 'maxim of will', which commands the particular obligation to act, is thus written $Ny'Oy\zeta'$, which reads, 'At least one subject has ruled: At least one subject must accomplish the said indeterminate action.'

As regards the end of the second part of the statement of the law, *can always also be valid as the principle of a universal legislation*: it names the predicate that is always attributed to the 'maxim of your will', at least if the action that the will commands in accordance with this maxim is just (or moral). This predicate is *the principle of a universal legislation*. The principle of a legislation is a norm. If the legislation is universal, this norm is decreed by any subject declaring norms. Moreover, the obligation thus elevated to the status of a universal norm is evidently the same one that commands the agent designated at the beginning (*Thou*) to accomplish the (indeterminate) action in question in the first part of the statement. Ultimately Kant does not intend only for that agent at least to be made to submit to the said universal legislation, but any agent whatever. Hence we will write the predicate in question $\forall x(Nx'Ox\zeta')$.

The expression *can always be valid as*, which links the predicate to the subject of this second part of the statement of the moral law, is to be understood: 'Each time that $NyOy\zeta$, then it is necessary that $NxOx\zeta$'. We must not let ourselves be deceived by Kant's use of the modal verb *can* (*können*). It cannot here have the force of probability, or even of very great probability, which it can elsewhere denote in French, as in German;[71] such meaning would ruin the scope of the law that Kant would have 'fundamental' and that would then merely be very likely. The fact that the particular maxim *can always be valid as* a universal principle signifies that every time there is the maxim, then it is valid every time, as that principle. What commands the meaning of the necessity that we attribute to the modal verb is the adverb *always* (*jederzeit*, every time), which is the temporal index of the universality of a proposition, as *necessary that* is its modal index. So we will express this meaning by the sign of implication (or logical conditional): *If p, then q*, or $p \supset q$. This provides the following expression for the second part of the statement of the moral law: $(Ny'Oy\zeta') \supset (\forall xNx'Ox\zeta')$, that is, 'If at least one subject has ruled: The said subject at least must accomplish the said indeterminate action, then any subject whatever has ruled: Any subject whatever must accomplish the said indeterminate action.'

Let us finally come to the operation by which the preceding statement, which expresses the second part of the statement of the fundamental law, finds itself modified into the complete statement. The question is to know how this second part is articulated with the first. The articulation of the Kantian statement is *in such a way that (so, dass)*. This is of the greatest importance for Kant, since it is what comes to determine the action, otherwise indeterminate, that the subject makes for himself the obligation of accomplishing, and since the determination takes place (as Kant repeats) only through the 'form' of the maxim and not through its 'matter'. Now, what Kant calls the 'form' of the maxim is none other than the second part of the statement of the law that we have just described. It is only if the norm bearing on the obligation to accomplish an action can be decreed as a universal norm that the accomplishment of the said action can be obligatory. It follows that the subjective obligation is legitimate, that is, constituting the object of a norm, only if it can also constitute the object of a universal norm.

The operator that unites the two parts of the Kantian statement is thus that of equivalence (or of biconditionality): *p if, and only if, q*, or *p ≡ q*.

Do whatever it is if, and only if, the norm of what you must do is also a universal norm. Or to put it more rigorously: 'At least one subject must accomplish such-and-such an action if, and only if, one subject at least having ruled: At least one subject must perform the said action, then any subject has ruled: Any subject must perform the said action.'

To write this, we will replace the sign of the indeterminate action with the sign of the determinate action, since the complete statement of the law henceforth allows us to determine (formally) the action to be accomplished. We get the following expression:

$$Cy\propto \equiv [(Ny'Oy\propto') \supset (\forall x Nx'Ox\propto')].$$

We find in many of Kant's explanations confirmation of the proposed reading of the expression *in such a way that* as an operator of equivalence. This operator is not a simple conditional (or inference). For the moral law does not only say, 'If the norm of such-and-such an action is a universally obligatory norm, then you must perform this action.' It also says, 'If you must accomplish such-and-such an action, then the maxim of your will (= your particular norm) is a universally obligatory norm.' Not only *if p, then q*, but also *if q, then p*. That the universality of the norm is a condition of validity of the action is something that no one can fail to understand in the second *Critique*. But we cannot restrict ourselves to this simple condition; the morality of the act must also be a condition of the universality of the norm.

The first condition is to be understood as the determination of the will by the pure law, that is, by pure reason in its practical usage. The second condition is to be understood as the determination of the law by pure will, that is, again by pure reason in its practical usage. In effect, practical reason is both legislation (that is, pure synthesizing power and, so to speak, power to enunciate a nature) *and* at the same time efficient causality, that is, power to produce and power, so to speak, to institute a nature. As legislation, it requires universality as the condition of any obligation to act. As causality, it requires pure will, that is, freedom, which emancipates its effects from nature as explained by theoretical reason, which places them in a suprasensible nature.

Thus the equivalence indicated by our operator appears to be merely the transcription into the conventions of logical notation, of the identity admitted by Kant between reason that rules and reason that wills. The reciprocal implication, or biconditionality, between these two powers appears clearly in a phrase like the following: 'Pure practical laws are . . . necessary, if freedom is assumed, or inversely freedom is necessary, because these laws are necessary, as practical postulates.'[72]

The same applies for Kant's insistent emphasizing that will is pure only if it is 'absolutely' and 'immediately' determined. Then 'it is all one (*einerlei*) with pure practical reason'.[73] This immediate identity is only possible if the will is guided solely by the legislation of reason, which has universal value. If will, then reason, that is, universality; and if reason, then will.

Levinas against Kant

What have we shown by this? That a prescriptive statement, the obligatory symbolized by O, is equated with the description of this statement, which makes of it a norm N – on one condition only, it is true. This is that the norm of particular obligation can be rewritten as a universal norm: but this condition can itself be entirely expressed in the logic of norms and does not make any new obligation appear, only an implication of propositional logic attributing a change of quantifier to the subject who enunciates the norm.

This equivalence of the prescriptive and the descriptive in the statement of the law was prepared, so to speak, by the inversion of the practical Deduction, and above all by the reversal of usage of causality. The latter is valid as a model for any synthesis of elements in the descriptive statements of science. When Kant detects its new usage in the prescriptive statements of morality, he declares it to be inverted as to its effects: in theoretical reason, causality synthesizes the givens; in practical reason it produces them. But this reversal now seems to be something other than an inversion of direction on one and the same axis.

A simple inversion of that sort would result from a reciprocal transformation. A reciprocal transformation manifests in particular the property of transforming an implication $p \supset q$ in such a way that where R symbolizes the transformation in question, we have $R(p \supset q) = q \supset p$. This transformation is situated in the realm of propositional logic and affects only the form of the statements.

But that is not true of the Kantian *Widersinnige*. The transformation noted by Kant escapes from propositional logic: in displacing the cause from the 'noumenon' side on the basis of the 'phenomenal' position accorded to it by theoretical reason, it does not operate, or does not only operate, as a reciprocal transformation, inverting the order of the premise and the conclusion in the statements; nor for that matter does it operate as any one of the other three transformations admitted by propositional logic. What it introduces as the premise of that conclusion (i.e., the prescriptive statement of the moral law) is the 'subject' of the enunciation of this statement itself.

The practical Deduction does indeed start out from the moral law, as from an ideally tested premise, but only in order to deduce it and substitute for it a premise that is untested even ideally and that is even inconceivable – namely, will. If will remains 'unintelligible', it is because it cannot be placed in a propositional statement, that is, in a discourse with a denotative function, arising from theoretical reason and having nothing to do with this genre of unintelligibility. When Kant says that will, if it is pure, prescribes the law, he keeps it in principle outside the statement of that law – which is marked by the imperative form of that statement. Hence the will does indeed occupy the place of the subject of the prescriptive enunciation, which escapes *ex hypothesi* from any descriptive statement (i.e., from all intelligibility).

This 'absolute exteriority' of that which commands, so precious to Levinas but also to Kant, is precisely what Kant causes to vanish, by identifying the power of the subject of the practical enunciation with causality and by conceiving causality as the same category that permits theoretical reason to form its denotative expressions well. Or in other words, by identifying reason as prescriptive will with reason as descriptive causality.

In the language we are using here, we will say, then, that what is at stake in the discourse of Levinas is the power to speak of obligation without ever transforming it into a norm.

Pragmatic analysis of the Kantian statement of moral law

To clarify the scope of what is at stake, let us go back to the pragmatic point of view, in which we have noted,[74] that the addressee of an order is in a quite different situation from the addressee of a discourse of knowledge. The discourse of knowledge is a genre of discourse that authorizes, and even encourages, the addressee to begin to speak, either to proffer in his turn some statement on the same 'subject' (i.e., the same reference) as the first enunciator, or to comment on what the latter has said about this same reference, or to mix the two in a composite discourse. But the recipient of an order has hardly any latitude, at least not if he means to restrict himself to the world of prescriptions: he can only carry it out or not carry it out. If he argues about it, comments on it, negotiates over it, he inevitably substitutes for the order received the 'image' of this order that the negotiation, commentary, or argument take as their reference, and he escapes *ipso facto* from the universe of prescriptions into that of denotations.

Now we have just seen that the insertion of an order into a statement declaring that order to be a norm is a particular case of the above situation. The one, whoever he is, who promotes an obligation to the dignity of a norm is an addressee of that order who takes it as the reference of his discourse and, in so doing, moves into the position of addresser of a new statement, the commentary that makes the order into a norm. It is of course conceivable that he did not gain knowledge of that order directly but was told of it; it could be objected that the order thus did not reach him equipped with its executive power, but was already neutralized and repeated as a quotation in a descriptive discourse. This is possible; but the situation is then merely displaced: someone, whoever he is, necessarily, rightly or wrongly, must not have 'taken upon himself' the order he heard, so that this order could be made the object of a commentary, even if this commentary consisted of a declaration that the order were valid as a norm.

Such, in particular, is the situation of the enunciator named Kant in respect of the moral law. We have just described the statement of the moral law in the conventions of Alchourrón and Kalinowski. If we now had to write the Kantian statement that declares this law to be the 'fundamental law' of practical reason, that is, a norm *par excellence*, it is clear that we would have to place before our expression of the law a supplementary prefix such as $Nk'-'$. This prefix belongs to the logic of norms and reads '*Kant has ruled: '-''* where the symbol '$-$' designates the statement of the law, properly speaking.

The complete Kantian statement would then be expressed:

$$Nk'Oy\alpha \equiv (Ny'Oy\alpha') = (\forall xNx'Ox'\alpha')'.$$

This reads (omitting the outer quotation marks so as to simplify the notation):

A subject named Kant has ruled: 'One subject at least must perform the action α if, and only if, one subject at least having ruled: One subject at least must perform the action α, then any subject has ruled: Any subject must perform the action α.'

A reading like this brings out that Kant – one at least of the addressees of the obligation y – comes to occupy the position of an addresser, inasmuch as he sets up the first obligation as a norm.

The same goes for the reader of the *Critique of Practical Reason*. By reading Kant's commentary, he makes himself the addressee not of the obligation enunciated by the moral law encased in this commentary (as an 'image' of itself) but of the discourse by which Kant raises this obligation to the dignity of a norm. As the addressee of denotative propositions, he is required to understand but not to do. He can comment on the commentary in his turn and thus pass into the position of enunciator by the same right as Kant.

This substitution appears legitimate in the case of the reader of the *Critique of Practical Reason:* what he reads is not an order but the declaration that the order *Act in such a way that. . .* is a norm. Now, the statement of an obligation is not an obligation. In this respect, it seems that the reader of Levinas is in a position no different from that of the reader of Kant. If he reads the order *Do before understanding* in this or that book by Levinas[75] it is, so to speak, understood (*entendu*) that he will not stop understanding (or reading) in order to do and that he 'must' understand this statement, not as a command but as the quotation or image of that command reported in Levinas' metalanguage.

There is no difference between the two readers in this regard: the one, like the other, is authorized by his position as reader of a book of philosophy to neutralize the executive force of the order that he reads there and to place himself in the position of possible commentator; but the same does not hold true of the two 'authors'.

Kant can denote the moral obligation as a norm because universality is already implied in its formula. When 'Kant has ruled: "One subject at least must accomplish such-and-such an action, etc.",' he is doing nothing other than applying to the order *Act in such a way that* . . . the argument *from the moment that the obligation to which you are submitted can be universalized as a norm.* Kant's commentary can denote the order as a norm since this order is executive only on condition that it has been denoted as a norm by the one who is to execute it. Kant can comment on it as a norm since that is what the agent must already have done in order for his action to be moral. To speak in formal terms, the *k* that we have made appear in the *Nk* is a case of the *Nx* that the *Ny* must imply for the obligation to be valid.

For the moment we will not follow this clue any further, despite its importance. Let us be content to observe that the moral imperative, which on the one hand is set up as a universal norm by Kant and on the other hand equates the obligation with the universal norm in its statement, appears to rest on a *petitio principii,* belonging to the first type recognized by Aristotle, when 'one postulates the very thing one has to demonstrate'. Kant has to demonstrate that the statement of the moral law is universally valid. Now, by introducing into this statement the biconditional *if and only if.* . .what else is he doing but postulating that the maxim, if it is valid, becomes the moral law?

Yet, if we re-establish the different levels of language the *petitio principii* is not certain:

Object language: *Do that.*
Metalanguage 1: *Do that iff/Do that/is universalizable.*[76]
Metalanguage 2: *Do that iff/Do that/is universalizable/is universalizable.*

The first level of language here is prescriptive; the second, that of the metalanguage or commentary, establishes the equivalence of prescriptive and denotative; the third, which cites the second, is purely denotative. For there to be a *petitio principii,* the metalanguages (1) and (2) would in reality have to be of the same species and at the same level. This would be the case, for example, if the last statement, that is, the Kantian commentary, were prescriptive and if one could substitute */that/* for the expression */Do that iff/Do that/ is universalizable/.* In that case the statement would be: *Do (= Say)/Do that iff/Do that/ is universalizable iff/ Do (= Say) //that// is universalizable,* where the last */that/* is substituted for the first complete expression between bars. Intuitively transcribed, and with simplified quotation marks, we have: *Say [Statement of the moral law] iff [Say (Statement of the moral law)] is universalizable.*

Obviously, this is not the Kantian statement: Kant does not order his reader to declare the statement of the law obligatory on condition that it is universalizable. Kant does not order his reader to do anything practical. That the reader *may* or *must* say something about the statement of the moral law is not on account of a permission or an obligation; it is a modalized inference. The reader of the book is placed before a universe of denotative statements, to which the third-order statement fully belongs. The prescriptive statements that he encounters in the Kantian commentary are always only 'images' of themselves. Hence it is legitimate to assert that what saves the Kantian statement from the *petitio principii* is the recourse to denotative metalanguage.

'Obey!'

But this recourse is at the same time a kind of scandal, since it rests on the equivalence, in the second-order statement, of a prescriptive and a descriptive statement: this is the scandal that Levinas denounces in a sentence we have already quoted.[77] For this equivalence is nothing other than the ego's infatuation with knowledge. By promoting the order he receives to the dignity of a norm, the addressee of the prescription subordinates the obligation that is linked to the prescription to the comprehension that what he understands (the maxim of the action) can be understood, and hence executed, by everyone. The order he receives is really an order only if it is mediated by a denotative metastatement. In consequence, the addressee of the moral law ceases to be in the place of the *Thou* to whom the prescription is addressed and who is expressed in the statement of this law by the second-person imperative, and he comes to occupy the place of the *I* who delivers the opinion that this prescription is or is not universalizable. By the fact of this displacement, the other from whom he receives the order – that other whom Kant, however, admits is 'inscrutable' and whom Levinas strives to maintain in his transcendence – finds himself 'placed in symmetry' with the ego. The irreducibility of the prescriptive is ruined, if it is true that it assumes an ineffaceable dissymmetry between the addresser and the addressee of the order.

This supposition, which governs the whole discourse of Levinas like a kind of metaprescription of alterity, can be expressed by the following statement: *That /Thou/ shalt never be /I/!*[78] Among the numerous occurrences of it that can be found in his books, the following is a philosophically inspired one:

The differences between the others and me. . .depend on the I-Other orientation conjuncture, on the inevitable *orientation* of being 'on the basis of oneself' towards 'the Other' . . . Multiplicity in being, which refuses totalization, but takes form as fraternity and discourse, is situated in an essentially asymmetrical 'space'.[79]

But it is Levinas the commentator on the Talmud[80] who seems to grasp most closely the metaprinciple of asymmetry:

> The incomparable character of an event like the giving of the Torah [is that] it is accepted before it is known ... The deed in question ... is not simply the opposite practice to theory, but a way of *actualizing without beginning with the possible* ... They execute before having understood: ... To understand a voice that speaks to you [is] *ipso facto* to accept the obligation in respect of the one who is speaking ... In this impossibility of hiding from the imperious call of the creature, the assumption does not in any way go beyond passivity.[81]

The question, then, is to know how to formulate a first-level prescriptive statement, expressed in the natural language of orders, that would satisfy the metaprinciple *That/Thou/shalt never be /I/!*

Let us start again, according to the rapid description we made at the outset,[82] from the situation of the commentator who finds himself faced with the works of Levinas: if he understands it, he must not understand it, and if he does not understand it, then he understands it.

In the batch of 'paradoxes' that have come down to us from the principal adversaries of Plato and Aristotle, the Megarians and the Cynics, there exists a prescriptive statement that appears to produce a similarly contradictory effect. This is the order *Disobey!*

Aristotle notes it in the following context. Among the procedures of refutation used by the sophists, he gives the name *paralogisms* to those that, operating *exo tès lexeôs,* do not (or do not only) play on the *lexis* (or *dictio*) of the statement but make bad usage of the categories of thought.[83] In this way, a subset of these paralogisms rests, according to Aristotle, on a confusion of the absolute and the relative in attribution: *to haplôs versus kata ti,* or *to haplôs versus pè.* An example of a statement that plays upon such a confusion is ...: *If the nonbeing is opinable* (= the possible object of an opinion), *then the nonbeing is.*[84] In order to refute this sophism it is sufficient to reintroduce the obfuscated category *relation.* For, says Aristotle, 'it is impossible for contraries and contradictories, affirmation and negation, to belong absolutely (*haplôs*) to the same object, but there is nothing against each of the two (properties) belonging to it in some way or in a certain regard or in a certain manner.'[85] There then follows a further example of the same paralogism: 'Is it possible for the same [subject] to obey and disobey the same [order or subject]?' Aristotle rejects such a possibility by a lapidary argument: 'He who disobeys does not simply obey, but he obeys in something.'[86]

One can thus reconstitute the statement aimed at by the Stagirite as *Disobey!* However, this order is a paradox only on one condition, namely that it be understood as a complete statement. What does this mean?

Let us examine the case of its affirmative correlate: *Obey!* Customarily this statement is understood by its addressee as an abbreviation of a complete statement: *Obey the order that you have received in another connection!* One can thus distinguish two orders here: a first order, which carries the instruction about the act to be performed (*Close the door!*), and a second order (*Obey!*), which recalls that the first order is executive. Note that the sequence *first order, second order* must be conceived as a logical rather than a chronological succession: the expression *Obey!* can, in 'real' time, precede the order that gives the instruction, without this reciprocal transformation of the sequence's affecting the logical properties of its terms. In particular, the reminder of the order has in both cases an exclusively perlocutionary function: it orders its addressee not to perform an action but to receive the anterior or ulterior prescriptive statement in an attitude of carrying it out or, in other words, of being obliged by this statement.

One can always reject the expression *Obey!*, taken in isolation, because it is an incomplete statement, lacking an instruction. That is how Jean-Michel Salanskis[87] compares its inconsistency to that of an axiom such as *If a, then b. And a.* It is known that in order to make this axiom executable, Lewis Carroll's tortoise[88] demands a new instruction *c*, expressed as *If a, then b. And a. Then b.* But this instruction *c* must in turn be introduced into the reference that allows us to conclude *b. If a, then b. And a. And c. Then b.* This constitutes a new instruction *d*. And so on.

It is the same, observes Salanskis, for *Obey!* if we claim that it is a complete statement. Let *O* be the order *Obey!* and *e* its execution. This gives: *If O, then e. And O.* The instruction needed in order for the order to be executed is *If O, then e. And O. Then e.* But this instruction (which is here an order *O'*: *Obey the 'Obey'!*) introduces itself into the previous inference as a supplementary condition for the execution of *O*: *If O, then e. And O. And O'. Then e.* And soon the execution of the order will always be postponed, or – there will always be one instruction lacking.

One can use this argumentation (leaving aside for the moment the temporal properties of the expression *Obey!* which we will discuss elsewhere) the better to distinguish an interesting property of the statement *Obey!* This is the same property that Salanskis notes, we believe, in classifying this statement among the protodoxes. It is not one of the well-formed expressions, which satisfy a set of lexical and syntactical rules fixed in the metalanguage of deontic logic. It is one of the expressions that, in the natural language, allow us to gloss the metalinguistic symbol O, which also reads 'It is obligatory that . . . ' This symbol is an operator whose property is to change the proposition or proposition root placed on its right into an obligation. By itself it could not constitute one of the well-formed expressions of deontic logic: those are (in monadic logic) of the form '$O(p)$', where p is a well-formed expression of propositional logic.[89] The logician makes clear, as well, that among the other expressions that are not well-formed deontic expressions are 'those which repeat (iterate) a deontic operator'.[90] He thus excludes as inconsistent not only an expression like 'O' but also an expression like '$O(O)$'. Thanks to this exclusion, the logician declares himself secured against some 'paradoxes', which he does not name, but which we can guess.

There is thus a temptation simply to place the symbol O in the lexicon of the metalanguage that allows us to speak about the language of commands. But this situation is unsatisfactory because of the confused usage in it of the word *metalanguage*. According to the acceptation of Russell and Tarski, it is defined as a second-order language in which it is possible to decide the truth value of expressions belonging to the first-order language. The operator O in no way fulfils this function, not even for the sake of the interest that might accrue to it as a result. That is because, once again, the propositions it permits us to put into form are not descriptive or attributive but prescriptive. If there exists some metalanguage relating to prescriptive propositions, it must no doubt be denotative as we have said; but then the operator of obligation, if it is part of it, does not there fulfil the same function as the truth functions imported from propositional logic. These alone enable us to declare that a relation between two prescriptive statements is true because, for example, one can infer the one from the other or false because, on the contrary, the one and the other are contradictory (operator of exclusion). But the operator of obligation, taken in itself, neither derives from the claim to speak truly when we encounter it in the prescriptive expressions of the natural language nor allows us to decide the validity of those expressions when we consider it as a deontic operator. It is indispensable, on the other hand, in whatever form of words it may occur, to the formation of prescriptive expressions. On the hither side of all alethic validity, it is the prescription that accompanies any instruction so as to make it obligatory.

Is this *hither-side* (*en-deçà*) what Levinas means to signify by his *beyond* (*au-delà*)? Perhaps; but even then we must not forget what such a statement has as its pragmatic correlate, which Levinas calls 'passivity'.[91] Kant said of the *Ich denke* that it accompanies all our representations. This remark merely circumscribes what we previously called the enunciative clause.[92] But the *Thou shalt* or the *Obey!* could not in the same way accompany all our prescriptions. The form of the statement of obligation is not only different from that of a statement in propositional logic but it also does not derive from the philosophy of enunciation alone. Because of the use that it necessarily makes of the second person, the prescriptive necessarily connotes a pragmatic – which is not the case for reflexives.

It follows that the enunciative clause cannot figure in the universe of prescriptive statements, for lack of an enunciative instance capable of making its very assertion an expression or a part of an expression. The exclusion of this clause has not at all the same function as the exclusion to which propositional logic proceeds in order to sanitize its field. Here this exclusion signifies that an expression can be considered prescriptive only from the point of view of its addressee. Whether or not one executes the order contained in it is another question; in any case, it is received as obligation and seizes the one who receives it (or dis-seizes him, as we would prefer to say) as its 'obligee'. Such is the condition that Levinas calls, among other names, 'hostage'.[93]

The expression *Obey!* seems then to cover several of the properties that Levinas attributes to the ethical situation. It is an absolutely 'empty' proposition, since it is not provided with an instruction to make it executable, not even the meta-instruction of universality conceded by the Kantian statement of the moral law. It is not executable, but it is that which renders executory.

So it is not understood (*entendue*) in the sense of being comprehended (*comprise*), but only in the sense of being received. However, it is never in fact received in its own right but merely hidden in the form of complete or 'full' prescriptive statements, that is, instructives. So it is indeed a 'simple form' as in Kant, but this form is not that of universality, which is denotative; it is that of obligation, which is pragmatic. According to Levinas, 'it' is not obligatory because 'it' is universal; 'it' is simply obligatory. Thus, 'it' is to be done *before* 'it' is understood. In this way, the Lord requires of Israel not obedience but rather obligation towards Him, before he instructs the people as to what they will be obliged to do.[94] In this way the domination of knowledge, that is, the infatuation with the enunciation, is interrupted.

In saying this, we place the accent on a pragmatic property of prescriptives that seems indeed to correspond to the metaprinciple of alterity *That /Thou/ shalt never be /I/!* which we took as our guide. For to find oneself placed in the pragmatic position of being obliged is incommensurable with the position of enunciation, even of enunciating prescriptives. This incommensurability is the same as that of freedom with the condition of being a hostage. If there is freedom, it always and necessarily plays itself out on the enunciative instance. But the ethical and political question does not begin with that of the freedom enjoyed by the '*I*'; it begins with the obligation by which the *Thou* is seized. Not with the power to *announce* . . ., but with the other power, which in the West is regarded as a powerlessness[95] – that of being *bound to* . . .

This is so much so that, in the end, there is not even any need to have recourse to the negative form *Disobey* in order to restore faithfully the discomfort in which any addressee of an order finds himself. That would give too much credit to the power of the enunciative clause by itself. It alone can allow us, in the universe of denotative propositions, to transform any negative statement into an assertion; it is thus the safeguard of the profundity of paradoxes, if not of their validity, in this universe. But in the universe of prescriptions, it is not necessary to resort to the negative form of the statement (as in *Disobey,* or *Do not understand,* or *Do nothing but command*) in order to reveal the power that is attached to them and that preoccupies Levinas. For this power is not polarized on enunciative spontaneity but on receptivity to the order, on prescriptivity. The Megarians and the Cynics seek by means of paradoxes to shake the system of knowledge from the inside; for the Jews, the point is to escape from it. The simplest prescription, instructively empty but pragmatically affirmative, at one stroke situates the one to whom it is addressed outside the universe of knowledge.

At least two questions are left hanging: How does Levinas' commentary on this situation, a situation incommensurable with denotations, escape the trap of denotative metalanguage? How does his reader receive the commentary? Must we not revise the assimilation we made of Levinas' reader and the reader of the second Kantian *Critique*?

NOTES

1 See 'Hegel et les Juifs', in *Difficile liberté*, 2nd edn (Paris: Albin Michel, 1963), pp. 304-8 (henceforth *DL*).
2 See *Quatre lectures talmudiques* (Paris: Editions de Minuit, 1968) (henceforth *QLT*).
3 *DL*, pp. 268, 234; *Autrement qu'être ou au-delà de l'essence* (The Hague: Martinus Nijhoff, 1974), pp. 6-9, 58-75, 195-205 (henceforth *AEAE*)/ *Otherwise Than Being or Beyond Essence*, tr. A. Lingis (The Hague: Martinus Nijhoff, 1981), pp. 5-7, 45-59, 153-61 (henceforth *OBBE*).
4 *AEAE*, p. 8/*OBBE*, p. 7.
5 On the 'there is' and on insomnia, see *De l'existent à l'existence* (Paris: Fontaine, 1947), pp. 93ff. (henceforth *DEE*)/*Existence and Existents*, tr. A. Lingis (The Hague: Martinus Nijhoff, 1978), pp. 57ff. (henceforth *EE*); *Totalite et Infini* (The Hague: Martinus Nijhoff, 1969), pp. 114ff. (*TeI*)/ *Totality and Infinity*, tr. A. Lingis (The Hague: Martinus Nijhoff, 1969), pp. 140ff. (henceforth *TI*).
6 Aristotle, *Refutation of the Sophists* 167a1, 180a32; *Rhetoric* 1402a5.
7 B. Russell, *My Philosophical Development* (New York: Simon and Schuster, 1959), ch. 7.
8 See *TeI* pp. 81-160, *Interiorité et economie*/*TI* pp. 109-186, 'Interiority and Economy'; *DEE* passim/*EE* passim.
9 *TeI* p. 122/*TI* p. 148; emphasis added.
10 Cf. J.L. Austin, *How to Do Things with Words* (New York: Oxford University Press, 1968); P. Grice, *Logic and Conversation* (unpublished, 1968); H. Parret, *La Pragmatique des modalités* (Urbino: Università di Urbino, 1975)..
11 G.W.F. Hegel, *Phänomenologie des Geistes* (Hamburg: Meiner, 1952), p. 19/*Phenomenology of Spirit*, tr. A.V. Miller (New York: Oxford University Press, 1979), pp. 9-10.
12 Hegel, *Phänomenologie*, p. 21/*Phenomenology*, p. 11.
13 Terms borrowed from J. Habermas, '*Vorbereitende Bemerkungen zu einer Theorie der kommunikativen Kompetenz*', in Habermas and Luhman, *Theorie der Gessellschaft oder Sozialtechnologie – Was leistet die Systemforschung?* (Frankfurt: Suhrkamp, 1971). See J. Poulain, *Vers une pragmatique nucléaire de la communication*.
14 On the properties of philosophical or 'speculative' statements, see V. Descombes, *L'inconscient malgré lui* (Paris: Minuit, 1977), pp. 142-78.
15 *DL*, p. 379/'Signature', tr. M.E. Petrisko, ed. A. Peperzak, *Research in Phenomenology 8* (1978), pp. 188-9.
16 Hence the necessity to remove the writing of a Blanchot or a Roger Laporte (who are for Levinas the expression of *proffering*) from aesthetics and to class them on the side of ethics. This can be confirmed by reference

to E. Levinas, *Sur Maurice Blanchot* (Montpellier: Fata Morgana, 1975), p. 78 n. 3; and E. Levinas, *Noms propres* (Montpellier: Fata Morgana, 1976), pp. 133-7.

17 Aristotle, *On Interpretation* 17a3; cf. *Nicomachean Ethics* 1138b15-1140a24.

18 See J. Rey-Debove, *Le Métalangage* (Paris: Thèse de Doctorat d'Etat, Universitá de Paris VIII, 1977).

19 G Kalinowski, *Du métalangage en logique* (Urbino: Universitá di Urbino, 1975), p. 24.

20 'We say "the order orders this" and we do it; but also "the order orders this: I must . . . " We transfer it now into a proposition, now into a demonstration, now into an act' (L. Wittgenstein, *Philosophical Investigations*, §459).

21 See Von Wright, 'Deontic Logics', *American Philosophical Quarterly 4* (1969), no. 2.

22 Wittgenstein, *Philosophical Investigations*, §22; R.M. Hare, 'Imperative Sentences,' *Mind 58* (1949), pp. 21-39; H. Keuth, 'Deontische Logik . . . ', in *Normenlogik*, ed. Lenk (München: K. G. Sar, 1974), p. 68.

23 The symbolization preferred by G. Kalinowski, *Du metalangage en logique*, pp. 18-19, and taken up by C.E. Alchourrón, 'Logic of Norms and Logic of Normative Propositions', *Logique et analyse 12* (1969), p. 245.

24 Cf. Wittgenstein: 'Here we mean: an order would be the image of the action which was executed in accordance with this order; but also an image of the action which must be executed in accordance with it' (*Philosophical Investigations* §519).

25 See J.L. Gardies, *La Logique du temps* (Paris: PUF, 1975), p. 29.

26 *DL*, p. 260. [*Genesis* 21:14-19 - Ed.]

27 Cf. 'Humanisme et an-archie', in *Humanisme de l'autre homme* (Montpellier: Fata Morgana, 1972), pp. 72-82 (henceforth *HAH*).

28 See *AEAE,* pp. 57, 210-18/*OBBE*, pp. 44, 165-71; cf. the critique by Sextus Empiricus of categorical syllogisms.

29 'Where would the Jew get the strength of his refusal . . .? the *No* requires a criterion. Rabbi Yossi will give the required sign: "Let the waters of the cave of Pamais be changed into blood! and they were changed into blood" (Sanhedrin 98a) . . . The men who see cannot turn their eyes away from the innocent blood which they are diluting' (*DL*, p. 278).

30 'In the just war waged upon war, tremble - yea, shudder - at each instant, because of this very injustice' (*AEAE*, p. 233/*OBBE*, p. 185).

31 *Tel*, pp. 161ff./*TI*, pp. 187ff.; *HAH*, pp. 57-63; *AEAE*, pp. 125-30/*OBBE*, pp. 99-102. [The next paragraph begins the portion of Lyotard's article that appears in *Textes pour Emmanuel Levinas*, ed. F. Larvelle, pp. 127-50 - Ed.]

32 *Tel* Section I (pp.1-78), pp. 187ff./*TI* Section I (pp. 31-105), pp. 212ff.

33 '[The Other] commands me like a Master. A command which can concern me only insofar as I am a master myself; consequently a command which commands me to command' (*Tel*, p. 188/*TI*, p. 213).

34 *AEAE* ch. IV (pp. 125–66)/*OBBE* ch. IV (pp. 99–129).
35 E.g., *TeI*, p. 193/*TI*, p. 217. Unless we read Spinoza transparently, as that which shelters the word of the law from demonstrative discourse, as Levinas means to do via S. Zac's *Spinoza et l'interpretation de l'ecriture* (Paris: PUF, 1965). Cf. *DL*, 'Avez-vous relu Baruch?', pp. 148–59.
36 E.g., *TeI*, pp. 274–5/*TI*, pp. 298–9. And the following: 'None of the generosity which is supposed apparently to be in the German term *"es gibt"* was shown between 1933 and 1945. This has to be said!' (*DL*, p. 375).
37 Except, of course, if he chooses the alternative hypothesis, which is to begin by defining the conventions thanks to which the metalanguage will be defined in which we can say whether the statements of the object language are true or false.
38 'Exteriority is not a negation, it is a marvel' (*TeI*, p. 269/*TI*, p.292).
39 One can see the importance of the conventions of notation in these matters. The methodological remarks of J. Rey-Debove, *Le Métalangage*, pp. 15–18, are particularly illuminating for the philosopher, as is her analysis of the Metalexicon, ch. 3.
40 *DL*, p. 260.
41 Concerning pardon, see, e.g., *TeI*, pp. 259–60/*TI*, pp. 282–3.
42 Immanuel Kant, *Kritik der praktischen Vernuft* in *Werke in Sechs Bände*, Bd VI (Insel Edn, 1956), I §8/*Critique of Practical Reason*, tr. L.W. Beck (Chicago: University of Chicago Press, 1949), Part I, Bk. I, ch. I, §8 (144).
43 *TeI*, p. 192/*TI*, p. 217.
44 Kant, *Kritik*, pp. 155–65/*Critique*, pp. 152–60.
45 Ibid., p. 161/p. 157.
46 Ibid., p. 160/p. 156.
47 Ibid., p. 160/p. 157. This is why Kant attributes to it a sort of credit, '*Diese Art von Kreditiv*' (Ibid., p. 162/p. 158).
48 Ibid., p. 161/p. 157.
49 Ibid.
50 See *QLT*, second lesson, '*La tentation de la tentation*' ('The Temptation of Temptation').
51 'Imperialism of the Same', 'effrontedly before the non-Ego', *TeI*, p. 59/*TI*, p. 87.
52 Kant, *Kritik*, p. 141/*Critique*, p. 142.
53 Ibid., p. 156/p. 153.
54 Ibid., p. 170/p. 164.
55 Ibid., p. 157/p. 154.
56 Ibid.; and again: 'This moral law must be the idea of a nature which is not given empirically, but which nevertheless is possible via freedom: the idea of a supra-sensory nature' (Ibid., p. 158/p. 154).
57 See, e.g., *TeI*, 'Moi et dependance', pp. 116–25/*TI*, 'I and Dependence', pp. 143–51; *AEAE* 'La Proximité,' pp. 102–24, 'La Signification et la relation objective', pp. 167–95/*OBBE* 'Proximity', pp. 81–97, 'Signification and the Objective Relation', pp. 131–52.

58 '*Ein merkwürdiger Kontrast*' (Kant, *Kritik*, p. 155)/ 'A marvellous contrast' (*Critique*, p. 153).

59 Ibid., p. 162/p. 158.

60 Ibid., pp. 158-9/p. 155.

61 Ibid.

62 'In the former [nature to which will is submitted], the objects *must* be (*sein müssen*) the causes of the representations . . . while in the latter [nature submitted to a will], the will *must* be (*sein soll*) cause of the objects' (Ibid., p. 158/p. 155).

63 Ibid., pp. 165-73/pp. 160-6.

64 Ibid., p. 170/p. 164.

65 Ibid., p. 171/p. 164.

66 Ibid., p. 140/p. 142.

67 Von Wright, 'Deontic Logics', p. 136.

68 Kant, *Kritik*, p. 146/*Critique*, p. 146.

69 See Alchourrón, 'Logic of Norms and Logic of Normative Propositions' and Kalinowski, *Du métalangage en logique*.

70 See above, 'Prescriptives Against Denotatives'.

71 On the linguistic value of modals, see: Culioli, 'Modality', in *Encyclopédie Alpha* (1970), p. 168; and his 'Ébauche d'une theorie des modalities', paper given to the Societé de Psychanalyse, May 6, 1969; and his Seminar at the École Normale, 1972-3.

72 Kant, *Kritik*, p. 160/*Critique*, p. 156.

73 Ibid., pp. 141, 171/pp. 142, 164.

74 In above, 'The Enunciative Clause'.

75 Particularly *QLT*.

76 Using 'iff' to indicate the biconditional. The statements have been simplified on purpose here, at the risk of being inexact.

77 *TeI*, p. 192/*TI*, p. 217 (see note 43 above).

78 /*Thou*/and/*I*/being autonyms in this statement, we will write them in italics and between oblique strokes, in keeping with the conventions adopted. Cf. Rey-Debove, *Le Métalangage*, pp. 17-18.

79 *TeI* pp. 190, 191/*TI*, pp. 215, 216.

80 To be more exact, on the tractate *Chabat* 88a-88b. The passage in the *Chabat* that Levinas comments on is given in French in *QLT* pp. 67-9.

81 *QLT*, pp. 91, 95, 98, 104-5, 108.

82 See above, 'Commentary and Persecution'.

83 Aristotle, *Refutation of the Sophists* 165b24.

84 Aristotle, *Refutation of the Sophists* 167a1.

85 '*Pè méntoi ékatéron è pros ti è pôs* . . . ' (Aristotle, *Refutation of the Sophists* 180a26ff).

86 '*Oud'ho apeithôn peithétai alla ti peithétai*' (Aristotle, *Refutation of the Sophists* 180b1).

87 Jean-Michel Salanskis, *Autochronie et effets* (unpublished); 'Genèses "actuelles" et genèses "serielles" de l'inconsistant et de l'hétérogène'

(*Critique 379* (December 1978), 1155-73).

88 Lewis Carroll, 'What the Tortoise Said to Achilles', *The Complete Works of Lewis Carroll* (New York: Modern Library, 1960), pp. 1225-30.

89 At least this is the position taken by Von Wright, 'Deontic Logics'. Cf. N. Rescher, *The Logic of Commands* (London: Routledge & Kegan Paul, 1966), chs. 2 and 3.

90 Von Wright, 'Deontic Logics', p. 136.

91 See, among others, *AEAE*, pp. 141-3/*OBBE*, pp. 111-12.

92 See above, 'The Enunciative Clause'.

93 See, e.g., *AEAE*, pp. 150-1/*OBBE*, pp. 117-18.

94 See *Exodus*, Ch. 19.

95 Cf. the expression 'X has no lesson to learn from anyone'. We find the exact opposite view of this infatuation in the Levinasian theme of reading, study, of the *to learn*, and finally, in that cardinal idea that the other is by virtue of its position the master of the *I*, *no matter where the prescription comes from, because it transcends the freedom of the I.*

Translated by Ian McLeod

17

Universal History and Cultural Differences

It is not advisable to grant the genre of narrative any absolute privilege over other discursive genres when we come to analyse human phenomena, and particularly the phenomena of language (ideology); it is still less advisable to do so when we adopt a philosophical approach. Certain of my earlier reflections ('Présentations', 'Lessons in Paganism', and even *The Post-Modern Condition*) may have succumbed to this 'transcendental appearance'. It is, on the other hand, advisable to approach one of the great questions posed for us by the historical world at the end of the twentieth century (or the beginning of the twenty-first) by examining some 'stories' or 'histories'. For to declare the world to be historical, is to assume that it can be treated in narrative terms.

The question I am thinking of is as follows: can we continue today to organize the multitude of events that come to us from the world, both the human and the non-human world, by subsuming them beneath the idea of a universal history of humanity? I do not intend to discuss this question as a philosopher. Even so, the formulation calls for certain clarifications.

1 I begin by saying: 'can we *continue* to organize...?' The word implies that this was previously the case. I am in fact referring here to a tradition: that of modernity. Modernity is not an era in thought, but rather a mode (this is the Latin origin of the word) of thought, of utterances, of sensibility. Erich Auerbach saw its dawnings in the writing of Augustine's *Confessions*: the destruction of the syntactic architecture of classical discourse and the adoption of a paratactic arrangement of short sentences linked by the most elementary of conjunctions: *and*. Both he and Bakhtin find the same mode in Rabelais and then in Montaigne.

For my own part, and without attempting to legitimate this view here, I see signs of this in the first-person narrative genre chosen by

Descartes to expound his method. The *Discours* is another confession. But what it confesses is not that the ego (*moi*) has been dispossessed by God; it confesses to the ego's attempts to master every *datum*, including itself. The *and* that links the sequences expressed by his sentences leaves room for contingency, and Descartes attempts to graft on to it the finality of a series organized with a view to mastering and possessing 'nature'. (Whether or not he succeeds is another matter.) This modern mode of organizing time is deployed by the *Aufklärung* of the eighteenth century.

The thought and action of the nineteenth and twentieth centuries are governed by an Idea (I am using Idea in its Kantian sense). That idea is the idea of emancipation. What we call philosophies of history, the great narratives by means of which we attempt to order the multitude of events, certainly argue this idea in very different ways: a Christian narrative in which Adam's sin is redeemed through love; the *Aufklärer* narrative of emancipation from ignorance and servitude thanks to knowledge and egalitarianism; the speculative narrative of the realization of the universal idea through the dialectic of the concrete; the Marxist narrative of emancipation from exploitation and alienation through the socialization of labour; the capitalist narrative of emancipation from poverty through technical and industrial development. These various narratives provide grounds for contention, and even for disagreement. But they all situate the data supplied by events within the course of a history whose end, even if it is out of reach, is called freedom.

2 Second clarification. When we say, 'Can we continue to organize . . .', we at least accept, even if the (implicit) answer is negative ('We cannot') . . . we at least accept that a *we* still exists, and that it is capable of thinking or experiencing this continuity or discontinuity. And the same question also asks what this *we* consists of. As the first person plural pronoun indicates, it refers to a community of subjects: you and I or they and I, depending on whether the speaker is addressing other members of the community (you/I) or a third party (you/they and I) for whom the other members it represents are designated by the third person (they). The question then arises as to whether or not this *we* is independent of the Idea of a history of humanity.

Within the tradition of modernity, the movement towards emancipation is a movement whereby a third party, who is initially outside the *we* of the emancipating avant-garde, eventually becomes part of the community of real (first person) or potential (second person) speakers. Eventually, there will be only a *we* made up of *you* and *I*. Within this tradition, the position of the first person is in fact marked as being that of the mastery of speech and meaning; let the people have a political voice, the worker a social voice, the poor an economic voice, let the particular seize hold of the universal, let the last be first! Forgive me if I over-simplify.

It follows that, being torn between the present minority situation in which third parties count for a great deal and in which you and I count for little, and the future unanimity in which third parties will, by definition, be banished, the *we* of the question I am asking reproduces the very tension humanity must experience because of its vocation for emancipation, the tension between the singularity, contingency and opacity of its present, and the universality, self-determination and transparence of the future it is promised. If that is indeed the case, the *we* which asks the question 'Shall we continue to think and act on the basis of the Idea of a history of humanity?' is at the same time raising the question of its own identity insofar as it has been established by the modern tradition. And if the answer to the question has to be no (no, human history as a universal history of emancipation is no longer credible), then the status of the *we* which asks the question must also be reviewed.

It seems that it is condemned (but it is only in the eyes of modernity that this is a condemnation) to remain particular, to remain (perhaps) *you* and *I*, and to exclude a lot of third parties. But as it has not (yet) forgotten that they were potentially first persons, and were even destined to become first persons, it must either mourn for unanimity and find another mode of thinking or acting, or be plunged into incurable melancholia by the loss of an 'object' (or the impossibility of a subject): free humanity. In either event we are affected by a sort of sorrow. The work of mourning, Freud teaches us, consists of recovering from the loss of a love object by withdrawing libido from the lost object and restoring it to the subject, withdrawing it from them and restoring it to us.

This can be done in several ways. Secondary narcissism is one such way. Many observers say that this is now the hegemonic mode of thought and action in the most highly developed societies. I fear that it is simply a blind (compulsive) repetition of an earlier period of mourning, of the period in which we mourned God, of the very period which gave rise to the modern world and to its project of conquest. To pursue that conquest today would simply mean perpetuating the conquest of the moderns, the only difference being that the notion of reaching unanimity has been abandoned. Terror is no longer exercised in the name of freedom, but in the name of 'our' satisfaction, in the name of the satisfaction of a *we* which is definitely restricted to singularity. And if I judge this prospect intolerable, am I still being too modern? Its name is tyranny: the law which 'we' decree is not addressed to *you*, to you fellow-citizens or even to you subjects; it is applied to *them*, to third parties, to those outside, and it is simply not concerned with being legitimized in their eyes. I recall that Nazism was one such way of mourning emancipation and of exercising, for the first time in Europe since 1789, a terror whose reason was not in theory accessible to all and whose benefits were not to be shared by all.

Another way to mourn the universal emancipation promised by modernity might be to 'work through' (in Freud's sense) not only the loss of the object, but also the loss of the subject who was promised this future. This would not simply be a matter of recognizing that we are finite; it would be a way of working through the status of the *we* and the question of the subject. What I mean is this: avoiding both the unthinking dismissal of the modern subject, and its parodic or cynical repetition (tyranny). This working-through will, I believe, inevitably lead to the abandoning of the linguistic-communication structure (I/you/he/she) which, consciously or otherwise, the moderns endorsed as an ontological and political model.

3 My third clarification pertains to the words *'can we'* in the question 'Can we continue to organize events on the basis of the Idea of a universal history of humanity?' As Aristotle and linguists know, when it is applied to a notion (in the present case the notion of the pursuit of a universal history), the modality of *can* simultaneously entails the affirmation and the negation of that notion. That the pursuit is possible implies neither that it will take place nor that it will not take place, but it certainly implies that the fact of its taking place or not taking place will take place. The content or the *dictum* (the affirmation or negation of the notion) is uncertain; the subsequent *modus* is, *de facto*, necessary. We recognize here Aristotle's thesis about contingent futures. (But they still have to be dated.)

But the expression *we can* does not merely connote possibility; it also indicates capacity. Is it within our power, our strength or our competence to perpetuate the modern project? This question indicates that the project requires strength and competence if it is to be sustained, and perhaps that we may lack that strength and competence. This reading should inspire an inquiry, an inquiry into the defaillancy *(défaillance)* of the modern subject. And if we argue the case for its defaillancy, we must prove it, by referring to facts or at least to signs. Their interpretation may well give rise to controversy, but they must at least be subjected to the cognitive procedures used to establish facts or to the speculative procedures used to validate signs. (I refer here without further explanation to the Kantian problematic of hypotoses, which plays a major role in Kant's politico-historical philosophy.)

Without wishing to decide immediately whether we are dealing with facts or signs, it seems difficult to refute the available evidence of the defaillancy of the modern subject. No matter which genre it makes hegemonic, the very basis of each of the great narratives of emancipation has, so to speak, been invalidated over the last fifty years. All that is real is rational, all that is rational is real: 'Auschwitz' refutes speculative doctrine. At least that crime, which was real, was not rational. All that is proletarian is communist, all that is communist is proletarian: 'Berlin 1953, Budapest 1956, Czechoslovakia 1968, Poland 1980' (to mention only the obvious examples) refute the doctrine of historical materialism: the workers rise up against the Party. All that is democratic exists through and for the people, and vice versa: 'May 1968' refutes the doctrine of parliamentary liberalism. If left to themselves, the laws of supply and demand will result in universal prosperity, and vice versa: 'the crises of 1911 and 1929' refute the doctrine of economic liberalism. And 'the 1974–9 crisis' refutes the post-Keynesian adjustments that have been made to that doctrine.

The enquirer finds in the names of these events so many signs of the defaillancy of modernity. The great narratives are now barely credible. And it is therefore tempting to lend credence to the great narrative of the decline of great narratives. But, as we know, the great narrative of decadence is there in the very beginnings of Western thought, in Hesiod and Plato. It dogs the narrative of emancipation like a shadow. And so nothing has changed, except that greater strength and competence are required if we are to face up to our current tasks. Many believe that this is the moment for religion, the moment to reconstruct a credible narration which will tell the story of how the *fin de siècle* was wounded, and of how its scars healed. They point out that myth is the original genre, that the thought of origins appears in myths in all its originary paradox, and that we must restore the ruins to which rational, demythologizing and positivist thought has reduced it.

This does not seem to me to be the right direction at all. In any case, it should be noted that in this brief description the term *can* has undergone a further modification, as is evident from the use I have just made of the word *right*. The answer to the question 'Can we perpetuate the great narratives?' has become 'We *must* do this or that'. 'Can' also has the meaning of having the right, and in that sense the word introduces into thought the universe of deontology; it is as easy to move from right to duty as it is to move from permissible to obligatory. And what is at stake here is the contingency of what follows on from the situation I have described as the defaillancy of modernity. There are several possible ways to follow on, and we have to decide between them. Even if we decide nothing, we still decide. Even if we remain silent, we speak. Politics depends entirely upon how we follow on from one sentence to the next. This is not a matter of the volume of discourse, nor of the importance of the speaker or the addressee. One of the sentences which are currently possible will become real, and the real question is: which? A description of defaillancy does not give us even the beginnings of an answer to that question. This is why the word *postmodernity* can refer simultaneously to the most disparate prospects. These few remarks are simply intended to indicate the antimythologizing manner in which we must 'work through' the loss of the modern we.

It is now time to turn to the subject indicated by the title of this exposé. I wonder if the defaillancy of modernity, in the shape of what Adorno called the collapse of metaphysics (which for him found its concentrated expression in the failure of the affirmative dialectic of Hegelian thought when confronted with the Kantian thesis of obligation or the event of the insensate annihilation known as Auschwitz) . . . I wonder if this defaillancy might not have to be related to resistance on the part of what I will term the multiplicity of worlds of names, on the part of the insurmountable diversity of cultures. I will end by approaching the question in these terms, by returning to and reformulating certain aspects which I have already touched upon, and which concern the universality of our great narratives, the status of the *we*, the reason for the defaillancy of modernity and, finally, the contemporary question of legitimation.

A child or an immigrant enters into a culture by learning proper names. He has to learn the names used to designate relatives, heroes (in the broad sense of the word), places, dates and, I would add, following Kripke, units of measure, of space, of time and of exchange-value. These names are 'rigid designators'; they signify nothing or can, at least, acquire different and debatable significations; they can be linked to sentences from totally heterogeneous regimes (descriptive, interrogative, ostensive, evaluative, prescriptive, etc.) and they can be included in incommensurate discursive genres (cognitive, persuasive, epideictic, tragic, comic, dithyrambic, etc.). Names are not learned in isolation; they are embedded in little stories. The advantage of a story is, I repeat, that it can contain within it a multiplicity of heterogeneous families of discourse, provided that it expands, so to speak. It arranges them into a sequence of events designated by the culture's proper names.

This organization has a high degree of coherence, and its coherence is further reinforced by the mode of the narrative's transmission, and that mode is particularly visible in what I will, for convenience, term 'primitive' societies. André Marcel d'Ans writes: 'Amongst the Cashinahua, any interpretation of a *miyoi* (myth, tale, legend or traditional piece of writing) begins with a set formula: "This is the story of . . . as I have always heard it told. In my turn I will tell it to you. Listen to it." And the recitation invariably ends with another formula: "Here ends the story of . . . He who told you it was . . . (Cashinahua name), who is known to the whites as (Spanish or Portuguese name)." ' The ethnologist tells us whites how the Cashinahua story teller tells Cashinahua listeners the story of a Cashinahua hero. The ethnologist can do so because he himself is a (male) Cashinahua listener. He is a listener because he has a Cashinahua name. The import and recurrence of the stories is ritually determined by strict rules. All the sentences in a story are, so to speak, pinned to agencies which have been named or can be named in the Cashinahua language. Whatever its regime, each of the universes presented by each of these sentences refers to a world of names. The hero or heroes, places, the sender and the receiver are meticulously named.

In order to hear these stories, one must have been named (all males and prepubertal girls can listen). In order to tell them, one must have been named (only men can tell stories). In order to have a story told about one (to be a referent), one must have been named (stories can be told about any Cashinahua; there are no exceptions). By putting the names into stories, narration protects the rigid designators of a common identity from the events of the 'now', and from the dangers of what follows on from it. To be named is to be recounted. In two ways: every story, no matter how anecdotal it may seem, reactivates names and nominal relations. And by repeating that story, the community reassures itself as to the permanence and legitimacy of its world of names thanks to the recurrence of that world in its stories. And certain stories are explicitly about the giving of names.

If we raise the question of the origin of tradition or of authority amongst the Cashinahua in positive terms, we are faced with the usual paradox. A sentence is, one might think, authorized only if its sender enjoys a certain authority. What happens when the authority of the sender derives from the meaning of a sentence? By legitimizing the sender described by its universe, the sentence itself gains legitimacy in the eyes of the addressee. The Cashinahua narrator derives his authority from telling stories in his name. But his name is authorized by his stories, and especially by those which recount the genesis of names. This *circulus vitiosus* is common.

We see here the discursive workings of what might be called a 'very large scale integrated culture' [English in the original]. Identification reigns supreme. A self-enclosed culture eliminates scraps of stories and elements that cannot be integrated by making sacrifices, taking drugs (as amongst the Cashinahua), or by fighting wars on its borders.

Mutatis mutandis, the self-identification of a culture involves this same mechanism. Its dismemberment, in a situation of colonial, imperialist or servile dependency, signifies the destruction of its cultural identity. On the other hand, this mechanism is also the principal strength of guerrillas fighting for independence, as narrative and its transmission provides resistance with both legitimacy (right) and logistics (mode of transmission of messages, identification of places and moments, use of natural elements within a cultural tradition, etc.).

We have said that the power of the narrative mechanism confers legitimacy: it encompasses the multiplicity of families of sentences and of possible discursive genres; it could always be actualized, and still can be; being diachronic and parachronic, it ensures mastery over time, and therefore over life and death. Narrative is authority itself. It authorizes an unbreakable *we*, outside of which there can only be *they*.

Such an organization is in every respect the complete opposite of that of the great narratives of legitimation that characterize Western modernity. The latter are cosmopolitical, as Kant would put it. They are concerned of course with the 'transcendence' of particular cultural identities in favour of a universal civic identity. But how that transcendence takes place is far from obvious.

There is nothing in a savage society to lead it to dialecticalize itself into a society of citizens. To say that it is human and already prefigures a universality is to admit that the problem has been solved; the humanist presupposes the idea of a universal history and inscribes particular communities within it as moments within the universal development of human communities. This is also, *grosso modo*, the axiom of the great speculative narrative as applied to human history. But the real question is whether or not there is a human history. The epistemological version is the most prudent, but it is also the most disappointing; in accordance with the rules of the cognitive genre, anthropology describes savage narrations and their rules without pretending to establish any continuity between them and the rules of its own mode of discourse. In its Lévi-Straussean version, it may introduce a functional, or in other words 'structural' identity between the myth and its explanation, but it does so at the cost of abandoning any attempt to find an intelligible transition between the two. Identity, but no history.

We are familiar with all these difficulties, and they are trivial. I recall them simply because they may allow us to take better stock of the import of our contemporary defaillancy. It is as though the immense effort, signalled by the name of the Declaration of Rights, that has been made to strip peoples of a narrative legitimacy which lies, so to speak, downstream in historical terms, and to make them adopt as their sole legitimacy the Idea of free citizenship, which lies upstream ... it is as though an effort that has, in various ways, been going on for two hundred years, had ended in failure. We might even find a harbinger of its failure in the very designation of the author of a declaration with a universal import: 'We, the French people'.

The labour movement provides a particularly convincing example of this failure. Its theoretical internationalism meant of course that the class struggle did not derive its legitimacy from local popular or working-class traditions, but from an Idea that was to be realized: the idea of the worker emancipated from the proletarian condition. But we know that as soon as war broke out between France and Germany in 1870, the International broke up over the Alsace-Lorraine question, that in 1914 both French and German socialists voted war credits in their respective countries, and so on. By beginning the construction of socialism in one country and by abolishing Comintern, Stalinism openly ratifies the superiority of national proper names over the universal name of 'soviets'. The rise of independence struggles after the Second World War and the recognition of new national names seem to indicate a strengthening of local legitimacies and the disappearance of any prospect of universal emancipation. Newly 'independent' governments enter the sphere of influence of either the capitalist market or the Stalinist-style political apparatus, and the 'leftists' who were fighting for universal emancipation are eliminated without mercy. As the current slogan of the far right in France has it: *French first* (which implies that freedom comes second).

It might be said that this retreat into local legitimacy is a reaction to and a form of resistance against the devastating effects imperialism and its crisis are having on particular cultures. This is true; it confirms the diagnosis, and makes it worse. For the rebuilding of the world market after the Second World War and the immense economic-financial battles now being waged by the multinational companies and banks, with support from national states, to win that market offers no cosmopolitan prospects. Even if the partners in this game could boast of having reached goals set by the economic liberalism or the Keynesianism of the modern age, it would be difficult to give them any credit, as it is perfectly clear that their game is doing nothing to reduce the inequality of wealth in the world, and is in fact increasing it, that it is not breaking down national barriers but using them for speculative economic and financial ends. The world market is not creating a universal history in modernity's sense of that term. Cultural differences are, moreover, being promoted as touristic and cultural commodities at every point on the scale.

And what, finally, is the '*we*' which tries to think this situation of defaillancy, if not the kernel, the minority, the avant-garde which prefigures today the free humanity of tomorrow? When we try to think that, do we simply condemn ourselves to being negative heroes? It is at least clear that one figure of the intellectual (Voltaire, Zola, Sartre) has disintegrated as a result of this defaillancy. That figure was once supported by the recognized legitimacy of the Idea of emancipation, and it was, for better or worse, part of the history of modernity. But the violence of the critique addressed to education in the 1960s, followed by the inexorable degradation of educational institutions in all modern countries, clearly shows that knowledge and its transmission have ceased to exercise the authority which once made people listen to the intellectuals when they moved from the professorial chair to the public platform. In a world in which success means saving time, thinking has only one disadvantage, but it is an irredeemable disadvantage: it makes you waste time.

Such, in simplified form, is the question I ask myself, or which has to be asked. I do not intend to answer it here, but merely to discuss it. Certain elements which I have not noted in this exposé may become more explicit in the course of the discussion. Now that the age of the intellectuals, and that of the parties, is over, it might, without wishing to be presumptuous, be useful, on both sides of the Atlantic, to begin to trace a line of resistance against our modern defaillancy.

Translated by David Macey

18

Judiciousness in Dispute, or Kant after Marx*

> War itself, if it is carried on with order and with a sacred respect for the
> rights of citizens, has something sublime in it . . .
>
> Immanuel Kant, *Critique of Judgement*

At seventy-four, Kant complained to Hufeland of having suffered for
two years from an 'epidemic head cold accompanied by a *heaviness of
the head (Kopfbedrückung)*'.[1] This morbid state accompanies thought,
rendering it painful 'inasmuch as thought is the maintenance
(*Festhalten*) of a concept (the unified consciousness of related representations)'. Kant explains that the mind has the power, by force of
sheer human will, to master illnesses taking the form of spasms,
cramps, coughing, sneezing, insomnia, and hypochondriac paralysis.
But in the case of this inflammation of the head, he confesses, one has
the sensation of a 'spasmodic state of the organ of thought (the brain) –
a sort of oppression'. This state apparently does not weaken either
thought or reflection themselves (*das Denken und Nachdenken*), nor
does it affect memory (*Gedächtnis*) in respect to what was previously
thought (*das ehedem Gedachten*). But 'in the explanation (be it written
or oral) where it is necessary [here, by a *lapsus* that proves the malady
he describes, Kant omitted the *it is necessary*] to secure against
distraction a solid collection of representations in their temporal
sequence, it [this headache] produces an involuntary spasmodic state
in the brain, a certain inability to maintain a unified consciousness of
these representations during their succession.' 'This is what happens
to me,' he adds,

---

* This essay was first published in Jean-François Lyotard, *La Faculté de Juger*, Editions de
Minuit (1985), pp. 65–105.

I always begin a discussion (*Rede*) by preparing the listener or reader for what I am going to say. I direct attention first to the object I am aiming at, and then to the object from which I take my point of departure. Without this dual direction there would be no coherence in the discussion. But when I come to linking the second object with the first, I suddenly (*auf einmal*) have to ask my listener, or myself: Where was I? Where was I going? This lapse is due less to a mental flaw or even to a flawed memory than to a defect in one's presence of mind (*Geistesgegenwart*) in making connections. This involuntary distraction is a most trying defect, and one that should be avoided in writing, especially philosophical writing, since it is not always easy to look back at one's own point of departure in philosophy.

Jean-Luc Nancy analyses this 'fainting spell' of discourse from the perspective (as Kant would say) that is his own: the perspective of the impossibility, or at least the undecidability, of a properly philosophical presentation (a *Darstellung*); the impossibility of a presentation of thought. His argument, transcribed in Kantian terms, is that any philosophical treatise worthy of its name must seek to furnish a 'direct presentation' of the entire system of thought. Since, however, this entire system is hypothetically a whole, and since the whole is the object of an Idea which cannot be directly presented, then the philosophical treatise can only *indicate* the speculative object that is the system. The treatise can furnish one or more *signs* of the system, but cannot provide through schemas or examples any intuitions about it. It follows that, considered as a perceptible (that is, artistic or literary) work, philosophical discourse (*Rede*), whether spoken or written, is always found lacking in respect to the connections that assure the maintenance of the system. It is thus itself afflicted with a spasmodic ailment. The feeling inspired in connection with this torturous distraction must consequently be a sublime one. This sign (or should we say symptom?) that is the discursive cramp provokes in the reader or listener three sensations: first, the pleasure deriving from reason's infinite capacity to formulate an Idea (namely that of the systematic whole of thought); second, the pain born of the inability of the faculty of presentation to furnish an intuition of this Idea in philosophical discourse; and finally, the benefit arising from this disorder among the faculties. This latter benefit (which is not a secondary gain, but rather the ontological stakes of criticism) lies in the fact that the convulsion in which 'before' and 'after' lose their co-presence in the discourse is also a signal that discourages the transcendental illusion by which the Idea of the presentation of the system itself in its entirety would claim to be realized in some written or oral discourse.

This is the reason why the condition that constitutes an illness or even a torture for the empirical patient named Kant (a patient who suffers only because he is susceptible to this transcendental illusion, especially as the author or presenter of philosophical discourse) also constitutes a 'transcendental health'.[2] This illness comprises even that ontological health which *is* criticism. I would thus like to begin by saluting in this agitation – which is the emblem of a busy life and of the syncopated rhythm of health – the shadow cast over experience by the critical condition, or what anthropologists would call its judicious complexion. To judge is to open an abyss between parts by analysing their *différend*;[3] this act is marked by the camera obscura of that complex feeling Burke called 'delight'.

Always, in the Kantian text on man, be it the *Anthropology*, the *Quarrel between the Faculties*, the historico-political works, or the critique of teleological judgement, health – whether that of the body, of the mind, of institutions, or of 'the organization' in general – is presented as a *Wechsel*. That is, as an alternation, an exchange between two poles, a thrust inhibited by an obstacle, a movement to and fro, a race from one point to another and then back again, a visceral *vibrato*, an excitation of the life force. In section 25 of the *Anthropology*, causes capable of increasing or diminishing sensory impressions are ranked in a hierarchy ranging from contrast to novelty to the *Wechsel* and beyond, on a scale of increasing intensity. Section 79, which deals with the emotions, announces at the outset that through certain emotions, such as laughter and tears, 'nature mechanically promotes health'. At the end of the paragraph, Kant spares, in the name of mirth, even the court jester, the *Hofnarr* whose task it is to spice with laughter the meal of the elite; his situation, Kant writes, 'is, whichever way one takes it, either above or beneath all criticism.'[4]

If we remember the 'quality of the satisfaction in our judgements upon the Sublime' that Kant analyses in section 27 of the *Critique of Judgement*, we recognize the same extreme agitation that gives this judgement an ontological advantage over the sense of the beautiful. Here, the agitation is attributable to the transcendental subject rather than to the empirical individual. Kant writes: 'The mind feels itself moved (*bewegt*) in the representation of the Sublime in nature', while in aesthetic judgements about the beautiful, it is in a state of restful contemplation. This sublime motion 'may be compared to a vibration (*Erschütterung*); that is, to a quickly alternating attraction towards and repulsion from the same object.'[5] We know that in this movement the imagination is repelled by reason as if by an abyss where it would perish, while at the same time it is attracted to it. That the mind, eluding all forms of exemplification, is reserved for Ideas is evinced in the insufficiency and impotence of the faculty of presentation. From the very beginning of the 'Analytic of the Sublime' in section 23 of the same *Critique*, the same transcendental agitation characterizes that indirect pleasure, that delight which is the sublime, and which is born, Kant writes, from 'a momentary checking (*Hemmung*) of the vital powers and a consequent stronger outflow of them'.[6]

Agitation does not serve here simply as a predicate distinguishing one pleasure from another within the realm of human experience. It is, rather, a transcendental feeling, a distraction or a dispersion in the strict sense of the word *Zerstreuung*. As a paradoxical feeling, like pleasure in pain or even pleasure through pain, this agitation is one of the conditions of possibility for the human experience of the sublime. The 'subject' that is thus affected is not an individual human in experience, but rather the subjective entity, itself unpresentable, to which Kant persists in attributing the power of Ideas and presentations as if these were faculties of that entity. It is evident that this 'subject' is still far too heavily patterned on human experience, and that there remains much that is analogically 'humanist' or anthropomorphic in what is, after all, scarcely even a series, but more precisely a dispersion, a *Zerstreuung*, of conditions of possibility for sensation, for positive knowledge, speculation, ethics, the beautiful, the sublime. We shall see that it is precisely this persistence of what Kant called, in 1770, his 'phenomenology' in his subsequent critical strategy that motivates our own *différend* with his thought. But we must grant that with Kant, an emphasis is placed on the sublime with an energy unprecedented in the already long tradition of meditation on the sublime that had begun, at the latest, with Boileau's translation, in 1674, of the treatise of the pseudo-Longinus. The accent is placed on the dispersion of the subjective entity and on the paradox which results. What Kant calls the 'freeplay' of the faculties, in respect to reflective judgements in general, is in the case of the beautiful immediately harmonious. In the case of the sublime, it is harmonious through meditation. Kant writes in section 27 of the *Critique of Judgement* that the play between imagination and reason in the sublime is 'harmonious through their very contrast (*Kontrast*)', and that if there exists a subjective purposiveness, it is paradoxically produced '*durch ihren Widerstreit*': through this conflict.[7] The appeal to judgement results from a conflict between faculties. Two phrases from heterogeneous regimes, here, imagination and reason, do not succeed in agreeing about an object that gives rise to a feeling of the sublime. Their conflict is signalled by a sign, an eloquent silence, and by a feeling that is always an agitation, that is, an impossible phrase.

These analogies between the transcendental and the anthropological are admittedly debatable in themselves, and yet are properly critical in the Kantian sense, as are signs, symbols, and monograms. It is by means of these analogies that we are led to suspect that critical activity itself – the activity that is at work in reflective judgement and that should constitute the object of a Critique of critical reason, and which is in fact surreptitiously woven into the three (or four) written Critiques – we are led to suspect that this activity falls less under the sign of a jury or judge acting according to a body of laws or jurisprudential provisions than under the sign of the agitation of an uncertain and shaken watchman who is always on guard as to cases and rules – a sentinel.

The analogy with the tribunal occurs frequently in the Kantian text. It decrees a happy ending for the fiction of the war of doctrines that is sketched in the first Preface of the first Critique, but goes no further. The indifference (*Gleichgültigkeit*) towards questions of metaphysics resulting from the episodes of this war is not entirely negative; it also attests to a 'profound way of thinking', a 'strength of judgement, an *Urteilskraft*' which purportedly anticipates the institution of a tribunal: 'This court of appeal is no other than the *Critique of Pure Reason*.'[8] The battlefield, the arena (*Kampfplatz*) where metaphysical combat takes place, thus becomes a courtroom. And the verdict will be rendered 'according to (*nach*) the eternal and immutable laws' of reason. The triumphant tone of this text from 1781 makes the act of judging appear to be no more than the subsumption of a given case under a predetermined concept. The fiction of war does not explain why criticism did not come into play at the very beginning, in order to spare thought the useless torment of dogmatic quarrels; it doesn't even raise the question.[9] We can only surmise that the welcome birth of critical philosophy must have taken place at the cost of these misfortunes. From a polemical point of view the discipline of pure reason suggests what may be the purpose of these wars, or of this single war lasting two thousand years. By an excellent disposition of nature, these wars promote the development of investigational reason as well as critical reason. Such a purpose ought to suffice in forbidding the exercise of any censure in speculative controversies. It is in this sense that Kant writes: 'There really is no antithetic of pure reason.'[10] Once again, criticism puts an end to war, replacing it by 'the peace of a legal status, in which disputes [our *différend*, our *Streitigkeit*] are not to be carried on except in the proper form of a lawsuit.'

We should note, however, one small indication of an unexpected critical reward. Even if the champions of various doctrines are allowed to fight at will, reason can only benefit from the struggle in its progress towards criticism. However painful the battle for the combatants, we who are firmly ensconced in the critical position (if we can call it a position) can observe the struggle in peace (*geruhig*) and even make of it an entertaining pastime.[11] If he is a judge at all, the Kantian judge takes a strange, ironic, Lucretian pleasure in the chicanery.

Thrown into polemics with Schlosser fifteen years later, Kant abandons his materialist or stoic irony to adopt a 'critical' sense of humour. The figure of the judgemental instance becomes in Kant's writing less judicious than ever. The subject of the portrait is the critical philosopher who, as a man, partakes in the realm of experience. The figure is once again anthropological; it belongs to the 'physiological knowledge of man' which, according to *Anthropology from a Pragmatic Point of View*, 'aims at the investigation of what natures makes of man.'[12] Since, with criticism, nature makes something of the thinking man, there must thus be a physiology or a physics of a philosophy that judges. Here is what physiological anthropology discovers in the philosophical mind: a penchant (*Hang*) or even an impulse (*Drang*) to reason or ratiocinate (*vernüfteln*), to argue, and, in the excess of the *Affekt*, to quarrel (*zanken*). The combative complexion of reason is probably 'a wise and beneficial disposition of nature', since, by unsettling the validity of the arguments of both empiricists and idealists, this combat arouses the critical spirit, leading it to institute critical philosophy. The familiar schema is thus repeated; with the tribunal, one hopes, peace will replace war. This anticipation is much encouraged by the title of a small work published in 1796, *Proclamation of Imminent Peace in Philosophy*.

And the first section of this work does in fact establish the serene perspective of this permanent peace. But even before the second section can acknowledge that with the Schlossers the aforementioned perspective was disturbed, the promised peace itself offered something unexpected.

Critical philosophy, Kant writes, 'is a permanently armed state (*ein immer bewaffneter Zustand*) aimed at those who wrongly take phenomena to be things in themselves.' (I would add: equally aimed at those idealists who treat things in themselves as phenomena.) This armed state 'always accompanies the activity of reason'. If 'the perspective of perpetual peace among philosophers' does indeed arise in respect to the Idea of freedom, it is not because philosophers manage to arrive at a consensus on this Idea, but rather because this Idea can be neither refuted nor proved, while at the same time there exist the most pressing of practical reasons for admitting the principle of freedom. That is why this peace presents in addition (*Überdem*) yet another privilege (*noch ein vorzug*): that of 'always keeping in a state of alertness or agitation those of the subject's forces that aggressions [like Schlosser's] seem to put in danger'. At the same time this restless peace is a means of 'promoting, thanks to philosophy, nature's plan to continually revive the subject and defend it against the sleep of death'.[13] In nature's plan, philosophy is thus 'a means of reviving (*Belebungsmittel*) humanity in light of its ultimate goal'. If, therefore, someone like Schlosser launches an attack on philosophy, he unintentionally contributes to the reinforcement of the 'combative disposition or constitution (*die streitbare Verfassung*) which is not war, which in fact can and should prevent war', but which is not on the other hand the peace of a graveyard.

From an anthropological point of view, the benefit deriving from philosophy is immediately physical: health, *status salubritatis*. But as human health is simply the incessant movement between illness and cure, the salutary effect of philosophy is not that of a regime which would protect a stable health against illness; it also requires a treatment which will re-establish health. Kant recalls that Cicero tells of the Stoic Posidonius who cured himself, before Pompey's eyes, of a violent attack of gout by means of a lively dispute (*durch lebhafte Bestreitung*) with the Epicurean school. A good dialectical argument on liberty, one which purports to refute the adversary (although the *Critique of Practical Reason* accords neither combatant the victory) at least results in the body's health. Kant confesses to Hufeland in the third *Quarrel Between the Faculties* that with age he has begun to suffer from cramps that prevent him from sleeping, and that are generally considered to be symptoms of gout. He writes: 'One feels at that moment a sort of spasm in the brain – something like a cramp.' To overcome his insomnia, Kant fell into the habit of fixing his thoughts on some object: 'For example,' he writes, 'on Cicero's name, which calls up many associations' (*Nebenvorstellungen*). The course of these associations suffices to turn his mind from the disorders afflicting it, permitting him to sleep. Firmness in this sort of resolution (aided by a proper regimen) should see one through episodes of gout as well as convulsions, epileptic attacks, and even podagra.[14]

Kant leads us to think that we are dealing here with the Stoic therapeutics leading to apatheia. If apathy comes into play here, however, it would necessarily be Sadic – that is, an agitated apathy. Kant writes: 'The act of philosophizing, even though one is not a philosopher, is a way to fend off a number of undesirable feelings. At the same time it is an agitation (*Agitation*) of the mind that introduces into whatever occupies it an interest that is independent of external contingencies. Although it is merely a game, this interest is nevertheless powerful and profound; it prevents the vital forces from stagnating.'[15] If one is not intelligent enough for philosophy, even as unskilled work, then any other 'pointless amusement' would render the same therapeutic service.[16] For example, one might make sure that none of the clocks in one's house chimed at the same moment. This practice definitely prolonged the life of one old man (presumably from Konigsberg), while it made money for the clockmaker. In this way, the lover of parachronisms who creates 'cramps' in chronology thereby revives his forces and prolongs his own life. The lover of abysses, for his part, either listens for or provokes convulsions among the mental faculties, which serves to keep him alert. Looking for passages (*Übergange*) where there are none, he lives long and well, accomplishing the ends that nature pursues by means of the philosophical condition.

In this way, the exercise of judgement can be considered stimulating. The root of the word *gescheut* (judicious) is *scheiden:* to separate. The judicious spirit described by the *Anthropology* (section 46) no longer conjures up the image of a venerable magistrate armed with a code to be used in settling contested issues. We see, rather, a sort of insomniac night watchman, a vigilant sentinel who defends himself against the torpor of doctrines by the practice of criticism. Doctrines weave a spell that prefigures death; the spasm is a salutary illness because it shakes us out of the doctrinal torpor. And if insomnia in turn becomes an illness, then sleep becomes the critical antidote, permitting the agitation to transfer to another domain while the vital forces are at rest. This domain is that of the imagination: dreaming is in animals as in man that agitation which nature maintains even in rest in order to prevent that very rest from spilling over into death.[17] The critical sentinel is alternately an insomniac and a dreamer in the same way that he lives in the city and in the country, writes stories and poems, works and rests, travels and stays home; and in the same way that he likes to gamble because he feels both fear and hope, he goes to the theatre because he finds both apprehension and joy there, he smokes because tobacco is harmful but at the same time arouses new thoughts and sensations; and in much the same way, he works because although work is painful, it is less so than idleness, and vice versa, he rests even though it is painful because it is less painful than working.[18]

This agitation is without end, except that one does die after all. But we die in spite of the agitation, not because of it. It promotes long life, which is the only objective symptom of good health, since health is like the voice of God: 'One can certainly *feel* well, basing his judgement on a sensation of well-being, but one can never *know* that he is well.'[19] Health is the object of an Idea, not of a concept of the understanding. At least old age allows us to say that we *have been* healthy. Not only does judging make for long life, old age is reciprocally necessary for good judgement. Judgement is that 'understanding which comes only with the passage of time'.[20] Judgement cannot be learned, but only exercised; its development is called *Reife*, maturity, because it is a fruit that nature cultivates in the mind. Judgement is a macrobiotic prescription. How should we judge? Often and intensely. Since it makes for a long life, we should judge a great deal. For the more we judge, the better we judge.

What maintains the health of the critical watchman? The war of doctrines is salutary in that it comprises a game, an exercise serving to sustain a state of agitation. But war in itself is bad; the only benefit deriving from war lies in its mechanics: confrontation, contestation, alternation, *Wechsel*. This becomes all the more evident when wars are replaced by commercial transactions. Money is good not because it enriches, for then we would have to presuppose 'that riches mean happiness', but because it allows for dispersion (*Zerstreuung*). Take, for example, the dispersion of the 'Palestinians who live among us', as Kant writes in a note to section 46 of the *Anthropology*. Their world-wide diaspora, which is also termed *Zerstreuung*, is not a curse but a blessing. The manuscript of this note originally read: 'Therefore the greatest disaster of the state turned into the greatest luck of its citizens . . . . Provided that riches means happiness.'[21]

The diaspora is a convulsion. It can be salutary, provided one doesn't slumber under the effect of the remedy it offers (for example, money). The watchman's power of discernment is not brought to bear upon the content of the doctrines presenting their respective pretensions. This power of discernment is logical; it is brought to bear upon the relationship of the rule (or of meaning) to the individual case. It asks the question: what are the claims made by the doctrine – truth? goodness? beauty? the common interest? Analysis delimits the stakes, and the stakes situate a regime of phrases or sentences. What is at stake in an imperative phrase is not whether it is true, but whether it is obeyed. In a work of art, what is at stake is not the work's ethical value, but its ability to elicit pleasure. Analysis elaborates the subtle conditions of the respective stakes: the conditions involved in the obligation to obey an order, and the conditions governing the pleasure that a work of art must produce. These conditions are not found in experience in the general sense. Ethical and aesthetic experience are not experience in a strict Kantian sense, but are the effects, in experience, of that which is not empirical. The diversity of these experiences is only possible because there exist diverse regimes of phrases calling for validation, and thus necessarily cases which are themselves diverse in their modes of presentation. This is what Wittgenstein calls 'grammatical remarks' when he notes, for example, in section *717* of the *Zettel*: 'You cannot hear God speaking to others; you can only hear Him if He speaks to you. This is a grammatical remark.' Is it a *lapsus* or a deliberate paradox that this remark is in the second person?

The critic thus moves between rules and cases, not between doctrines. There lies the real war, the right war, the true *différend*, the *Streit* and the *Widerstreit*. And the *différend* between the academic faculties of 1798 is a *différend* between mental faculties, that is, between regimes of heterogeneous phrases. The case must be found for the rule, or the rule for the case, and that is not something that can be learned. It is something that is only exercised; it is what we call judgement. If it cannot be learned, neither can it be taught. For it is, as Kant explains in section 42 of the *Anthropology*, the 'faculty of distinguishing whether something is under the rule or not'. Teaching, on the other hand, consists of communicating rules: 'Therefore, if there were any doctrines concerning judgement, then there would have to be general rules by which we may distinguish whether or not something agrees with the rule. Such a process would ask questions *ad infinitum*.'[22] This argument had already been presented in the introduction to the 'Analytic of Principles'.[23]

How can we know if a given case comes under a given rule if the subsumption of the case under the rule has not previously been determined, as it is in the schema? We don't *know* it, but we are able to discover it. In section 44 of the *Anthropology*, Kant writes that judgement is 'the faculty of discovering (*ausfinden*) the particular for the universal (the rule)'. What about finding the rule for the particular case? This, he writes, is the work of the *ingenium*, of the *Witz*, which 'succeeds in thinking (*ausdenken*) the general for the particular'. These two movements within the realm of critical agitation are due solely to talent. The most important aspect of this talent is, in both cases, acuteness, or *acumen*: judgement 'concentrates on detecting the differences within the manifold as to partial identities,' while the *Witz* 'concentrates on marking the identity within the manifold as to partial differences'. Each culminates in 'noticing either the smallest similarity or dissimilarity'. If we pursue the minute difference, we have a sense of exactitude (*Genauigkeit*), but if we pursue infinitesimal resemblances, we enjoy the *Reichtum des guten Kopfs,* the fertility of a good mind, which produces the blossoms of intelligence. With its blossoms Nature is at play, while it tends to business with its fruit. We usually judge the talent for games to be inferior to the talent for business; the inventor of rules is only the artist of criticism; its real head of state is the inventor of cases.

This distribution of roles is somewhat at odds with the rigid, militaristic hierarchy established in section 42 of the *Anthropology* in respect to the three faculties of knowledge. Understanding is right (*richtig*); reason is well-founded (*gründlich*); judgement is exercised (*geübt*). The first, understanding, is sufficient for the domestic or civil servant whose task it is to follow orders. A general, on the other hand, needs reason in order to devise (*ausdenken*) the rule for potential cases. It is the subordinate officer who needs judgement, for he is given general rules that he must apply to particular cases. This hierarchy of talents reappears in section 43; it had previously been mentioned in 1784 in a text entitled 'What Is Enlightenment?'[24]

This stratification of tactical intelligence is clear-cut in appearance only. Is the devising of a rule for a case ultimately an act of reason or of *ingenium*, otherwise known as *Witz*? And if we consider judgement as a game without rules, isn't it, too, in search of the rule? Or must we limit judgement to the search for cases? The judgement of the critical watchman, at least, doesn't settle for simply discerning cases that fit a given rule; it isn't satisfied with providing examples or exemplary representations for various pre-established regimes of phrases. The critical watchman's judgement also seeks to discover, for a given case, a rule that it doesn't know. For example, what rule could govern cases as apparently disparate as the emotion produced by tragedy, or political pathos, or intellectual heroism, or the feeling of guilt? If these are cases, then they are also phrases, albeit complex ones, which obey certain rules of formation that are in themselves complex. Or, inversely, what about a rule for which there are no cases? The question posed by criticism presupposes a possible relationship between these extremes. All in all, at least one case – however singular it may be – does exist for at least one rule. It is this presupposition – that is, that we must not neglect singularities or existences – that provides the motor force for the 'Critique of Teleological Judgement'.

But there are all sorts of *différends,* and they are not all equally lighthearted. What diverts the observer of the first 'Conflicts of the

Antithetic' in the *Critique of Pure Reason*? It is the futility of the
dogmatic arguments offered on all sides. This futility results from an
illusion which causes one regime of presentation to be taken for
another. Does the world have a beginning? Is there an absolutely
unconditioned totality? The thesis and antithesis are consistent in
relation to negation; they are not intrinsically contradictory. However,
cases for either one cannot be directly presented: no palpable fact, no
here and now can be found to prove the disputed phrase. The illusion
derives from a certain confusion as to the nature of the presentable.
Phrases from the dialectic of reason do not have as their object (or, as
we would say, as their referent) something that could also be the object
of a designation, of a phrase that says 'here it is'.

The conflict (*Streit*) of reason with itself in its dialectical usage
cannot be resolved (*nicht abzuurteilenden*) before the tribunal of
reason. We would be arguing about nothing (*um nichts*) if we indeed
meant by 'something' the possible object of a designation.[25] This isn't,
at bottom, a true *différend* according to the rules of knowledge
established in the Analytic, rules that are invoked by both sides. It is
not a true *différend* because it can be dispelled – that is, thrown outside
the realm of knowledge. It is dispelled by analysis. Both the defender
of the thesis and the defender of the antithesis concerning the infinity
of the world can produce a given, a 'this'. Subsequently, thanks to what
Kant calls the regressive synthesis of the conditioned (*les conditionnés*),
they can produce another 'this' which will precede the first, and so on.
Each one thus undertakes to retrace the series of conditioneds
themselves, with one seeing this series as endless and the other
disagreeing. The rule they obey in so doing is the one which dictates
that the synthesis of a given fact must always take as its point of departure the conditions of that fact. The term 'rule' is taken here in the
strict Kantian sense, as a regulative rather than a constitutive
principle.

The position (*Anstellung*) of this synthesis is not in the series, but
rather in the admonition 'and so on', which dictates the repeated
application of a given operation to its own results.[26] The explanation of
empirical facts is no more than the application to referents furnished
by designation, i.e., 'given *a*', of the operation Kant called empirical
synthesis. This operation proceeds by implication: 'if *a*, then *b*'; and so
on: 'given *b*; and if *b*, then *c*'. The explanation is thus infinite (or inde-
finite – we won't pursue the distinction here) by reason of the 'and so
on' included in its formulation. As to whether the world itself is
infinite or not, we cannot know (*savoir*) this in the sense that we
perceive it or are aware of it (*connaître*). For the world is a totality of
givens, and thus the object of an Idea. But this object cannot itself be

designated. Even if it were capable of designation, it would necessarily fall under the rule of explanation governing all objects of designation. Thus the *différend* that Kant calls mathematical is not at all settled, but simply dismissed as the product of an illusion or mistake common to both parties.

When it comes to causality through condition and through freedom, it's a different matter entirely. Kant thematizes this difference between *différends* in the following way: the quarrel (*Streithandel*) can be dismissed (*abgewiesen*) in respect to the world because its object, which is the cosmological series of phenomena, derives from a synthesis that is *homogeneous* with itself, and because both sides make the same mistake as to the position this synthesis should be given. But with causality through freedom, a *heterogeneous* position (*Anstellung*) is introduced into the series of conditions. This position is doubly heterogeneous if the above analysis is pursued: first, any cause (or condition) classified as free causality cannot be demonstrated. Second, Kant's empirical synthesis, or the admonition to apply the operation to its own result, is excluded. The free act is not demonstrable; its reasoning is not repeatable. Not only is the totality of the series of conditioneds not presentable here and now, but there exists in this series a conditioned for which is postulated a condition that is not presentable here and now.

At this point, if the critical watchman is sensitive to differences between *différends* (which are nevertheless grouped together under the single rubric of the Antithetic), he will stop smiling and enjoying himself as he did with the false *Streit* between idealism and empiricism over the issue of the world. In that case, the watchman was able to discern the identical in what appeared to be different or even opposite: that is, the same illusion which situates in the referent what actually belongs to a set of rules (designation, implication, repeated application). In the *différend* concerning freedom, the watchman discerns the differences in things that appear to be similar. The two sides don't speak in the same idiom, although they are talking about the same thing. And since they don't speak in the same idiom, both sides can be right.[27] Which means that the same 'this' can be shown by one side to be implied by a 'that' which is also implied and can also be designated. At the same time, the same 'this' can be designated or at least invoked by the other side as the result of a 'that' which can neither be designated nor implied, in its turn, in a regressive synthesis.

If the tribunal were competent to judge questions of knowledge, it would have to declare a mistrial. For even the tribunal would have to decide in favour of the defender of determinism who, since he speaks the language of the tribunal, makes himself perfectly understood. The court in question decrees that arguments must be implications with no free play, that demonstrable proofs must be produced, and that the procedure for administering the proofs must be capable of reiteration as often as necessary. This tribunal can *know* (*connaître*) nothing of the cause that the defender of freedom advocates. As Kant writes, 'the judge himself supplies perhaps the deficiency (*Mangel*) of legal grounds (*Rechtsgründe*).'[28]

In the same passage we learn, however, that the judge will 'supplement (*ergänzt*)' this deficiency, will fill in where the law defaults, so that the *différend* 'may be adjusted (*vergleichen*) to the satisfaction (*Genugtuung*) of both parties.'

What might be the constitution of this supplement, this complement? Does it consist in the establishment of another tribunal, one that would be competent to pass judgement on freedom's suit? This seems indeed to be the case, since a new Critique was established to examine the suit. This institution requires a complement to right that would be based on the regime of cognition, since a rule must be devised (*ausdenken*) under which the case for free action can be presented. Yet the only relationship that could possibly exist between this rule of presentation and the rule governing the presentation of 'this' that allows for the validation of knowledge is an *analogical* relationship. The analogy consists in the necessity, in both, of a *type* borrowed from cognition: that of the universal legality inscribed in the categorical imperative.[29] In fact, the only presentation capable of validating the ethical phrase according to its own stake – lawful prescription – would not be some 'this' that could be designated, but rather a feeling – that is, a sign whose designation must remain problematic. This means that without the possibility of direct presentation, the question 'Is it true that freedom exists?' can find no answer in the regime of cognitive phrases. It also means that in the regime of ethical phrases, it is not truth itself that is at stake, but the obligatory nature of truth. From the first to the second Critique, the heterogeneity is such that it comes to bear upon the very stakes of the phrases involved. It would seem that here the dispute is not over nothing, but rather over two entirely different things.

But this way of 'filling in' the law, of supplementing right's deficiencies in the area of freedom does not, finally, result in completeness. Far from filling out the jurisdiction of knowledge, the institution of a second Critique dealing with right creates an abyss between the two sides of regimes of phrases and, at the same time, between the two jurisdictions. This separation or insulation which continues to proliferate in the third and 'fourth' Critiques, in what I have called elsewhere an archipelago of regimes of phrases, is in fact the opposite of a completion. But this completion is nevertheless called for; and despite appearances, it is not only or essentially called for by the Idea of a system. It is called for by the nature of the real – and not illusory – *différend* opposing the cognitive phrase to the moral phrase. This *différend* is real not only because the two sides speak in different idioms, but because they make their claims in respect to the same case.

The separation between regimes of phrases is not in itself new. We can assume provisionally that it corresponds, *grosso modo,* to the divisions made since Aristotle among the various disciplines within philosophy. From a doctrinal point of view, this division would propose the reunification of the disciplines into a systematic whole as the task of the philosopher, or at least of the modern philosopher. But here a litigation occurs, stemming from a *différend* between two of the said disciplines in respect to the same case. This *différend* assumes first of all some sort of claim – call it rivalry or jealousy – whose stakes are the case which each side claims. This claim then assumes that a given case, at least before criticism sets it straight, is capable of belonging to two or more different regimes. Even after it has established separate jurisdictions, criticism is still impelled to demand, as Kant does in the second introduction to the third Critique (although we might concede that he does so to satisfy the system's demands), that despite the abysses separating heterogeneous regimes, whatever is presented as a referent for the various phrases deriving from the respective regimes must at least be compatible with all admitted phrases. There must exist between the phrases, a *Zusammenstimmung,* a concordance of voices. The passage (*Übergang*) from one to the other must be possible '*ohne Abbruch zu tun*', with injury to none.[30] This is clearly, if not distinctly, expressed when Kant writes that 'the concept of freedom is meant to actualize in the world of sense the purpose proposed by its laws'.[31]

Any critique of the Critique must in its turn take note of this demand for compatibility. It can go in two completely divergent directions. And it is in our suspicion as to this divergence that we most feel our own divergence, our *différend*, with Kant. For the required compatibility – that is, the liability of a single referent before several different critical tribunals – can dictate one of two things: either that the extreme equivocacy which criticism discovers in the referent need not destroy the referent's identity as a fact (or a real human act when we are dealing with the Third Antinomy); or that the dissociation of the entire field of all objects into domains or territories separated by abysses can be restored to a unity that is at least teleological, through a movement subordinated to an ultimate end. In the first hypothesis the unity of the referent is called for by the very possibility of a confusion of regimes (by the possibility of error), and thus by the possibility of discerning between regimes through criticism. In the second hypothesis the unity of the field, which can only be postulated as an ultimate end, is called for by the *Idea* of systematicity. This unity does not necessarily compel that a single, Leibnizian world be formulated for all the phrases; with Kant, in fact, it remains simply a field. But this unity does require that the phrases' heterogeneity, while conserved, must at least be ordered towards a single end comprising the object of an *Idea*.

The deficiency supplemented by the judge of the Third Antinomy, which is the dynamic antinomy *par excellence*, is not the missing identity of the referent. For it is supposed that a given fact can give rise to controversy as to its causality, which is considered to be conditioned for one side, and free for the other. The judge remedies the absence of a universal tribunal, of a final judgement before which the regimes of knowledge and of freedom can be, if not reconciled (for they will never be reconciled), then at least put into perspective, ordered, and finalized according to their difference. This supplementation is so evidently on the order of a reconciliation between phrases themselves, and not between their referents, that it must be attributed to nature rather than to the world in the Kantian sense.[32] Nature is the object of the Idea of objective purposiveness, and this is in turn called for by reflective judgement in its attempts to account for the singular existences that the lawfulness of a 'mechanically' determined world does not explain. But inversely, if the activity of precise discernment (*Genauigkeit*) – or, in other words, the attention paid to *différend*s that is at work in criticism – could assume this function of supplementation through the objective purposiveness of a certain nature, then that activity or attention would itself be a means used by nature to achieve its own final purpose.[33] This purpose must be accomplished by man because he is the only being in the world that is not entirely conditioned.

Therefore if the critical watchman believes it is possible, in the absence of legal provision, to pronounce a sentence on the *différend* concerning freedom, it is because the Idea of a natural purpose authorizes critical philosophy to do so. But then, what authorizes critical philosophy to find in this Idea of natural purpose the authorization to judge without law? Since what is in question is an Idea – that of nature and thus of purpose – the critic can designate no 'this' to validate that authorization. But he can present an 'as if this' – that is, a sign. As always, the sign is a sensation, a feeling. Does the feeling that signals (and only signals) the possibility of judgement even in the absence of law constitute a sensation of good health? In other words, is it the sensation of passing quickly from life to death and from death to life: the delightful vertigo of leaping above (*au-dessus*) the abyss rather than over (*par-dessus*) it? And would we have to call this sensation the sign of judgement, as when Kant elsewhere calls enthusiasm for the French Revolution a 'sign of history'?[34] But the sensation of health thus described is only anthropological; it has to do with what nature seeks in the empirical individual who judges. We must further acknowledge that the critic can use this sensation as proof (*Beweisen*) of the existence, outside law, of a right to judge. But he can only admit to the existence of this right according to the Idea of a nature pursuing its ends even in the process of supplementation.

According to this development, then, the example permitted by the schema authorizes knowledge by providing the concept (or descriptive scientific statement) with the direct presentation of a perceptible given – that is, by providing a case for the rule. If this is the case, then the question that follows is: whether all other regimes of phrases (whether dialectical, ethical, aesthetic, or political) are validated only by means of indirectly perceptible givens, which in Kant's work have several names that I have grouped here under the term 'sign'. But the value of signs for the critical watchman, apart from the fact that they liberate the play of judgement for their subject (finding the case for the rule and the rule for the case), lies in the frank presupposition of a sort of intention or purposiveness on the part of whatever uses signs. A sort of subject has to be assumed, which Kant does under the name of 'nature'. But it is an 'as if' subject which signals, at least for the philosopher, and by means of the sensation he experiences – cramps, fainting spells, that is to say, *health* – that a quasi-phrase is taking place under the auspices of a given sign; and that the meaning cannot be validated by procedures applicable to knowledge. Is it possible to make judgements on signs without presupposing, even problematically, such an intention? That is, without prejudging?

This presumption or presupposition, even in the qualified form Kant lends it, is at once too consistent, and not consistent enough. It is not consistent enough if we want to know how to judge. For then we would have to establish this quasi-subject who makes signs as though it were a subject. The critical philosopher would have to become speculative, but speculative in the sense intended by absolute idealism: not only must the subjectivity of his thought become substance, but the objectivity of the object must be transformed into a subject. But then signs would cease to be signs. Signs would no longer be needed. Nor for that matter would feelings. There are concepts, and there are realities; the former exist for themselves (*pour soi*). This is, at least, the principle of speculative thought. In fact, as Adorno writes, reality now serves only as a reservoir of examples for concepts.[35]

On the other hand, however, the Idea of a nature that sends signs to the critical watchman weighs a little too heavily; it is too rough an instrument when it comes to analysing and elaborating *différends*. Today we would say that this Idea masks by closing too quickly the wound suffered by the referent when the unity of language totters under the blows administered by the Critique. If we do away with this overly consoling Idea, we are left with the naked convulsions of the *différends*. Without hoping that this Idea might bring about health (the sign of judgement), or that it would mark some progress for the better (the sign of history), we at least wonder how it is possible. We have already said that *différends* could only take place if a given case could belong to at least two systems of heterogeneous phrases (which Kant called the synthesis of the heterogeneous).

Those of us for whom the *différend* strikes a blow at the referent must necessarily reverse the question. Given: two phrases that criticism establishes as belonging to heterogeneous regimes. How can we know that in spite of their heterogeneity, these phrases, as is supposed in all quarrels, are talking about the same referent? Take the descriptive statement 'That door is closed' and the order 'Close that door'. In the universe presented by each sentence, it is not only the meaning that undergoes an obvious modification in passing from one regime to the other, but also the sender and the addressee. The entity that receives an order is not expected to act upon it in the same way as the entity to whom a description is addressed. As for the entity (whatever it may be) who declares the door open, it is not situated by this declaration in the same way as the entity who orders it closed. Different things are expected of each party. This expectation is in no way a psychological state, but rather an anticipation of the enunciations or acts (if we provisionally allow this term) that normally follow description or prescription. This 'normality' corresponds to what I have called the regimes of phrases, in the same way that the meaning presented by (or deriving from) the form of the phrase corresponds to those phrases. It is thus provisionally accepted that there is only one meaning, a 'pure' or 'proper' meaning. Normally, for example – that is, purely or properly – an interrogative sentence (including, in the case of an oral sentence, the curve of intonation) presents the meaning of a question, or a questioned meaning. The sender and receiver are consequently situated as two poles, between which a meaning presented as suspended *there* should be presented as established *here*. Whether or not the intended connection is actually made, or even whether it is made more often than not is another question, and one that cannot be treated here.

Let us return to the referent. How can two heterogeneous phrases be made in respect to the same referent? Doesn't the referent meet with the same fate as the other instances in the universe of phrases – such as the sender, the receiver, or the meaning – when the regime of phrases changes? How can it be determined that the door referred to in the statement 'This door is open' is the same door presented by the sentence 'Close that door'? Doesn't a descriptive sentence call up its referent differently than a prescriptive sentence? Isn't being the object of a piece of information entirely different from being the object of some future transformation? An order, as René Thom has noted, is not a piece of information.[36] If the referent is an instance in the universe presented by a phrase (and what else could it be?); if the instances of these universes of phrases are simply poles across which various expectations play themselves out in the manner described; and if these expectations are finally different according to the differences in regimes of phrases, then we would be able to conclude that the instance called the referent is not the same in both declarative and prescriptive sentences.

The question is even more pointed if the entity involved in phrases from heterogeneous regimes is not involved, in both regimes, in the same type of instance. It is here that we rediscover heterogeneity in the Kantian use of the word. The door in the preceding example served as a referent in both sentences. But how can we know that we are talking about the same entity when we say: 'Albert is going to leave Marie'; and to whom we say: 'Albert, think before you act'; or about whom we say: 'What courage Albert has!' and who himself says: 'I think it would be best if I left Marie'? These shifts in instance, added to the heterogeneity of the phrases, seem to complete the dissolution of the identity of that entity who answers to the name of Albert.

Certainly in questioning the identity of this entity through the various instances and regimes, we too take it to be the referent of our inquiry; the examples cited here are cited in order to argue the said inquiry. In respect to philosophical inquiry, the situation of that referent often causes the investigator to admit with no further debate the reality of the entity in question, and to conclude that the various enunciations cited are only variations on the meaning allowed by the

substance or substratum called Albert, which is from that moment
held to be real. This is an error. The investigator's phrase is the 'nth'
(here, the fifth) in a series along the lines of 'What then is the reality of
Albert?' This sentence, which belongs to the interrogative regime, has
in itself no privilege enabling it to endow the entity named Albert with
a real identity. This is a frequent error in philosophical discourse: its
nature as phrases about phrases causes it to disregard referential value,
as Frege would have said; or, as we might say, the stakes inherent in
each of these phrases. Herein lies the error of the Hegelian speculative
discourse in particular; it places all phrases, regardless of the regime to
which they belong, within the regime of cognitives, thus making
pronounced sentences into autonomous quotations. Instead of the
order 'Close the door,' the Hegelian tribunal (or, as it is called, the
tribunal of the world) can only know the interrogative-descriptive
sentence 'Was the door really ordered closed?' The synthesis of the
heterogeneous has no difficulty in being effected on this level of
metalanguage.[37]

Once we have rejected this speculative refuge, the question remains:
does the entity bearing the name of Albert really exist? As the referent
of a description, this entity derives from what can be called, in the
Kantian sense, a judgement based on experience. As the receiver of a
prescriptive phrase, it falls within the province of practical reason. As
the occasion for evaluation, it belongs to the sphere of ethics or
aesthetics. As we have seen, Kant poses the problem of the incompatibility of these different phrases in the dramatic terms of a leap above
abysses. Here, however, the problem must be presented in its most
urgent form: are the ethical Albert and the 'conditioned' Albert the
same entity? What we term the 'referent' is for Kant called the 'object'.
For Kant, objects are always objects of litigation; they are always put
into play in legal proceedings. But they are always put into play for
their meaning, which will determine the regime of phrases to which
they belong. Are they also put into play for their reality?

We know that for Kant, the reality of the object comes under the
safeguard of direct *Darstellung*. This presentation (and I use the word
in its Kantian sense) complies with the regime of perception. The
forms of the latter are rules which transform enigmatic sensory matter
into given facts situated in time and space. We would say today that
Kant's direct presentation, once it is divested of its phenomenological
trappings,[38] corresponds to a designatory or ostensive phrase, one on
the order of: 'Here is the case.' For, as Kant knows, a referent is only
designated as real in order to prove an assertion. The ostensive phrase
is an indispensable moment in a line of reasoning: it appeals to reality

344 *Judiciousness in dispute, or Kant after Marx*

for the validation of an argument. The ostensive sentence declares: 'There is, here and now, this thing that confirms the validity of what I am saying.' It implies the use of deictics or their equivalent. Deictics designate reality; they designate the referent of the ostensive sentence as being endowed with an 'extra-linguistic' existence. But deictics also connect the whole universe presented by the sentence where they are used to a 'present' spatio-temporal 'origin', something like I-here-now.

This origin does not itself constitute any sort of permanence. Presented or co-presented (that is, presupposed) along with the universe of the sentence in which deictics are evident, it appears and disappears with that universe, that is, with that sentence. That which was before the here-and-now is, here and now, the *here and now of a moment ago*. The same goes for the 'I'. How then can an ostensive sentence serve as proof in arguing an assertion? In order for the citing of a case to carry the weight of a proof, it must be accompanied by some means of repeating the presentation of that case. But repeating the same deictic is not sufficient for citing the same case a second time. The validation of a cognitive phrase requires, at least, that a given referent be locatable in an unchanging place and time. The validation can only do this by means of referentials that are independent of the phrases' occurrences, and which thus are not deictics. The *here*, the *now*, and the *I* must be replaced or at least completed by designators of place, person, and time that will be independent of the sentence that presents them.

The problem posed is thus that of finding a designator that will always indicate the same referent independently of the time, place, or person of the designation. It doesn't seem plausible that this problem could find a solution in the domain of transcendental or phenomenological philosophy, at least insofar as it comprises a philosophy of the subject. I do not intend to reopen here the discussion of the general aporia of the *Ich denke* in its relationship with time, nor do I want to deal with the enigma of schematism. The elaboration of these two questions has become a philosophical staple. As it is more precisely a question of *Darstellung* and of the possible constancy, through what Kant called the *Zeitreihe*, or temporal series, of the designated referent, I will only note here that the difficulty is treated in the first 'Analogy of Experience'. This is the one that is entitled, in the second edition of the *Critique*, the 'Principle of Permanence of Substance' (and no longer, as in the first edition, simply the 'Principle of Permanence'). The revised version is also found in the 'Refutation of Idealism', which was similarly added in 1787. The argument of the Analogy is the following: any change in time presupposes that time is a permanent, changeless form. Now, Kant writes that 'time, as a form of internal intuition, cannot be perceived in itself.' Permanence must thus be located in external objects, as substance. Kant's 'Refutation', as modified by a note in the second preface, directs this argument at Descartes' problematic idealism: there is no empirical determination of self-consciousness that does not presuppose a permanent substance. And this permanent substance 'must therefore be something external, and different from all my representations.'[39] It follows that the determination of my existence in time proves the existence of objects in space.

We can certainly designate the permanence of the referent in various ostensive phrases as 'substance', since, as Kant himself notes, 'the proposition that substance is permanent is tautological.'[40] But what is not tautological is the fact that substance or subsistence is a *thing*. In saying *thing*, Kant certainly can't mean the thing in itself, but only something which isn't caught up in a temporal series of 'representations'. (We are now back to the heart of the problem of preservation and convulsion in presentation: hysteria and 'heaviness of the head' are, after all, a sort of 'cramp' in time, and in this sense perhaps constitute an ontological endeavour.)

The problem is thus: given that 'I', 'here', and 'now' are designators that depend on the ostensive phrases supporting them, how can we find independent designators without falling back on the concept of a permanent substance which can itself receive no validation by designation?

Nor is this the only problem raised by the synthesis of the heterogeneous – that is, by the constitution of the *différend*. The problem as we have just delimited it consists only in the synthesis of referents of demonstrative phrases, and particularly in their identity throughout their succession. This synthesis essentially corresponds to what Kant called experience. But the heterogeneity of regime existing among phrases that we assume to present a single entity – whether or not that entity occupies the position of a referent – seems necessarily to constitute a new attack on the unity of experience. Take, for example, the event: Albert opens the door and leaves. How can it remain an event if we are able to attach to it all the various phrases from heterogeneous regimes that I cited earlier: 'He's going to leave Marie'; 'Think before you act'; 'What courage!'; 'I think I should leave Marie.' Or others, such as Marie's 'You'll regret it', and of course our own: 'Albert opens the door and leaves'?

It is precisely on the question of this specific diversity that judgement must be exercised. Judgement must recognize and bring to light the abyss that exists between these sentences: their incommensurability. The problem of the identity of the referent of ostensive phrases (in this case named Albert) is, in this respect, only a preparation for the problem of judgement. Of course, this latter problem would not be raised at all if the entity named Albert were not the same in the various universes presented by the sentences cited. But showing that it is the same entity – that is, solving the problem of the identity of the referent named Albert – does not solve the problem of the synthesis of the heterogeneous. In fact, it only makes it more acute. The entity named Albert must be the same not only in order to make knowledge possible, but also in order to make possible the coexistence of those worlds that Kant calls fields, territories, and domains[41] – those worlds which of course present the same object, but which also make that object the stakes of heterogeneous (or incommensurable) expectations in universes of phrases, none of which can be transformed into any other. *Ohne Abbruch zu tun.*

One striking feature of philosophical discourse in most of the forms it borrows (for it borrows from other genres, literary and otherwise) is that it avoids, on principle, any use of proper names in its arguments. The names of authorities and adversaries that nevertheless remain persist only as the names of arguments. I will not examine here the reasons offered to justify this exclusion. More often than not, none are offered. It seems to go without saying that in philosophical discourse we are not operating on the level of names. On the other hand the discourses of history, of the great classical or romantic poetic genres, of geography, of biology, anthropology, palaeontology, or physics would simply be impossible without proper names, however different their usage may be in the various discourses. Even the 'hard' sciences must use them. For example, if electrical science recognizes a 'Joule's Law', it does so not only to honour the physicist who discovered the variables governing the intensity of electrical current, but also because this name designates an experimental procedure that can be repeated by an 'I' at any time and in any place. For the permanent conditions of the procedure's execution are strictly determined, and have up to now always permitted the observation of identical results. But what does 'strictly determined' mean? It means that once the names of measurements (of duration, extent, weight, volume, or intensity) have been fixed and acknowledged, the variables constituting the experimental schema can be introduced in named quantities by means of these measurements. Thus the repetition that assures the validity of Joule's Law can be only executed thanks to the stability of the names of measurements (of systems of units in physics) which must be considered as a network or proper names.[42]

No evidence of any order can be admitted as proof unless it is accompanied by names that permit it to be reiterated. It does not suffice to say: 'I was there.' We have to be able to say who, when, and where; that is, we have to give the names that make it possible to locate the *here* of 'there' in a world of place names; to locate the *now* of 'then' in a world of dates; to locate the *I* of 'he or she' in a world of personal names. In addition, for each of these worlds, we must give the names of measurements (of duration and extent at least) that situate the names in respect to each other in a repeatable fashion, so that a journey in this network can be retraced from the 'here-now-I' of the phrase pronounced.

If it is true that all referents are litigations, and that judging is finding the case for the rule (and probably also the rule for the case), then judgement cannot be passed if the case, the object of litigation, is not attested to. And the case can be attested to only by its positioning in a world of names, which permits the evidence to be repeated as often as desired. Any tribunal requires names in order to establish the reality of a referent. The reconstruction of a crime serves as a model for any assertion of or about the reality of a referent.

This is why the detective story whose hero is a criminal trying to erase any clues provided by names (dates, places, people, measurements) constitutes, as Kracauer suggests, an archetypal form of the ontological question in the modern or postmodern age.[43] In the classical age, tragedy was the form taken by that question. What distinguishes modernity is that the destruction of identities and the assassination of experience through the effacement of proper names is a willed effect. The psychoanalytic investigation should also be examined in this light. Freud's passion for the cryptic inscription, for the *rätselhaften Inschriften* that he deciphered at night in the *Fliegende Blätter* had much more to do with the style, or more precisely the genre, of the *Traumdeutung* than his rereading of *Oedipus Rex* or *Hamlet*. Causing proper names to be forgotten (an amnesia which is also one of the first signs of old age) is the perfect crime because it prevents the reconstruction of the crime. This is the criminality of the unconscious: a solitary confinement in which one finally forgets oneself; where the self, grown nameless, can no longer even take itself to be another in the momentary salvation of a pseudonym like that taken by Nietzsche, Hölderlin, or Wilde, but can only drift into anonymity. And if measurements are also proper names, then Assassination must be considered the art most admired by the unconscious. It was Thomas de Quincy who watched over Kant's last *lapsus*, in the *Kantswake*.[44]

I would be tempted to think that in blinding the proper name and its function in the establishment of reality, philosophical discourse can only be one of two things: either it is dogmatic because it must assume a permanent thing or some absolute witness (which is a non-sense, or *unsinnig* in Wittgenstein's sense); or it is autistic because it is incapable of taking the step which leads from the deictic of the ostensive phrase to the reality of the referent. The latter incapacity is evident in Kant's impossible schematization, which can only furnish the possibility of experience, and not experience itself; it is also evident in the impossible constitution of the other in the course of the *Fifth Cartesian Meditation*, from which there can only be derived a *him* or a *you* dependent on the constitutive direction of the *I*.

Like executions or death sentences, there are ways of summarily putting an end to reality's trial. But the trial is nevertheless without end, affording neither summation nor sleep. And while it is true that this trial makes an appeal to proper names, it doesn't necessarily follow that their application puts an end to the *différends* in question. In fact, the opposite happens. For names are, as Kripke characterizes them,[45] constant quasi-deictics; in this sense they are what Kant would call *analoga*. But they are *analoga* of deictics, not semantic equivalents of given facts. Proper names are empty, but they are, in a certain sense, empty twice. They are first either empty of meaning or too full of meaning, which is in effect the same thing; and they are also empty of reality.

A name is no proof of the reality of the referent that bears it. As Louis Marin has noted, we show our inheritance from Pascal's nominativism when we say 'That's Caesar' both when we meet the man bearing that name, and when we see his profile on a coin.[46] A fictional universe is a world of names in which, more often than not, all the referents named can be located or situated in respect to each other. Sometimes it takes no more than a name to achieve the effect of reality – for example, the longitude and latitude of the island of Utopia in Thomas More's story. Or the names Waterloo and Napoleon in *The Charterhouse of Parma*. This proves at the very least that the same name can provide one indicator in the world of names comprised by Stendhal's fiction and another in the world of names verified by historical science – and this without wronging either world. This entanglement provides a good example of a *différend*: is Napoleon the emperor of France, or is he the Ideal of political reason for Fabrice and Julien? We consider that a referent for a given name is real when we can attach to a nominative phrase such as 'It is Rome' the corresponding ostensive phrase: 'And here it is.' While we certainly cannot simply settle for designation, neither can we do without it.

But we should recall that elsewhere the nominative phrase 'It is Rome', whether it be an acknowledgement or a baptism, is always appealed to in a search for the proof of a meaning – that is, in a legal argument. This meaning doesn't necessarily have to be introduced by a sentence taken from the realm of descriptive phrases. We would naturally respond with the designation '*This* door' when asked 'What door are you talking about?' But this question could just as well be linked to phrases from regimes as heterogeneous as that of description: 'The door is open', or exclamation: 'What a door! It's always open!', or narrative-interrogative: 'Did he open the door?', or simply narrative: 'It was at that moment that he opened the door.' What is certain is that the answer – the designation '*This* door' – does not provide sufficient proof of the reality of the referent of these sentences. Between the said designation and the sentence or sentences cited above there must be interposed a nominative phrase on the order of: 'You know, the Eastern door of Albert's house at Villeurbanne.'

The case is clear in the now proverbial examples of Aesop or Plutarch: *Hic Rhodus, hic salta. Salta* presents meaning within the regime of prescription. *Rhodus* gives the name, while *hic* serves as the articulation, marking the designation. And since it is an order – the order to jump – that must be validated, *hic* also signals a state of urgency. The question of the reality of the referent is thus never resolved by a single phrase falling under a regime specifically charged with this duty; it is always resolved by the play, or free play, of three phrases: one carrying the meaning, one carrying the name, and the third carrying what Kant calls the presentation. This tripartite complex is not without complications. Once again, however, the question of the reality of the referent is no more than a stage in the problem that concerns us here: the problem of the *différend*. Therefore, I will not dwell on the first question. As for the second, I will note only that, unlike a concept (or an essence) or a deictic, the proper name undergoes no changes in its value as a designator when placed in any instance in the universe of phrases, or when placed in the most heterogeneous of regimes. We have seen that this is the case for Albert. For example, in a descriptive phrase, Albert is situated, as a predicate, in the instance of meaning: 'She has stopped loving Albert.' In an interrogative, he is situated in the instance of the referent: 'Was Albert here?' Or Albert can occupy the position of the addressee in an imperative: 'At this moment, I opened the door' (taken from Albert's diary or memoirs). It is precisely because its value as a designation remains constant that the proper name lends itself so aptly to *différends*.

The plasticity of the proper name is evidently᾽ limited by its inclusion in one or more worlds of names, as well as by the place constitutively assigned to it among other names according to spatial, temporal, and anthroponymic distances which themselves have names: kilometres, decades, generations, degrees of kinship. And this place is in constant agitation. Within these limits, nevertheless, a nondeterminable swarm of meanings can descend upon a name without changing its capacity for designation. From among this swarm, of course, certain of the attributed meanings will be singled out by means of the name's relationship with the other names given, and also by means of designators. Even then, however, the swarm of possible meanings still remains enormous at any given moment; nor will it ever be ended. No one could have known in 1932 that Karol Wojtila would one day become Pope, just as no one could have known, around 340 BC, that one of the meanings attached to the referent named Aristotle would be that a French philosopher at the end of the twentieth century would show how the ontology contained in Aristotelian metaphysics is not a science, but rather a dialectic. In other words, names are very capable of accommodating future contingencies, as well as ambiguity, polysemy, and even contradiction. This accommodation is possible because names are neither definable essences nor designators of essences (although Leibniz believed the opposite to be true, just as Kripke still does to some extent). Names only designate landmarks which indicate procedures for reiteration, but which, in so doing, also allow the institution or attempted institution of new networks in which the given names will be included.

The nominative phrase thus presents a double advantage: first, that of corresponding to a necessary moment in the procedures for establishing the reality of the referent; second, that of making possible an infinite number of *différends* concerning the referent. Kantian *Darstellung* - designation - is insufficient for the first task, that of establishing reality. And it seems to constitute an obstacle to the second task, that of promoting *différends*. Kant is condemned, by a transcendental aesthetic that is also phenomenological, to make a distinction between direct presentation and analogical presentation. This distinction causes him to accord an excessive privilege, which is otherwise inexplicable, as is his schematization, to the cognitive phrase. At the same time, this distinction sets in orbit outside the sphere of the perceptible all those 'objects' that are not objects of knowledge. In this way, the question of the *différend* is not posed with its full cutting force, but can be blunted in the Idea of a reconciliatory end.

The question of the *différend* has to do with language rather than anthropology. In spite of all appearances, what is at stake in *différends* is not the satisfaction of 'human' interests or passions. To allow this claim would be to presuppose some sort of nature which, be it human or not, would have to obey a purpose. And this idea is much too rough, too pathetic, or too heroic to account for *différends*. It would be just as futile to replace the *anthropos* by a *logos* if it were only in order to attribute anew to the logos some 'nature' – whether expressive, communicational, or 'poetic' – which would assure its ultimate unity. It does not even suffice to say, as Wittgenstein does, that: 'Language (*die Sprache*) is a labyrinth of paths (*ein Labyrinth von Wegen*),' because this still supposes that someone walks there, even if it is only to get lost. What Wittgenstein subsequently adds comes closer to the *différend*: 'You approach from *one* side, and you know your way about; you approach the same place from another side and no longer know your way about.'[47] Wittgenstein uses the same verb (*sich auskennen*) that serves in section 123 of the *Philosophical Investigations* to present the problem of philosophy: 'A philosophical problem has the form,' he writes, of the expression, 'I don't know my way about.' Kant said: 'Where was I? Where was I going?' This spasm in the labyrinth of legal arguments attests to the fact that language is not 'something unique'[48] in the sense that it is composed of phrases from heterogeneous regimes, phrases which should forbid any recognition of 'the same place', the same referent.

But neither can it be said that no one knows that 'here' is the same place as 'there'. The possibility of identifying a referent does exist – certainly not by direct presentation, but by the procedures that we briefly indicated, and which are fixed paths marked in the labyrinth: pieces of paper. This identification is required by the validation of cognitive phrases; it still takes place, at least as a demand. Why? In order to put an end to *différends* both theoretical and practical. But it is precisely in the attempt to bring an end to *différends*, to transform war into a litigation and pronounce a verdict that will settle the dispute, that a *différend* can manifest itself. It manifests itself by a feeling. Even damages for which reparations have been made can evidently arouse a feeling of irreparable wrong. The purposiveness thus undoes itself, and peace remains an armed state.

I will term a 'wrong' any damage accompanied by the loss of the means to prove the said damage. We can recognize in this 'wrong' what Marx said in 1843: 'a class with radical chains, a class in civil society that is not of civil society, a class that is the dissolution of all classes, a sphere of society having a universal character because of its universal suffering and claiming no particular right because no particular wrong but unqualified wrong (*ein Unrecht schlechthin*) has been perpetrated upon it.'[49] To explain why I had to introduce this word here would take too long – would be interminable. At any rate, this word is diverted here from the perspective that was Marx's at that time: a perspective that was still Feuerbachian – that is, humanist, Lutheran, and perhaps still dialectical. But it is perhaps the most decisive way of marking the break with Hegel's philosophy of right – a break that has not yet been either reversed or *aufgehoben*, which is why 'Marxism has not finished.'[50] Indirectly, it marks the break with a thought that proposes mediation or reconciliation: with the Kantian Idea of the *Zusammenstimmung*. Whatever suffers a wrong is a victim. It is in the nature of a victim to be incapable of proving that a wrong has been suffered. For the judge says to the victim: one of two things is possible; either you are the victim of a wrong, or you are not. If you are not, you are either mistaken or you are lying when you testify that you are a victim. If you are a victim, and since you can testify to this wrong, as I am informed is the case here, then this wrong ceases to be a wrong. It becomes a damage; and you are mistaken or lying when you testify that it is a wrong.

Faurisson complained that he had been lied to about the existence of gas chambers. To verify that a place is a gas chamber, he would only accept, he declared, 'a former prisoner capable of proving to me that he actually saw a gas chamber with his own eyes.'[51] According to Faurisson, then, there can be no direct witness to a gas chamber other than its victim; and there can be no victim except a dead victim, for then this gas chamber would not be what Faurisson's opponent claims it to be. Thus, no place can be identified as a gas chamber, because there can be no eye-witness.

This argument is called the dilemma, and was known by the sophists, notably Protagoras. It provides the mechanism for the Epicurean maxim: if death is there (at Auschwitz), you are not there; if you are there, death is not there. In both cases, it is impossible for you to prove that death is there.

This double bind also provides the mechanism for the lawyers' arguments in the great political trials of Berlin or Moscow: if you are a communist, you are in agreement with the Politburo; if you are not in agreement with the Politburo, you are not a communist. In either case, there is no way of proving that a disagreement exists within communism. But the double bind also provides the key to positivism in its generality: only that which can be validated under the regime of cognitives is real. If for some reason you are deprived of the means to prove the damage you have suffered, then your judge cannot 'reconstruct' the damage; that is, he cannot accomplish a reiteration of the case through the accepted procedures. Your case is thus dismissed. Extended to all statements, this criterion is called performativity. It compels any plaintiff to prove any damage he alleges according to the rules of cognition – that is, according to technological science. If the regime of phrases to which the plaintiff belongs is different from that of cognitive phrases, and thus necessarily different from that of the only tribunals he can appeal to, then he is certain to lose his suit. This is the case, for example, with a philosophy whose regime of phrases, if indeed there is one, cannot by hypothesis be limited to the cognitive regime. In *The Quarrel Between the Faculties*, Kant marks his position as that of the impossible witness of *différends*, as the judicious position. In so doing, he fully assumes the inferiority which necessarily results in respect to disciplines armed with a code.

What forbids any 'return' on our part to Kant is capital, or the power of indifference. Marx is himself a name around which many *différends* have arisen, and which still provides material for litigation and vengeance. But something in Marxism has not finished being critical, has not stopped demanding that we be judicious. With Marxism, the *différend* has been transmitted by a reception that is at once sharp and blurred. It is sharp because Marxism has welcomed a rejected feeling, that of class hatred, and has sought to invent the idiom for which that passion was at a loss. But the reception becomes blurred when Marx insists on furnishing proofs of a wrong for which no one can point out a case, and, moreover, when the wrong is treated as the only one whose reparation, through revolution, could put an end to most *différends* – or, in its Stalinist version, to all of them.

Contracts and agreements between socioeconomic partners do not preclude (indeed, they presume) the fact that the wage earner or his representative must have spoken – and will continue to speak – of his work as if it were the temporary transfer of merchandise, or the 'service' which he owns. Marx terms this situation 'abstraction' (but the term is deceptive: what 'concrete' does it imply? what more real reality does it oppose to the provable reality of earning wages?); this 'abstraction' is nevertheless required by the idiom in which the litigation is decided: 'bourgeois' social and economic law, the language of capital. Unless he makes use of this language, the worker cannot exist in the domain governed by it; he would be a slave, for example. By using this language, he can become a plaintiff. But, precisely because he does use it, he cannot stop being a victim. Does he indeed possess the means of establishing that he suffers some damage, not because his salary or the conditions of his salaried work are unjust, but from the very fact of wage-earning itself? No. How can he – or anyone – *know* (*savoir*) that the wage earner is something other than the owner of an ability which he rents out to his employer according to the conditions of social legislation? How could the arbitrating magistrate understand that the worker's 'being', his Idea, is a force that creates surplus value, and that his real name is the proletariat (according to Marx)? The arbitrator does not need to know what the worker is, or what his Idea is; he needs to know what he owns and what he is exchanging. For the judge, it would seem impossible for the worker to have nothing, since his employer is in the process of buying something from him. Moreover, as Kant would add, the referent 'labour force' is perhaps the object of a concept, but since no intuition can be subsumed within it, this concept is a concept of reason – an Idea. No direct perception is possible for a case that could validate this concept or the phrase that signifies it; the worker's counsel will never be able to furnish proof of it.

The arrangement worked out between the different sides by the arbitrators – even if we assume no denial of justice on their part – cannot accede to the petitions of the other phrases, which we can call Marxist, but which also relate to the same name, that of the wage earner. This phrase belongs to a regime which is not that of the phrases by which judgement is rendered. A wrong and a victim therefore exist by the mere fact that the wage earner's suit is tried in a language whose regime excludes the very Idea that a labour force capable of creating value could be associated with the name 'wage earner'.

How can we know that the wage earner's name is also that of a proletarian, in the Marxist sense? We don't know any proletarians, but we can form the concept of one. We cannot point to an example of a proletarian. The proletariat is the object of an Idea, and this Idea is elaborated reflexively, taking signs as a point of departure. And signs, as Kant shows in respect to the French Revolution,[52] are feelings. But in order to signal that a noncognitive regime of phrases is attached to names given in the various worlds of names, a feeling must be inexplicable, like free action. Class hatred – at least as it is usually understood – is explainable. What escapes the administration of cognitive proof, and can serve as the sign of a phrase from another regime, is the feeling of solidarity manifested by spectators who are not themselves involved with the actors in the class struggle. In the same text from 1843, Marx seems to support this view when he writes: 'No class of civil society can play this role [of emancipation] unless it arouses in itself and in the masses a moment of enthusiasm, a moment in which it associates, fuses, and identifies itself with society in general, and is felt and recognized to be society's general representative.'[53] Without this solidarity, Kant would continue, there is no sign that the proletariat is the object of an Idea. The empirical establishment of even an international association of workers takes the place of this feeling of solidarity. Kant would say that such an association obeys, like all organisms, the principle of a technical purposiveness.

That is at least how the critical watchman would judge the case after a full century of Marxism. But this watchman would also add: other objects of Ideas are possible, and they must be constructed reflexively, taking as a point of departure signs that derive from other names. For example: what is the object of an Idea whose sign arose out of the 1968 movements to elicit the solidarity and enthusiasm of many people who had no stake in the events, and who were at a considerable remove from them? This object has not been elaborated reflexively. The movement has merely been explained; it has been placed, for judgement, under the regime of proof. The wrong to which it was perhaps trying to testify has not found its idiom.

What has been lost, at least for the critical philosopher, with this century of Marxism (and Hegelianism), is the speculative principle of the Result. There is no contradiction between two phrases attached to the same name but deriving from heterogeneous regimes; they can both be 'true'. The 'truth' may not even be at stake in these phrases. Their synthesis – the result – cannot be the object of a concept; the very principle is absurd. Moreover, when the advocate of synthesis claims to produce proofs of it, absurdity makes way for terror.

What has perished here, along with Marxism, as the victim of the transcendental illusion, is a principle symmetrical to that of the Result: the principle of the origin. This principle only recognizes as fundamental the *différend* in which work is at stake. The watchman wonders: the Algerians are not the proletariat; but were they not victims of a wrong merely by the fact that they were unable to express, either in the framework of French constitutional law or international law, the damage they suffered by being French? Or the Quebecois, who are not the proletariat, by being Canadian? Or women, who are not the proletariat, by being at best placed under the same judicial regime as men?

A certain form of Marxism objects to this Idea of a multiplication of *différends*: none is fundamental, it would say; capital accommodates them all, transforming them one by one into litigations that are judged according to the criteria of performativity. The means used to make this judgement is a universal measure applicable to all entities, regardless of the regime of statements from which they derive: money. This is evident in the new technology of language, which has as its corresponding unit of measure the bit of information. The response to this objection is the argument that the totality of phrases, like the whole in general, is an Idea. This is why capital can only be the 'virtual' totality of phrases. Capital's madness, or even its sanity, its transcendental illusion, is perhaps that the enigma of will, which is (since Descartes) the infinite, seeks to transform itself into experience. Thus there results a confusion of regimes of phrases. The task of the critical watchman is clear: illusion must always be dissipated. Yet that task is also obscure: that very dissipation may be an illusion.

Hidden within the litigations and the verdicts is a wrong that can be threatening (but even this isn't sure, for the Antithetic tells us that there are false *différends* that are merely amusing). Through these litigations and verdicts, phrases – and thus meanings – are attached to names. As a result, other heterogeneous phrases that were attached to the same names can be dismissed. Proper names are indeed, if not passages, then at least points of contact between heterogeneous regimes. Taken to the extreme, this threat of a wrong promises to strike from history and from the map entire worlds of names: extermination of the Communards, extermination of counter-revolutionaries, extermination of the Armenians.. The final solution. The purposiveness that the twentieth century has witnessed has not consisted, as Kant had hoped, of securing fragile passages above abysses. Rather, it has consisted of filling up those abysses at the cost of the destruction of whole worlds of names. A Polish adage says that when the people and the government disagree, the government changes peoples. Capital is that which wants a single language and a single network, and it never stops trying to present them. The means capital employs to diminish the *différends* is what Marx called the *Gleichgültigkeit,* or the indifference, of money. This 'equivalent value' conceals surplus value in the same way that equality hides *différends*.

Vengeance hovers around names. Vengeance does not precede legal cases; it follows them. It can invoke no right, for right is always 'right' according to a tribunal that is unique and that demands proofs, names, and measurements. What cries out for vengeance are the forbidden phrases of defence, phrases that have suffered a wrong because they can only make an appeal to feelings. A *différend* takes the form of a civil war, of what the Greeks called a stasis:[54] the form of a spasm. The authority of the idiom in which cases are established and regulated is contested. A different idiom and a different tribunal are demanded, which the other party contests and rejects. Language is at war with itself, and the critical watchman posts guard over this war. The name 'Palestine' belongs to several worlds of names. Within each of these worlds, several regimes of phrases quarrel over the name 'Palestine'. Here we have an analogon of language: not simply the complexity of a large city, but the complexity of a large city at war. In 1956, at Budapest, the names of the streets were changed to mislead the Soviet tanks; the government doesn't change peoples, the people change names: this is the clandestine. And this is why philosophy must remain in arms. The armed state that is philosophical peace procures health neither for humanity nor for philosophers: it is the health of language.

In the *différend*, something cries out in respect to a name. Something demands to be put into phrases, and suffers from the wrong of this impossibility. This affect comprises the silence, the feeling, that is an exclamation; but, because it has to, it also makes an appeal, through its ellipses, to possible phrases. Humans who believe that they use language as an instrument of communication and decision learn, through the feeling of pain that accompanies the silence of interdiction, that they are conscripted into language. The 'delight' that they also feel at this conscription does not derive from any hope of thereby increasing their power, but only from the hope of permitting other phrases, perhaps heterogeneous.

NOTES

1 *The Quarrel Between the Faculties*, Kant, *Werke* (Frankfurt: Insel-Verlag, Wilhelm Weischedel), 6: 389–90. [All references are to this edition. Where possible, I have used a standard English translation of the Kantian texts cited. These references follow the author's references to the German edition – Tr.]

2 The expression is borrowed from Jean-Luc Nancy, *Le Discours de la syncope* (Paris: Flammarion, 1976), p. 74.

3 Translator's note: I have chosen to leave *différend* in the French throughout the text. The term denotes at once a difference of opinion, a quarrel, a dispute, or a state of discord. The term *différend* connotes both the subtlety of a difference and the antagonism of a dispute.

4 6: 599. *Anthropology from a Pragmatic Point of View*, tr. Victor Lyle

Dowdell (Carbondale: Southern Illinois University Press, 1978), p. 172.

5 5: 345. *Critique of Judgement,* tr. J. H. Bernard (London: Macmillan, 1914), p. 120.

6 5: 329. Bernard, p. 102.

7 5: 346. Bernard, p. 121.

8 2: 13. *Critique of Pure Reason,* tr. F. Max Müller (Garden City, NY: Anchor Books, 1966), p. xxiv.

9 Obviously, the theme of the war between doctrines has long been a rhetorical staple of preambles in general, and of prefaces to philosophical works in particular. Hume makes use of it in the introduction to *A Treatise of Human Nature.* But he doesn't intend to put an end to the war with a verdict; he simply wants to win it with a decisive blow: 'instead of taking now and then a castle or village on the frontier, to march up directly to the capital or centre of these sciences [the human sciences], to human nature itself; which being once master of, we may everywhere else hope for an easy victory' (London: Dent, 1911), p. 5. This Blitzkrieg strategy did not exactly achieve the anticipated success. This was for the most part due to Kant's parry. But the strategy was destined to have another success, at once less 'clear' and more fearful: the installation, in the course of two centuries (including, as it has been shown, to some extent with Kant himself), of the human sciences in the place of metaphysics, as well as the installation of positivism at the heart of methodology, whatever may have been Hume's own thoughts on the subject.

10 2: 640. Müller, pp. 481, 486.

11 2: 636. Müller, p. 484.

12 Preface, 6: 399. Dowdell, p. 3.

13 3: 409.

14 6: 381–3.

15 6: 377.

16 *Opus postumum,* Liasse 11, fo. 5, p. 3.

17 6: 381–3.

18 Dowdell, pp. 132–3.

19 6: 374.

20 Dowdell, p. 93.

21 Ibid., p. 102.

22 6: 519. Dowdell, p. 102.

23 2: 184. Müller, pp. 118–19.

24 6: 55–7.

25 2: 467. Müller, p. 350.

26 The problem is posed in this way by Wittgenstein in the *Tractatus,* sections 5.251 to 5.254, but only in respect to the logical-mathematical series.

27 2: 488, 491. Müller, pp. 366, 371.

28 2: 486–7. Müller, p. 365.

29 4: 157, 186–91. *Critique of Practical Reason,* tr. Thomas Kingsmill Abbott (London: Longman, Green, 1909), pp. 133, 159–63.

30 This expression recurs frequently in Kant's text. It signifies the minimum requirement for compatibility among the regimes. Its French translation (*sans en léser aucun*) was suggested by Jean-Pierre Dubost.
31 Vol. 2, Introduction, in fine. Bernard, p. 13.
32 2: 408. Müller, p. 302.
33 2 (KUK), section 84. Bernard, pp. 359–61.
34 6: 357.
35 *Dialectique négative*, tr. *Groupe Collège de philosophie* (Paris: Payot, 1978), avant-propos.
36 *Modèles mathématiques de la morphogenèse* (Paris: Editions 1018, 1974), p. 186.
37 See J.-F. Lyotard, 'Essai d'analyse du dispositif spéculatif', *Degrés*, nos 26–27.
38 In a letter to Lambert dated 2 September 1770, Kant terms 'phaenomenologia generalis' the entirely negative science in which the value and limits of these principles of perception would be determined. The fourth part of Lambert's *Nouvel Organon* is called 'Phenomenology'.
39 2: 254–7. Müller, p. xiv.
40 2: 222. Müller, p. 150.
41 Introduction, 2: 245. Bernard, p. 11.
42 Saul Kripke, *La Logique des noms propres*, tr. Jacob and Recanati (Paris: Payot, 1982), pp. 42–4.
43 Siegfried Kracauer, *Le Roman policier*, tr. Rochlitz (Paris: Payot, 1981), pp. 38ff.
44 *Les Derniers Jours d'Emmanuel Kant*, tr. Pierre Legris and Marcel Schwobt (Paris: Gallimard, 1973).
45 Kripke, *La Logique*, pp. 36ff.
46 Marin, *Le Portrait du roi* (Paris: Editions de Minuit, 1981).
47 Wittgenstein, *Philosophical Investigations*, 3rd edn, tr. G. E. M. Anscombe (New York: Macmillan, 1958), section 203, p. 82e.
48 Ibid., section 110, p. 47e.
49 'Contribution to the Critique of Hegel's "Philosophy of Right"', in *Critique of Hegel's Philosophy of Right*, tr. Annette Jolin and Joseph O'Malley (Cambridge: Cambridge University Press, 1971), p. 141.
50 See Jean-François Lyotard, 'Pierre Souyri, le marxisme qui n'a pas fini', *Esprit 13* (1982), no. 2.
51 *Le Monde*, 16 January, 1979, and Serge Thion, *Vérité historique ou vérité politique?* (Paris: Librairie La Vieille Taupe, 1980).
52 Section 5, 6: pp. 356ff.
53 Marx, 'Contribution', p. 140.
54 Nicole Loraux, *L'Invention d'Athènes* (The Hague: Mouton, 1981), pp. 200–4 and Index: Stasis; in, L'Oubli dans la cité, *Le Temps de la réflexion* (1980), 1:222ff.

Translated by Cecile Lindsay

19

Discussions, or Phrasing 'after Auschwitz'

I

This lecture has been entitled 'Discussions'.[1] Such a title announces a genre of discourse, the *dialéktikè*, the theses, arguments, objections, and refutations that Aristotle's *Topics* and *On Sophistical Refutations* analyse and seek to bring within norms. The 'greater' dialectics, speculative dialectics, dismisses this genre as frivolous: 'Objections – if they really are connected to the thing against which they are directed – are one-sided determinations ... These one-sided determinations, insofar as they are connected to the thing, are *moments of its concept;* they are thus brought forth in their momentary place during the latter's exposition, and their negation within the dialectic immanent to the concept must be demonstrated ... ' This is so much the case that in regard to a work which seeks to compile objections, such as the one undertaken by Göschel (the author of the *Aphorisms* commented upon here by Hegel), 'Science could demand that such work be superfluous, since it would arise only through thought's lack of culture and through the impatience proper to the frivolity of defective thought.'[2] Science, in the Hegelian sense, does not simply brush aside the *dialéktikè* as did Aristotelian didactics. It encloses the *dialéktikè* within its own genre, speculative discourse. In this genre, the *two* of *dialéktikè*, which is what provides material for paralogisms and aporias, is put into the service of the didactic end, the *one*. There is no true discussion.

But this phrase[3] (the speculative phrase) is a phrase which is nevertheless up for discussion. The fact that this is so is 'our' entire affair, an affair of linking phrases (*une affaire d'enchaînement de phrases*). Is not oneness the aim of and therefore the law for the linkings of phrases? Does not man, the 'we' in 'our' affair, owe his unique (his singular) name solely to the fact that he links together his propositions in the direction of making them one?

On this question, here are two chains of phrases. One bears Derrida's signature. Here are some of its links:

There will be no unique name, even if it were the name of Being. And we must think this without *nostalgia*.

Such a *difference* would at once, again, give us to think a writing without presence and without absence, without history, without cause, without *archia*, without *telos*, a writing that absolutely upsets all dialectics, all theology, all teleology, all ontology.

What might be a 'negative' that could not be *relevé?* And which, in sum, as negative but without appearing as such, without *presenting* itself, that is, without working in the service of meaning, would work? but would work, then, as pure loss?

What is difficult to think today is an end of man which would not be organized by a dialectics of truth and negativity, an end of man which would not be teleology in the first person plural.[4]

These are so many objections, or rather disjections, made to unobjectional thought. The Latin word, *disjectio*, more or less covers the meanings of *dissemination* and *deconstruction*. Neither the former nor the latter are sufficient to obtain 'some dislocation without measure'.[5] Consider, by way of proof (here is an argument), the definition of the deconstructive strategy: 'an *overturning* of the classical opposition [between terms such as speech/writing, presence/absence, etc.] *and* a general *displacement* of the system.' This double operation, presented as the 'only condition' capable of giving to deconstruction 'the means with which to *intervene* in the field of oppositions that it criticizes, which is also a field of nondiscursive forces',[6] could, if taken literally, just as well be (here is a refutation) a definition of the work of speculative dialectics itself.

The other chain of phrases, which links up with the former, bears the name of Adorno and the colours of negative dialectics. Here are a few of its linkages:

It lies in the definition of negative dialectics that it will not come to rest in itself, as if it were total. This is its form of hope.

Dialectics is obliged to make a final move: being at once the impression and the critique of the universal delusive context, it must now turn even against itself.

Discussions, or phrasing 'after Auschwitz'

According to its own concept, metaphysics cannot be a deductive context of judgements about things in being, and neither can it be conceived after the model of an absolute otherness terribly defying thought.

[Metaphysics] would be possible only as a legible constellation of things in being (*als lesbare Konstellation von Seiendem*).

[Metaphysics] would bring [things in being] into a configuration in which the elements unite to form a script.

The smallest intramundane traits would be of relevance to the absolute (*Relevanz fürs Absolute*).

Metaphysics immigrates into micrology. Micrology is the place where metaphysics finds a haven from totality.

These phrases are taken from the end of *Negative Dialectics*.[7] It is stated there that 'the micrological view cracks the shells of what, measured by the subsuming cover concept [this is directed against Hegel], is hopelessly isolated and explodes its identity, the delusion that it is but a specimen' (ND 408).

The question of the specimen (*l'exemplaire*) is decisive. It is the question of the name. What conceptual name does the so-called proper name bear? By what intelligible, dialectical phrase can the factual name be replaced? What does a proper name *mean to say (veut dire)?* According to Adorno, this is the speculative question. This question presupposes, moreover, a reversal by which the particular becomes an example of the generic. That is why he writes, in the Preface to *Negative Dialectics:* 'Part three elaborates models of negative dialectics. They are not examples; they do not simply elucidate general reflections ... the use of examples which Plato introduced and philosophy repeated ever since: as matters of indifference in themselves' (ND 8).

Now, in this third part, which is entitled *Models (Modelle)*, the section, 'Meditations on Metaphysics', begins by, let's say, a micrology whose title is 'After Auschwitz'. Here, and in adjacent passages, are to be found the following phrases:

After Auschwitz there is no word tinged from on high, not even a theological one, that has any right unless it underwent a transformation.

If death were that absolute which philosophy tried in vain to conjure positively, everything is nothing; all that we think, too, is thought into the void.

In the camps death has a novel horror; since Auschwitz, fearing death means fearing worse than death (ND 367, 371).

If one discusses or disputes what is indisputable *(indiscutable)*, speculative thought, is it only out of impatience, frivolity, and lack of culture? Is 'Auschwitz' and 'after Auschwitz', that is, Western thought and life today, something which disputes speculative discourse? If so, is it frivolous? If not, what happens to and what becomes of the speculative which would not be speculative? What then is the discourse, named 'Auschwitz', which disputes the speculative? Or which seeks, without success, to dispute it? This question of the end, death, and aim of speculative dialectics, is also necessarily that of the ends of man, of 'our' ends.

(I will not speak about Marxism. It is twice implicated in the question: once, on the side of *speculatio*, and once, on the side of *disputatio*.)

II

'After' implies a periodization. Adorno counts time (but what time?) from 'Auschwitz'. Is this name that of a chronological origin? What era ends and what era begins with this event? This question appears ingenuous when it is remembered what kind of disintegration the dialectic inflicts upon the idea of beginning in the first chapter of Hegel's *Science of Logic,* and already in the second Kantian antinomy. Has Adorno forgotten this?

'Auschwitz' is a model, not an example. From Plato to Hegelian dialectics the example, says Adorno, has the function in philosophy of illustrating an idea; it does not enter into a necessary relation with what it illustrates, but remains 'indifferent' to it. The model, on the other hand, 'brings negative dialectics into the real' (ND xx). As a model, 'Auschwitz' does not illustrate negative dialectics. Negative dialectics, because it is negative, blurs the figures of the concept (which proceed from affirmation), scrambles the names borne by the stages of the concept in its movement. This model responds to this reversal in the destiny of the dialectic: it is the name of something (of a para-experience, of a paraempiricity) wherein dialectics encounters a non-negatable negative *(un négatif non niable),* and abides in the impossibility of redoubling that negative into a 'result'. Wherein the mind's wound is not scarred over. Wherein, writes Derrida, 'the investment in death cannot be integrally amortized'.[8]

The 'Auschwitz' model would designate an experience of language which brings speculative discourse to a halt. The latter can no longer be pursued 'after Auschwitz', that is, 'within Auschwitz'. Here would be found a name 'within' which we cannot think, or not completely. It would not be a name in Hegel's sense, as that figure of memory which assures the permanence of the *rest* when mind has destroyed its signs. It would be a name of the nameless (there are other such names, such as, according to Adorno, the 'intelligible character' of the Kantian moral act: 'the impulse to do what is just', which justly remains unintelligible [ND 297, translation modified]). It would be a name which designates what has no name in speculation, a name for the anonymous. And what for speculation remains simply the anonymous.

Why say that this anonym designates an 'experience of language', a 'para-experience'? Is that not to insult the millions of real dead in the real barracks and gas chambers of real concentration camps? It can be surmised what advantages a well-led indignation can derive from the word of reality. And what is spawned by this indignation is the embryo of the justice-maker. It is this indignation, however, with its claim to realism, which insults the name of Auschwitz, for this indignation is itself the only result it derives from that collective murder. It does not even *doubt* that there is a result (namely itself). Now, if this name is a nameless name, if Auschwitz does not provide an example but a mode, it is perhaps because nothing, or at least not all, of what has been expended in it is conserved; because the requirement of a result is therein disappointed and driven to despair; because speculation does not succeed in deriving a profit from it, were it the minimal one of the beautiful soul. That all this is an affair of language is known only too well by asking the indignant ones: what then does 'Auschwitz' mean to say to you (*que veut donc dire 'Auschwitz' pour vous*)? For one must, in any case, *speak* (*dire*). Some argue over the number of dead in concentration camps: is that what it is, to speak 'after Auschwitz'?

'An experience of language, a para-experience.' The word *experience* is *the* word of Hegel's *Phenomenology of Mind:* the 'science of the experience of consciousness'. And experience is the 'dialectical process which consciousness executes on itself'.[9] In the sphere which belongs to it, experience supposes the speculative element, the 'life of the mind' as a life which 'endures death and in death maintains its being' (PM 93). This sojourn liberates the *Zauberkraft* [magical force – tr.] of the mind, the power to convert the negative into Being, the *göttliche Natur des Sprechens*.[10] Can one still speak of experience in the case of the 'Auschwitz' model? Would that not be to presuppose the 'magical force'? Is the death named (or not named) 'Auschwitz', this sojourn wherein the reversal, the old paradox of the affirmation of non-Being, can take place? Adorno writes: 'Since Auschwitz fearing death means fearing worse than death.' What can make death not yet the worst is its being not simply the end but only the end of the finite and the revelation of the infinite. Worse than this magical death would be irreversible death, or simply the end – including the end of the infinite.

That could not therefore be said to be an experience, since it would have no result. Its not having a speculative name does not, however, prevent one from talking about it. The question raised by Auschwitz is that of the texture of the text which 'links onto' Auschwitz. If this text is not the speculative one, what might it be? How can it authorize itself, if it is not thanks to the *Umkehrung* [reversal – tr.]? It is thanks to the move which passes the thing, the *res* (*die Sache*), from the position of referent in the universe of an unmediated phrase to that of addressor and addressee in the universe of a phrase 'linking onto' the preceding one that the second phrase is in effect authorized. It is authorized on account of the fact that what is formulated about the referent of the first phrase is formulated by it (the referent), as addressor, and addressed to it, as addressee. Apart from this movement, how can Auschwitz, something which is thought from the outside, a referent placed only 'near itself' (*an sich*) (*auprès-de-soi*) 'for us' *(für uns)*, be interiorized, suppressed (*supprimé*)[11] as an unmediated position or pre-supposition, and show itself to itself, know itself in the identity (be it ephemeral) of a for-itself (*für sich*)? In the absence of this permutation, there is according to Hegel only chatter, emptiness, subjectivity, arbitrariness, at best regression towards 'ratiocinative' thought, towards the discourse of the understanding, towards the 'modesty' of finitude. Now this modesty, he writes, because it is subjective vanity erected into an absolute, is 'wickedness'.[12]

Nevertheless, in contending that one must speak about 'Auschwitz' and that one can speak about it truly only if the anonymous object of the phrase becomes its subject and consequently names itself, this summons to express the result of 'Auschwitz', to speculate on the anonym, is an intimidation that prejudges the nature of the object. If the name hidden by 'Auschwitz' is the death of the magical 'beautiful death', how could the latter, which sustains the speculative movement, repossess itself after the former and sublate it? And supposing it was the case, on the other hand, that 'after Auschwitz' speculative discourse has died, does it follow that only subjective chatter or the wickedness of modesty remains in its place?

This alternative is formulated only within speculative logic. In accepting the alternative, one perpetuates that logic. But if this logic is to be perpetuated, one might as well attribute the magical force of the negative to 'Auschwitz' and already make of it an example of the 'beautiful death'. For the opposite hypothesis, that of subjective chatter, is in this case excluded by its very construction.

Is it possible that some kind of discourse, some kind of logic, sprung from the anonym 'Auschwitz' would be maintained 'afterwards' which would not be its speculative result? One would have to imagine the following: that the cleavage introduced into Western thought by 'Auschwitz' does not go outside of speculative discourse, that is (since the latter has no outside), that it does not determine its effect inside that discourse as an incomplete, invalid, or unexpressed exit, as a kind of neurotic stasis on a figure (that of 'Auschwitzian' death) which would only be, all things considered, but a moment. Rather, this cleavage would breach speculative logic itself and not only its effects, would jam the functioning of certain of its operators but not all of them, would condemn that logic to the disarrangement of an infinity which would be neither the good one nor the bad, or which would be both at once. This is how Derrida imagines the 'breach' (*fêlure*) of the philosophical tympanum: 'By means of this breach . . . , the bloodiness of a disseminated writing comes to separate the lips, to violate the embouchure of philosophy, putting *its* tongue into movement. . . . A necessarily unique event, nonreproducible, hence illegible as such and when it happens. . . .'[13] Would 'Auschwitz' be a name for this illegibility? As such, how does it enter into the 'legible constellation' fabricated by Adorno's micrologies?

III

In making of the name 'Auschwitz' a model for and within negative dialectics, Adorno suggests that what meets its end there is only affirmative dialectics. But in what way is the dialectic affirmative? In the *Philosophical Propaedeutics* of 1809, Hegel makes a distinction within logic between 'the dialectical side or side of negative reason' and 'the speculative side or side of positive reason'.[14] This distinction is made again in the 1830 *Encyclopaedia*: 'In the dialectical stage these finite determinations suppress themselves and pass into their opposites. . . . The speculative stage, or stage of positive reason, apprehends the unity of determinations in their opposition – the *affirmative*, which is involved in their disintegration and in their transition.'[15]

This distinction is not respected everywhere in Hegel's opus. In fact, how could it possibly be respected in a discourse whose resources are found precisely in the negative as the magical force that converts non-Being into Being? What ought to be surprising, rather, is that the opposition should have been made at all and that it should be maintained apart from its own dialecticalization, like a concession made on the side to the understanding. This opposition is a trace, the scar of a wound in speculative discourse, a wound for which that discourse is also the mending. The wound is that of nihilism. This wound is not an accidental one; it is absolutely philosophical. Scepticism (of the ancient kind, it should be understood) is not just one philosophy among others; it is, writes Hegel in 1802, 'in an *implicit* form . . . the free aspect of every philosophy.' Hegel continues:

When in a given proposition expressing reasoned knowledge, one has isolated its reflective aspect, that is, the concepts enclosed within it, and when one considers the way in which these concepts are connected, then it necessarily appears that these concepts are sublated (*relevés, aufgehoben*) at the same time, or that they are united in such a way that they contradict each other; otherwise, the proposition would not be one of the reason, but one of the understanding.[16]

In paragraph 39 of the 1830 *Encyclopaedia,* Hegel refers to the 1802 article as if he still approved of it.

In paragraph 78, however, a stern corrective is placed upon the philosophical liberty to dissolve determinations: 'Scepticism, made a negative science and systematically applied to all forms of knowledge, might seem a suitable introduction, as pointing out the nullity (*Nichtigkeit*) of such assumptions. But a sceptical introduction would be not only an unpleasant but also a useless course; and that because Dialectic, as we shall soon make appear, is *itself an essential element of affirmative science*' (HL 111-12; translation modified, my emphasis). This corrective has already been given in the Introduction to the *Phenomenology of Mind:* 'Scepticism always sees in the result only *pure nothingness,* and abstracts from the fact that this nothing is determinate, is the nothing of *that out of which it comes as a result*' (PG 74, PM 137).

Animals are given in the *Phenomenology of Mind* as examples of wisdom in regards to the truth of sense-certainty: they despair of the latter's reality and they eat it up *(zehren sie auf)* (PG 91, PM 159). Scepticism is unpleasant because it is the animality of the mind, its stomach, so to speak, which consumes determinations. Such is the wounding fascination exerted by nihilism, a consumption or consummation that leaves no remains. The balm and the exorcism are as follows: to make this distressing negativity work for the production of an affirmation. To close up the tympanum. Is the anonym 'Auschwitz' a model of negative dialectics? Then, it will have awakened the despair of nihilism and it will be necessary 'after Auschwitz' for thought to consume its determinations like a cow its fodder or a tiger its prey, that is, without leaving a result. In the sty or the lair that the West will have become, only that which follows upon such a consumption will be found: waste, shit. So must be spoken the end of the infinite, as an endless repetition of *Nichtige*, as a 'bad infinity'. You wanted blood, you get shit.

What would a result of 'Auschwitz' consist in? What is a *result*? In the same paragraph 82 of the *Encyclopaedia*, Hegel goes on to write: 'The result of Dialectic is positive, because it has a *determined content*, or because its result is not *empty and abstract nothing*, but the negation of *certain specific determinations* which are contained in the result – for the very reason that it is a resultant and not an *unmediated nothing*' (HL 119; translation modified). The *Resultat* – a word whose root is *salt-*, *saltare*, *sauter* (to jump) (as in *insult* or *exult*) – is a rebound, a rebounding: something is in motion, it encounters that which stops it; transformed, it re-bounds (*re-saute*).

What is in motion? Let us say, a signifier in search of its signified. For example, what does one say in saying *Being (Être)?*[17] What makes the word falter? Its opposite. In saying *Being*, one says *nothing*, therefore one says nothing. Here, ratiocinative thought is blocked and lacks a result. It holds onto the propositional form, it wants to attribute a determination to the propositional subject, *Being*, and it finds nothing to predicate except nothingness, the contrary of Being. Now, this predication is forbidden to ratiocinative thought by its major rule, the principle of non-contradiction.

But if there is an aporia here, it is by reason of the rules that have been fixed for this language game: a rule for forming terms, a rule for forming phrases, a rule for linking phrases. Let us examine the rules of the game. Here, in short, are those necessary for the speculative one:

1   A rule for forming terms. Terms enter into a dialectical phrase only on the condition that they have at least two signifieds, and if possible, mutually opposing ones. The model is given by *aufheben*.[18] But this condition is amply satisfied in natural languages, the speculative capacity of each being measured according to the amount of its words in *Doppelsinnigkeit* (double meaning), in *Zweifelhaftigkeit*

(uncertainty), and no doubt also in *Verzweiflung* (despair, not only of the kind inflicted on the translator, but also the nihilistic despair before the flight of the signified).

2   A rule of immanent derivation, which defines negative dialectics, and which could be formulated thus: *if p, then non-p; if non-p, then p, p* being indifferently a term or a phrase (PG 53–5; PM 113–15). The figure of Epimenides or Russell's antinomy will be recognized here, the figure that threatens every attributive or propositional logic, the anti-principle of contradiction.[19] (A prescriptive analogue of this figure is given by Aristotle's *Do not obey*.) The elaboration of the double *if, then,* even if performed by an aporetic mind (that of the understanding), already contains the result, but only as it is performed, only as it is given *in* the operation of the elaboration itself. The double implication, that is, the elaboration of the equivocacy of the signifieds and the sceptical course through doubt, *is* the result: the implication is dialectic. But it fails to say so.

3   A rule of expression. The movement of the double immanent derivation must express itself in a single phrase or term which designates the unity of the dialectical movement. The movement *through* which, according to the second rule, the determinations are first dissolved, must express itself (this is the *ausdrücken*), give itself a name, address to itself the news of its name. It is then that it becomes a *Resultat*.[20]

This summary, it will have been noticed, transcribes the operators of speculative discourse into the discourse of phrase games; it turns speculative discourse into a phrase game, of which it gives the rules of formation and linkage. The question is to know whether or not this transcription – and what it presupposes in turn – escapes the grasp of speculative discourse. In pursuing this transcription, have we not taken an exterior 'point of view' towards that discourse? Are we not dealing with an opinion, with a subjective *Meinen*, which arises from the understanding, or indeed from logical empiricism? The stakes are important: that of the necessity of making linkages from one phrase to the next. Or yet again: that of the homogeneity of phrases in their apparent heterogeneity, of their common, although contradictory, *relevance*[21] to a single genre. Or else, if we proceed in a reverse manner, what is at stake is the possibility, as Derrida writes and italicizes, 'of an other [of the philosophical phrase] which is no longer *its other*'.[22] Would the anonym 'Auschwitz' have that name: not that of non-linkage, but of a linkage which is other than 'result'?

IV

It would be a question, in sum, of evading the *Resultat*, of conceiving – and thus, of already making work within this very conception – a dialectics which would not be a moment in speculative discourse. This dialectics would obey, for example, the rules of equivocacy and of immanent derivation; it would ignore the rule of expression. But how could this be possible? Is it not necessary that, in all cases, that which is in question *name* itself, that this name be *its* name? And how could it be named unless it is that Self itself which gives its name to itself? How then can dialectics stay negative? Is it not possible that what is being sought under the name of negative dialectics is just another way of fitting together phrases, and that the name it gives itself then is deceptive? The breach would be covering a fracture.

The question of the necessity of making linkages will be raised in relation to a strong point in the articulation of phrases: that of the *we*. In 'our' societies, the pronoun of the first person plural answers in principle to the question of sovereignty. It is the supreme argument of authority, or rather of authorization. It is, in fact, the link which is supposed to bind series of prescriptive phrases (such as articles in codes, court rulings, laws, decrees, ordinances, circulars, and commandments) to their legitimation. A prescriptive phrase is formulated as follows: *It is an obligation for x to accomplish act* $\propto$. A normative phrase has the following formulation: *It is a norm edicted by y for x to accomplish act* $\propto$.[23] This norm is considered legitimate, in 'our' societies, if it is admitted that *x* and *y*, the addressee of the prescription and the addressor of the norm, must be the same. The legislator submits to the obligation. The obligated one legislates. The former says, *I decree that I must*; says the latter, *I decree that I must*. The four instances (addressor and addressee respectively for the normative and the prescriptive) being perfectly commutative, obligee and legislator are thus united in the same *we*. This is how the figure of autonomy is constructed.

This construction is not self-evident, however. The first person plural has been pulled out of a hat because two first person singulars were put into it. But in the hat, there were also some *hes* and some *yous*. It has been demonstrated by Benveniste to what extent each of these personal pronouns presents in and of itself a phrase universe *(univers de phrase)* different from that of the others.[24] But here, to boot, the pronouns are included in phrases belonging to heterogeneous families. Since the category of the *we* belongs to the problematics of enunciation, let us first examine the question of its formation in that regard.

From the point of view of the legislator, the normative phrase is formulated, *I decree as norm that* . . . , and the prescriptive phrase, *They (the French, the deportees, etc.) must accomplish act* $\propto$. From the point of view of the obligated, the respective formulations are, for the normative phrase, *They (the legislator, the SS etc.) decree as norm that* . . . , and for the prescriptive phrase, *I must accomplish act* $\propto$. Thus is expressed the one-sidedness of the subjective phrase. The description which uncovers this one-sidedness shows that while *I* and *he* are indifferently applied to the same name (what is *I* for oneself is *he* for another), the proper names (the SS, the deportees) remain unchanged and unexchangeable. Subjective singularity does not rebound.

The heterogeneity of the phrases reinforces this immobilization. The normative phrase, *I (or He) decree(s) as norm that* . . ., is declarative and belongs to the genre of descriptive statements. A descriptive invites the addressee to situate himself, at the time of a subsequent occurrence, on the addressor instance. This is the rule of *homologia* or of consensus. A: *The door is shut.* The addressee consents to this by saying, *The door is shut.* Addressor and addressee can easily say a 'we' which unites then an *I* and an *I*. Such is not the case in the prescriptive phrase. In response to the command, *Shut the door,* the addressee cannot indicate his consent by saying, *Shut the door,* to the addressor of the command. There is dissymmetry in the case of prescription: the *I* and the *you* are not easily unifiable here.

Before proceeding further, I must clear up a misunderstanding that threatens to arise. In the following, as in the preceding, observations, one might suspect a 'wild', unquestioning use of certain notions borrowed from pragmatics, specifically those of addressor and addressee. In reality, no *use* at all is being made of them. What is presupposed in these observations is rather a manner of speaking (which I'm not naming, let's say, a phrase game; that is already the whole question) circumscribed, very poorly but sufficiently, by the following phrases:

If there is one phrase, then there are several phrases. A phrase presents a universe. No matter what its form, a phrase entails a *There is (Il y a)*, whether it is marked or not in the form of the phrase. What is entailed by a phrase is that it presents. A phrase is an event, *ein Fall,* a token. It presents a universe constituted by instances (referent, addressor, addressee, sense) which can be marked or not in the form of the phrase. The phrase is not a message passed from an addressor to an addressee who remain independent of it. The latter are situated in the universe that the phrase presents, together with the referent and the sense. To present phrases as messages is what a phrase does (in the theory of communication); to present a context is also what a phrase does (in sociology or in pragmatics). The phrase universe is not presented to something or someone as if to a subject. The presentation is that there is a universe. There are as many universes as there are phrases, as many situations of instances as there are phrase universes, that is, as many as there are forms of phrases. Space and time are situations of instances in phrase universes. The presentation entailed by a phrase is not itself presented in the universe that the phrase presents; another phrase may present that presentation, but this last phrase also entails a presentation which it does not present. One could call the presentation 'Being'; it can be qualified as *absolute*, but it is thereby presented. Therefore, it is situated in the universe of the phrase that presents it, and is relative to that phrase universe. Being is only as if presented (*comme présenté*), that is, it is presented as an existent (*étant*), as non-Being. There is no synthesis of the presentations which are entailed; there is only a synthesis of presentations insofar as they are themselves presented in a phrase which synthesizes them. (There is no transcendental time.) 'Now' can only be presented (as 'the now' of a given phrase). The 'now' entailed in a phrase is not presented in the universe that the phrase presents. The linking of one phrase to another requires still another phrase, to present the linkage. This linkage is a necessary one if it follows rules of derivation whose result is termed necessary. These rules are themselves presented. A phrase can co-present several universes along with the one it presents (equivocation).

That should suffice. I will add the following: *phrase* comes from Greek *phrazō*, root *phrad*, which, if I am not mistaken, has no etymological correspondent in Latin. *Phrazō* is to *legō* as *telling* or *declaring* is to *speaking*. An archaic meaning of the word seems to be *to indicate*. Liddell and Scott cite an interesting occurrence of this meaning in Herodotus: *phōnēsai men ouk eikhe, tē de kheiri ephraze:* 'unable to express her meaning through speech, she indicated with her hand.' Whence it follows that *to phrase* is not to give voice (*phonein*).

I will also add the following: the preceding phrases imply a displacement of man. In them, man is not understood as the subject matter which needs to be signified, that is, as the referent. For this reason, these phrases do not arise from the human sciences, nor from pragmatics in particular. They reverse the relationship of phrase and context: the latter belongs to the universe presented by the phrase. As the occasion arises, men (proper names) come to occupy given instances in phrase universes. The phrase, *The meeting is called to order*, is not performative *because* its addressor is the person who chairs the meeting; rather, that person is the chair of the meeting *to the extent that* the phrase is performative. Man is not what is; what is, is what is presented, an existent, situated at a given instance. It might be objected that the delimitation of the phrase universe into instances remains nonetheless anthropological, linguistic. Not at all, for it is not man who articulates language, but language which articulates not only the world and sense, but also man. To articulate is not anthropocentric. No more than *to phrase* is. Is this structuralist? No, not that either. Speech (*langage*) is not language (*langue*). While the latter is understood as a structure made up of codes, the former is composed of moves in games. The rules for phrase games are not structures of language.

V

Returning now to the problem of the *we*, we find that language very naturally authorizes the synthesis of *I* and *he* in the pronoun of the first person plural, that synthesis providing one of the pronoun's linguistic values (the other is the synthesis of *I* and *you*). But while the philosophy of the subject of enunciation feeds, and feeds upon, this analysis of personal pronouns, it comes up against an old problem, that of the non-I. There is something of the non-I in the *we*. To this philosophical obstacle, pragmatics adds the heterogeneity between two phrase games: the descriptive and the prescriptive.

If 'Auschwitz' has no name, is it not because it is the proper name of para-experience, that of the impossibility of forming the we? Is it not the case that in concentration camps there is no plural subject? And is it not further the case that for want of this plural subject, there can remain 'after Auschwitz' no subject which could presume to name *itself* by naming this 'experience'?

It will be objected, first of all, that the theoretical and philosophical difficulty of forming a *we* is horridly aggravated when the prescription and the norm take the summary form, *Die, I decree it,* which the SS authorities pronounced to the deportees. The content of the command would be the cause for the failure of the *we*.

This case is far from unique, however. Public authority (familial, political, military, partisan, denominational) does on occasion address the order to die to its own addressees. But if they are *its own* addressees, it is because, through some procedure whose institutional form is not important here, this authority is *their own*. Here again then, a *we* acts to unite the addressee of the command with the addressor of the phrase that makes of that command a norm. This *we* makes it possible for one to die both on command and 'freely' or 'knowingly'. The command, *Die,* can undergo different modalities: *Die rather than escape* (Socrates in prison), *Die rather than be defeated* (Thermopylae, the Paris Commune), etc. These modalities in no way alter the principle according to which the command is executory as long as the commutation of instances in the two phrases is said to be possible. (But in which phrase in this said?)

Whatever the modality (including degree zero) that affects it, the prescription, *Die,* nevertheless presents a difference between itself and other phrases of the prescriptive family. For the content of the command, if we follow the logic of phrase games, is such that if the addressee obeys, his proper name will no longer be able to figure among the instances of addressor and addressee in ulterior unmediated phrases. It will only be able to figure on them at the referential instance. If, however, this proper name can still be found upon the instances of addressor or addressee, it will be in mediated phrase universes (citations, prosopopoeia, chronicles, accounts of all kinds) in which are reported phrases wherein this proper name was, or will supposed to have been, the addressor and addressee. This immobilization clause in the game (i.e. death) in particular prohibits the addressee of the command *Die* – if he obeys it – from later shifting to the position of addressor in a normative phrase of the type, *I decree as norm that...*

The only exit offered him as an escape from the situation of exclusive (whether mediated or unmediated) referentiality that is his death is to identify with a *we* (whatever the latter's name might be, the issue being unimportant here) capable, as the instance of addressor and addressee, of legitimizing all possible commands starting with the one ordering him to die. By shifting from one phrase universe to another, by rebounding from that of the final prescription to that of the first legitimation, he eludes the death sentence and is able, for that very reason, to die. He exchanges his particular name for a collective pronoun.

As opposed to the moment of the life-or-death struggle and of domination described in the *Phenomenology of Mind,* 'self-consciousness' does not here have to discover that 'life is as essential to it as pure self-consciousness' (PM 234), for the life in question here is that of the *we.* In the cities of ancient Greece, this identification formed the outline of funeral orations pronounced in honour of citizens dead for the city. The 'beautiful death', the epideictic theme *par excellence,* the one Plato lampoons in *Menexenus,*[25] is what reconciles the two ways a man can meet his end: his *eschaton* and his *telos,* his ending as incompletion and his completion as un-ending, his *Die* and his *Do not die*, his finitude as living being and his infinitude as legislator, as speaker of the law.

(To put the final touch on the *Zweideutigkeit*, on the equivocation dear to speculative language, and thus to give wit its due measure of enjoyment, it will be noted that the respective semantic fields of the two Greek words encroach on each other: not only does *teleō* correspond to Latin *perficere*, accomplishment, but *telos* also means death, as well as the tax payment which is the price for the passage to citizenship. In this passage, what passes away is finitude and what comes to pass is the recognition of the citizen's infinitude as legislator.)

In 'Auschwitz', it is not the *Die* which remains nameless and leaves no result but the fact that the reconciliation of the name in the prescription and the pronoun in the norm, of the finitude of death and the infinity of law, is prohibited. The one who commands the death is exclusively other than the one to whom the command is addressed. The former does not have to account to the latter, and the latter does not have to legitimize the former. The two phrase universes have no common application. What the prescriptive phrase presents (the command to die), the normative phrase does not (whence the 'We knew nothing about it' of the so-called legislators); what the normative phrase presents (*So says the law*) remains unknown in the universe of the prescriptive phrase *Die* (whence the 'Why do they do it? This cannot be' of the victims).

Nevertheless, we are not dealing with an accident but with a death sentence. For want, however, of a *we* which would make of that command a law, it cannot obligate. The command cannot be obeyed. 'It is proper to man to *know* his law,' writes Hegel in the *Encyclopaedia*, and therefore 'he can truly obey only such known law – even as his law can only be a just law, as it is a *known* law' (HP 260; translation modified). 'Auschwitz' would be the name of this impossible phrase wherein the law is not known, wherein it cannot be just, wherein the command cannot obligate, wherein man loses what is proper to him, namely, his *we*. At Auschwitz and afterwards, one does not 'know' how to die (ND 365–73). It is the death of the beautiful, infinite death: finite death. One administers (*On administre*).

Why then say '*after* Auschwitz'? Because out of the disjoining – or unlinking – of legitimation and obligation (which is what prohibits the formation of a *we* or destroys its figure), it would not even result that *we* are condemned to browse and ruminate over the nullity of determinations. For, what would be this *we*? From merely negative dialectics, deprived of the operators of positive reason, a *we* – no more than any other result – cannot *result*, in order to say or do anything at all. There would not even be a spirit, a spirit of the people or a spirit of the world, which are *wes*, to repossess the name 'Auschwitz', to think it and to think itself inside it. The name would remain empty, in a mechanical memory, abandoned by the concept. It is in this way that that name would be anonymous. And that 'after Auschwitz' would not mean a rebound, but the repetition of a *Metrum* to which no accent would come to provide rhythm:[26] and it would not mean anything *(il ne voudrait rien dire)*.

VI

Is it not possible to try, however, through some painful paradox, through some inhuman – other than human – exertion, to draw a result from this irreparable death? (But would this be a result?) The result would be drawn by saying that this death's sense, the identification of another *we*, proceeds from its non-sense, from the impossibility for the addressee of the Auschwitz *Die* to identify himself with the legislator who makes of that command a norm. By saying that, the impossibility of the reversal bears witness to the disparity between the finite and the infinite, that the failure of the mediation reveals the infinitude of that which decrees this death. By daring to say that within the extermination order emanating from the SS (an order to which it is impossible to be obligated, and in relation to which one can only be a victim), a request nevertheless makes itself heard thanks to this impossibility, an identification thanks to non-identification. What if the abhorrent buffoonery, as David Rousset has called it,[27] of administered genocide, had existed negatively, *in order to* recall that it is only through a dialectical imposture that there is a *we* capable of bringing together the obligated one and the legislator? What if the abasement and the abject dispossession of which the deportees were victims had been marks of the absolute alterity and transcendence of every request (of every prescription) for the addressee it enjoins? Is infinitude not that which escapes identification? Does it not take place as the absurd, as what is beyond one's capacities, as the intolerable, as the command Abraham received, as the 'marvel' in Emmanuel Levinas's sense of the word? A *we* can perhaps identify itself on the basis of this non-identification: a community of addressees alert to the 'marvel', the condition Levinas calls that of the 'hostage'.[28]

This *we* would not be ethical in the sense of *Sittlichkeit* [ethical life – tr.], nor even in the sense of morality, if by morality one persists in identifying, as Kant does, pure will with reason in its practical use. This identification, objects Levinas, turns out to preserve a basic intelligibility at the addressor's pole of the moral law,[29] even if Kant himself admits that the power there is an 'inscrutable one'.[30] The new *we* is founded upon the ruins of positive reason and its attendant humanism. This prohibits philosophy from describing the prescriptive situation. The true *we* is never *we*, never stabilized in a name for *we*, always undone before being constituted, only identified in the non-identity between *you* – the unnameable one, who requests – and me, the hostage. This *we's* relation to infinitude is not at all to understand the law, but to let itself be possessed by it in the mode of a dispossession, to be 'passive' to the request the law makes.[31] Is this a result, that which results from 'Auschwitz'?

It cannot be a speculative result. Even when dialectical thought is not constituted speculatively, it proceeds to reduce the thought of the absolutely other. The infinity of the Jews, writes Hegel (in Frankfurt, a little before 1880), is a purely 'ideal' master, a master who does not make one work and who is merely the reverse image of his servant. The latter, Abraham, cannot have a mediated relationship with nature because 'he wants *not* to love'; his finitude is that of an animal, but a denatured one. Judaism is what does not arrive at the contradictory unity of determinations. The mind and nature, a people and outsiders, domination and servitude, the family and the State, hate and love, the finite and the infinite are maintained in their unmediated exteriority the one to the other.[32] Henri Meschonnic writes that the phrases devoted to Judaism in *The Spirit of Christianity and its Fate* perpetrated an 'anthropological murder' which Hegel never repudiated.[33] Which he could not repudiate, so much does speculative thought always need to exclude the otherwise-than-being *(l'autrement qu'être)* in order to leave the field clear for mediation.

It is at least advisable to concede that this exclusion can only proceed through inclusion. The Frankfurt phrases, which denied *relevance* and result to Judaism, were not inscribed in the project of a 'final solution' to the Jewish question. They were inscribed in a dialectical movement according to which thought judged oppositional and discontinuous, the thought of finitude and of the bad infinity (to which thought, according to Hegel, Kantianism also belongs), can only find expression because 'we', Greeks and Christians who are in possession of the beautiful totality and of love, can give it that expression, albeit in a contradictory way. This movement is fully expressed, and takes on its properly speculative turn thirty years later in the Berlin *Lectures* on the philosophy of history and the philosophy of religion. There, Judaism becomes necessary in its place; it is not yet what we are, but we needed it to have been what it is: 'In this process which detaches it from its abstract particularity and situates it in its rank among the figures of universal mind, Judaism thus obtains its relative justification.' Mr Bernard Bourgeois writes this without further ado *(sans phrases)*.[34]

Speculation inflicts upon the figure of the marvel and of the hostage, as it does upon all figures, a defiguration which supposedly commutes that figure into its properness (*son propre*). The phrase *Listen, Israel, par excellence* and by its own avowal, does *not know* what it says. To know what it says is to report it, that is, to bring it into a rapport with other phrases. The command contained in the phrase is then suppressed and gives way to a description of the command, something not contained in that phrase. This description, however, reciprocally alters the value of the command: it ceases to be executory, becoming a merely reported prescription. It is not a matter of obeying the prescription or not, but of understanding it and of acquiescing or not to its description. Speculative description takes the command as the referent of its phrase; and the phrase of the impossible commandment (of the impossible *we*), stripped of its referential and pragmatic, that is, practical value, conserves only its value of signification: it becomes the image or autonym of itself. The speculative argument (but, as has been stated, speculation does not even need to be argued) says that if knowledge is the issue, the neutralization of the object is its necessary condition. This neutralization also takes place, so the argument goes, in the reflection of a Kant or a Levinas, but it takes place badly, because it is ignorant of itself. If 'Auschwitz' speaks, it is in order to say not the unintelligible but the intelligible, and it becomes necessary to speculate. If it does not speak, if death is senseless *(insensée)* there, it is because one does not speculate.

VII

What would be a speculative analysis then, that is, with result and gain, of the *Die* at 'Auschwitz'? And what happens in that analysis to the *we*?

Die, I decree it is understood as an unmediated, presupposed phrase. As has been seen, a first analysis dissolves it into two phrases: *Let them die, it's our law,* and *Let us die, it's their law.* From this, one cannot pass directly to the *we*, contrary to what subjective thought (philosophy of enunciation) affirms. For the *I* of the deportee, the *he* of the legislator remains exterior. This exteriority is that of every situation of obligation posited in terms of subjectivity. The opposition between the infinitude (or the universality) of the law and the finitude (or the particularity) of the obligee cannot be overcome.

The *I* of the one would have to become a *he for himself* and not only for the other. The infinity of the legislator would have to become *for itself* the finitude (of a good conscience, of the absence of risk, of force); the finitude of the obligated one would have to become *for itself* the infinity (that he knows and wants the law ordering his death).

The two poles of the opposition disappear then, however; they become identical, each one containing the finitude and the infinity of the other. They can be confused. But the obligation and the command have also disappeared. There is a *we*, but it is empty, or abstract, the mere addition of an *I* and an *I*. This abstraction is the work of a thought which is exterior to the obligation, which has transformed each of the *I*s into a *he*, which has placed them within its own phrase universe as its referent. This external thought is that of the philosopher of understanding, who stands above the battle between the command and its impossibility. It is he who effaces the differences, he for whom the respective points of view are inessential and become interchangeable, he through whom the *we* is instituted as an abstract solution.

This separate *we* cannot be one wherein the contradiction of obligation expresses itself in its resolution. What 'we' have just said, 'we' have said *as if* 'we' were in turn the legislator and the obligee, the infinity of the one and the finitude of the other, then the finitude of the first and the infinity of the second. 'We' have thus effected what we were seeking. 'We' were seeking a *we*, that *we* was what was sought, and therefore what sought itself. It expresses itself at the end just as it effected itself from the beginning. It is not the sum of the *I*s comprehended within the command of the norm; it is the contradictory movement that goes from one to the other.

The name of this movement is obligation, for the latter is nothing more than the contradiction that has just been traversed. This contradiction can only be traversed because 'we' are able to traverse it, that is, because there is already obligation. But the obligation is at first only 'near itself' and 'for us', for an external, abstract *we*. It is only truly what it is when it is 'for itself', in the expression of itself, when the movement by which it is effected names itself.

In exploding the contradiction of *Die, I decree it*, 'Auschwitz' does not fall into unintelligibility; it effects the obligation, but in its impossibility. Its speculative result is . . . the analysis that has just been carried out; the anonym 'Auschwitz' receives therein its speculative baptism.

It would not be very opportune to object that this dialectical deduction in turn presupposes what it deduces, that is, the *we*. One could look for the *we* that packs the *Phenomenology of Mind;* one could show that 'it articulates natural and philosophical consciousness with each other', that it 'is the unity of absolute knowledge and anthropology, of God and man, of onto-theo-teleology and humanism'.[35] Such is without a doubt its at once presupposed and supposed equivocacy within the phenomenological field. But this is because this field is that of the experience of consciousness, wherein, as the *Encyclopaedia* states, '[the 'I'] is one side of the relationship and the whole relationship' (HP 153). This equivocacy vanishes when logic, or objective mind, is involved, that is, when speculative discourse is extended to objects which are not part of consciousness. In these cases, the *we* is seen to occupy the necessary though subordinate place of the abstract moment, of the moment of exteriority. The place of the other of speculation (i.e., the understanding) within speculation. On the other hand, the *we* does not appear in the supreme moment, that of the Idea of philosophy, which is said to be 'near and for itself *[an und für sich]*' (HP 315; translation modified). No *we* is needed then in order for this idea, which is God, to express its relation to itself.

In the 1830 edition of the *Encyclopaedia*, the expression *für uns, for us,* is generally combined with the expression *an sich, near itself (auprès de soi)*. Together, these expressions mark the abstract moment in the development of the concept, wherein is maintained the exteriority between the object of thought (the *self [le soi]* which is near itself) and the subject (the *we* that posits this self). The speculative moment, on the contrary, comes when this exteriority is dissolved, when the *self* comes 'in the place of' the *we* (which is no longer there), when the object of thought becomes the thought which objectifies itself as well as the object which thinks itself, the *für sich*, the *for itself (pour soi)*. This distinction is evidenced by, among others, the difference between a cause and an aim: 'It is only when near itself, or for us, that the cause is in the effect made for the first time a cause, and that it there returns *into itself*. The aim, on the other hand, is expressly stated as containing the determinations *in its own self* – the effect, namely, which in the purely causal relation is never free from otherness. . . . The aim then requires to be speculatively apprehended . . .' (HL 268; translation modified). Similarly, in the case of reciprocal action, *die Wechselwirkung,* it is at first just 'near themselves' and 'in our reflection' that the determinations of this form of actuality are 'null and void' *(nichtige)*; the *Wechselwirkung* only attains its unity when the unity of the determinations 'is also *for itself*', when reciprocal action itself suppresses each determination by inverting it into its opposite (origin and effect, action and reaction, etc. [HL 218; translation modified]). The price paid for speculation is the suppression of the *we* as an identity that thinks or speaks for the outside.

The first *Realphilosophie* of Jena teaches that 'the sign as *something actual* (must) thus directly vanish' and that 'the name is in itself something, it *persists*, without either the thing or the subject. In the name the *self*-subsisting reality of the sign is nullified.'[36] The *I*, the *he*, the *you*, the *we* are signs, as are all pronouns; identity cannot take place in them. Identity takes place in names, in the case of 'Auschwitz' the name of obligation, and it takes place at the cost of the designification of signs, of the destruction of pronouns. This is how 'the thing works'.

And if there is not even a name, if the name of 'Auschwitz' is a nameless name, does it follow that the thing does not work? The thing is more complicated, it also devours names. For names are again only what memory makes out of signs.[37] Memory, though, is itself 'the one-sided mode of thought's *existence*', its 'mechanical' side, thought which is 'for us or near itself', as the *Encyclopaedia* recalls (HP 223; translation modified). On the contrary then, if there were nothing but names the thing could not work precisely because the machine of names, nominalism, would work in its place and because, as Jean-Luc Nancy has written, 'the disappearance of sense would resemble the death of Molière.'[38] Derrida 'risks' the 'proposition' according to which 'what Hegel *could never think*, is a machine which would work.'[39] Machines work through a loss. Speculation is a machine that gains, and it is therefore a deranged machine. The 'thing' only works by throwing its gains – including names and pronouns – out of kilter.

This throwing out of kilter is a necessity which is itself a purposiveness (*finalité*). 'Reason,' it is written in the Preface to the *Phenomenology*, 'is *purposive activity*', '*das zweckmässige Tun*' (PG 26, PM 83). The model for this purposiveness is borrowed from Aristotle. The speculative game only appears monstrous from the perspective of the understanding, but the understanding fails to recognize its presuppositions accepting them as evidences, as axioms, or as conditions of possibility. It admits first phrases. There are none. The first is also the last. One begins with philosophy's need for a figure in which the mind is only 'near itself', but every phrase is needed in order to express this object of need and to suppress the need, in order for the mind 'to become for itself what it is near itself' (HP 25; translation modified). In the speculative phrase, the purposiveness of the for-itself is what guides the rebound. The aim is the 'reconciliation of the self-conscious reason with the reason which *is* in the word – in other words, with actuality' (HL 8). This aim is *ceaselessly* attained, and for that reason it is never attained. If it is attained, it is not attained. When it is not attained, it is attained nonetheless. This rule is that of immanent derivation and of negative dialectics. Here, the rule has been applied to the aim, that is, to the result. But a dialecticalized aim is still just as much an aim. The teleology has merely sophisticated itself.

VIII

The *we* is not what resists; what resists is mind proceeding towards itself. The latter's infinitude throws the phrase-stages out of kilter in order to express them. The *we* phrase is such a phrase-stage. The linkages are always made on the same side, that of expression, of gain over infinity, of infinite gain.

There is nevertheless something presupposed in this way of proceeding. In the Preface to the first edition (1817) of the *Encyclopaedia*, Hegel criticizes 'a *manner* of dealing with philosophical objects which has become habitual, and which consists in *presupposing a schema*' in such a way that 'by the strangest of misunderstandings, the necessity of a concept will have been sufficiently demonstrated by means of fortuitous and arbitrary connections.'[40] The presupposition of speculation is that one is the aim; or, to state it better, that the aim should be set on the one. This presupposition supports the third of the rules we isolated, the rule of expression. To make two out of one is negative reason; to make one out of two is positive reason.

Now, this is the presupposition only of speculative discourse. *One* is the aim because the aim of this discourse is its own origin, its engenderment, as true. The only true *Umkehrung*, the one ceaselessly found in all the figures of this discourse, is the one which shifts the entire universe of the unmediated phrase, not onto the referential pole of the philosophical phrase (that is the operation of the understanding), but onto its addressor and addressee poles. There, the phrase is transformed into its for-itself, that is to say, it is transformed into the philosophical phrase. The *Resultat* is to be had for this price.

This is a rule in a phrase game, namely, the rule of expression in the speculative game. This rule is permitted by individual languages. It violates Aristotelian logic and propositional logic. It endows the philosophical phrase, however, with something these logics cannot give it: the engenderment of itself as true.

One cannot object to the functioning of this rule on the grounds that 'it doesn't really work that way'. Only the following objection can be raised: that although it is a rule in a phrase game where the self-engenderment of the phrase is, in fact, what is at stake, *this rule cannot itself engender itself.* The objection is not that of a logical paradox as in Russell, but that of the limitation of formal systems as in Gödel.[41] If one says that the rule of engenderment *results* from the analysis of what happens in dialectical analysis (as we have suggested in the case of obligation), then one presupposes the rule, under the name of result.

The condition whereby the engenderment of the rule is what is at stake in a language game is the rule in the philosophical game insofar as it has, as one says, 'imperfect information' with regards to its rules.[42] But insofar as the rule is what is at stake in the game, *it is not* the rule, and the game is played without its consideration. And when it is 'identified' as the rule of the game that is being played, that rule *is no longer* whatever is at stake in the philosophical game.

One will recognize in this last statement the dialectical phrase *par excellence.* The dialectical phrase is not, however, the speculative phrase. The above statement excludes the game where *the loser wins.* At the level of rules, there operates one where *the winner loses*; it is called Maxwell's demon, Brillouin's argument, Gödel's theorem.[43]

The position of the third rule, the speculative rule, remains necessarily presupposed. This is not the case for the rule of equivocacy and of immanent derivation. A rule like, *Equivocate (or dialecticalize) every phrase, including the present one,* implies that the operators of equivocacy and of dialectics apply to the rule itself. This self-application corresponds to the following rule: in philosophical discourse, every phrase which presents itself as its rule can be put back into play through equivocation and dialecticalization.

This rule is only permissive. It corresponds to scepticism. Philosophical discourse entails another rule, which is prescriptive. This rule prescribes that philosophical discourse identify the rule which is its own. In no way does it declare what this last rule might consist in. In particular, it does not presuppose that this rule is that of identity (*Selbst*). Nor even that this rule is identical to itself (the prescriptive rule). In the philosophical game there can be no rule which anticipates the nature of the aim.

The fact that identity is the aim cannot be engendered from the rule that makes identity into an aim. The speculative rule, *Engender every phrase as the expression or identity of the preceding ones, including the present one,* is impossible. For taken as a rule, this phrase is logically the first one, and has no precedent. It cannot then be the expression or identity (*Resultat*) of those phrases which precede it. It is understood that, for Hegel, this 'beginning' can only come at the end, as a result, after the phrases of which it presents itself as the expression or final identity. Moreover, it can only appear as this final result because it has been presupposed from the beginning, as the rule for the linking of the first phrase (itself) with the following phrase and those afterwards. Now, taken as a first phrase, it is senseless. If, however, it is not applied from the beginning (to itself), there is no need to find it at the end, and thus it is not the *Resultat*; not having been engendered as such, it is not the rule that is sought.

All that the rule for philosophical linkage can prescribe is that what is at stake in philosophical phrases is a rule (or rules) to be sought, without it being possible to announce yet what this rule says. It follows that from one phrase to the next, the alterity each time stays intact. The *one* implied in *One phrase* (see above, section IV) is not a one abstracted from all other phrases, through which it would lose itself in order to rejoin itself, but one with others. *With* indicates at least two types of relation: the others within the one, the one amongst the others.

The others within the one: the qualitative infinity. As it stands, a phrase is perfect, its sense is complete (thus Hegel can write that 'in a concept there is nothing further to be thought than the concept itself' (HL 6-7; translation modified)). Thus, a phrase is finite; it only presents what it presents. This *only* implies therefore that a phrase also co-presents something else, which it does not present. Other possible universes are copresent with the one it presents. They are copresent, not as something missing in it (for why would a phrase 'want' to present everything?), but as what exceeds it (its equivocacy): copresent universes are always implied, presupposed, connoted, etc. The interrogative, *Can you come see him?* copresents, among others, a universe which could also be presented by a prescriptive such as, *Come see him.* This last universe, however, is not presented by the interrogative.

The other phrases are incommensurable with this phrase; otherwise, each would be indiscernible from the others. The fact that the others would be *with* the phrase in question – *in* it – turns the latter into an infinity of thought, an *infinitum actu,* analogous to the one which Spinoza describes to Lewis Meyer[44] and which Hegel reconsiders in his *Science of Logic* under the title of the 'good infinity'.[45]

The other phrases' heterogeneity in relation to the phrase in question consists in their incommensurability or untranslatability. The abyss which separates the two Kantian *Critiques* is a trace of this heterogeneity at the very moment when it is annihilated by the project to present complementarity. The 'late' Wittgenstein is more radical:

one language game cannot be translated into another. But Wittgenstein keeps to (empirical) descriptions, leaving aside only his notion of an inexpressible.

The one amongst the others: the quantitative infinity. The surplus of others within the one indicates a necessity, the only one, which is to link up the other phrases to the one. The linkage is regressive-progressive, dialectical in the paralogistic sense, when and only when it *aims* (here is the aim) to formulate the other phrases that are within the one (the philosophical language game). Were those phrases already there? To apprehend them is to formulate them; and formulated, they are *there no longer*. The precursor arrives too late. This phrase here is destroyed. Another, which is now this phrase here, presents a universe reputedly copresented by the 'preceding' one. (Here, Hegel would write that the concept 'suppresses its presupposition, but at the same time, it is the concept alone which, in the act of positing itself, makes its presupposition' (HL 221; translation modified)).

But the linkage does not have to be linked this way. To *Can you come see him?* can be linked the following phrases: *Why not?; You think so?; My car isn't working; Of course; I can't;* and many others including, *How is Chantal?* So goes conversation, the *Konversation,* the chat, the aggregate (*Aggregat*) of phrases rejected in the Preface to the *Phenomenology.* A conversation is also a diversation.

To link is to disjoin. The calm completeness of the infinity *actu* at rest within a phrase becomes discontinuous. (There is still too much substantialism, too much *rest,* in the idea that a phrase is deferred from itself *[se diffère]*.)

The one (a phrase) is not first, nor last, nor both; it is amongst the others which are within it.

The *absolutely other* is a phrase which designates the incommensurability between the universe of the prescriptive phrase (request) and the universes of the descriptive phrases which take it as their referent.

'Auschwitz' is an abhorrent model for this incommensurability. The notion of incommensurability has been elaborated by Kant, by Wittgenstein (in his 'Lecture on Ethics'[46]), by Levinas. But in a one-sided way. For this lack of measure (*démesure*) (in the sense that rational activity is an activity measured by its aim, *zweckmässig*) is not the exclusive privilege of prescriptive phrases. It can be at work in all linkages, in all the alterities between phrases, to the extent that each of these alterities is *what happens,* is the case, *der Fall.* And perhaps every phrase, even if it is 'well known', recognizable, harbours the force of what falls (*fallen*), of what runs you over (*ce qui vous court dessus*) (*occur*). This lack of measure indicates that the being-with of phrases is neither a being-as nor a being-together, nor even a being-without. It indicates that reason is not sufficient (to make links in accordance with an aim); that the joust, the *agōn*, of phrases is perpetual; that justice is – nevertheless and *justly* because it is a matter neither for treastises nor for systems (for simple repetitive linkages) – always possible, albeit as prudence (what Aristotle calls *phronesis*): the prudence to make or speak the linkage 'that suits' in a particular case, without there being known what the rule of suitability is.

'If there are margins, is there still *a* philosophy, *the* philosophy?' asks Derrida.[47] There is no longer any philosophy if it presupposes the phrase of self-engenderment. If that phrase is not presupposed, is philosophy aimless, endless, and therefore truthless? Is it nihilistic? empiricist? modest? It might be as follows: with a phrase, the attempt to link on a phrase which presents universes copresented by the former; and thus to 'invent' rules for the linkings of phrases; and with a rule, in turn, to link on a phrase . . .

The following remarks, transcribed by Jean-François Lyotard, are taken from the discussion which took place after the reading of 'Phrasing "After Auschwitz"' at Cerisy.

Derrida states that he finds himself in agreement with the talk, that he does not want to 'yield to this pathos' (of agreement), that he seeks to 'link on, no, not to link on, but to add phrases'. He wonders if 'the question' is not that of 'the multiplicity of proper names', if 'the very grave stakes of what Lyotard has given to think' are not 'the fact that there are several proper names'. He wonders, first of all, about the 'schema' presupposed by Lyotard's discourse centred upon Auschwitz; and he thinks he perceives that 'in referring to this nameless name, in making a model of it, that discourse risks reconstituting a kind of centrality,' a *we* for this occasion, one which is certainly not that of speculative dialectics, but which is related to the unanimous privilege 'we Western Europeans' grant Auschwitz in 'the combat or the question' we oppose to speculative dialectics, to 'a certain kind of Western reason, etc.'. The risk is that this *we* 'would consign to oblivion or would brush aside (*latéraliserait*) proper names other than that of Auschwitz and which are just as abhorrent as it,' names which have names, and names which don't. 'And my worry,' says Derrida, 'is that a certain *we* reconstitutes itself in reference to what you have said so admirably about Auschwitz.'

Derrida then formulates 'another worry', which resembles the less dramatic or 'more formal' one he feels when he reads Levinas: 'Despite all the indisputable things he says about the utterly-other *(le tout-autre)*, about the hiatus, the relation to the utterly-other gives rise to linkings of phrases.' This difficulty, Derrida calls in a text devoted to Levinas, *'sériature'*. By the same token, we have 'to make links historically, politically, and ethically with the name, with that which absolutely refuses linkage'. Derrida asks: 'If there is today an ethical or political question and if there is somewhere a *One must*, it must link up with a *one must make links with Auschwitz . . . (Il faut enchaîner sur Auschwitz)*. Perhaps Auschwitz prescribes – and the other proper names of analogous tragedies (in their irreducible dispersion) pre-scribe – that we make links. It does not prescribe that we overcome the un-linkable, but rather: because it is unlinkable, we are enjoined to make links. I do not mean to say that one must make links in spite of the linkable; I mean to say that the unlinkable of Auschwitz prescribes that we make links.' If Lyotard was able to move us, it is because the presupposition shared by all is that Auschwitz is intolerable and therefore that one must say and do something, so that it does not, for instance, start over again . . . .

Finally a couple of 'ancillary' words on difference. Refusing the nascent pathos of this subject, Derrida states:

I would say with a smile that of course the word seems to imply some nostalgia. It is nonetheless an economical word which has a *Zweideutigkeit* upon which I do not wish to dwell but with which I can reckon *(compter)*. One of the two senses can imply nostalgia, but the other does not imply nostalgia very much, if at all; I have explained myself on this point elsewhere. I do not say this in order to correct an interpretation – that would be absolutely ridiculous here – I say it in order to break with the kind of pathos of agreement in which I have been up until a little while ago, and in order to try to understand, no matter how far this agreement may be pursued, what the fundamental difference of tone or affect is between what you say and what I would say. In regards to nostalgia, I said that I wanted to break with it, but I guard (and I assume this guardednesss because that's the way it is), I guard a nostalgia for nostalgia, and that is perhaps a sign that when I say, 'Nostalgia would be better,' I continue to, etc. You, on the other hand – and I was very sensitive to this again today, I have always been sensitive to this in reading you, but I was again even today when I have never felt myself closer to you – you have a style, a mode and a tone of rupture with nostalgia (and with everything it brings or connotes) that is resolute, trenchant, wilful, etc., and I thought to myself that perhaps this, and nothing more, was what was fundamentally at play in this question.

Lyotard recalls, first of all, that he was tempted to suggest, perhaps in 'too resolute' a fashion, that 'every phrase, if it is apprehended as an occurrence in the strong sense of the term, can become a model' (German: *Modell (mold)* specifies Maurice de Gandillac). In this sense, there can be innumerable name-models, and Derrida is right to underscore this because there ensues a considerable displacement in how one thinks about history. Then, to the objection of breaking too quickly with dialectics, Lyotard answers: 'On the contrary, while working on this talk, I had the feeling of making a enormous effort to try not to break with dialectics.' Whence the accent on the 'One must make links', presented as the sole necessity and sole enigma. He strove not to let this 'One must' slip into a philosophy of the will. But neither does he believe that it arises (*relève*) from ethics: 'the "One must" is much more stupid than that.' One must make links after Auschwitz, but without a speculative result. As for the question about the *we*, he is inclined to think in the Hassidic tradition reported by *Gog and Magog*, in the sense of the impossibility for a community to conceive the following: 'We would merely be hostages of the 'One must make links', '*we* are not in possession of its rule, *we* seek it, *we* make links in seeking it; it is thus the stakes but not the rule for the linkage.' This *we* works, or has to work no matter where 'to vary all the rules of linkage whatever they might be, in music, in painting, in film, in political economy' in a way not unrelated to Derridean dissemination. This quest for the rule of linkage is a quest for the intelligible. Adorno speaks of the legible, Derrida of the illegible. This is a radical divergence, and yet 'if *we* are the community of hostages of the "One must make links", it is that we are learning to read, therefore that we do not know how to read, and that for *us*, to read is precisely to read the illegible.'

As for the question of nostalgia, Lyotard says to Derrida: 'I will not intervene because, after all, you have turned it into an affair of idiosyncrasy.' Derrida: 'Something like that.' Lyotard: 'Then, I would be indiscreet if I were to intervene in your nostalgia just as you were indiscreet to intervene in my resoluteness' (laughter). Derrida: 'It was a little more than an idiosyncratic comparison . . . : in the resolute break with nostalgia, there is a psychoanalytic-Hegelian logic, a rigid relation, not very well regulated' (laughter); 'there is perhaps more nostalgia in you than in me' (laughter). 'This is the suspicion rooted in the question about style' (laughter). Lyotard: 'Do you have the right rule then?' Derrida: 'No.' Lyotard observes that he did not speak about Heidegger, even though ontology is evidently what is implicated in the idea of a phrase game wherein what is at stake is that a phrase present the entailed presentation. This omission is not due to an excess of 'resolution'; rather, it is that the interest of phrases (in the Kantian sense of the interest of reason) does not appear to him to be on the side of ontology. The notion of interest is a little narrow, but it introduces what is at stake in a justice or justness (*justesse*) where one did not expect to find it. Derrida observes that the relation to nostalgia is always badly regulated, and that 'to dismiss it purely and simply' is a case of a bad rule. Lyotard says he had hoped to evoke Derrida's agreement by proposing a less nostalgic acceptation of difference (laughter), which he sees emerging in the development of his work. Derrida acknowledges this shift, but he repeats that 'in your case it is the face that breaks away from nostalgia' that is mostly seen.

NOTES

1 Translator's note: This paper is a transcript of a lecture given by Jean-Françqis Lyotard in 1980 on the occasion of the colloquium, 'Les fins de l'homme: à partir du travail de Jacques Derrida', Cerisy-la-Salle.
2 Hegel, *Aphorismen über Nichtwissen und absolutes Wissen im Verhältnisse zur christlichen Glaubenserkenntnis. Von Karl Friedrich Göshel*, in *Werke in zwanzig Bänden* (Frankfurt: Suhrkamp Verlag, 1970) XI pp. 380–1.
3 Translator's note: At the risk of some awkwardness and confusion, I will translate the French word *phrase* by its English cognate rather than by the semantically more correct *sentence*. English *phrase* like French *phrase* can be used without appreciable semantic difference either as a noun or as a verb, whereas *to sentence* is a verb used only in a juridical sense, as when one speaks of 'sentencing someone to death'. The explicit content of this essay would seem to make even a neologistic use of the verb, *to sentence*, undesirable and possibly dangerous. *Phrase*, on the other hand, is a term of very wide extension and encompasses utterances at various levels between word and sentence. My hope then is that wide applicability of the term, *phrase*, will open a space wherein Lyotard's notion of phrase can more forcefully take on the precise formulations he gives it in the course of the essay. These formulations (especially those in section IV) show that what is being considered under the rubric 'phrase' is *not* a grammatical – nor even a linguistic – entity, but a *pragmatic* one, and that the essay's central concern is with the possibility or impossibility of phrasing certain things, that is, of being able or not to make certain phrases. As Lyotard

says at the end of section IV, 'the rules for phrase games are not structures of language'.

4 Jacques Derrida, *Margins of Philosophy*, tr. Alan Bass (Chicago: University of Chicago Press, 1982). The citations are taken from, respectively, 'Différance' p. 27; 'Ousisa and Grammē' p. 67; 'The Pit and the Pyramid' p. 107; 'The Ends of Man' p. 121.

5 Derrida, 'Tympan' p. xxvi.

6 Derrida, 'Signature Event Context', p. 329.

7 Theodor Adorno, *Negative Dialectics*, tr. E. B. Ashton (New York: The Seabury Press, 1973) pp. 406–8. Hereafter cited as ND in the text.

8 Derrida, 'The Pit and the Pyramid' p. 107.

9 Hegel, *The Phenomenology of Mind*, tr. J. B. Baillie (New York: Harper & Row, 1976) pp. 144, 142. Hereafter cited as PM in the text.

10 Hegel, *Phänomenologie des Geistes, Werke* III, p. 92; hereafter cited as PG. Also PM, p. 160.

11 Translator's note: *Supprimer* is how Jean Hyppolite translates *aufheben* into French.

12 *Hegel's Philosophy of Mind: Being Part Three of the ENCYCLOPAEDIA OF THE PHILOSOPHICAL SCIENCES (1830)*, tr. William Wallace (Oxford: Clarendon Press, 1971) paragraph 386, 22–3. References to the German text will be to *Enzyklopädie der philosophischen Wissenschaften in Grundrisse*, ed. F. Nicolin and O. Pöggeler (Hamburg: Felix Meiner, 1959). Hereafter cited as HP in the text.

13 Derrida, 'Tympan' xviii.

14 Hegel, *Texte zur Philosophischen Propädeutik, Werke* IV, 12. The passage is from paragraph 12 of the section entitled 'Philosophischen Enzyklopädie'.

15 *Hegel's Logic: Being Part One of the ENCYCLOPAEDIA OF THE PHILOSOPHICAL SCIENCES (1830)*, tr. William Wallace (Oxford: Clarendon Press, 1975) para. 81, p. 115 and paragraph 82, p. 119; translation modified. Hereafter cited as HL in the text.

16 Hegel, 'Verhältnis des Skeptizismus zur Philosophie'. *Aufsätze aus dem Kritischen Journal der Philosophie, Werke* II, p. 229.

17 Hegel, *Wissenschaft der Logik, Werke* V pp. 82–4; *Science of Logic,* tr. A. V. Miller (London: George Allen & Unwin, 1969) pp. 82–4.

18 See Jean-Luc Nancy, *La remarque spéculative* (Paris: Galilée, 1973).

19 Translator's note: The antinomy in question is more commonly known by the 'paradox of the liar' wherein it becomes impossible to know whether a liar who claims to be lying is telling the truth or lying. See Lyotard's discussion of this paradox in his 'Sur la force des faibles', *L'Arc 64* (1976), pp. 4–12.

20 The reader will forgive this synopsis. Its excuse is the brevity of life, as Protagoras would say – the brevity of even a long lecture. A slightly less summary exposition is given in 'Analysing Speculative Discourse as Language-Game', tr. G. Bennington, *Oxford Literary Review 4*, 3 (1981), pp. 59–67, reprinted in this volume (ch. 15).

21 Translator's note: The word *relevance* here is to be understood not only in the English sense of pertinency but also as a neologism derived from Derrida's translation of *Aufhebung* as *relève*.

22 Derrida, 'Tympan', p. xiv.

23 See Georges Kalinowski, *La logique des normes* (Paris: PUF, 1972).

24 Emile Benveniste, *Problems in General Linguistics*, tr. Mary E. Meek (Coral Gables: University of Miami Press, 1971).

25 See Nicole Loraux, *L'invention d' Athènes: Histoire de l'oraison funèbre dans la 'cité classique'* (Berlin: Mouton/De Gruyter, 1981).

26 I refer to the threat which, by Hegel's avowal, hangs over the speculative phrase, and which Jean-Luc Nancy has studied in *La remarque spéculative*. The concept's unity always threatens the difference between the subject and the predicate of a proposition, just as metre threatens accent (PM, p. 120).

27 David Rousset, *Le pitre ne rit pas* (Paris: Christian Bourgois, 1979). See also *Les jours de notre mort* (Paris: U.G.E., 1974).

28 Emmanuel Levinas, *Totality and Infinity*, tr. A. Lingis (Pittsburgh: Duquesne University Press, 1969), p. 292; *Otherwise Than Being, or Beyond Essence*, tr. A. Lingis (The Hague: Martinus Nijhoff, 1981), pp. 117-18.

29 Levinas, *Totality and Infinity*, pp. 216-19.

30 '*Unerforschlichen*' in the German. Immanuel Kant, *Critique of Practical Reason*, tr. L. W. Beck (Indianapolis: Liberal Arts Press, 1956), p. 49.

31 Levinas, *Otherwise Than Being*, pp. 111-12; *Quatre lectures talmudiques* (Paris: Gallimard, 1968).

32 Hegel, *The Spirit of Christianity and Its Fate*, tr. T. M. Knox, *Early Theological Writings* (Chicago: University of Chicago Press, 1948), pp. 182-205, 253-61.

33 Henri Meschonnic, *Le signe et le poème* (Paris: Gallimard, 1975) pp. 109-10.

34 Bernard Bourgeois, *Hegel à Francfort* (Paris: Vrin, 1970) p. 118. Levinas protests against this in *Difficile liberté* (Paris: Albin Michel, 1963).

35 Derrida, 'The Ends of Man' p. 121.

36 Hegel, *First Philosophy of Spirit*, ed. and tr. H. S. Harris, *System of Ethical Life and First Philosophy of Spirit* (Albany: State University of New York Press, 1979) pp. 221-2.

37 Hegel, *First Philosophy of Spirit*, p. 221.

38 *La remarque spéculative* p. 157. Nancy's commentary deals particularly with paragraph 462 of the *Encyclopaedia*. Translator's note: It will be recalled that Molière met his death on stage while performing *Le malade imaginaire*. Nancy explains his analogy as follows: 'To play knowing that it is only a play *and* that a fearful, mortal actuality is at play in this play, such would be the almost intolerable experience of Hegelian discourse ...' (p. 157).

39 Derrida, 'The Pit and Pyramid', p. 107.

40 Hegel, 'Vorrede zur ersten Ausgabe (1817)', *Encyclopädie*, pp. 20-1.

41 Translator's note: According to Gödel's theorem, the internal logical consistency of a formal system cannot be proved within the system.

42 Translator's note: The reference is to Anatol Rapoport, *Fights, Games, and Debates* (Ann Arbor: University of Michigan Press, 1960), pp. 152–4.

43 Translator's note: The problem of Maxwell's Demon posits a case wherein the second law of thermodynamics (commonly known as the theory of entropy) could be reversed by the existence of a being small enough to separate and redirect individual molecules according to their velocity. Brillouin solved this problem by his notion of information as negative entropy or 'negentropy'. In other words, the information gained in a scientific experiment is itself only gained by an even greater gain in entropy.

44 Spinoza, letter to Lewis Meyer, 20 April 1663, letter 29 in *Correspondence, The Chief Works of Benedict de Spinoza*, tr. R.H.M. Elwes (New York: Dover Publications, 1951) II, pp. 317–23.

45 Hegel, *Wissenschaft der Logik*, pp. 291–3; *Science of Logic*, pp. 249–51 ('The Specific Nature of the Mathematical Infinite').

46 Translator's note: 'A Lecture on Ethics', *The Philosophical Review 74* (1965), pp. 3–12.

47 Derrida, 'Tympan' p. xvi.

Translated by Georges Van Den Abbeele

20

The Sign of History

Under the somewhat enigmatic title, 'The sign of history', I am going to suggest an introduction to a reconsideration of the historico-political reality of our time. In order to do this I shall appeal to the critical thought of Immanuel Kant. I hope that you will see why this detour is necessary as you follow it with me.

Anyone who tries to reflect on historico-political reality today (as always) comes up against names – proper names. These names form part of the treasure of phrases that he has received in his share of language and that he must continue by allowing new phrases. For we have all of us a sort of debt, or a sort of rivalry, with respect to names.

These proper names have the following remarkable property: they place modern historical or political commentary in abeyance. Adorno pointed out that Auschwitz is an abyss in which the philosophical genre of Hegelian speculative discourse seems to disappear, because the name 'Auschwitz' invalidates the presupposition of that genre, namely that all that is real is rational, and that all that is rational is real. Budapest '56 is another abyss in which the genre of (Marxist) historical materialist discourse seems to disappear, because this name invalidates the presupposition of that genre, namely that all that is proletarian is communist, and that all that is communist is proletarian. Nineteen sixty-eight is an abyss in which the genre of democratic liberal discourse (republican dialogue) seems to disappear, because this name invalidates the presupposition of that genre, namely that all that concerns the political community can be said within the rules of the game of parliamentary representation. The crisis of over-capitalisation that the world economy has been suffering since 1974 and will suffer for some time to come invalidates the presupposition of the discursive genre of post-Keynesian political economy, namely that a harmonious regulation of needs and the means to satisfy them in work and in capital, with a view to the greatest enjoyment of goods and services for all – that this regulation is possible and on the way to being achieved.

One is tempted to close these wounds as quickly as possible, to forget these names, to re-establish these genres in their respective pretensions to universal validity in terms of historico-political reality, and to carry through to completion the project of 'modernity', as Habermas puts it. From all sides we are being urged to restore confidence in one or other of these genres. The philosopher tries, rather, to take his inquiry further, although in fact these names show him no direction to take, but only directions not to take. He sees that he is dealing with a sort of *fission* affecting the unity of the great discourses of modernity.

At the same time, this fission affects the rules of philosophical discourse itself. The genres available to this discourse – the Treatise, the Manual, the Meditation, the Discourse, the Dialogue, the Lecture, the Manifesto, the Diary – which are so many ways of proceeding in thought, seem to the philosopher to damp the echo of this fission with the deafness of established forms. For these genres of philosophical discourse have their rules for the formation and linking of phrases, and their rules for the presentation of objects (examples) which can validate these phrases.

The philosopher who is willing to echo the shock associated with these names of history thus discovers or rediscovers that, whatever the genre involved, philosophical discourse obeys a fundamental rule, namely that it must be in search of its rule. Or, if you prefer: its rule is that what is at stake is its rule. How to form phrases and how to link them together is the question of literature too: philosophy adds to this question that of knowing what sort of presentation can validate those phrases and linkings. The philosopher discovers or rediscovers that his discourse takes place only in order to find out how it has the right to take place: and thus that it takes place *before* that finding-out, and that he therefore judges without any criterion (in the absence of established rules) that such and such a phrase is philosophical and that such and such a case permits it to be validated. Philosophical discourse is waiting for its criterion.

By describing the current situation of thought in this way, we cannot fail to encounter the critical reflexion of Kant. Indeed, we are already in his company. The name 'Kant' (it is not the only one) marks at once the prologue and the epilogue to modernity. And as epilogue to modernity, it is also a prologue to postmodernity. The historian assigns to this name a definite chronological place (the end of the eighteenth century), but the philosopher accords this name (and others) the status of a sign, a sign of thought, which is not only determined by its historical context, but which 'gives food for thought' with respect to many other historical contexts, with respect to the context which is ours.

The philosophical phrase according to Kant is an analogon of the political phrase according to Kant. It can be this analogon only insofar as it is critical, and not doctrinal. The doctrinal, or systematic, phrase must come after the critical phrase: the rule for it is to be found in the regulation implied by the idea of system, and is an organ of the organic body of doctrine – a legitimated phrase. In order to establish its legitimacy, it has been necessary to judge its pretension to validity: if it has the pretension of speaking the truth, this means judging if and how it manages to do so; if its pretension is that of speaking the just or the good, this means judging if and how it manages to do so; and so on. These judgements bearing on the respective pretensions of the various families of phrases (cognitive, ethical, juridical, etc.), and these verdicts which establish the respective validity of each of them in its field, territory or domain are the work of the critique. It is well known that Kant often symbolizes the critical activity as that of a tribunal or a judge. But this judge cannot simply be a magistrate, for he has at his disposal no code of law, criminal or civil, nor even a collection of already-judged cases, for the conduct of his enquiry or the formulation of his verdict. He does not judge pretensions with the yardstick of an established, incontestable law. This law must in its turn come under his examination. From this point of view, critical philosophy is in the position of a juridical authority which must declare: 'this is the case, this phrase is the right one' (with respect to the true, the good, even the just) – in this position, rather than in that of an authority (in any case entirely illusory, and in the first place illusory for Kant himself) which would only have to apply, without further ceremony, an already established rule to a new piece of data. This does not mean that this authority has at its disposal no criterion by which to make its evaluations, but that the applicability of the criterion in the given case is itself subject to evaluation. And then either one must admit a regressive search for criteria of criteria *ad infinitum*, or else place one's faith in that 'gift of nature' called judgement, which allows us to say, 'here, it is the case'. Now, according to Kant, it is the case of philosophy, as critical philosophy, to say 'it is the case'.

Next, how does the critical philosopher judge that it is the case when there is no intuition to present for the case? In the *Critique of Judgement*, Kant makes a distinction between two modes of presentation, or hypotyposes. For determinant judgements, that is when we are dealing with descriptive phrases, either these phrases are experience-phrases (empirical concepts), and intuition presents them with objects as *examples*, or else they are knowledge-phrases, and pure intuition presents them with objects as *schemata*. When we are dealing with Ideas (of the world, of the beginning, of the element, of the first cause or origin, of God and of course of historical totality), in which case intuition cannot, by definition, present anything as an object, presentation takes place indirectly by analogy: 'One submits an intuition such that with respect to it the procedure of the faculty of judgement is simply analogous with the procedure it follows when it schematises.' The form of presentation, that of the intuitive mode (the schema) is drawn out from the concept which can be intuited (since this latter is absent), and under this form is placed another intuition, 'equally empirical', which would, in sum, allow the validation of the Idea if it were a concept of the understanding. In other words, the non-cognitive phrase, which is descriptive but dialectical, is presented with an 'as if' referent, that is, one which would be its referent if the phrase were cognitive. This indirect presentation is called symbolic presentation, or presentation by symbols, and makes use of *analoga*.

In this way the critical philosopher can continue judging a phrase, even when there is no empirical case directly presentable for its validation. Through the analogy all properly philosophical (i.e. critical) phrases operate like an external critique, and *must* do so, at least if they are striving for conformity with their Idea. It is because it has to judge, and more particularly to find *analoga* (symbols or others) for its Ideas (including the Idea of itself) that philosophy cannot be learned: 'At most, one can learn to *philosophize*.'

It remains to argue the assertion that this reflecting condition is analogous with that of the political, as Kant sees it.

Kant's historico-political texts are, *grosso modo*, scattered through the three *Critiques* and a dozen or so opuscules. The Critique of Political Reason was not written. It is legitimate, within certain limits yet to be determined, to see in this dispersion, whatever its 'cause' (demanded too hastily by the phrase of understanding, the cognitive phrase), the sign of a particular heterogeneity of the political as an 'object' of phrases. This heterogeneity of the object is already noticeable in the third *Critique*. Here the faculty of judgement is provided not with one specific object, but with at least two – art and nature. I say 'at least', because of the problem (which might be the whole problem) of knowing whether this faculty of judgement is indeed a faculty. Kant has previously given this word 'faculty' a precise meaning – a potential of phrases subject to a group of rules of formation and presentation (in the Kantian sense), when it was a matter of sensitivity, understanding and reason for theoretical matters, of reason alone for practical matters. But in fact judgement intervenes already and necessarily, every time one has to say that 'it is the case': in other words in order to establish presentation – in cognitive phrases under the rule of the schema, in dialectical argumentative phrases under that of the *symbol*, and in prescriptive phrases (in evaluation of responsibility and morality) under that of the *type*.

In the Introduction to the third *Critique*, the dispersion of families of phrases is not only recognized, but is dramatized to such an extent that the problem is that of finding 'transitions' (*Übergänge*) between these heterogeneous types of phrases. And because of its very ubiquity which I have just recalled (that is, the fact that it is called on every time a phrase has to be validated by a presentation), the 'faculty' of judgement is seen as a potential of interfaculty 'transitions', to such an extent that it is given a major privilege over other faculties when it comes to unification, and simultaneously a major defect when it comes to knowing what object would be specific to it – this defect is that it *has* no determined object. This is why we might wonder if it is indeed a faculty of knowledge in Kant's sense. In all the families of phrases, however heterogeneous they are with respect to each other, what Kant obstinately calls the 'faculty of judgement' is the determination of the right mode of object-presentation for each of these families.

Suppose we had to present an object for the Idea of the proliferation of the faculties seen as capacities for having objects (as domains, territories or fields): this object with which to validate the dispersion or fission of the faculties can only be a symbol – I would suggest that of an archipelago. Each family of phrases would be like an island, and the faculty of judgement would be (at least in part) like a ship-fitter or an admiral, sending out expeditions with the job of presenting one island with what they had found ('invented', in the etymological sense) on the others. This task-force or venture-force has no object, but requires a *milieu*: the sea, the *Archepelagos*, the major sea as the Aegean used to be called. In the Introduction to the third *Critique*, this sea has a different name, that of the 'field', the *Feld*: 'To the extent that concepts are referred to objects without one's considering whether a knowledge of these objects is possible or not, they have their field, which is determined solely according to the relationship of their object to our faculty of knowing in general.' And the end of the same Introduction tells us that this faculty of knowing *in general* includes the understanding, the faculty of judgement, and reason. All these faculties find their objects in the field, some marking out a territory, others a domain: the faculty of judgement marks out neither, but looks after the transitions between those of the others. So this faculty is, rather, that of the *milieu* in which all marking-out of limits to legitimacy takes place.

More still, it is what allowed territories and domains *to be* marked out, and what established each family's authority over its island. And it could do this only because of the commerce it keeps going between them.

At this point we ought to establish this on the basis of cases drawn from critical activity itself. We would examine how, and at the cost of what transitions, the beautiful can stand as a symbol of moral good, as explained in the third *Critique*. How, and at the cost of what transitions, the maxims of ethical action, the categorical imperative, as Kant writes in the second *Critique*, 'must withstand the test of the form of a natural law in general', i.e. how and at what cost the pure 'Act' is accompanied by the analogical '*so dass* (meaning "in such a way that" and/or "as if") the maxim of your will could be laid down as the principle of a universal legislation'. Here the transition is called a *type*: Kant writes, 'Natural law serves only as a *type* for a law of freedom'. Were it not for this *type*, which results from a transfer from nature to the will, the imperative would provide no guiding thread, but would simply prescribe action without suggesting any regulating Idea (that of a supersensible nature, of a community of practical, i.e. free, beings) to guide the judgement of what must be done. We would examine as further cases of transitions other strange objects of Kant's thought, such as the Ideas of the imagination, which result from a transition from Reason to imagination by inversion: these are intuitions without a concept, whereas the Ideas of Reason are concepts without a sensory intuition. Or again – and these are perhaps more paradoxical – we would examine the ideals of sensibility, which Kant calls 'monograms', and which are 'inimitable models of possible empirical intuitions', that is, 'floating designs', 'incommunicable phantoms' inscribed in the sensibility of painters (and physiognomists), which do not to be sure give them determined rules (of plasticity, for example), but which nonetheless direct their judgement in matters of sensibility.

The importance of the philosophy of the beautiful and the sublime in the first part of the third *Critique* lies both in the de-realization of the object of aesthetic feelings, and in the absence of a real aesthetic faculty of knowing. The same thing holds, perhaps even more radically, for the historico-political object, which as such has no reality, and for any political faculty of knowing, which must remain inexistent. The only things that *are* real (i.e. that for the concept of which intuitions can be presented) are phenomena, all of them both conditioned and conditioning. The series of these phenomena, which makes up the history of humanity (and not even its natural history, only its cosmological history), is never itself given. This series is not given, but is the object of an Idea and, insofar as it is a human world, comes under the same antithetics as the cosmological series in general.

In general in Kant's work the cognitive phrase, with its double criterion of pertinence (with respect to negation or the principle of contradiction on the one hand, and to intuitive perception on the other), is opposed to vain hopes, false promises and prophecies. It is used to refute the right of insurrection and to condemn the violent substitution of a new authority for the old one. The argument runs as follows: the existence of the 'common being' (*das gemeine Wesen*) is the referent of a phrase which is either cognitive (of the understanding) or objective-teleological (finality in organized beings). This common being's proximity to Good is judged in a subjective-teleological phrase (moral finality in rational beings). Revolution breaks open (*Abbruch*) an existing common being: another cannot fail to replace it (by natural law). The heterogeneity of the two families of phrases is not modified. Revolutionary politics is based on a transcendental illusion in the political domain, confusing what can be presented as an object for a cognitive phrase and what can be presented as an object for a speculative and/or ethical phrase – in other words it confuses schemata or examples with *analoga*. The progress of a common being for the better is not to be judged on the basis of empirical intuition, but on the basis of signs.

The expression 'sign of history' is an outstanding example of the complexity of the 'transitions' which have to be made in order to phrase the historico-political. The question posed (against the Faculty of Law) is whether it can be asserted that the human species is progressing continuously for the better, and if the answer is yes, *how* it can be asserted.

The first difficulty lies in the fact that such a phrase has as its referent a part of human history yet to come, and is thus a phrase of *Vorhersagung*, of anticipation, a prognostic. Kant immediately distinguishes it from the *Weissager's* (fortune-teller's) phrase, by showing that, following the rule for cognitives, there can be no direct presentation of the object of this phrase when it bears on the future.

So we shall have to change our family of phrases in order to produce the required demonstration. We shall have to look in the experience of humanity, not for an intuitive *datum* (a *Gegebene*) (which can only validate the phrase describing it, and no more), but for what Kant calls a *Begebenheit*, an event, a deal (in the card-playing sense) – a *Begebenheit* which would only indicate (*hinweisen*) and not prove (*beweisen*) that humanity is capable of being not only the cause (*Ursache*) but also the author (*Urheber*) of its progress. More precisely, explains Kant, this *Begebenheit* delivered in human historical experience must indicate a cause the occurrence of which remains undetermined (*unbestimmt*) with respect to time (*in Ansehung der Zeit*) – and we recognize in this rule the clause stating the independence of causality by freedom from the diachronic series of the mechanical world. This is the price to be paid for being able to extend this cause's possibility of intervening to past and future too.

And this is still not all. The *Begebenheit* must not itself be the cause of progress, but only an index (*Hindeutend*) of progress – a *Geschichtszeichen*. Kant immediately makes clear what he means by sign of history: '*signum rememorativum, demonstrativum, prognosticum*'. The *Begebenheit* we are looking for will have the job of 'presenting' causality by freedom along the three temporal directions – past, present and future. What is this enigmatic, even contradictory 'fact of being delivered'? We might expect some heroic deed to be the looked-for 'deal' bearing witness to the power of free causality. But such a heroic deed is still only a *datum*. Certainly it can be given several readings (descriptive phrase, dialectical phrase), but this only means that it is an equivocal object which can be seized on by one or other of these phrases indifferently. Here the critical judge's requirements go further, to the extent of seeming paradoxical. He is not satisfied with letting the advocate of determinism and the advocate of freedom or finality be reconciled by an arrangement satisfying both, but leaving the decision whether to phrase one way rather than the other indeterminate (in the sense of contingent). The *Begebenheit*, which is a *datum in* experience at least, if not *of* experience, must be the index of the Idea of free causality. With this *Begebenheit* we must get as close as possible to the abyss to be crossed between mechanism on the one hand and liberty or finality on the other, between the domain of the sensory world and the field of the supersensible – and we should be able to leap across it without suppressing it, by fixing the status of the historico-political – a status which may be inconsistent and indeterminate, but which can be spoken, and which is, even, irrefutable. This is the price to be paid for being able to prove that humanity has a natural inclination to use its reason, and for being able to anticipate with certainty a continuous progress of its history for the better.

At this point Kant goes off on what can seem to be an unexpected detour in order to present this *Begebenheit*, but this detour also allows the most minute location of this 'as if object', the historico-political, and the location most faithful to its complexity. We have, he writes, a *Begebenheit* satisfying the conditions of the problem, and which is not a great deed:

> We are here only concerned with the way of thinking (*Denkung-sart*) of the spectators (*Zuschauer*) as it reveals itself (or betrays itself, *verrät*, as one betrays a secret) in public (*offentlich*: a public use of thought then, in the same sense as the article on the *Aufklärung* distinguishes a public use of reason) on the occasion of (this is how I translate *bei*, which does not mean *in*) this drama of great transmutations (*Umwandlungen*) (this drama, *dieser Spiel*: which drama? Kant will give the example of the French Revolution, the text dates from 1795), in which is expressed a taking of sides (a participation, a taking up, *eine Teilnehmung*) for one set of antagonists against their adversaries, a taking of sides so universal and yet so disinterested – even at the risk that this taking of sides can be of disadvantage to them (the spectators) – that it provides the proof (*beweist*) (because of its universality) that there is a character of mankind as a whole and (because of its disinterestedness) that this character is a moral one (*moralisch*) at least as a disposition (*Anlage*), and this character not only allows us to hope for human progress, it is already this progress, insofar as its scope is within reach of what is possible at present.

Kant adds that the recent Revolution of a people which is *geistreich*, rich in spirit, may well either fail or succeed, accumulate misery and atrocity, it nevertheless 'arouses in the heart (*in den Gemütern*, in the spirits) of all spectators (who are not themselves caught up in it) a taking of sides according to desires (*eine Teilnehmung dem Wunsche nach*) which borders on enthusiasm (*Enthusiasm*) and which, since its very expression was not without danger, can only have been caused by a moral disposition within the human race'.

I will not give a detailed commentary on this text which contains in condensed form Kant's thought (maybe the whole of his thought) on the historico-political. I shall simply make three observations, the first on the nature of enthusiasm, the second on its value as a *Begebenheit* in the historical experience of humanity, and the third on its links with critical thought. All three observations will be made in accordance with the clause controlling the elaboration of the *sign of history*, that is, that the meaning of history (i.e. all phrases pertinent to the historico-political field) does not only show itself in the great deeds and misdeeds of the agents or actors who become famous in history, but also in the feeling of the obscure and distant spectators who see and hear them and who, in the sound and fury of the *res gestae*, distinguish between what is just and what is not.

The first observation is that according to Kant the enthusiasm they feel is a modality of the sublime feeling: *sublime feeling* rather than *feeling of the sublime* since, if we are to believe the third *Critique*, 'it is not the object which must be named sublime, but the disposition of the mind provoked by a certain representation which occupies the reflective faculty of judgement.' The imagination attempts to provide an object given as a totality in intuition, i.e. to provide a presentation for an Idea of reason (for the totality is the object of an Idea: for example, the totality of practical rational beings) – the imagination fails, and thus feels its impotence, but at the same time discovers its calling (*Bestimmung*, its destination), which is to realize its accord with Ideas of reason by providing a suitable presentation. The result of this inhibited accord is that instead of having a feeling for the object, we have on the occasion of this object a feeling, 'for the Idea of mankind in us as subjects'. In this text from paragraph 25, the feeling Kant comments on is that of respect. But the analysis works for any sublime feeling inasmuch as it involves a 'subreption' (*Subreption*) which substitutes a regulation (which is in fact a non-regulation) between the faculties of a subject, for a regulation between an object and a subject.

The regulation of the sublime is a non-regulation. By contrast with taste, the regulation of the sublime is good when it is bad. The sublime involves the finality of a non-finality and the pleasure of an unpleasure:

> We discover a certain finality in the unpleasure felt in proportion with the extension of the imagination necessary if it is to fit with what is without limit in our power of reason, i.e. the Idea of an absolute whole, and consequently also in the non-finality (*Unzweckmässigkeit*, the non-affinity, the incommensurability in terms of the goal) of the power of the imagination for the Ideas of reason, and the arousing (*Erweckung*) of these Ideas ... The object is apprehended as sublime with a joy which is only made possible by the mediation of pain.

Even the most extensive imagination cannot manage to present an object which could validate or 'realize' the Idea. Whence the pain: from the inability to present. What is the joy which, nonetheless, is grafted onto this pain? It comes from the discovery of an affinity in this accord: even what is presented as being very big in nature (including in human nature and in the natural history of man, such as a great revolution) is still and will always be 'small compared with the ideas of reason'. What is discovered is not only the infinite scope of Ideas, which are incommensurable with any presentation, but, also, the calling of the subject, 'our' calling, which is that of having to supply a presentation for the unpresentable and thus, in terms of Ideas, to go beyond anything that can be presented.

Enthusiasm itself is an extreme form of the sublime feeling: the attempt to provide a presentation not only fails, thus giving rise to the tension I have described, but also, so to speak, is reversed or inverted so as to provide a supremely paradoxical presentation, which Kant calls a 'simply negative presentation', and which he characterizes with some audacity as a 'presentation of the infinite'. We have here the most inconsistent of all 'transitions' – blind alley. Kant even ventures to give examples of it: 'There is perhaps no passage in the Old Testament more sublime than the commandment: Thou shalt not make graven images, nor any representation of things on high in heaven, below on earth, and under the earth ... Only this commandment can explain the enthusiasm that the Jewish people, in the period when it was flourishing, felt for its religion when it compared itself with other peoples, or the pride inspired by the Mahometan religion.' And he continues, 'It is the same with the representation of the moral law and the disposition to morality within us.'

What is required of the imagination, for this abstract presentation which presents nothingness, is that it should 'unlimit' itself. The fact remains that this extreme painful delight called enthusiasm is an *Affekt*, a powerful affection; and that as such it is blind and thus cannot, writes Kant, 'serve as a satisfaction for reason'. It is even a *dementia*, a *Wahnsinn*, in which the imagination is 'unleashed'. As such, it remains of course preferable to the *Schwärmerei*, to the tumult of exaltation, which is a *Wahnwitz*, an *insanitas*, a 'disorder' of the imagination, an 'illness deeply rooted in the soul', whereas enthusiasm is a 'passing accident which can affect the most healthy understanding'. The *Schwärmerei* gives rise to an illusion, to 'seeing something beyond all limits of sensibility', i.e. to thinking that there is a presentation when there is not. It makes a non-critical transition which is comparable to the transcendental illusion (the illusion of knowing something beyond all the limits of knowledge). Enthusiasm, on the other hand, sees nothing, or rather sees *the* nothing and refers it to the unpresentable. Although it is to be condemned ethically as pathological, 'it is aesthetically sublime since it is a tension of forces due to Ideas, which give the soul an *élan* which acts much more powerfully and durably than the impulsion given by sensory representations.'

Historico-political enthusiasm thus borders on *dementia*. It is a pathological attack and as such has in itself no ethical validity, since ethics requires one to be free of all motivating pathos, allowing only the apathetic pathos which accompanies obligation and which is called respect, and not the *Affektlosigkeit* which is still too sublime, and which Kant proceeds to discuss immediately in his study of the sublime. And yet the pathos of enthusiasm in its episodic outbursts retains an aesthetic validity; it is an energetical *sign*, a tensor of the *Wunsch*. The infinite nature of the Idea draws all other capacities (i.e. all the other faculties) to itself, and produces an *Affekt* 'of the vigorous type', which is characteristic of the sublime. The 'transition', then, does not take place; it is a 'transition' in transit, and its transiting, its movement, is a sort of agitation on the spot, in the blind alley of incommensurability, above the abyss, a 'shaking', writes Kant, 'that is the rapid succession of repulsion and attraction for the same object'. And this is the state of the *Gemüt* of the spectators of the French Revolution.

Second observation: this enthusiasm is the *Begebenheit* looked for in the historical experience of humanity in order to validate the phrase, 'Humanity is continually improving'. Great changes such as the French Revolution are not in principle sublime in themselves. As objects they are like those spectacles of physical nature on the occasion of which the spectator feels the sublime: 'It is rather in its chaos and its disorder (if grandeur and force manifest themselves) in its wildest and most unbridled devastation, that nature best provokes Ideas of the sublime.' What best determines the sublime is the indeterminate, the *Formlosigkeit*: 'the sublime of nature . . . can be as if without form or figure'; 'no particular form of nature is represented therein.' The same must be the case for the Revolution, and for all great historical upheavals – they are the formless and figureless in historical human nature. Ethically there is nothing valid about them: on the contrary they come in for critical judgement as we have seen; they are the result of a confusion (which is the political illusion itself) between the direct presentation of the *Gemeine Wesen* and the analogical presentation of the Idea of a Republican contract.

As an event in the historical nature of mankind, the Revolution belongs to the residue of data, the remainder made up of singularities and existences waiting for a phrase once the cognitive phrase has taken charge of what belongs to it in the intuitions it can subsume under regularities, in the mode of the presentation of examples. This remainder is waiting for the teleological phrase, and yet its lack of form looks as if it ought to cause the absolute failure of this phrase. But in the enthusiasm aroused in the *Gemüt* of the spectators by this formlessness, this failure of all possible finalization is itself finalized. The *dementia* of enthusiasm for the Revolution and the revolutionary party bears witness to the extreme tension felt by spectating mankind – a tension between the 'nullity' of what is presented to it and the Ideas of reason – i.e. the Idea of the Republic which unites the Idea of autonomy, of the people and that of peace between States. What is given in this *Begebenheit* is thus a tension in the *Denkungsart* occasioned by an object which is almost pure disorder, which has no figure, which is however extremely big in historical nature and which is a sort of abstraction refractory to all functions of presentation – even by *analoga*. But because of these negative properties of the object which is the occasion of this tension, it proves all the more indubitably by the very form it imprints on feeling, that it is polarized, '*aufs Idealische*, towards something Ideal, *und zwar rein Moralische*, that is something purely moral, to which the concept of right is similar'.

Third observation: Kant writes in the third *Critique*, 'All that matters in the resolution of an antinomy is that two propositions which apparently contradict each other do not in fact do so, and can be maintained alongside each other even if the explanation of the possibility of their concept surpasses our faculty of knowing.' Let us call this solution *parathetical*.

What are, notably, involved in the parathetical solution of the Antinomy are also the senders and addressees of the various families of phrases. In principle their situation is regulated, i.e. subject to determination, according to the way the referent is presented by the phrase. This is at least what was established by the *Analytic* of the first *Critique*. But in certain cases, and in the first place that of the ethical phrase, only the situation of the addressee is regulated – the sender of the moral law remaining indeterminable. (In fact the situation of the referent is regulated too, since one of the properties of the ethical phrase is that the sender must bring the referent into existence – the referent being the action prescribed by the imperative.) In other cases, and in the first place that of the aesthetic phrase, what is regulated is the fact that there *is* no rule, since there is no determinable presentation of the referent. And yet this rule of non-regulation nonetheless appeals to a possible agreement between sender and addressee of the ethical phrase about a referent which is, however, never directly presentable. There is thus a bond of 'communicability' between them, which is not subject to the rule of presentation which is valid for the cognitive phrase. This communicability is required 'as a duty, so to speak', and taste is the faculty which judges it a priori. The *sensus communis* is thus in the aesthetic field *like* the totality of rational practical beings in the ethical domain. It is an appeal to the community made a priori, judged without a rule of direct presentation: simply the ethical community is mediated by a concept of reason, the Idea of freedom, whilst the aesthetic community of the senders and addressees of the phrase on beauty is immediately situated in feeling, in that it is a priori to be shared between those senders and addressees.

Enthusiasm as a '*Begebenheit* of our time' is thus phrased according to the rule of the aesthetics of the most extreme mode of the sublime. Extreme firstly because the sublime is not only a disinterested pleasure and a universal without a concept, but also because it involves a purposiveness of anti-purposiveness and a pleasure by pain, as opposed to the feeling of the beautiful, the purposiveness of which is without purpose, and the pleasure of which is left to the free accord of the faculties amongst themselves. With the sublime we go a long way into heterogeneity, so that the solution to the aesthetic antinomy appears to be more difficult for the sublime than for the beautiful.

A *fortiori* more difficult when we are dealing with enthusiasm, which is at the extreme limit of the sublime. Kant recognizes that 'the disposition of the mind supposed by the feeling of the sublime requires *eine Empfanglichkeit* to Ideas (that the mind be susceptible to Ideas, sensitive to Ideas)'. And a little later, 'The judgement on the sublime in nature (of human nature too) needs a certain culture', which does not mean that it is produced by that culture, for 'it has its foundation in human nature'. Kant says no more on this subject in this paragraph. But this allusion to culture is cleared up in the critique of teleological judgement in the paragraph dealing with the ultimate aim of nature. Here (as in many of the political opuscules) Kant refutes the thesis that this goal could be the happiness of the human race, and shows that it can only be its culture. 'To produce in a rational being the general aptitude for the aims which please him (and consequently in his freedom), that is culture.' Culture is the ultimate aim pursued by nature in the human race because culture is what makes men more 'receptive to ideas', and is the condition which opens the door to thinking the unconditioned.

In the same paragraph Kant makes a distinction between the culture of skill and the culture of will: and in the former, between the material and the formal culture of skill. Now the formal development of the culture of skill requires the neutralization of conflicts of free beings on the individual scale, by means of a 'legal power in a totality called *bür-*

gerlich Gesellschaft, civil society'. And if men get ahead of the plans of natural providence, the development of the culture of skill requires the same neutralization, but this time on the scale of the State, by means of a 'cosmopolitical totality, *ein weltbürgerliche Ganzes*', the federation of States. In this way the enthusiasm which is publicly revealed on the occasion of the French Revolution – firstly because it is an extreme sublime feeling, secondly because this feeling already requires a formal culture of skill, and finally because this culture in turn has as its horizon civil and perhaps international peace – this enthusiasm, then, in itself, 'not merely allows us to hope for human improvement, but *is* this improvement, insofar as its scope is within reach of what is possible at present'.

So not just any aesthetic phrase can provide the proof (*beweisen*) that humanity is in constant progress in improvement – but only the phrase of the extreme sublime. The beautiful will not do: it is only a symbol of the good. But because the sublime is the affective paradox, the paradox of feeling (of feeling publicly) in common a formlessness for which there is no image or sensory intuition – because of this, the sublime constitutes an 'as if' presentation of the Idea of civil and even cosmopolitical society, and therefore of the Idea of morality; where however there can be no such presentation in experience. This is how the sublime feeling is a sign. This sign does no more than indicate a free causality, but it nonetheless counts as proof for the phrase affirming progress: since spectating mankind must *already* have made progress in culture to be able to feel this feeling, or in other words to make this sign, by its 'way of thinking' the Revolution. This sign *is* progress in its present state, as far as can be, although civil societies are not, far from it, close to the Republican regime, nor States close to world-wide federation.

The faculty of judgement at work in critical philosophy (in Kant writing the *Contest of Faculties*) sees a sign of history in the enthusiasm of the people for the Revolution, because it is a proof of the progress of the faculty of judgement in mankind as a whole as a natural species. However, this faculty appeals to the anticipated bond of the *sensus communis* and, in feeling, mankind judges the Revolution to be sublime, despite its lack of form. This sign is indicative when it is evaluated against the rule of presentation of the phrases of historical knowledge: it is a simple *Begebenheit* among the *Gegebene* of historical data open to intuitions. But in the family of the strange phrases of judgement it is a proof for the Kantian phrase which judges that there is progress, since it is *itself* this phrase of the people, which is not 'spoken', to be sure, but which is publicly expressed as a feeling which can in principle be shared, on the occasion of an 'abstract' *datum*. Kant's reflecting phrase, 'there is progress' does no more than reflect the 'there is progress' of the people, which is necessarily implied in their enthusiasm.

This is why Kant can continue rather solemnly: 'Without the mind of a seer, I now maintain that I can predict (*vorhersagen*) from the aspects and precursor-signs (*Vorzeichen*) of our times, the achievement (*Erreichung*) of this end, and with it, at the same time, the progressive improvement of mankind, a progress which henceforth cannot be totally reversible.' For, adds Kant, 'a phenomenon of this kind in human history *can never be forgotten* (*vergisst sich nicht mehr*)'. No politician (the politician of politics, whom Kant calls the 'political moralist') would have been 'subtle enough to extract from the previous course of things' this capacity for improvement in human nature, discovered by enthusiasm. He adds, 'Only nature and freedom combined within mankind in accordance with principles of right, have enabled us to forecast (to promise, *verheissen*) it; but only in non-determined fashion in terms of time, and only as a chance *Begebenheit*.' The aspects of intemporality and fortuitousness remind us of the necessarily, determinedly indeterminate character of the 'transition' between nature (i.e. the Revolution and the pathological aspect of the feeling it arouses) and freedom (i.e. the tension towards the moral Idea of absolute Good which is the other, universal and disinterested, aspect of the same feeling).

'There is progress': the critical judge can legitimate this phrase every time he can present a sign to be a referent for this assertion. But he cannot say *when* such 'objects' will present themselves, because historical sequences forming a series only give data to the historian (data which are at best statistically regular) – and never signs. The historico-political only presents itself to assertions through *cases* which operate not as examples, still less as schemes, but as complex hypotyposes (perhaps what Adorno was asking for under the name *Modelle*); the most complex being the most certain. Popular enthusiasm for the Revolution is a highly validating case for the historico-political phrase, and thus permits a very certain hypotyposis, for the simple reason that it is itself a highly *improbable* hypotyposis (recognizing the Idea of the republic in a 'formless' empirical *datum* in which 'grandeur and force' are revealed). As for the philosophy of history which cannot even be considered in critical thought, it is an illusion born of signs being a semblance of examples or schemes.

It seems to me that the *datum* (which can only be a *Begebenheit*) which we are dealing with, the *Begebenheit* which marks what has been called 'postmodernity' to designate our time, is (if you will allow me to use a symbol – but the critical judge *must* allow me to use it) – this *Begebenheit* is the feeling produced by the fission of the great discursive nuclei I mentioned at the beginning of this lecture.

As the *Begebenheit* Kant was faced with was occasioned by the French Revolution, the *Begebenheit* we shall have to think through as philosophers and moral politicians, and which is in no way homologous to the enthusiasm of 1789 (since it is not aroused by the Idea of one purpose, but by the Idea of several purposes or even by Ideas of heterogeneous purposes) – this *Begebenheit* for our time, then, would induce a new type of sublime, more paradoxical still than that of enthusiasm, a sublime in which we would feel not only the irremediable gap between an Idea and what presents itself to 'realize' that Idea, but also the gap between the various families of phrases and their respective legitimate presentations.

At the beginning of this lecture, I named certain events which provide a paradoxical, negative occasion for this highly cultivated community sense to reveal itself publicly: Auschwitz, Budapest 1956, May 1968 . . .

Each one of these abysses, and others, asks to be explored with precision in its specificity. The fact remains that all of them liberate judgement, that if they are to be felt, judgement must take place without a criterion, and that this feeling becomes in turn a sign of history. But however negative the signs to which most of the proper names of our political history give rise, we should nevertheless have to judge them *as if* they proved that this history had moved on a step in its progress; i.e. in the culture of skill and of will. This step would consist in the fact that it is not only the Idea of a *single* purpose which would be pointed to in our feeling, but already the Idea that this purpose consists in the formation and free exploration of Ideas *in the plural*, the Idea that this end is the beginning of the *infinity of heterogeneous finalities*. Everything that fails to satisfy this fission of the single purpose, everything that presents itself as the 'realization' of a single purpose, as is the case with the phrase of politics, of the 'political moralist', is felt not to be up to (*angemenen*), not akin to (*abgezielt*) the infinite capacity of phrases given in the feeling aroused by this fission. And when I say: not commensurable, this is the least one can say. This pretension to realize a single purpose can, as we know, be threatening enough to embalm what is already dead, as is the case in Red Square, or to give life to a fable by terror and massacre, as under the Third Reich.

The idea of commensurability (in the sense of affinity with no rule to act as an established criterion) is of decisive importance in Kant's thought, and especially his thought about the historico-political. But for us today it moderates too strongly the event of fission. The exploding of language into families of heteronomous language-games is the theme that Wittgenstein, whether he knew it or not, took from Kant and which he took as far as he could towards rigorous description. For Kant's judge it is not enough to decide one way or the other; he must also admit at least the coexistence of heteronomous phrases. The obligation to compromise presupposes an attraction or general interaction of families of phrases, despite or because of their heteronomy.

Kant pulls the idea of this drive to commerce between phrases down onto that of a subject which otherwise would fall to pieces, and of a rationality which otherwise would be in conflict with itself and no longer worthy of its name. We today – and this is part of the *Begebenheit* of our time – feel that the fission given in this *Begebenheit* attacks that subject and that rationality too. Since Marx, we have learned that what presents itself as unity for the phrases of the postmodern Babel, as something that is capable of verifying them, at least in experience subject to concepts and direct presentation – we have learned that this is the impostor-subject and blindly calculating rationality called Capital, especially when it lays hold of phrases themselves in order to commercialize them and make surplus-value out of them in the new condition of the *Gemeinwesen* called 'computerized society'. But in the unnamed feeling I have suggested we make the *Begebenheit* of our time, we can easily find what we need to judge the pretension of Capital's phrase to validate all phrases according to its criterion of performativity, and the imposture which puts that phrase in the place of the critical judge – to judge this pretension and this imposture, to criticize them and to re-establish the rights of the critical tribunal – which will, however, not be the same as the tribunal of Kant's critical philosophy. For we cannot judge them according to the Idea of man and within a philosophy of the subject, but only according to the 'transitions' between heterogeneous phrases, and respecting their heterogeneity. This is why a philosophy of phrases is more 'akin' to this *Begebenheit* than a philosophy of the faculties of a subject. But then, what can *a* tribunal be? Is the only purpose of the reflective function which is ours to transform, as Kant thought, dispute (*différend*) into litigation, by substituting the law-court for the battle-field? Is not its aim also that of emphasizing disputes, even at risk of aggravating them, of giving a language to what cannot be expressed in the language of the judge, even if he is a critical judge?

NOTE

'The Sign of History' was first delivered as the inaugural Michel Benamou memorial lecture at the Center for Twentieth-Century Studies, Milwaukee, in 1982.

Translated by Geoff Bennington

Select Bibliography of English Translations of Lyotard's Writings

1963 'Algeria'. *International Socialism*, Summer 1963, no. 13, pp. 21–6.

1974 'Adorno as the Devil', tr. R. Hurley, *Telos, 19*, pp. 127–37.

1975 'For a Pseudo-Theory', tr. M. Ron, *Yale French Studies*, 52, pp. 115–27.

     'Beyond Representation', tr. J. Culler, *The Human Context VII*, 3, pp. 495–500.

1976 'The Tooth, The Palm', tr. A. Knapp and M. Benamou, *Sub-Stance, 15*, pp. 105–10.

1977 'Jewish Oedipus', tr. S. Hanson, *Genre*, Fall, *10* (3), pp. 395–411.

     'Energumen Capitalism', tr. J. Leigh, *Semiotext(e)*, 2, 3, pp. 11–26.

     'The Unconscious as Mise-en-scène', tr. J. Maier. In M. Benamou and C. Carmello (eds), *Performance in Post-Modern Culture* (Madison, Wisc.: Coda Press), pp. 87–98.

1978 'Acinema', tr. P.N. Livingston and J.-F. Lyotard, *Wide Angle 2*: 3, pp. 52–9.

     'Notes on the Return of Capital', tr. R. McKeon, *Semiotext(e) 3*: 1, pp. 44–53.

     'One of the Things at Stake in Women's Struggles', tr. D.J. Clark, W. Woodhill and J. Mowitt, *Sub-Stance 20*, pp. 9–17.

     'Lesson Concerning the Secret Nature of Languages' (Teacher's Manual), tr. I. McLeod, *The Oxford Literary Review 3*: 1, pp. 35–7.

     'On the Strength of the Weak', tr. R. McKeon, *Semiotext(e)*, *3*: 2, pp. 204–14.

1979 'The Psychoanalytic Approach'. In M. Dufrenne (ed.), *The Main Trends in Aesthetics and the Sciences of Art* (New York: Holme and Meir), pp. 134–49.

     'That Part of the Cinema Called Television'. *Framework*, Autumn, 11, pp. 37–9.

1981 'Use me', tr. M. Feher and T. Gora, *Semiotext(e)*, *4*:1, pp. 82–5.

'Theory as Art: A Pragmatic Point of View', tr. R. Vollarth. In W. Steiner (ed.), *Image and Code* (Ann Arbor: University of Michigan Press), pp. 71-7.

'Analysing Speculative Discourse as Language Game', tr. G. Bennington, *The Oxford Literary Review*, 4:3 pp. 59-67.

'The Works and Writings of Daniel Buren. An Introduction to the Philosophy of Contemporary Art', tr. L. Liebmann, *Artforum*, Feb. 1981, pp. 56-64.

1982 'Endurance and the Profession', tr. C. Gallier, S. Ungar and B. Johnson, *Yale French Studies, 63*, pp. 72-7.

'Presenting the Unpresentable: The Sublime', tr. L. Liebmann, *Artforum, 20*:8, pp. 64-9.

1983 'Answering the Question: What is Post-Modernism?', tr. R. Durand. In I. Hassan and S. Hassan (eds), *Innovation and Renovation* (Madison, Wisc.: University of Wisconsin Press).

'The Dream-Work does not Think', tr. M. Lydon, *The Oxford Literary Review, 6*: 1, pp. 3-34.

'Fiscourse Digure', tr. M. Lydon, *Theatre Journal, 35*: 3, pp. 333-57.

'Passages from *Le Mur du Pacifique*', tr. P. Brochet, N. Royle and K. Woodward, *Sub-Stance 37*:8, pp. 89-99.

'Presentations', tr. K. McLaughlin. In A. Montefiore (ed.), *Philosophy in France Today* (Cambridge: Cambridge University Press), pp. 116-35.

1984 *Driftworks* (New York: *Semiotext(e)*).

'Philosophy and Painting in the Age of Their Experimentation: Contributions to an Idea of PostModernity', tr. M. Brewer and D. Brewer, *Camera Obscura*, no. 12, 1984, pp. 110-25.

The Postmodern Condition, tr. G. Bennington and B. Massumi (Manchester: Manchester University Press).

'The Differend, the Referent and the Proper Name', tr. G. van den Abbeele, *Diacritics 14*:3, pp. 4-14.

'Longitude 180 Degrees W or E'. In *Arakawa*, Mailand, Edizione Nava Milano.

1985 'The Sublime and The Avant-Garde', tr. L. Liebmann, G. Bennington and M. Hobson, *Paragraph, 6*, pp. 1-18.

'The Tensor', tr. S. Hand. *The Oxford Literary Review, 7*:1, pp. 25-40.

'Les Immatériaux'. *Art and Text*, April 1975, pp. 47-57.

Just Gaming with J.-L. Thebaud, tr. W. Godzich (Manchester: Manchester University Press).

1986 'Defining the Postmodern, etc.', tr. G. Bennington. In *Postmodernism* ICA Documents 4 & 5.

'Levinas' Logic', tr. I McLeod. In R.C. Cohen (ed.), *Face to Face with Levinas* (Albany: SUNY Press), pp. 117-58.

'Discussions, or Phrasing "After Auschwitz",' tr. G. van den Abbeele. Center for Twentieth Century Studies, University of Milwaukee, Working Paper no. 2.

'Rules and Paradoxes and Svelte Appendix', tr. B. Massumi, *Cultural Critique*, no. 5, pp. 209–19.

'A Success of Sartre's', introduction to D. Hollier, *The Politics of Prose: Essay on Sartre* (Minneapolis: University of Minnesota Press), pp. xi–xxii.

1987 'Notes on Legitimation', tr. C. Lindsay, *The Oxford Literary Review*, 9, pp. 106–18.

'The Sign of History', tr. G. Bennington. In D. Attridge and G. Bennington (eds), *Post Structuralism and the Question of History* (Cambridge: Cambridge University Press), pp. 162–80.

'The Thought Police', with J. Rogozinski, tr. J. Pefanis, *Art and Text*, 26, pp. 24–32.

'Judiciousness in Dispute, or Kant after Marx'. In M. Krieger (ed.), *The Aims of Representation* (New York: Columbia University Press).

1988 *Peregrinations: Law, Form, Event* (New York: Columbia University Press).

'A Memorial to Marxism', tr. C. Lindsay. An afterword to *Peregrinations*.

'Sensus Communis', tr. G. Bennington and M. Hobson, *Paragraph*.

Index